BATH FESTIVAL OF BLUES

SATURDAY JUNE 28th
RECREATION GROUND · PULTENEY STREET ENTRANCE

with

FLEETWOOD MAC
JOHN MAYALL
TEN YEARS AFTER
LED ZEPPELIN
THE NICE
CHICKEN SHACK
JOHN HISEMANS COLOSSEUM
MIKE ABRAHAMS BLODWIN PIG
KEEF HARTLEY · GROUP THERAPY
LIVERPOOL SCENE · TASTE
SAVOY BROWN BLUES BAND
CHAMPION JACK DUPRE
CLOUDS · BABYLON
PRINCIPAL EDWARDS MAGIC THEATRE
DEEP BLUES BAND · JUST BEFORE DAWN
COMPERE JOHN PEEL

IN CASE OF BAD WEATHER THERE WILL BE A SUBSTANTIAL AMOUNT OF UNDER COVER ACCOMODATION

REFRESHMENTS AND HOT SNACKS WILL BE AVAILABLE ALL DAY

12 NOON TO 11 P.M.

TICKETS IN ADVANCE ALL DAY 18'6 EVE.ONLY(6-30 P.M.) 14'6
ON THE DAY ALL DAY 22'6 EVE.ONLY(6-30 P.M.) 16'6

PINK FLOYD
at 3 p.m.

THE WHO
at 8 p.m.

PRICES : 8/- 12/- 16/- 20/-

TICKETS : Union Box Office and other Agencies after 16th Feb

Midsummer merry-making at Pleasure Acre **PORTBURY** FRIDAY 30th JULY

JOHNSON HALL YEOVIL

THURS 18th SEPT
FOLLOWING THE SUCCESS OF 'AUTOBAHN'

KRAFTWERK

IN CONCERT WITH

A.J. WEBBER

DOORS OPEN 8PM. LICENSED BAR. ADVANCE·
TICKETS £1·20 FROM ACORN RECORD SHOP, RADIO
HOUSE, MINNS MUSIC CENTRE. AT DOOR ON NIGH

CW01391539

BRISTOL BOOKS

Bristol Books CIC, The Courtyard, Wraxall,
Wraxall Hill, Bristol, BS48 1NA
www.bristolbooks.org

The West's Greatest Rock Shows 1963-1978
Written and researched by Robin Askew

Published by Bristol Books 2024

ISBN: 978-1-909446-39-7

Copyright: Robin Askew

Design: Joe Burt

.skew has asserted his right under the Copyright, Designs and
nts Act of 1988 to be identified as the author of this work.

served. This book may not be reproduced or transmitted in any form or in any means
prior written consent of the publisher, except by a reviewer who wishes to quote brief
onnection with a review written in a newspaper or magazine or broadcast on television,
radio or on the internet.

P record for this book is available from the British Library.

ristol Books is grateful to Bristol Ideas for their support.

over: David Bowie image copyright Los Angeles Times Photographic Collection at the UCLA Library.
Marsha Hunt copyright Tony Byers.

THE WEST'S GRE...
ROCK S...

1963-19...

LOST, FORGOTTEN AND
UNTOLD EYE-OPENING
THE GIGS YOU'LL WISH

Robin ...
Pat...

All rights ...
without th...
passages in ...

A C...

ROBIN ASK...

TRIGGER WARNING:
This book contains sex, drugs
and rock'n'roll

To the late Al Read and Freddy Bannister, without whom
many of these great shows would never have happened.

Also to Sue, who continues to put up with me even though I once
abandoned her in the St. John Ambulance tent after she passed out at the
Monsters of Rock festival, because I didn't want to miss a minute of Slayer.
(Hey - they were playing *Raining Blood*.)

CONTENTS

INDEX OF SHOWS

1966

1967

1968

1969

1970

1971

1972

1973

1974

1975

1976

1977

1978

INTRODUCTION

On October 7, 1987, I went to see Guns n' Roses at the Colston Hall. It was one of just five UK dates on the *Appetite For Destruction* tour. This turned out to be the only UK tour by the band's classic line-up before they hit the stadiums and imploded. The Hall was half-full and the only other hack there was the *Bristol Post*'s 'pop correspondent'. He was not impressed, writing that these "foul-mouthed rockers" would not be welcome in Bristol again. When I tried to do the Jon Landau "I have seen the future of rock and roll" thing on my then editor, he turned down my offer of a review because he'd never heard of Guns n' Roses. If memory serves, he was more interested in a band called The Woodentops, who were deemed to be The Future of Indie for at least the next ten minutes. Six months later, the Gunners were the biggest band in the world. In his interesting and perceptive book *Uncommon People: The Rise and Fall of the Rock Stars*, David Hepworth writes: "It remains the case that when fashion editors think of a rock star they think of Axl Rose in 1987. Nobody has ever looked more the part."

Anyhow, I can occasionally wow impressionable young people with the story of how I was actually at this show, bootleg recordings of which can be found across the internet - and, indeed, how I saw Queens of the Stone Age at the Fleece (half-full) and Nine Inch Nails at the Bierkeller (about 300 punters, including Island Records boss Chris Blackwell). But if an even older, gnarlier rocker is present, he or she will invariably say, "That's really great. But I remember seeing David Bowie supported by Thin Lizzy at the Locarno/Jimi Hendrix at the Colston Hall/Pink Floyd at the Corn Exchange."

So that's me well and truly trumped, then. Bastards! If I had a time machine, I wouldn't be bothered with the Battle of Hastings, the birth of the alleged baby Jebus, and all that guff. I'd nip back and witness rock history being made. I once calculated that the optimum year in which to be born was 1950. That way you'd be hitting your teens just as The Beatles turned up to change the world, be old enough to enjoy all the free love of 1967, and then savour the incredible flourishing of creative music at a time when baffled but wealthy record companies were chucking money at bands and giving them plenty of time to find their feet.

Nostalgia for other people's youth is a concept for which there ought to be - and probably is - a German word. Speak to those who were there and some will acknowledge their immense good fortune at finding themselves in the right place at the right time. Others will insist that it was all awful, and it has to be acknowledged that not every one of these is a sad, bitter old git or ghastly trend-chaser eager to be down with the kids by disavowing the unfashionable music of their youth. But the yearning for this possibly mythical past now seems to transcend generations. I've often found myself talking to teenagers who also wish they'd been around to savour 1972.

Indeed, you can continue to hear the music of The Beatles, the Stones, Pink Floyd, Genesis, Fleetwood Mac, AC/DC, The Who, Thin Lizzy, Jimi Hendrix, Led Zeppelin, Frank Zappa, David Bowie, Deep Purple, T. Rex, Black Sabbath, Roxy Music, Bob Marley, Queen, Steely Dan and many, many more performed live locally by the plethora of covers bands/tribute acts (delete according to prejudice) who make a comfortable living from keeping it alive. While there are performers paying tribute to everyone from Amy Winehouse to Nirvana and Rammstein, the market remains dominated by music from the sixties and seventies. Some of the bigger acts - such as the Bootleg Beatles, Illegal Eagles, Australian Pink Floyd and The Musical Box - play to crowds the same size as those pulled by the original bands half a century or more ago, occasionally in the same venues. Make of the tribute act phenomenon what you will, but it can't be denied that the music continues to appeal to audiences of all ages.

So if I had that time machine, these are the local gigs I'd go to. Just a few clarifications before we start. I'm not suggesting for a moment that this is a definitive collection of the Greatest Gigs That Ever Happened Round These Parts. It's limited to a 15-year period and concentrates on rock, specifically classic rock, metal, prog and their precursors - plus those jazz, folk, blues, soul and occasional reggae artists with crossover appeal. Maybe a legendary trad jazzer pitched up to tootle and parp his way through a gig at some long demolished local venue back in the 1950s. Or perhaps a disc jockey played a record particularly well at a rave in 1991. But I wouldn't know about that. If your taste is for indie, punk, world music or trip hop, no doubt your list will be very different. So feel free to compile your own, or consult those who have written far more authoritatively and with much greater enthusiasm for these genres than I could ever muster. The local punk and new wave movements, for example, have been superbly chronicled by Mike Darby's excellent Bristol Archive Records.

Anyone who's ever read a rock biography will be familiar with the sentence that reads: "Band/artist X then embarked on a 19-date UK tour before returning to the studio to record their next album." But hang on a minute. What happened on that tour? How did they go down in the regions, away from the metropolitan tastemakers? What sort of venues did they play? How much naughtiness did they get up to on the road? Focusing on the thriving scene in Bristol, Bath and surrounding areas, I've set out to answer these questions and more by delving into the regional and student press, none of which has been digitised, and quizzing band members, promoters and punters. It's astonishing how many incredible stories about major stars have been lost, forgotten or simply never told before. In these pages, you'll find accounts of stage mishaps, petty officialdom, eccentric promoters, multiple instances of rock'n'roll misbehaviour and several riots (including the UK's first outdoor pop riot). And, of course, that great local pre-internet rite of passage: camping out overnight at the Colston Hall to secure front row seats for your favourite band, from rebellious schoolgirls in 1964 to teenage heavy metal fans in 1978.

Along the way, you'll be plunged into the sights, sounds and - oh, yes - smells of the sixties and seventies regional club scene. There's the Corn Exchange, where rock history was made on multiple occasions in the 1960s; the Granary Club, Bristol's vibrant, pleasingly lawless counterpart to London's Marquee; and the extraordinary, none-more-seventies Boobs, where you could have seen artists as diverse as Quo, Faust and Bob Marley and the Wailers performing alongside plastic palm trees - and still have change from a quid. It all amounts to a very different prism through which to view rock history.

To step back into the sixties, particularly the early part of the decade, would be quite a culture shock for those of us used to our favourite bands playing three hour wig-outs at ear-splitting volume accompanied by retina-frazzling lightshows. These days, all but the most extreme rock bands attract all-ages audiences. Back then, older generations tended to be aghast and punters over the age of 25 were generally thin on the ground. Then there were those exotic gangs of yesteryear to contend with, ranging from the Teds to the Mods, who could be vocal in their disapproval of acts that failed to conform to their particular subcultural requirements. And they had plenty to disapprove of, as the Colston Hall's programme was filled with package tours, many of them absurdly mismatched - none more so than the mind-boggling Walker Brothers/Jimi Hendrix/Englebert Humperdinck show. What's more, the sound was crap, the lighting basic and there were two houses each night. The combination of under-powered amplification and over-excited teenage girls meant that your chances of hearing anything played by the likes of The Beatles or Stones were slim indeed.

Another surprise for modern audiences might be the youthfulness and social backgrounds of many of the sixties acts. Today, we're used to what seems like a monoculture of posh musicians with stage school educations, often in their late twenties and early thirties, whose ambitions extend no further than to make tasteful music that never threatens to quicken the pulse but secures them fawning colour supplement profiles, a slot on *Later... With Jools Holland* and a Mercury Prize nomination.

When Stevie Wonder first played Bristol, he was fourteen years old. Steve Winwood was fifteen. Gary Moore was sixteen. Many of the most raucous and thrilling rock groups turning up at the Corn Exchange and Bath Pavilion were still in their late teens. Those working behind the scenes were often not much older. Joe Boyd told me he was "a very green 21-year-old" when he made his debut as a tour manager at the Colston Hall at the start of 1964's American Folk, Blues and Gospel Caravan jaunt, finding himself thrown in at the deep end on a mission to corral the much older, often cantankerous and frequently feuding artists.

A large proportion of the early bands were working-class kids taking full advantage of the social mobility afforded by what became the Swinging Sixties. Indeed, nice, well brought up middle-class boys who chose not to fake it like the Stones often found themselves very much in the minority. The young Reginald Dwight, for example, who slogged round the same circuit with Long John Baldry's Bluesology and went on to become one of the biggest stars of the seventies, often found himself feeling distinctly uncomfortable among the ruffians. "In the six-strong line-up, fat Reggie was the odd man out - quiet, neat and self-contained, inhabiting his own little patch of order amid the travelling chaos," writes Philip Norman in his definitive biography, *Sir Elton*.

There was also a great deal more racial diversity than you might perhaps expect. Virtually all of the great black artists who laid the foundations of rock played shows in Bristol during the 1960s. Lippmann and Rau's annual touring American Folk-Blues Festival brought astonishing packages to the Hall Formerly Known as Colston, building up a large and loyal audience through the decade and beyond. Acts ranging from Screamin' Jay Hawkins to Sister Rosetta Tharpe, Muddy Waters and John Lee Hooker also performed in local club venues, although details tend to be poorly recorded because these musicians were of less interest to the local press than white beat boom combos. And as we shall see, on one memorable occasion the Ike and Tina Turner Revue played shows in Bath and Bristol on the same evening.

The prevailing view in the early days was that pop music was just a passing fad and it wouldn't be long before audiences saw sense and went back to the crooners. To make as much loot as possible before everything went tits-up, promoters crammed as many bands as they could onto the big Colston Hall bills, sent each act on stage to play a couple of hits and then promptly hauled them off again. There was always the danger of missing your favourite band if you turned up late or went for a swift piss. Even musical giants like Chuck Berry and Jimi Hendrix were granted as little as 20 minutes for their headline performances, while openers frequently got just eight minutes. There must have been someone standing at the side of the stage with a stopwatch.

The world of pop was also so volatile that bands' fortunes often changed markedly between a tour being booked and it actually taking place, leading to enormous backstage rivalries. As we'll see, many of the biggest names in rock started out on these tours. David Bowie, for example, was at the bottom of the bill for two Colston Hall packages in 1969. At the first of these he didn't sing a note; at the second he was heckled.

If you're wondering why acts like The Who, The Move, Pink Floyd and

David Bowie did so many gigs in Bristol during this era, often separated by just a few weeks, that's because they were playing to completely different audiences. Venues like the Locarno, Granary and Corn Exchange were open to everyone, but for a long time only students were permitted access to the Victoria and Anson Rooms. This was rigorously policed in order to keep the oiks out. Local papers would occasionally carry angry letters from ordinary gig-goers who'd been repulsed along with the rest of the riff-raff, demanding to know why these shows were publicised. The standard reply was the rather optimistic one that students might be avid readers of the *Western Daily Press*. To save the University of Bristol and/or University Union the bother of issuing a press release in response to this, here's one I made earlier: "Wouldn't happen today... community engagement... diversity... inclusion... blah blah..."

What's particularly striking about the seventies is how diverse rock became. Let's take one genre by way of example. Sadly, just as the terms 'indie' and 'alternative' are now used as cynical branding exercises to confer unearned moral and artistic superiority upon bland music that is neither independent nor the alternative to anything, so 'prog' has too often been devalued by self-appointed arbiters to apply to a narrow range of music played in a specific style. Flip through these pages and you'll be reminded that a glorious panoply of acts were originally united, often somewhat uncomfortably, under this broad banner, from ELP, Yes, Pink Floyd and King Crimson to Magma, Gentle Giant, Soft Machine, Roxy Music, the Mahavishnu Orchestra and the great Krautrock explosion. While today's purists would only acknowledge bands operating in the same musical postcode, these people don't even occupy the same artistic continent.

There's another reason for compiling this book now. Each time the local press writes about The Rolling Stones in Bristol, an intern is dispatched to unearth the old story about Mick Jagger being denied entry to the Grand Hotel restaurant in January 1964 because he was improperly dressed. This might indeed have happened, although it's a yarn that bears all the hallmarks of an Andrew Loog Oldham publicity stunt. But there are some much more interesting local stories about the Stones, as we shall see. The trouble is that the people who are able to give us these first-hand accounts are, not to put too fine a point on it, dropping like flies. Indeed, *Classic Rock* magazine sometimes devotes more space to obituaries than it does to live reviews.

Sadly, some of those with key roles in the local sixties and seventies music scene are also no longer with us to share their memories. I was fortunate to be able to speak to two of them, promoter Freddy Bannister and Granary entertainments manager Al Read - both of whom were generous with their time and stories - when I wrote for local what's on magazine *Venue*.

What's more, when the Colston Hall's website underwent one of its many anniversary revamps, a half-hearted historical timeline was introduced. This, frankly, was a travesty, littered with incorrect dates and missing shows of enormous significance. The unfortunate impression given was that the hall's management - or, more likely, their highly remunerated consultants - either didn't know or didn't care about the musical history that was made within its walls. I can only hope that this book will go some way towards correcting that.

It's also instructive to go back and see how these shows were reviewed by the local press. Given the speed of change in what would now be referred to as youth culture, we should perhaps not be too harsh on the hacks whose verdicts seem hopelessly wrong. Back in the early to mid sixties, general entertainment journalists were struggling to come to terms with the notion that pop music and its screaming teenage audiences were here to stay - for a while at least. They seem to have decided that the best thing to do was to treat it as an exotic and slightly hairier branch of showbiz. The young lads - and they were mostly lads - who play this music might look a bit odd, but they're generally clean and pleasant and have some jolly tunes that aren't too far removed from the output of Tin Pan Alley.

No doubt the fact that the first wave of baby boomers had disposable income available to spend on news of their teen idols helped to spark the papers' interest in all things pop. On a good day, the *Bristol Evening Post* sold as many as 120,000 copies, reaching virtually every household in the city, and could afford to hire young reporters to help cover the pop beat. Indeed, the paper boasted of having its own Beatle in the form of mop-topped Roger Bennett, who was dispatched to hang off the Fabs' every word. The rival *Western Daily Press*'s Thursday *Teenpage* embarked on a seemingly ceaseless quest to find the hairiest groups coming to town. *Hairiest Yet!* screamed a 1964 headline, triumphantly announcing the arrival at the Corn Exchange of a band who were "even hairier than the Stones". The combo in question? The Birds, featuring 17-year-old future Stone Ron Wood.

Bristol United Press's lesser-known weekly *Week-End* magazine, meanwhile, held out against the barbarian hordes well into 1965. Pitched at an older readership (competition headline: Win the Wife a Washing Machine), this boasted a weird mix of picture spreads of society events, lifestyle guff and lurid *News of the World*-esque reports (pornography, the occult, ghosts/poltergeists, gruesome historic murders, etc). In September 1963, it mounted an investigation into the 'peculiar existence' of the beatnik (*Rebels in Ringlets*), as part of which reporter Mike Dornan donned a wig and clutched an acoustic guitar, looking remarkably like Neil the hippy from *The Young Ones*. He then set off into the night in the hope of being roundly abused by salt-of-the-earth Bristolians. Alas, he was to be disappointed, as few seemed to share the often splenetic weekly's prejudices.

"No-one made the slightest effort to throw me out," Dornan opined: "In one of the city's most respectable bars, when the barmaid asked me to stop playing my guitar, she was shouted down by cries of 'He's all right', 'He's a good 'un', 'This gentleman is entertaining us.'" Everywhere he went, people bought him drinks and, on one occasion, a full meal. Interestingly, *Western Daily Press* reporter Maurice Fells tried the same gambit three years later, with much the same result. In a Gloucester Road café, he was given a meal on the house. At a pub in the centre, the landlord offered him a free drink. The small price to pay? "Girls looked, giggled, men wolf-whistled, middle-aged ladies said my hairstyle was 'disgusting.'"

Week-End's attitude towards popular music is best summarised by a review of *Top of the Pops*, "the BBC's stamping ground for the long-haired shakers", which was published in March 1964. The show was described as a "ritual parade of the odd noises that pass under the title of pop" performed in front of a "jerking, twitching throng of teenagers… a crowd of cave man cuts, cowboy hats and sloppy looks… As for the pop tunes, whatever tune they had was drowned in discordant howling and stamping."

This wasn't just the view of pipe-smoking old squares. Before rock music swept it away virtually overnight, trad jazz was where it was at, daddy-o. It's hard to over-emphasise how huge the scene was locally. And the jazzers weren't going to go down without a fight, deploying their full armoury of snobbery and condescension. Nowhere was this more evident than in the student press, whose early sixties music coverage was dominated by jazz, with a side-order of folk (whose adherents were usually at war with one another over their arcane differences). In November 1963, Bristol University's student newspaper *Nonesuch News* attached a metaphorical clothes peg to its nose and ventured into the vulgar world of popular culture for a series of important articles. First up was pop music: "A natural reversion to primitivism for the lower orders and a nice novelty for the sophisticates." The uncredited, lip-curling author acknowledged teenagers' enthusiasm, enjoyment (or "mass-produced self-expression") and sense of ownership of the music pushed by "unscrupulous elements among their elders and betters", but warned of its "degrading, prostituting effect... The danger here is that... they start a disintegration of society as a whole; until the sound of their own music is a war cry." Hmm... on reflection, perhaps they could be onto something.

Local TV made an occasional stab at covering the local and national pop scene too. By far the most successful and longest running show was the *Discs A-Go-Go* groovy pop programme, a regional counterpart to Rediffusion's London-based *Ready, Steady Go!* from Television West and Wales (TWW) - forerunner of HTV and ITV West. Many of the bands appearing at the Corn Exchange would nip along to the Bath Road studio while they were in Bristol to perform or mime to their latest hits. Sometimes this would cause problems. The Byrds were so busy looking fab for the cameras in August 1965 that they didn't finish recording until 9:30pm, which meant they were greeted by some very disgruntled punters when they finally arrived on stage.

Presented by Kent Walton, who later became ITV's voice of wrestling, the weekly half-hour show was launched in 1961 and broadcast at 7pm every Monday. Jazz acts dominated until pop came along. Hordes of local teens would turn up to dance for the cameras and each would be rewarded with a badge bearing a jolly grinning fox logo. The cartoon fox had been created by Harry Hargreaves and was named Gogo - the proprietor of "the gayest coffee bar in town".

Among the artists who appeared over the next four years were The Moody Blues, The Kinks, The Yardbirds, The Animals, The Pretty Things, Donovan, The Beach Boys, Simon & Garfunkel, Ben E. King, Bo Diddley and, ahem, Gary Glitter (pitching up on the very first show in his unsuccessful first incarnation as Paul Raven).

Occasionally, ructions occurred. In 1964, Mandy Rice-Davies made a short-lived attempt to cash in on her Profumo affair notoriety by becoming a pop singer. Cilla Black was the big *Discs A-Go-Go* star of the week when Rice-Davies turned up unannounced at the Bath Road studio on the arm of local music promoter, journalist and general man about town Terry Olpin. The entire audience promptly turned their backs on the chirpy Scouse popstrel, who had to suffer the indignity of watching Rice-Davies sign autographs all evening. Flying into a rage, vengeful Cilla made a formal complaint to TWW management, which got Olpin fired from his role of selecting dancing girls for the show. He went on to found a local property rental empire. Fifty-five years later, Mandy's story was told in the 2019 BBC drama *The Trial of Christine Keeler*, which was shot on location in Bristol.

Alas, every single episode of *Discs A-Go-Go* was subsequently wiped. Yep, even the 1962 edition with The Beatles miming to *Love Me Do*. The only surviving show is a one-off edition broadcast in 1968 as part of an evening of programmes shown to mark the loss of TWW's franchise.

Discs A-Go-Go had initially been commissioned for a trial five-episode run. But it proved such a success that TWW managed to flog it to several other regional franchise holders, including Anglia, Ulster and Westward. Late in 1965, management made the foolish decision to replace their hit with a revamped programme boasting a bigger budget and taking a wider look at teenage life and fashions. It also had a local talent contest, painfully titled *Popportunity Now*.

Launched at 6:30pm on December 22, 1965, *Now!* was billed as "a swinging, trend-setting show". Musical guests on the first programme were Tom Jones and PJ Proby, while the host was a young man making his TV debut. His name? Michael Palin. He was joined by actress Wendy Varnals, who would later be strangled and decapitated by Peter Cushing in the 1968 Brit horror *Corruption* ("This is not a woman's picture! No women will be allowed in alone!").

Eight days later, the *Western Daily Press* published a damning and occasionally rather cruel takedown of the show, framed as a "tip to TWW programme controller Bryan Michie". Tony Crofts reckoned it "ought to forget about swinging right away, and perhaps it should not try too hard to be trend-setting, either." He didn't like the arrangement of the audience ("sitting glumly in leggy, spoggy rows on amphitheatre seats"), the dancers ("one of the girls is just too big and beefy for her shift") or the presenters

("Wendy Varnals must go"). Palin wasn't mentioned by name, but the one element that Crofts did enjoy was the cracks at the music press and pop stars - especially "a piece about the syrupy thanks of the Melody Maker poll winners", which made him laugh out loud. This sounds positively Palin-esque, but we'll never know because - you guessed it - the shows were wiped.

A few clips of Palin's filmed insert comedy skits survived, however. In the 2018 BBC documentary *A Life on Screen*, he recalled of *Now!* "Tom Jones was just starting. He'd come on every other week. [Not actually true. Records reveal that he was on the first and 15th shows.] Eric Clapton was there regularly... Although it may not have been the greatest show ever, it did pay me £30 a week and I got married in 1966 on that."

In 2023, Bristol's Slapstick festival of classic and silent comedy unearthed some more clips for its *Michael Palin: Beyond Python* event with the great man himself. One of these had him larking around the streets of Clifton in drag to the strains of *Second Hand Rose*.

One show was co-presented by Scouse comedy, poetry and music trio The Scaffold, who went on to have huge hits later in the 1960s with *Thank U Very Much* and *Lily the Pink*. "I don't know how they heard of us - maybe it was because of the Edinburgh Festival," mused Scaffold member Mike McGear - aka Mike McCartney, younger brother of Beatle Paul - when I spoke to him after The Scaffold's reunion at Slapstick.

Mike, who rather disarmingly continues to refer to his illustrious sibling as "our kid", doesn't recall The Scaffold performing on the show. Instead, they were there to introduce bands and film some comedy sketches. "There was one where we had to chase a pound note as it floated through the streets of Bristol. I can't remember the payoff. Another one had Roger McGough snogging a bird."

Palin, he recalls, was "just a young lad from Sheffield who was able to show off and do links - and so were we, so we got on very well."

The Scaffold were in Bristol for a couple of days to film their contributions and were particularly keen to hit the pub and sample the local beverage... scrumpy. Young Mr. Palin was equally keen to warn them off. "He said, 'Look this is serious stuff. You need to start off with half pints.'"

It wasn't long before the trio were necking pints and swiftly became the worse for wear. "The last thing I remember is someone saying: 'I'm a policeman...'"

Now! clearly had no trouble attracting major stars. Stevie Wonder, Lulu, Jimmy Cliff, The Yardbirds, Wilson Pickett and the Everly Brothers all made their way to the TWW studio. On what must have been a memorable occasion, The Animals and Arthur Mullard appeared on the same show. But in July 1966, after a little more than six months, *Now!* was canned. Palin departed for pastures new, joining forces with his old Oxford University chum Terry Jones to write for *The Frost Report*. Varnals went on to co-present with Barry Fantoni the BBC's national yoof programme *A Whole Scene Going* ("… reflecting the tastes and times of Britain's under twenty-ones"), a short-lived rival to ITV's hit *Ready Steady Go!* TWW, meanwhile, had one last bash at a pop show. The USP of *Herd at the Scene*, launched in September 1966, was that the pop groups would introduce their own music. It lasted for three episodes.

Just a few short years later, 'underground' bands turned up, attracting an entirely different type of punter. Those beat boom acts were faced with the prospect of hanging up their matching suits or updating their style and sound dramatically. The Traffic and Walker Brothers/Jimi Hendrix package shows at the Colston Hall in 1967 are striking examples of this existential crisis at play.

Having spent several years serving up a bizarre mix of enjoyably snarky commentary on pop groups in town and a somewhat creepy obsession with very young teenage girls, the *Western Daily Press*'s *Teenpage* took a different tack, reacting violently against hippies, psychedelia and 'flower power'. In a long editorial published on March 16, 1967, Ray Wood predicted that "the much-vaunted, earth-shattering trend of '67, psychedelic music, is going to be nothing but a great big light-flashing flop." Alluding to The Rolling Stones' Redlands drug bust a month earlier, he voiced disapproval of the music's 'pushers' and their attempts to "convey a turned-on feeling, representing the effects of hallucinogenic drugs". What's more: "Bringing drug terminology into pop lyrics had not helped the general show-business image, either." Fortunately, he foresaw an end to this nonsense, observing that "psychedelic music has caught the backlash and looks like losing out during a general cleaning-up of the pop world."

Teenpage's Canute-esque campaign against psychedelia continued with a broadside against Pink Floyd on April 13, 1967 ("I have never, ever heard such a load of noisy, boring monotonous rubbish hiding under the name of music," raged roving reporter Brian K. Jones in his *Long Thin Column*). Even the Fabs weren't immune. On June 22, Mr. Jones took aim at *Sgt. Pepper*, which contained, in his view, "just four worthwhile tracks", the rest being "psychedelic nonsense". "Please, Beatles," he concluded, "get back to the lyrics and melodies of the *Can't Buy Me Love* class. I just dread to think what your 'progression' will give us next."

In 1968, he described Tyrannosaurus Rex's debut album (deep breath) *My People Were Fair and Had Sky in Their Hair... But Now They're Content to Wear Stars on Their Brows* as "the biggest load of rubbish I have ever heard", prompting a bumper postbag of complaint. The big news of that eventful year, as far as he was concerned, was the short-lived rock'n'roll revival that saw portly, square-looking Bill Haley and his Comets arrive at the Locarno on May 23, more than a decade after his big hits. It's almost as though Bob Dylan wrote *Ballad of a Thin Man* specifically for this very Mr. Jones. To be fair to him, however, Jones eventually calmed down a bit when psychedelia gave way to progressive rock and heavy metal. He even found some nice things to say about Marc Bolan's glam rock makeover with T. Rex.

Meanwhile, something rather more interesting had been happening a little further down the page, though it only lasted for nine months in 1967. The paper's folk correspondent Gertrude (yes, just Gertrude) branched out from trad hey-nonny-nonny stuff to incorporate blues. Before long, she was also singing the praises of the Incredible String Band and Mothers of Invention, while expressing the hope that Bristol could soon boast a hippy club in the mould of London's UFO. Her *Folk Spot* column was also rebranded as *The Flowerpot* ("folk, blues and beyond"). "One great aspect of the underground Beautiful People scene is the mixing of so many art forms (i.e. pop, folk, blues, poetry, creative dance, light shows) from so many different cultures and the total involvement of all participants," Gertrude enthused on July 27. Perhaps she should have rolled one to relax her uptight colleagues.

The *Bristol Evening Post* seemed similarly confused and appeared to suffer something of a crisis in trying to work out what was going on. But at least the paper made an effort. They'd noticed that tastes were changing and changing fast. A case in point was Herman's Hermits who would once have packed the Colston but attracted only "a smattering" of fans to their disastrous 1969 show, while 'underground' bands Jethro Tull and Ten Years After were "outstanding successes". The Hall's Entertainments Manager, Kenneth Cowley, took a suitably progressive approach, describing underground music as "maturer, deeper. Pop is better for it." The *Post* noted that while "hippies arouse deep feelings of hatred among the respectable public," the Colston was welcoming them with open arms. "They certainly look very odd," conceded Mr. Cowley, "but they don't come to take part in the frenzied fan worships we used to see not so long ago. They are extremely polite."

By 1969, *Teenpage* had a new editor, Penny Weston, and broadened its horizons slightly. But some of these features were quite jaw-dropping. On January 2, 1969, for example, Ms. Weston introduced readers to Bristol's latest exciting competitive dating game: Blacklisting. The rules were very simple. White teenage girls hang out in local West Indian clubs trying to notch up as many 'coloured' boyfriends as possible. Naturally, the 'coloured' lads were delighted. But all the girls interviewed opted for anonymity. 'Attractive blonde shop assistant' Gillian, 17, said her dad would beat the living daylights out of her if he found out: "He's worse than Alf Garnett."

"They are more domineering and independent than other boys," swooned another girl of her many dates. "But I would not marry one as I feel they are unreliable and lazy."

Oh…

Later that year, *Teenpage* found an imaginative way to combine its two greatest obsessions: pop music and fruity teenage girls. They'd actually held a Teenpage Ball the previous year, but this was a much bigger one. Taking place in the swanky Mayfair Suite in the New Bristol Centre, it took the form of a beauty contest combined with a concert featuring the UK's hottest new band. The band in question? Deep Purple, fresh from the Albert Hall, where they'd performed Jon Lord's *Concerto For Group and Orchestra*. This had much to commend it, but was not widely noted for its teen appeal.

The lively, occasionally bizarre *Teenpage* was mothballed and long-serving reporter Brian K. Jones pensioned off in June 1971. In its place, the paper launched a twice-weekly column titled *Oyez!* (WDP executives clearly taking the view that a term used as a call for silence by crusty court officials would prove irresistibly appealing to the region's pop kids). This lacked all the spark and fun of its predecessor and was mostly concerned with local bands of no consequence. By the mid-seventies, the *WDP* seemed to have lost interest in popular music altogether.

For the student press of the late sixties sit-in era, gigs (or 'dances' as they were usually described) had become 'happenings' or 'freak-outs' - with the ubiquitous John Peel frequently wafting around backstage - or even revolutionary acts in which The Kids took on and were often beaten down by The Man. See, for example, the very different ways in which the great Small Faces riot at the Colston Hall in 1968 was reported.

It's important to remember that not all audiences got the memo about the underground takeover. While groovy scenes were developing in Haight-Ashbury and Carnaby Street during the Summer of Love, it took a long time for these to penetrate the English provinces. There's a great photograph from the *Daily Mirror* of Jimi Hendrix's first Bristol show in February 1967. Across the pond, 30,000 freaks had just gathered for the Great Human Be-In in Golden Gate Park, long-haired kids were being hassled by the pigs on Sunset Strip and the peacocking Beautiful People were gearing up for June's Monterey Pop Festival. But the *Mirror*'s snap, taken from behind Hendrix to show the Locarno audience, reveals that Bristol's teens were dressed as though it was still 1963. And even into the late sixties, when 'serious' former teen idols like Steve Winwood were bloviating about their move into more progressive music, they continued to be drowned out by battalions of screaming teenage girls at the Colston.

That said, we should also bear in mind that many local venues had strict dress codes throughout the sixties and beyond. The Locarno only lifted its code in June 1970 with the launch of its progressive rock series, the announcement that audiences could now wear what they liked being a major selling point. Over at the Top Rank (later Papillons, Romeo and Juliets, Syndicate, Odyssey, The Works and, currently, SWX), punters had to wait until 1972 for the dress code (including the ties-only rule) to be relaxed under new management. Similarly, the start of the new weekly Boobs night at Tiffany's that March was marked with an announcement that "for these special performances there will be no limitations on dress".

The development of more sophisticated and powerful amplification equipment also proved a matter of concern to the old guard of journalists. Few *Post* reviews of seventies rock shows at the Colston Hall failed to remark that the awful racket was way too loud, seemingly heedless of the only sensible thing Ted Nugent ever said: "If it's too loud, you're too old!"

There are those who claim that a similar revolution to the underground takeover took place in the late seventies with the advent of punk. I would argue, controversially, that this has been grossly exaggerated and does not bear close scrutiny. That's not to deny the cultural significance of the punk movement. It's also true to say that there were some big tours by major punk acts, especially in 1977. At the same time, record companies made life very difficult indeed for mid-level bands, while rising acts who declined to conform to the new orthodoxy - such as Iron Maiden, Def Leppard and Diamond Head - had to bide their time until their popularity could no longer be ignored. Technically, all three started out as indie acts, since their earliest recordings were DIY releases on their own labels.

But the prevailing narrative that claims 'boring old farts' were seen off by the filth and the fury overnight during punk's Year Zero runs up against some inconvenient facts. As we shall see, the likes of ELO, AC/DC, Thin Lizzy, UFO, Ritchie Blackmore's Rainbow, Steve Hillage, Lynyrd Skynyrd, Hawkwind, Fleetwood Mac and Rush all did a roaring trade locally during the punk years. On one night in 1977, Peter Gabriel and Camel played sell-out gigs in Bristol on the same night, at the Hippodrome and Colston Hall respectively. What's more, the charts were full of disco and soft rock, with punk barely registering. Major acts like the Stones, Bob Dylan, Queen, Led Zeppelin and even the disgraced Eric Clapton actually increased their audiences during the punk years. Even more gallingly for those expectorating revolutionaries, each of the apex prog bands (Yes, Genesis, ELP, Pink Floyd) were completely unaffected and enjoyed their biggest hit singles long after the movement's 15 minutes had expired. And globally, five of the top ten biggest selling albums of all time were released in 1976 and 1977. None of these were by The Clash. In fact, they were by the Eagles (twice), Fleetwood Mac, The Bee Gees and Meat Loaf. Furthermore, back in 2020 the BPI compiled a chart of the most streamed songs from 1977. The top six places were taken by ELO, Fleetwood Mac, Queen and Bob Marley. Not a single punk recording registered in the top ten. When the Official Chart Company undertook a similar exercise in 2022, it was found that the most-streamed songs from 1976 and 1977 were both by Fleetwood Mac - *Go your Own Way* and *Dreams* respectively. (Indeed, the OCC's year-by-year anlaysis revealed a striking disparity between the views of self-appointed tastemakers and actual popularity, with the critically reviled likes of Journey, Toto, Bon Jovi and Bryan Adams - artists whose music could only be heard in rock clubs and on specialist radio shows on release in the early 1980s - now taking their places among the nation's favourites.)

The truth is that the music punk was supposed to wipe off the face of the earth not only survived but remains in rude health today. This isn't something that can be said of trad jazz or the beat boom acts who failed to evolve in the late sixties.

This will earn me few friends, but you may be forgiven for detecting a certain disdain for national music journalism. The experience of wading through piles of old inkies serves as a reminder that, with some notable exceptions, many hacks were more interested in posturing than writing about music - a phenomenon that became supercharged in the punk years. Many of their judgements have not aged well. These days, for example, the brilliance of Led Zeppelin goes virtually unchallenged. During their lifetime as a band, however, they were subjected to relentless bile and hatred. What's more, the most influential band of all time, Black Sabbath (step outside if you want to argue), were widely treated as a joke and, bizarrely, in some quarters AC/DC were considered to be a punk act. It's amusing to see some of the writers concerned continuing to ply their trade, having quietly 'updated' their opinions.

'I May Be Old, But I Got to See All the Cool Bands' reads the T-shirt stretched across the beer belly of many a smug old rocker. There are few experiences more unedifying than being cornered by a greybeard bore who hasn't been to a sweaty club for decades but is happy to pontificate *ad infinitum* about the supposed 'death of rock'.

Personally, I prefer the rival Homer Simpson design: 'Never Too Old to Rock!' To be clear: this book is not intended as an endorsement of the nostalgic view that everything was much better in the Good Old Days. It might have been tempting to reach that conclusion in the 1980s - acknowledged by all but Dylan Jones as the grimmest decade since the advent of rock - but there's no shortage of great music being made today by artists who face very different challenges to those experienced by their forebears. You might have to look a little harder to find it, but for my money the most adventurous, creative and exciting music can be found in the fields of global metal, extreme metal and modern prog. And the standard of musicianship displayed by these young bands is quite astonishing.

Similarly, while we have lost many great venues since the 1960s and 1970s, we have also gained others that are run by enthusiasts with a genuine - horrible buzz term alert! - passion for music. In Bristol, the Exchange, Thekla, Fleece and Louisiana spring to mind.

Finally, if you're looking for sneery, 'ironic', distancing phrases like 'dad-rock' or 'rawk', which are routinely used by a certain breed of snooty journalist who imagine themselves to be above this sort of thing, you're reading the wrong book. Bands have been selected for inclusion because I really like their music (or because there's an entertaining and/or illuminating story attached). Even Uriah Heep. *Especially* Uriah Heep.

Note: In 2020, the Colston Hall was 'rebranded' as the Bristol Beacon. Yes, it's not the greatest of names but at least it doesn't honour a dead slave trader. I've used the original name throughout, simply because that's what the Hall was called when these gigs took place.

1963

S exual intercourse begins, if Philip Larkin is to be believed, as the sixties belatedly kick off after the coldest UK winter in living memory... This is the tumultuous year of the Profumo affair, the Great Train Robbery, the assassination of JFK, Martin Luther King Jr's 'I Have a Dream' speech and the launch of *Doctor Who*... In the world of music, it's all about The Beatles, who release their first two LPs and top both the singles and albums charts. Little known combo The Rolling Stones also put out their first single, *Come On*. It peaks at number 21. The game-changing *The Freewheelin' Bob Dylan* comes out in May, but isn't a hit in the UK for another year or so... Locally, the four-month Bristol Bus Boycott led by Paul Stephenson eventually forces the Bristol Omnibus Company to back down on its refusal to employ black and Asian workers... Tony Benn renounces his peerage and wins nearly 80% of the vote in the subsequent Bristol South-East by-election... Russell Pascoe, 22, is strung up in Horfield prison for murder, becoming the third-to-last person to be hanged in the UK... Florence Brown becomes Bristol's first woman Lord Mayor... On the big screen, The *Day the Earth Caught Fire* and *The Quatermass Xperiment* director Val Guest unleashes a smallpox epidemic in Bath in his minor apocalypse flick *80,000 Suspects*. But there were fewer cinemas in which to see it. Twenty Bristol fleapits shut their doors for good between 1956 and 1965. This year it was the turn of the Tatler, which closed with *My Bare Lady* (winner of the coveted Anatomy Award at the Paris Nudist Film Festival). It's now the site of the Old Market underpass.

Gene Vincent
Bath Pavilion, 8 April 1963
The birth of rock'n'roll is beyond the scope of this book, but less-than-

sweet Eugene Vincent Craddock's 1963 show at the Bath Pavilion acts as the perfect scene-setter, introducing many of rock's key characters. One of the original leather-clad, gun-toting, hotel room smashing bad boys of rock who became a template for generations of surly frontmen, Vincent had played in the west many times on packages with the likes of Sam Cooke and Little Richard. When Eddie Cochran perished in a car crash outside Chippenham on the way back to London after a gig at the Bristol Hippodrome in April 1960, passenger and tour mate Vincent hobbled away with a broken leg. Legend has it that the first copper on the scene was a Wiltshire police cadet named David Harman. He later claimed that he learned to play the guitar by sneaking into the evidence room and twanging away on Cochran's Gretsch over several evenings. Harman subsequently adopted the stage name of Dave Dee and enjoyed a string of hits with his chums Dozy, Beaky, Mick and Tich. That same Gretsch had been briefly carried for Cochran earlier on the tour by adoring fan Mark Feld, who, as Marc Bolan, subsequently died in - cue: spooky music - a car crash. And while we're digressing into Cochran lore, it's probably worth mentioning the longstanding rumour that he fathered a love child while in Bristol, though this is probably bollocks.

Anyway, Gene Vincent's Pavilion show was one of the earliest gigs staged in Bath by Freddy Bannister - the great unsung hero of local music promotion. He put on all the big music events at the Pavilion and on Wednesday nights at the Bristol Corn Exchange and was also the man behind both Bath festivals and the later, legendary Knebworth festivals. In the early sixties, Freddy was promoting gigs all over the UK, but always considered the Pavilion his flagship venue. "Because we had a Monday night, it gave us a chance to get bands that you couldn't normally get to work," he told me. "When people brought in Americans for a tour, Monday nights were pretty dead so we had our pick."

Vincent's manager at the time was the fearsome Don Arden - father of Sharon Osbourne and the fella who once allegedly dangled Robert Stigwood by his ankles from a fourth floor office window to dissuade him from poaching the Small Faces. Arden appointed a burly former wrestler and bit-part actor as the star's driver and minder. This was Peter Grant, who went on to acquire his own notorious reputation as the manager of Led Zeppelin. According to Mark Blake's suitably hair-raising biography

Bring It On Home, Arden issued Grant with the instruction: "Make sure that fucker gets to the shows in one piece and stays off the whisky".

The identity of Vincent's backing band at the Pavilion is unclear but by the time he played the Colston Hall in a package with Jerry Lee Lewis the following month he was being backed by The Outlaws. A bunch of top session musicians put together by producer Joe Meek (of *Telstar* fame), their ranks included keyboard player Chas Hodges (later of Chas & Dave), drummer Mick Underwood (later of Ian Gillan's band) and an 18-year-old guitar prodigy from Weston-super-Mare named Ritchie Blackmore.

The Outlaws swiftly moved on and Mr. Be-Bop-A-Lula found himself back in Bristol playing a show at the Victoria Rooms on January 25, 1964, with his new backing band, The Shouts. University student paper *Nonesuch News* dispatched reporter Jo Holmes to review the gig by "one of the first exponents of rock" and grill him in his dressing room afterwards.

The show had been an eventful one with a certain amount of band nudity, which Jo described as their "strip and shout act" during which Vincent did "his best to seduce the microphone". Apparently, this was the first time they'd performed such an outrage on stage. Post-show explanations ranged from "we felt like doing something shocking" to "[we] did it for laughs". "It was the Bristol girls," added the drummer ("his fleshy torso now more modestly attired in a string vest").

Jo reported that Vincent "has the pathetic air of a cocker spaniel whose owner has just whipped him for no apparent reason. Moustached and taciturn, his manager [possibly Arden himself; Peter Grant appears to have been clean-shaven at the time] stood nearby, strategically placed (so we discovered) to enable him to communicate his displeasure in mysterious sign language."

"Assuming the combined role of country boy and southern gentleman," Vincent addressed her as ma'am and admitted that he was "kind of afraid of universities" because he thought students would be too intellectual to appreciate rock music. He also ventured his opinion of The Beatles ("an asset to rock'n'roll") and talked about his formative blues influences, but refused to be drawn on 'the colour problem': "Being a Southerner, I don't think you should ask me questions like that".

The Beatles

Bath Pavilion, 10 June 1963

The Fabs played their first headline show round these parts a couple of months after the release of debut album *Please Please Me* and a week before Paul McCartney's 21st birthday. "I booked The Beatles a few months before they actually appeared," Freddy Bannister told me. "I remember thinking that their price was an absolute liberty. I think they were asking £250, when I could get more established bands for £100."

Of the gig itself, he had two clear memories: "Paul and John peering through the holes in the stage curtains, looking worried and asking me what sort of crowd it was. The other one is going on stage to do my normal plug for next week's gig. I walked out in front of the curtains and literally got pushed back by the yelling and screaming. I decided there and then not to do my announcement and just said 'Here's The Beatles'. The curtain opened and I walked back into The Beatles as they were playing, which is something that will always stick in my mind."

Bristol musician Mike Tobin was there for this historic show, and he didn't even have to pay to get in. "As my band The Magnettes were one of the local groups that Freddy Bannister used as a support act regularly (he even included a photo of us in his book), we always got in free to his gigs. So it was that me and bass player Pete Evans (RIP) were mingling backstage on this night. Pete was a boffin - every band had one - and The Beatles were having problems with their PA system, so he fiddled with it and fixed it for them. There were two support bands: Chet & The Triumphs from Bristol and the Colin Anthony Combo from Bath. They both did a slot each, then The Beatles came on and did a set. Amazing as it may seem, the two support acts came back on and did another set before the headliners returned for another finale."

The following month, the Fabs headed west again on their summer seaside tour, staying in room 49 at the Royal Pier Hotel. They played 12 shows over six days at the Weston-super-Mare Odeon between July 22 and 27. Local fan Sandra Woodruff (nee Blaken), 16, managed to get several Beatles autographs on an underpants card (no, really), as well as taking photographs of them at the hotel. In 2022, her collection sold at auction for £11,360.

While in Weston, The Beatles were filmed and photographed larking about on Brean Down beach wearing striped Edwardian bathing costumes.

The Rolling Stones
Bath Pavilion, 11 November 1963

The Stones' first west country date on their very first headlining tour of the UK. Debut single *Come On* had been released in June, and this was local punters' first opportunity to see the Fabs' famously scruffy counterparts in the flesh. As usual at the Pav, the headliners played two sets. Support act tonight was Merseybeat act The Undertakers, fronted by a chap named Brian Jones, which must have been confusing. The Stones, meanwhile, returned to play the Corn Exchange on December 18.

The Beatles
Colston Hall, 15 November 1963

The Beatles had played to about a thousand people at the Colston back in March, low on the bill of a package tour. Eight months later, Beatlemania was in full swing when they returned for the first of their two Bristol headline shows. Martin Creasy's book *Beatlemania!* carries an extensive report of the shenanigans. Travelling up from Exeter, The Beatles hid in a Bedminster side street and phoned ahead to arrange an escort to the Colston. "Operation Get The Beatles into Colston Hall Safely was deemed a success," continues Creasy, "and the heat was off for at least a few hours until Operation Get them Out Again. There were literally hundreds of girls around Colston Hall for up to eight hours. Many had skipped work, risking the sack. The hall's famous red doors were now adorned with messages of love for various Beatles. Tickets were being hawked at inflated prices, along with Beatle photos, and local sweet shops sold out of jelly babies." [Trivia note: female fans used to pelt the Fabs with jelly babies after they foolishly remarked that these were their favourite sweets. Good job they didn't say gobstoppers.]

The *Bristol Evening Post* really went to town on Fab-mania ("They're here!" screamed the front page), revealing important details about the foursome's supper in their Exeter hotel the previous night (turkey, ham and Horlicks, apparently). Future *Radio Bristol* presenter Roger Bennett (billed as 'the *Evening Post*'s Own Beatle' on account of his moptop) had been dispatched to report on their 'battle against boredom' while trapped in their dressing room. He also got to witness the hysterical scenes at the Colston Hall show. "They are intelligent enough to write their own numbers. They are musicianly enough to play the right chords - and in tune too. And they are adult enough not to take the whole screaming affair too seriously," revealed Roger, before making a startling confession: "My jazz friends will kill me for this… But I LIKE THE BEATLES."

Carter-Lewis and the Southerners
Co-op Hall, November 1963

This lot were an early Brummie rock group who would hardly be worth mentioning if it wasn't for the fact that their guitarist was a young session musician named James Patrick Page. Yep, that's right, the 19-year-old Mr. Zoso himself played at the Co-op Hall, which was situated a few hundred yards from the Corn Exchange. The hall itself was a low-ceilinged room up on the first floor, necessitating much inconvenience for grumbling roadies and band members alike who had to haul their gear up the stairs.

John Carter and Ken Lewis were a pair of old-school songwriters who'd been talked into forming the Southerners purely to promote their material. Page joined them very briefly, along with future Pretty Things drummer Viv Prince. The guitarist swiftly moved on, while the Southerners eventually reinvented themselves as The Flower Pot Men. We'll meet them again when they pop up at the Colston Hall in 1967.

1964

The first student protests against the Vietnam War take place in New York and San Francisco... Cassius Clay is crowned Heavyweight Champion of the World and announces his change of name to Muhammad Ali... Race riots break out in Harlem, Philadelphia and Chicago... Martin Luther King Jr is the youngest-ever recipient of the Nobel Peace Prize... Harold Wilson becomes PM after Labour defeat the Tories at the General Election... The House of Commons votes to abolish the death penalty... BBC2 begins broadcasting and *The Sun* newspaper is launched... Mods and Rockers battle in Brighton... The Beatles mount a hugely successful invasion of the USA... Dr. Robert Moog unveils his synthesizer... *Top of the Pops* and Radio Caroline go on air to delight the nation's pop kids... The Kinks, The Animals and The Rolling Stones achieve their first UK number ones with *You Really Got Me*, *House of the Rising Sun* and *It's All Over Now* respectively... Labour peer Lord (Ted) Willis makes a speech in the House of Lords dismissing The Beatles and Stones as "a cheap candy floss substitute for culture"... Future Bristol University chancellor Dorothy Hodgkin becomes the third woman to win the Nobel Prize in Chemistry... A fella named Bill Bailey is born in Bath...1 Redcliffe Street, aka the Robinson Building, aka the DRG Building, is completed, bringing the 1960s modernist dream to Bristol... Angela Carter graduates from Bristol University with a degree in English Literature. She goes on to become an award-winning poet, novelist and journalist, and opens a folk club in Clifton... In early March, The Beatles head west to film sequences for *A Hard Day's Night*. They can be seen larking about on the Taunton to Minehead branch line and at Crowcombe Heathfield station on the West Somerset Railway, where they run alongside the train shouting, "Hey mister - can we have our ball back?" The film is released in July. If that doesn't appeal, *The Beauty Game* is also showing in cinemas. A very different Val Guest film, this is, er, a searing expose of the beauty pageant game. A pretty, working class Bristol typist is seduced with dreams of glamour by a sleazy photographer from the evil *Western Daily Press* while on holiday in Weston-super-Mare. Watch out for Sid James as a beauty contest judge in Minehead.

Billy J. Kramer and the Dakotas
Longleat House, 3 May 1964

It's the UK's very first outdoor pop riot! There had been riotous scenes at earlier indoor shows by The Beatles, Stones and even the future Sir Cliff. But this was the first outbreak of al fresco hormonal teen pop pandemonium, which succeeded in grabbing national and local front page headlines (*Riot at Longleat* screamed the *Western Daily Press*; *Big Probe Follows Riot Over Billy J* added the *Bristol Evening Post*; *Stately Home Stormed by Pop Fans* was the *Daily Mirror*'s take).

It all came about because the sixth Marquess of Bath, Henry Frederick Thynne, was starting to feel the pinch in the early 1960s. So he decided to organise some outdoor music events on the steps of Longleat House. The first show was by Acker Bilk in 1961. Legendary jazzman Acker's mellow mellifluousness was never going to inspire beatniks to storm the barricades and the event was judged a great success. But Thynne - a former Conservative MP, father of the one with the wifelets and a great admirer of Adolf Hitler - was keenly aware that a new sound was enthralling Britain's pop kids. So he set out to grab a slice of the lucrative beat group action.

Despite the American-sounding name, Billy J. Kramer and the Dakotas were part of the Merseybeat scene. Managed by Brian Epstein of Beatles fame, Kramer enjoyed a string of hits that were mostly written for him by John Lennon and Paul McCartney or were covers of their earlier songs. And by 1964, anything Fabs-related was liable to have teens pulling on their Beatle wigs and screaming uncontrollably.

Ever the huckster, Thynne became the first - and probably only - Lord to appear on *Top of the Pops*. Hosted by Pete Murray and Jimmy Savile, the March 18 1964 edition included The Rolling Stones (*Not Fade Away*), The Dave Clark Five (*Bits and Pieces*) and Cilla Black (*Anyone Who Had a Heart*). At number one that week was Billy J. Kramer and the Dakotas with *Little Children*. They turned up to mime to it in the studio and naturally his Lordship was eager to tag along to plug his upcoming show. Rather improbably, he claimed to be a "terrific fan" of Billy J and responded to jibes about his short back and sides by asserting: "I'm with it. I may look a square but I am more of an oblong." Alas, the BBC's tape was wiped, like so many others from that era.

The PR gambit worked. Some 7,000 (according to the *Post*) or 13,000 (according to the *Wiltshire Echo*) kids literally beat a path to Longleat, having paid 2/6d each for their tickets. The *Echo*'s colourful report said that they "choked six miles of roads from Warminster to Longleat; trampled acres of parkland; laid siege to the 16th century house and fainted in scores."

It started quietly enough. According to *Western Daily Press* reporter Peter Hiscocks, Kramer turned up at a rear entrance but was declined admission by a policeman who refused to believe he was a pop star. The delay caused the crowd to become impatient, so for some bizarre reason Lord Bath's PR man stepped up to the microphone to announce the presence of a WDP reporter on the steps in the hope that this would quell the over-excited teens. "There were some cheers," reported Hiscocks, whose ego was clearly wounded, "but some of the many angry teenage girls screamed, 'We don't want him, we want Billy.'

"As he passed me to go on to the steps, Billy J gave a faint smile and said 'I'm not worried'. But his face was pale and his hands trembled."

The seething mass of over-excited teens promptly surged forward and the 15 coppers on duty were unable to prevent them overwhelming the barriers. The star was "ordered off stage" by the rozzers within minutes, said the *Post*. The *Daily Mirror* had a different interpretation: "Billy J took one startled look at the mob and fled."

"Hysterical women, frightened girls and half-suffocated children were dragged from the screaming crowd by police and ambulance men," reported the *Western Daily Press*, adding that Longleat's banqueting hall was turned into an improvised casualty station. Three fans wound up in hospital, 'scores' required first aid and all the band's gear ("worth £300") was trampled underfoot.

"It was worth it," insisted 15-year-old 'injured pop girl' Jacqueline Joyce of Keynsham, pictured by the *Post* clutching her prize of a Billy J autograph while strapped to a bed in Bath's Royal United Hospital.

His Lordship rebuffed suggestions that his next show would have to be cancelled because of the furore: "… we'll be better equipped. Stronger barriers and barbed wire."

This hardly proved necessary given that his next booking was The Bachelors. Longleat continued to host outdoor pop shows for another year or so. The only event that rivalled Billy J was to come in August.

The Kinks
Corn Exchange, 27 May 1964

This is The Kinks' earliest recorded local headline show (they'd already come west on a package tour with the Dave Clark Five and The Hollies). It took place a couple of weeks before their first attempt at recording the career-making *You Really Got Me*, which they'd written back in March and were already playing live. That means this show was likely to have marked an historic occasion: the very first heavy metal song ever played in Bristol.

In his autobiography, *There Must Be a Better Way*, Freddy Bannister reports that next to the Small Faces, The Kinks were the most badly behaved band he put on, "normally turning up late, if at all, and on one memorable occasion the stewards had to break up a fight on stage when Mick Avory, The Kinks' drummer, hit Dave Davies over the head with a cymbal." Things got even worse between the brawling twosome after that. On stage in Cardiff the following year, Davies kicked over Avory's drum kit, prompting the drummer to brain him with a hi-hat stand and then run away, fearing he'd finally killed his bandmate. Davies was carted off to hospital, where he received 16 stitches.

In his rollicking latest volume of autobiography, *Living on a Thin Line*, Dave Davies elaborates on this key moment in Kinks history and the events leading up to it. "In Taunton, on 18 May, we had argued about the set list. I wanted to change things around a bit but Ray disagreed, and Mick sat on his arse refusing to comment either way. That was so typical of Mick at the time, like all he wanted to do was sit behind his drums and not communicate anything he felt about the band… I told him to stop being so lazy and tell us what he thought, and our argument escalated into full-on fisticuffs. The road managers had to prise us apart, but not before we had started laying into each other.

"That set the tone for the following evening in Cardiff which, after a glorious eighteen months in the spotlight, could have been the night The

Kinks fell apart under the weight of battling egos. Mick and I had tried to stay out of each other's way that day, but by the time we arrived at the Capitol Theatre in Cardiff and went onstage, emotions were once again running very high. We opened with *You Really Got Me*, but something inside me snapped in the middle of the next number, *Beautiful Delilah*. I glared at Mick. 'You're a useless cunt,' I yelled before telling him that his playing was shit and his drums would sound better if he played them with his cock. I made a gesture, like he was wanking on his drums, then kicked over his bass drum and the rest of his kit fell like dominoes. I turned back to the microphone and started singing again, like nothing had happened.

"Suddenly I'm lying on my back in the dressing room backstage, blood pouring from my head. I learned later that Mick had picked up his hi-hat and thwacked me on the back on my head. He considered his drums to be like sacred objects, and he took what I'd done very badly, like I had assaulted him personally. Apparently the audience had howled with laughter and, for Mick, there could be no bigger humiliation."

The Animals
Bath Pavilion, 29 June 1964

The Animals played in the west country many times back in the 1960s. But this was their most significant local show. On this very day, *House of the Rising Sun* - a song they'd begun playing while on tour with Chuck Berry a couple of months earlier - hit number one in the UK singles chart. Because email and social media hadn't been invented yet, they received a telegram at the Pavilion informing them of this feat. Eric Burdon and chums celebrated as any self-respecting young musicians would in the circumstances, by getting hog-snortingly drunk. Present at this one was Ken Pustelnik, who ran the Blues Club at the Dug Out and later became the drummer with legendary British blues-rockers the Groundhogs.

"The guitarist [Hilton Valentine] was so pissed that he lay on his back for the entire show. Everyone was going, 'Jimmy Page is in the wings'. [As a session musician, Page had played uncredited on many of the hits of the era, but not this one.] He wasn't. I went to have a look and there was nobody there. I thought that explains why the bloke on his back on stage is playing such awful guitar. But as a celebration, it was amazing. It was a real moment to be there. They were so happy."

The Rolling Stones
Longleat House, 2 August 1964

On April 22, 1964, the *Western Daily Press* carried a photograph that appeared to show a quartet of shamed dissidents who'd been captured by the agents of a brutal Third World dictator and were using their hands to shield their faces from the camera prior to being interrogated or executed. The text below revealed that they were, in fact, schoolgirls who'd been caught playing truant, having queued all night outside the Colston Hall for Stones tickets that went on sale at 8:30am. "The Beatles are all right, but we wouldn't stay up all night for them," said one of the unnamed female delinquents.

1964 was a big year for the Stones with a total of 206 gigs, taking in four UK tours and their first American one. They also released their debut album and three UK singles, including two number ones, and appeared on the first edition of *Top of the Pops* (performing *I Wanna Be Your Man*). Charlie Watts later observed that *Little Red Rooster* was the only blues single ever to top the UK chart.

The band played the Colston Hall three times that year (January, May with Gene Vincent and Jamaican teenager Millie, of *My Boy Lollipop* fame, and October), but the first house of the October show was one Stone short. *Western Daily Press* pop correspondent Brian K. Jones drew the short straw and was sent on stage to tell the screaming teens that his namesake would not be appearing. The more famous Brian Jones had been stuck in traffic on the A4 and eventually arrived in Bristol at 7:15pm. Realising that he had no way of getting safely into the Hall, he appealed to the local police traffic department for help. Alas, they refused to believe he was a Rolling Stone until he produced a press cutting bearing his photograph. Further trouble ensued when Jones and accompanying rozzers arrived at the Colston Hall to find the promoters had locked all the doors (no 'elf and safety back then, kids) to prevent the swarms of ticketless fans getting in. His police escort then had to physically carry Brian into the venue past hordes of hysterical girls who were throwing themselves onto their Z-car. Inside, his proud mum was waiting to see him, having travelled down from the Jones family home in Cheltenham. Further rock'n'roll mayhem ensued during the show when Charlie Watts ripped his trousers because "he was playing so hard", reported the *Western Daily Press*. After this eventful show, the Stones stayed overnight at the Webbington Hotel and Country Club.

Sandwiched between the Colston Hall appearances, this August Bank Holiday outdoor show was much more of an event. Anywhere between 16,000 and 24,000 fans (reports differ) paid 2/6d each to see the band play on the steps of Longleat House. Their debut album had just spent 12 weeks at the top of the chart.

The sixth Marquess of Bath celebrated the occasion of his latest big outdoor pop show by addressing the crowd while sporting an ill-fitting Rolling Stones wig. Although security had been beefed up after the Billy J. Kramer riot, and chicken wire had been erected around the house, 227 girls and seven boys were reportedly treated for minor injuries in the ensuing melee. This time, however, the show went on. But it didn't exactly end as planned.

On August 5, Bristol United Press's *Week-End* magazine carried a typically appalled report of what happened, illustrated with plenty of vivid photographs.

"Superintendent J.G. Fisher looked at the surging crowd of 24,000 teenagers and said: 'I'm disgusted. I cannot understand how any supposedly intelligent person can lend himself to this kind of thing.'"

Leading a battalion of 50 cops charged with keeping the peace, Supt. Disgusted of Warminster eventually decided to put a stop to these disgraceful scenes of wanton teenage disorder whipped up by the surly degenerates on stage. Alas, he little anticipated the root vegetable insurrection he was about to unleash. "He climbed the steps to the front door of the Marquess of Bath's 16th century mansion and spoke to the wild, unhealthy-looking youth called Mick Jagger, who is The Rolling Stones' singer," continued *Week-End*'s Iain Gallantry. "He told Jagger: 'You can sing one more song and that's the lot.'

"Jagger replied by singing two. A hail of missiles flew from behind the crush barrier - buns, tin cans, orange peel, shoes, bags, baskets, even a plastic bag filled with carrots."

Longleat's rose garden was used as casualty station. "At one time, I counted 63 people unconscious on the grass. They were laying them out in rows, like fish stranded on a beach. Two boys had been beaten by girls who wielded stiletto-heeled shoes."

The fearless reporter decided it was time to confront his noble lordship.

"Do you feel morally justified in creating a situation in which life is endangered?" he demanded.

"Nobody was killed," retorted Lord Bath.

"Do you feel morally justified in creating a situation in which people are crushed to the point of unconsciousness?" pressed the impertinent hack.

"I am not concerned with morals."

"It's their own fault if they come here and get hurt," added press officer Andrew Bowen. "They don't have to come."

The Longleat report was carried in the same edition of *Week-End* as an account of riotous scenes at a performance by notorious trouser ripper PJ Proby at Filwood Broadway three days earlier. Clearly civilisation was on the verge of collapse. Clearly too, *Week-End*'s readers craved the full horrible details to tut-tut over at the breakfast table. Hastily, the magazine's editor decided to cash in by slapping a full colour shot of the Stones on the cover of the following week's edition. There was nothing new to add, so they just ran a photo spread of pictures taken in Lord Bath's library, with a hundred words or so of further disparagement of 'Mike Jagger': "He is hardly pretty although he does his best to be with his hair... Our office girl thinks Mr. Jagger is 'marvellous'. An elderly colleague won't recognise his name."

The original article also generated a bumper postbag. "Congratulations on a fine report on the Bank Holiday Sunday riot at Longleat," wrote D. White of Bishopston. "Having had to suffer The Rolling Stones' sound day and night from my teenage son's record player, I decided to find out more about them. I went with the family to the 'concert'. Words are not needed from me to describe what went on but I am happy to say my son now seems cured of his devotion to The Rolling Stones. He was bruised by the screaming girls; his feet were trampled on; and he hardly heard a note the group sang. Now I am glad we went!"

"Whatever is Bristol *Week-End* coming to?" demanded A.G. Genty of Westbury. "Five pages plus the cover devoted to teenage hooliganism is more than I could bear. If these youngsters must behave in such a violent animal way, let them do so but spare others the displeasure of having to watch."

"If the Marquis of Bath thought a little more about people instead of his pocket the disgusting incidents would never have happened," added T.

Kinnear (Mrs) of Belmont Road, St. Andrews. "As for the police, they are mad to allow such events in the first place."

Among the screaming teenage girls at Longleat that day was a young music fan and dairy farmer named Michael Eavis, blissfully unaware that it was his destiny to create an outdoor event that would comfortably eclipse the Longleat pop series. "That was a great show," he recalls. "I don't remember seeing any rioting, but the Stones were terrific. They were really young back then too. I actually wound up playing chess with Lord Bath - not then, but much later. It turned out that he didn't make a penny out of the Longleat events and only succeeded in annoying the locals."

Of course, the same would be true of Farmer Eavis's first two festivals…

The Pretty Things
Bath Pavilion, 17 September 1964

The *Western Daily Press*'s ceaseless quest to find pop combos who were even surlier, hairier and more outrageous than The Rolling Stones took *Beat Diary* columnist Brian K. Jones to the Bath Pavilion on this grim and rainy night. At the start of their career, Phil May and co had just enjoyed a minor hit with their first single, *Rosalyn*. "The audience were interested but by no means enthusiastic about this long-haired group who make the Stones look like choir boys," reported Mr. Jones.

But he was delighted to find a handful of teenage girls standing outside the stage door, "probably soaked to the skin," having written such inspiring lipstick messages on the group's van as: 'The Pretty Things are fab', 'You're lovelier than the Stones' and the curiously non-specific 'I love you with the hair'. Among them were Christine Clarke and Margaret Kingsbury of Keynsham, who'd followed the band from Reading and Trowbridge. "Maybe their hair is long but it is in fab condition," vouchsafed Chris. "We found them great company which our mothers and fathers would approve of," added Margaret.

"Yes Margaret, I'm sure they would," noted the droll reporter.

"We were very lucky to have Brian K. Jones," former *WDP* Deputy Editor Peter Gibbs told me. "He was deeply involved in the Bristol music scene and I think he even ran one of the local clubs."

The American Folk-Blues Festival
Colston Hall, 20 October 1964

As anyone who's ever read a Rolling Stones biography will know, the young Mick Jagger and Keith Richards bonded over their love of American blues artists and decided to form a band. They weren't alone. All over the UK, young white musicians were turned off by the sterility of the British music scene and looked to black Americans for inspiration. The best compositions were covered and occasionally stolen, the results eventually being sold back to white American youth by the truckload. Back in 1962, German promoters Horst Lippmann and Fritz Rau hit on the idea of bringing some of these great American artists to Europe as part of a touring festival. Billed as "a documentary of the Authentic Blues", this was originally branded, rather unfortunately, as the American Negro Blues Festival. It regularly visited the Colston Hall in the 1960s, beginning in 1964 with a stellar line-up that included Lightnin' Hopkins, Howlin' Wolf, Sleepy John Estes, Willie Dixon and Sonny Boy Williamson. Fortunately, someone had the good sense to film the first few tours, which are available on DVD as *The American Folk Blues Festival: The British Tours 1963-1966.*

According to Bristol University student newspaper *Nonesuch News*, Willie Dixon set out his stall at the Colston Hall by announcing: "God created man. Adam had the blues in the Garden of Eden. So God created woman and put Eve in the Garden of Eden to comfort Adam. And Man's had the blues ever since."

Mike Tobin couldn't wait for the show to pitch up in Bristol. "The German promoters Lippmann and Rau had taken this tour around Europe the previous year, but only included one English date at The Fairfield Halls, Croydon. Not having much of a clue where Croydon was, four of us set off in my Mini and found our way eventually - no M4, of course, or M25. Having been totally blown away by what we saw and heard that night we were excited to see that the package was at the Colston Hall in 1964. We were not disappointed. Amongst others, Howlin' Wolf proved to be one of the most exciting artists we had ever seen and to this day remains a huge influence on my musical thinking."

Sister Rosetta Tharpe

Corn Exchange, exact date unknown, September/October 1964

There are depressingly few female rock musicians. There are even fewer black female rock musicians. Black female rock musicians who deserve a place on any serious Greatest Guitarists of All Time list? Just the one.

Sister Rosetta Tharpe was a bisexual gospel musician who's been described as the 'godmother of rock'n'roll'. Never knowingly generous with his praise, Chuck Berry once said that his entire career had been "one long Sister Rosetta Tharpe impersonation". Way ahead of her time, Rosetta was the original shredder who pioneered the use of distortion on the electric guitar decades before Jimi Hendrix came along. She first played in Bristol at the Colston Hall on April 29 1964 as part of the 'American Folk, Blues and Gospel Caravan' package promoted by Harold Davison. This had been the opening night of the tour, whose bill included Muddy Waters and the Reverend Gary Davis. Also present at the Colston in his first role as a tour manager was the callow, 21-year-old Joe Boyd. In his vivid autobiography, *White Bicycles*, Boyd recalls introducing the acts in "American MC-style tones". He also describes his relief at how well it was received given that the acts seemed to be feuding between and among themselves. "The hall was full, the crowd queued for autographs afterwards and all my preconceptions about British enthusiasm for the blues were confirmed," he writes.

Rosetta Tharpe was picked out as one of the highlights by an uncredited reviewer from Bristol University student newspaper *Nonesuch News*, who'd been unimpressed by headliner Waters ("could have done much better"): "Sister Rosetta Sharpe got a great reaction - surprising in view of the stuff she sang." No elaboration was offered.

While on that tour, she made an appearance on a bizarre Granada TV show in which a disused railway station in south Manchester had been mocked up to look as though it was in the Deep South. Needless to say, it pissed with rain, so Rosetta plugged in and played *Didn't It Rain*. Ten million jaws dropped across the country.

So when she returned to play a handful of UK dates later that year, everybody wanted to see her.

According to US National Public Radio's 2019 *Turning the Tables* series focusing on "eight women who invented American popular music", one excited press report of the Bristol show was headlined *Beatle Boosters*

Defect: Bristolites Dig Blues Singer Sister Tharpe and noted that fans even stood outside the Corn Exchange to hear her play.

One of the lucky punters who got in was Ken Pustelnik. "I was absolutely gobsmacked," he recalls. "Women guitarists at the time were mostly folk singers playing acoustics. It was rare to see them playing electric guitars. They'd generally plunk away and do a bit of rhythm. She had a semi-acoustic guitar rather than the Gibson with which she was later associated, and she was brilliant. Not only that, but she played really loud. In those days, a lot of people from America came with these little amplifiers. Even if they were playing at the Colston Hall they weren't loud. But she was absolutely hammering it and everyone was going, '*Yeah!*' It was like an unbelievable novelty, but also magic. That's the only way I can describe it.

"At the Corn Exchange at that time you had really mixed audiences. There were teddy boys, proto-hippies, us weirdos who were the beatnik lot and a lot of ordinary people. I'm not kidding: there were a whole bunch of people who wouldn't talk to one another on the street turning to each other and going, 'Bloody great, isn't it?' She had everyone in the palm of her hand. Amazing woman."

Needless to say, Rosetta never received the kudos she so richly deserved during her lifetime. Shamefully, she wasn't admitted to the Rock & Roll Hall of Fame until 2018, 45 years after her death.

The Beatles
Colston Hall, 11 November 1964

The Beatles' final show at the Colston was also the last night on their Autumn tour. Showbiz tradition dictates that pranks will be played on these occasions. In the words of the *Western Daily Press*, as the quartet played *If I Fell* at the climax of the second house a "mystery man opened a lighting vent in the roof and emptied a large bag of flour on the group. The audience went mad with delight as it dropped in a white stream on the unsuspecting Beatles. John, Paul, George and Ringo broke into fits of laughter as the cloud settled on them."

One person who was decidedly unamused was Hall manager Ken Cowley. The outraged official demanded to know how his iron ring of security had been breached. It hadn't been difficult. Turned out that no fewer than 17 schoolgirls, including ticketless 13-year-old Hilary Wiltshire, snuck in through a back entrance left open for the cleaners and crammed themselves into a toilet. Only when one of them coughed was their enterprising ruse rumbled.

As for the mystery flour bomber, the following day the *Evening Post* ran a story headlined 'How We Bombed The Beatles'. Three lads and a copper's daughter claimed they'd done it by shinning up a drainpipe, running across two roofs, dropping through a trapdoor and waiting for their moment.

The Fabs' favourite local reporter Roger Bennett, who'd been granted another exclusive interview prior to the show, wasn't convinced. With a tenacity that would have shamed Woodward and Bernstein, he mounted a special investigation that eventually unmasked the real culprit: a stagehand.

What Roger didn't know, or was perhaps complicit in concealing, was that the barrage of screaming often drowned out a very different side of those lovable, cheeky moptops. In Paul Rees's biography of John Entwistle, *The Ox*, he tells the story of The High Numbers (shortly to become The Who) supporting The Beatles at Blackpool Opera House a few months before this Colston Hall show. The bassist described how, as usual, it was impossible to hear a note of music above the noise, which had led to the Fabs becoming increasingly jaded by 1964. But those old theatre dressing rooms always had a speaker feed on the wall coming directly from the stage microphones. So after their set, The High Numbers settled back to listen to The Beatles. In notes written for his proposed autobiography, Entwistle remarked: "Soon, the four of us were crying with laughter at the words they were singing and which only we were able pick up on - *It's Been a Hard Day's Cock, I Wanna Hold Your Cunt...*"

Bristol's final tally? Twelve girls collapsed with what was described as "emotional stress" while a further two were intercepted attempting to make a more personal connection with the objects of their lust on stage.

Fascinating Fabs trivia note: In his exemplary Beatles book *One Two Three Four: The Beatles in Time*, Craig Brown tells the story of John Lennon being given a short back and sides by German barber Klaus Baruch. This was in preparation for the bespectacled moptop's role as Private Gripweed in Richard Lester's *How I Won the War*, which was filmed in 1966 and released the following year. Brian Epstein was so determined not to feed the collectors' market that he instructed road manager/personal assistant Neil Aspinall to personally supervise incineration of Lennon's clippings.

But wily Klaus clearly held on to some of them. Fifty years later, a four inch lock was put on sale by Heritage Auctions of Dallas. It went for £35,000 - three times the estimate - to Paul Fraser of Bristol. This proved a very canny investment for Mr Fraser of Paul Fraser Collectibles on Whiteladies Road, Clifton. On his website, he will now sell you a half inch single strand from the noggin of Dr. Winston O'Boogie for a princely £399. Your loot also gets you a photocopy of Lennon's signed call sheet and certificate of authenticity. The strand is presented on a display card inside a frame, ready to hang or stand. "We believe these to be the only strands of John Lennon's hair available on the market," the company notes. Should you be wondering, the current going rate for a full set of Beatles autographs on a single sheet or photograph, also available from Paul Fraser Collectibles, is in the region of £20,000-£30,000.

1965

State troopers attack civil rights demonstrators in Selma, Alabama… Ian Brady and Myra Hindley are charged with the Moors Murders… *Thunderbirds* and *The Magic Roundabout* make their UK TV debuts. Peter Watkins' *The War Game* doesn't, because it's pulled for political reasons. Despite winning an Oscar in 1966, the film isn't broadcast for another 20 years… Kenneth Tynan says 'fuck' on the telly. The BBC issues an apology. Mary Whitehouse launches the National Viewers' and Listeners' Association… Bob Dylan's *Like a Rolling Stone*, The Rolling Stones' *(I Can't Get No) Satisfaction* and The Who's *My Generation* make waves culturally. But the biggest selling single of the year is *Tears* by Ken Dodd… In Bath, the former head of the BBC's Bristol-based Documentary Unit, John Boorman, shoots scenes for his feature debut, *Catch Us If You Can*: a cheap knock-off of *A Hard Day's Night*, which has the Dave Clark Five fooling about on the Royal Crescent and at the Roman Baths… Premiering at the Bristol Old Vic is *The Killing of Sister George* - the first mainstream British play with lesbian characters… Portishead's Beth Gibbons is born in Exeter. Damien Hirst and Massive Attack's Robert Del Naja are born in Bristol. J.K. Rowling is born in Yate.

Chuck Berry/Moody Blues

Colston Hall, 15 January 1965

It's the great Colston Hall Teddy Boy Riot! One of the big moral panics of 1964 had been about mods and rockers battling it out on Brighton seafront. But round these parts, a slightly older subculture was still making its baleful presence felt well into 1965. Mike Tobin was there to see the draped and bequiffed dandies in action. "As always when any of the original American rock'n'roll stars played in Bristol, there was a contingent of local Teddy Boys in the audience. They were not known for their tolerance of any other form of music, nor were they afraid to exhibit their dislike of acts that dared to cross boundaries into new musical territory."

This was the second of Chuck Berry's two Colston Hall appearances in the 1960s (he'd been here with Carl Perkins and The Animals on May 28 1964). Such was the nature of the package tour system that even a musical giant like him, billed here as 'The King of Rhythm and Blues', barely had time to enjoy a swift duck walk before being told to sling his hook.

He was sharing the bill with five (count 'em!) other acts: The Moody Blues (who'd just hit number one in the UK charts with their debut single *Go Now!* - originally recorded by another black American artist: Bessie Banks), The Graham Bond Organisation, Long John Baldry and the Hoochie Coochie Men, and Winston G, and The Five Dimensions. Interestingly, the Graham Bond Organisation (whose ranks included the feuding pre-Cream Jack Bruce and already smacked-out Ginger Baker), were billed above The Moody Blues because the latter hadn't had their hit when the tour was booked. This reportedly led to a certain amount of backstage rancour. The tour was promoted by Robert Stigwood and the two houses at the Colston Hall started at 6:20pm and 8:45pm. Tickets were priced from five shillings (25p) to fifteen shillings (75p).

It was during the Moodies' set that Mike witnessed the whole thing kicking off. "They were a very good band, fronted then by Denny Laine. Although they were going down well with the majority of the audience (including me), the Teds weren't having any of it and massed at the front of the auditorium shouting abuse, threatening violence and ignoring the few stewards trying to quell them.

"At this point, the Moodies stopped playing and drummer Graeme Edge left his kit, walked to the front of the stage and pointed to his nose and then to the toe of his boot. He was cheered and clapped as he strode back to his drums, and they continued their set with no further problems."

As usual with American stars touring the UK at the time, Chuck was equipped with an English backing band, openers The Five Dimensions (best known for once having featured the young Rod 'The Mod' Stewart) doing the honours. (Interestingly, Long John Baldry's Hoochie Coochie Men had also, until quite recently, boasted peripatetic Rodney on vocals.) His audience-pleasing set included *Johnny B. Goode*, *Maybellene*, and

Nadine, underlining Chuck's huge influence on the British Invasion bands who were then starting to coin it in his homeland. The busy pioneering rock'n'roller even found time to record *Chuck Berry in London* for Chess Records during this tour.

A footnote: legendary local 'character' Mad Ernie, who used to run the Shakespeare pub in Totterdown, always said that seeing Chuck at the Colston Hall was his musical epiphany, leading to a lifelong obsession with Mr. Ding-a-Ling. He even claimed to have shared a stage with his hero. The truth was slightly less glamorous. He'd been violently ejected from a Berry gig in Swindon after mounting a one-man stage invasion.

Screamin' Jay Hawkins

Corn Exchange, Spring 1965 (exact date unknown)

Shock rock started here. Everyone from Screaming Lord Sutch (an obvious imitator) to Arthur Brown, Alice Cooper, Marilyn Manson and Rob Zombie owes a debt to Jalacy Hawkins, whose distinctive booming operatic vocals and extensive use of spooky stage props was revolutionary back in the early sixties.

Although Hawkins' biggest hit, the oft-covered (notably by Nina Simone and Creedence Clearwater Revival) *I Put a Spell On You*, had been released back in 1956, he didn't make it to the UK until this tour in early 1965, which was promoted by Don Arden.

Ken Pustelnik was at the Corn Exchange and reports that Bristol was treated to the full theatrical production, with the smoking skull on a stick, plenty of early pyro and a caped Screamin' Jay giving it the full OTT comic horror. "I remember the curtain going up to reveal the coffin on stage. The music started, the lid slowly opened and he emerged singing *I Put a Spell On You*. Brilliant!"

But why open with your best-known song rather than leave it till the end, as most bands would do today? "Because that immediately got our attention and he didn't let go until the end of the show."

Them

Corn Exchange, 10 February 1965

Nineteen-year-old George Ivan Morrison played his very first gig on British soil here in the west, claimed promoter Freddy Bannister - though this doesn't actually appear to be true. Them had recently scored a hit with the *Baby, Please Don't Go/Gloria* single. So was Van pleased to be here? Not exactly. "Even at this stage in his career he showed signs of his neurotic personality, asking endless questions about the size and behaviour of the audience," recalled Freddy.

Trivia note: the keyboard player on this tour was Peter Bardens - the only member of Them apart from Van Morrison who was deemed competent enough to record *Baby, Please Don't Go*. The guitar solo on the record was by the ubiquitous Jimmy Page. We'll meet Bardens again later as a founding member of ace proggers Camel.

But before we leave Van the Man, let's revisit an oft-told local anecdote with the proviso that it may prove to be embellished or entirely apocryphal. Van enjoyed recording at the Wool Hall in Beckington, just outside Bath, so much in the late 1980s and early 1990s that he eventually bought the studio. The story goes that during one of his many sessions there the staff mentioned that they were having a party later that evening and he'd be welcome to come along. Nobody actually expected the famously grumpy musician to actually turn up. But that's what he did. Alas, when he rang the bell, the door was opened by someone who didn't have a faintest idea that the man standing before him was the world's least starry rock legend. So he turned and shouted back into the room: "Did anyone order a cab?"

The Yardbirds
Corn Exchange, 3 March 1965

Want to see a really foul-tempered Eric Clapton? This was the show to be at. Things had been getting strained in The Yardbirds ranks just 15 months after Eric joined. The guitarist was devoted to the blues; the others, egged on by manager Giorgio Gomelsky, were seduced by the idea of pop success. Matters reached breaking point over the single *For Your Love*, written by future 10cc star Graham Gouldman. This was championed by bassist Paul Samwell-Smith, who considered himself to be the band's leader. Eric's brief contribution to the record was almost inaudible. "I knew it was the beginning of the end for me; I didn't see how we could make a record like that and stay as we were," he writes in his autobiography. "It felt to me that we had completely sold out."

"There was a horrible atmosphere," drummer Jim McCarty told Philip

Norman for his book *Slowhand: The Life and Music of Eric Clapton*. "At band meetings, it was always Eric against the four of us. On the way to and from gigs, he'd sit in the van with a long face, lost in his own little world."

It all came to a head backstage at this Corn Exchange show, where unspecified ructions took place. This proved to be Clapton's very last gig with The Yardbirds. He left the band just weeks before his 20th birthday, swiftly joining John Mayall's Bluesbreakers. His place was taken by Jeff Beck, who was later joined by Jimmy Page. Less than a month after Clapton's departure, *For Your Love* hit number one in the UK chart.

The Motortown Revue Tour
Colston Hall, 23 March 1965

I'm bending the rock criteria to include this one because of some fascinating stories. In the US during the early sixties, the Motortown Revue tours of the Chitlin' Circuit proved to be the making of Berry Gordy Jr's Motown Records, introducing the label's key artists to mostly African-American audiences. The label faced more of a challenge on the other side of the Atlantic. This was its first package tour to hit the UK, and Bristol was the first show outside London. "The fabulous" Supremes were the headlining act, with support from "the exciting" Martha Reeves & The Vandellas, Smokey Robinson & The Miracles, Earl Van Dyke and "the fantastic" Stevie Wonder. These days, Motown enthusiasts would kill to see such a line-up. Back in 1965, however, you couldn't give tickets away. Literally. Promoter Charles H. Lockier dished out 1,000 free tickets among the city's black community and still only a few hundred people turned up. Among them was future Granary Entertainments Manager Al Read. For years afterwards, Al would dine out on the tale of how he was seated by a young black boy while the opening acts played. The lad then got up to take his turn. That's right: Al was next to 14-year-old Little Stevie Wonder.

As for Lockier, he was a Bristol impresario of the old school who promoted classical and popular music shows, mainly at the Colston Hall, from the 1920s until his company went bust in 1966. He was behind all the early Beatles and Stones packages at the Colston. Before that he brought the likes of Ella Fitzgerald, Buddy Holly, Louis Armstrong and Count Basie to Bristol.

The Who

Corn Exchange, 19 May 1965

With just two original singles in the bag, *I Can't Explain* and the soon-to-be-released *Anyway, Anyhow, Anywhere*, the 'oo headed west. After a show at Bath Pavilion on May 17, they pitched up in Bristol for another Freddy Bannister gig. In Freddy's autobiography, he reports an unfortunate incident at the Corn Exchange in which one of his bouncers walloped Roger Daltrey for trying to sneak a girl backstage. Daltrey feigned injury in the hope of getting some sympathy, but Bannister saw through his ruse. According to Johnny Black's book *Eyewitness: The Who*, Pete Townshend wrote a little ditty called *My Generation* on this very day.

The Byrds

Corn Exchange, 11 August 1965

Another big coup for Freddy Bannister, who bagged two of the UK shows the Byrds played on the back of the success of their *Mr. Tambourine Man* cover (they hit the Bath Pavilion on August 16). Christopher Hjort's exhaustive book *So You Want to be a Rock'n'Roll Star: The Byrds Day by Day 1965-1973* reveals that DJ Annie Nightingale accompanied them on the train to Bristol. Alas, after all that hype, Freddy reckoned they were crap: "They looked fabulous - the absolute personification of the sixties, all capes and granny glasses. However, when they started to play it was a different matter. They were simply dreadful - nowhere near as proficient as any of our local support bands."

The *Western Daily Press*'s Brian. K. Jones, whose *Beat Diary* had been excitingly rebranded as *The Long Thin Column*, found himself in agreement: "…the verdict on these American chart toppers? Disappointing. At the Corn Exchange, their mediocre performance could possibly be excused by the fact that they were tele-recording at the TWW studios until 9:30pm."

Colin Gunning was in the audience. "The main thing I remember was that they were very, very late in coming on stage," he says. "The air of expectation started to dissipate rapidly and people were getting very disgruntled. I found the songs all rather samey."

The *WDP*'s Mr. Jones was still unimpressed by the Bath Pavilion show. "Their sound is much of a muchness. Each number sounded like *Mr Tambourine Man* except that the words were different. And their performance left much to be desired."

But an excitable reporter from the *Bath and Wilts Evening Chronicle* reported that the Byrds "bowled over an enthusiastic audience of screaming girls" and went on to remark, perhaps somewhat lasciviously: "In the dressing room before the show, these young starlets, who wear Beatle haircuts 'because we like long hair', were showing the signs of a vigorous string of one-night stands."

Bristol and Bath weren't just unlucky. Despite their lauded recorded works and influence down the generations, the sixties David Crosby-era Byrds were a notoriously awful live act. Many contemporary reviews damn them for being too loud and heavy. Imagine!

That said, one good thing did come out of this mostly disastrous first UK tour. On the flight into London, Gene Clark was inspired to write *Eight Miles High*, which also documented the band's experiences in Blighty (could "Round the squares, huddled in storms/Some laughing, some just shapeless forms" be referring to the Corn Exchange?) and is frequently cited as being the first psychedelic pop song. On its release the following March, the Byrds attempted unsuccessfully to avoid a radio ban by denying that the lyrics had anything to do with drugs. They were, of course, lying through their teeth.

Steampacket
Corn Exchange, 14 September 1965

Yep, young master Rodney Stewart played the Bristol Chinese R&B Jazz Club in the Corn Exchange alongside Long John Baldry, Julie Driscoll and Brian Auger in the first Steampacket tour of the UK. Mr. *Do Ya Think I'm Sexy* found himself in need of some chemical augmentation prior to the show, so he asked local support band The Magnettes if they could help him locate some "naughty sweeties". Band member Mike Tobin later recalled their blank looks and confusion. "He must have really dismissed us as hicks from the sticks with straw behind our ears."

"My main memory of that night is Rod Stewart singing a cover of *My Girl* by The Temptations," recalls punter Colin Gunning. "That was the stand-out: he did a really good job of it."

So what's with the Bristol Chinese R&B Jazz Club thing? Turns out it was a live music night run by a fella who styled himself 'Uncal' Bonny Manzi (catchphrase: 'Chop Chop'). As the name might suggest, he wasn't actually Chinese but a Cockney geezer from a showbiz background. Billed erroneously as "the most famous club in Europe", the club ran on Tuesday nights at the Corn Exchange, with Freddy Bannister generally having the Wednesdays for his more rock and pop-oriented shows. You couldn't get away with such cultural appropriation today, but Bonny used to hang the venue with Chinese lanterns, while his gig posters advertised 'fly lice' and, for some reason, crocodile sandwiches. Another feature of his club was that nurses got in for half-price. These days, he'd be described as "a character".

In November 1965, a couple of months after this show, Bristol University student newspaper *Nonesuch News* ran a rare profile of this "manager, compere and ticket puncher, the brains behind the business." Reporter Lofty Rye described him as having a "sharp Cockney face and frayed cuffs" and sporting his trademark battered boater. "Yes, the hat, the straw hat, it goes back years and years and years," he explained. "Muvver and farver used to be on the boards, song and dance act. They both used to wear these straw hats and this is sort of a lucky mascot - just a gimmick."

Bonny had been a trad jazz fan and described himself as the King of Jazz on account of running 14 clubs across the land - more than anyone else. But when the bottom fell out of the trad market so abruptly, he'd been forced to consolidate. By 1965, he had just four clubs left - three dominated by rhythm and blues and only one, in Brighton, devoted solely to jazz. So the Bristol Chinese Jazz Club had become the Bristol Chinese R&B Jazz Club. Bonny said he enjoyed R&B because it appealed to students and had a higher standard of musicianship than pop, against which he was, at the time, bravely holding out. "Four years ago, if you was a young good-looking man with a tight pair of trousers and twanged a guitar and had all the kids screaming at you, you were away. But after four years of listening to R&B, people must gradually become educated... And now they're beginning to appreciate the musicianship. They begin to look for chords and solos and all this type of thing and this is where you get a lot of them standing around and watching and listening."

1966

Time Magazine coins the phrase 'Swinging London'... England win the World Cup... Aberfan disaster takes place in South Wales... *Camberwick Green* and *Till Death Us Do Part* make their TV debuts. The BBC's *Cathy Come Home* is watched by a quarter of the British population... In the US, Anton LaVey founds the Church of Satan, *Star Trek* premieres on NBC, LSD is made illegal, Vietnam War protests continue and the Black Panther party is formed... Popular music undergoes a revolution. "1966 began in pop and ended in rock," writes Jon Savage succinctly in his book *1966: The Year the Decade Exploded*. The Beatles release *Revolver* and play their last show. John Lennon suggests the Fabs are more popular than Jesus, which doesn't go down well in the Bible Belt. Psychedelic rock enters the mainstream with the release of The Yardbirds' *Shapes of Things* and The Byrds' *Eight Miles High*. Frank Zappa and the Mothers of Invention put out their debut album, *Freak Out!* Jimi Hendrix arrives in London and releases his first single, *Hey Joe*. David Jones changes his name to David Bowie. Nobody notices... Locally, the Marquess of Bath unveils Longleat Safari Park and Tony Bullimore opens the Bamboo Club - billed as 'Bristol's premier West Indian entertainment centre'... Adge Cutler and the Wurzels release their first single, *Drink Up Thy Zider*, which was recorded at the Royal Oak in Nailsea... Seventeen-year-old Olivia Newton-John lives in Bristol for three months after winning an Australian talent contest. She stays with her aunt in a house just off Whiteladies Road and records her first single, *Till You Say You'll Be Mine*, for Decca Records... The New Bristol Centre opens in Frogmore Street, boasting the "cinema of tomorrow" (now the O2 Academy)... And the Severn Bridge finally connects South Wales directly to civilisation.

The Who
Bath Pavilion, 25 April 1966

The Who played in Bristol and Bath frequently on the way to hitting their peak as Britain's greatest live band. But eyewitness accounts of these incendiary early shows are few and far between. Brian K. Jones of the *Western Daily Press* pitched up for this one, which came just after *Substitute* hit number five in the chart.

A few days later, he published his vivid account of the show's climax. "Cymbals flew one way, the bass drum toppled from the rostrum and toppled towards the screaming teenagers pulling at the curtains in an effort to keep them open. Stage lights were flashing, first on and then off while we tried to work out whether vocalist Roger Daltrey, arms waving frantically in the middle of the stage, was in fact at the end of [*My*] *Generation* or intending to continue. Two road managers dashed on stage to replace the drum kit only to see Keith Moon kick over the tom-tom. In the wings, hall staff employees were attending as best they could to young girls overcome with Who emotion."

After the show, he buttonholed Pete Townshend and a rather pleased with himself Keith Moon. "Audiences like that are few and far between these days," enthused the crazed drummer. "We react to the crowd. A good reception and we do the sort of show we did tonight."

Townshend parried the standard question about instrument destruction: "I would quite happily smash my amp to pieces if the show was going that way."

A few days later, The Who were on the bill with The Beatles at what turned out to be the Fabs' last ever live performance in the UK, at the NME Poll Winners concert at the Empire Pool, Wembley.

Bob Dylan
Colston Hall, 10 May 1966

Legend has it that the 1965 Newport Folk Festival was the scene of the great showdown between old folkies and rockin' kids. The former, led by Pete Seeger, saw themselves as keepers of the flame of noble tradition and political radicalism, holding out against the Barbarians of commercialism. The latter thought the beardies were boring old musical conservatives. Some have even framed this as a battle between the New Left and the Old

Left. It all centred on Bob Dylan's electric headline performance with Mike Bloomfield and Al Kooper. This proved to be a key moment in the lives and careers of such important music industry figures as Jac Holzman and Joe Boyd, who were both present to witness the events as they unfolded. The folkies booed, while Seeger allegedly attempted to cut the power cables. But history was on the side of the rockers. Dylan was absent from the 1966 fest, which was the first one to lose money. Facing extinction, the companion Newport Jazz Festival eventually took a more dramatic turn, embracing hard rock in the form of Led Zeppelin and Jethro Tull.

The story of Dylan's performance, and the audience response to it, has been disputed in recent years. But when he pitched up in the UK for a run of 11 gigs the following year, punters and reviewers alike seemed eager to embrace the myth and voice their outrage accordingly. The Bristol show was the first English date, just ten days before the legendary "Judas!" incident at the Manchester Free Trade Hall. Each show comprised two full sets: an unaccompanied, seven-song acoustic one and an electric one for which Dylan was backed by The Hawks (who later became The Band). According to the *Rough Guide to Bob Dylan*, one hack grumbled of his only Bristol show that he was "sacrificing lyric and melody to the God of big beat" while another asserted that he was "buried in a grave of deafening drums".

Interestingly, The *Bristol Evening Post* decided that Dylan's performance merited considerably less attention than a new production by Bristol Old Vic Theatre School students. The paper's review of the latter dominated the page, while his Bobship had to settle for second place. Helen Reid was not impressed by the fella she dubbed "the bard of nihilism, hope, anti-convention and protest".

"During the first half, the audience patiently listened as he belched his way through half a dozen marathons," she sniffed. "Where was the Dylan stage presence we have heard so much about? Are a couple of short laughs really all he expects?"

Reid was even less impressed by the second half of the show, which she characterised as "beat music… with the volume turned on full.

"Two guitarists, a drummer and an organist accompanied Mr. Dylan. The resulting rivalry was wearying and not very enjoyable."

If anything, the *Western Daily Press* was even more damning. In his *Focus on Folk* column, Peter Gibbs demanded: 'Has Fame Spoiled Dylan?'

Gibbs reckoned that the "folk-singer prophet of the modern generation parted company with many of his fans at the Colston Hall" and branded the show a "noisy, blaring, ear-splitting disaster".

Dylan's arrival on stage had been greeted by the full house with "the type of applause reserved by fans for their idols." By the end, the clapping diminished and "some of the audience had already walked out - presumably in disgust". It was the second set that caused the offence, on account of the Hawks "who proceeded to bombard the audience with wave upon wave of amplified notes. Even Dylan joined in the punishment of his audience, gyrating with an electric guitar like a second-hand Rolling Stone." (Geddit?)

The only explanation he could think of for this "amplified din" drowning out Dylan's lyrics was that it had been imposed against his will. "Perhaps this exaggerated Top Ten sound has been forced upon him by others who want him to cash in on what they suppose to be a commercial sound," he sniffed. "But if so, why does the free-thinking, rebellious Dylan carry on with it?"

"He and the late lamented Robbie Robertson apparently used to get high on various substances before going out and playing the electric stuff," the now retired Peter Gibbs told me. "I do remember that, rather politically incorrectly, I described him as looking like an 'electric golliwog'. I was later told that he was so annoyed with my review that he threw it across his hotel room."

The novelist Angela Carter graduated from Bristol University and stayed on in the city to become part of the mid-sixties Clifton bohemian scene. She published *Shadow Dance*, the first book in her 'Bristol trilogy' in 1966, and also went to see Dylan that year. For some reason that no one seems to be able to explain, she chose the Cardiff Capitol Theatre show the night after the Colston Hall one and wrote a lengthy, vivid review for *London Magazine*. Carter took a very different view to that of the mostly male music critics of the time, prophetically hailing, if you'll forgive the cliché, the future of rock'n'roll.

"Bang, bang, drums, organ, amplified guitar. He does a black and white devil dance clutching a black and white amplified guitar and you can hardly hear a word he's singing. Maybe this is part of the plot. But it's all right, ma, he's only howling. Thus Bob Dylan, erstwhile Wonder Kid of Protest, demonstrated to packed and baffled theatres up and down the British Isles that he is approaching an artistic maturity of a most unexpected kind," she enthused.

"He has become a prophet of chaos and those who once accepted him as a blue-denim Messiah of a Brotherhood future once the times had changed may sense a personal betrayal. He attempted to pacify the old fans by doing the first half of his concerts in this country with acoustic guitar and mouth organ. ... the audience greeted the opening lines of Mr Tambourine Man with relieved recognition and a round of applause; he did not even give a thin smile in return but threw the song away as if he wished he could throw his harmonica after it. No introductions, no nothing. He scrambled through the troubadour of song bit.

"He began to jerk into life when the group came on in the second half and the noise bit began. This Dylan is clanging and vulgar, neon and plastic and, at the same time, blackly, bleakly romantic. And exhilarating, akin to reading The *Dunciad* or a strip cartoon version of *Wuthering Heights* while riding a roller coaster.

"Dylan is a phenomenon. He never used to be.... He's on his own (like a rolling stone or like a Rolling Stone) and what happens now should be best of all."

We can now judge for ourselves who was right as the entire Bristol show was released on CD in 2016 as part of the epic 36-disc *The 1966 Live Recordings* set.

Stephen E. Hunt's excellent book *Angela Carter's 'Provincial Bohemia': The Counterculture in 1960s and 1970s Bristol and Bath* tells of how Carter's friend Gary Hicks managed to blag his way into Dylan's suite at the Grand Hotel after the Bristol show, along with local writer and experimental playwright Michael Kullman, where they found the great man holding court to a dozen acolytes. "We stayed until 5am and helped fight off an attempt by the Bristol University rugby team to rough up Dylan - by putting some furniture against the door," he revealed. "They banged on it for a while and then went off."

"Stupidly, Kullman accused Dylan of going commercial with the electric guitar and Dylan responded by saying, 'You are the kind of guy who farts on his mother's cushions after Sunday lunch', i.e. accusing him of being a kind of pseudo beatnik."

A famous photograph taken the following day on Aust Ferry shows Bob looking rather glum. A couple of months after the Colston Hall show, he suffered the motorcycle accident that would keep him from playing live for another eight years.

Fast forward two decades to September 1986: "Excuse me, mate: do you want to get paid to watch Bob Dylan?" Local rock enthusiast Aidan Naughton was on his way to return some books to the Central Library when he was waylaid outside the Colston Hall with an offer he couldn't refuse. Dylan was in town for the second and final time, shooting concert scenes for the dismal film *Hearts of Fire*, which was released to critical derision the following year. Aidan didn't need to be asked twice. "There were about 200 extras playing audience members, some of whom had obviously been recruited in advance. But others, like me, were just plucked off the street. It wasn't really a gig, as they just did one tune over and over again. But Ronnie Wood, Ian Dury and Terry Williams jammed with Dylan between takes. The whole thing lasted for about three-and-a-half hours. We all got fed and I was paid £20. Dylan seemed to be in a good mood and was happily signing autographs."

Renowned Bristol-based pinhole photographer Justin Quinnell was also there that day, hoping to sneak some snaps. "We were told we couldn't bring cameras but I told them it was given to me as a prop. The day did seem to go on forever. During one break, I went down to ask Mr Dylan if I could take his photo but he was whisked away. I then noticed Richie Havens sat on the front row. I'd seen *Woodstock* many times while working as an usher at the Arts Centre Cinema (now the Cube) in 1977-78 . I caught his eye and instead of security being called, he stood up, strode towards me, shook my hand, offered me a seat beside him and proceeded to ask if I came from Bristol. I remember being completely dumbstruck at what a fantastic, lovely guy he was. He headlined Glastonbury the next year and died in 2013. Another star hit the heavens."

The Rolling Stones/Ike and Tina Turner Revue/The Yardbirds
Colston Hall, 7 October 1966

As we've seen, the Stones played the Colston three times in 1964. They also played here in 1965. But if you had to choose just one Colston Hall Stones show from the sixties, this would have to be it - the 10th of 12 dates on what turned out to be their last British tour of the 1960s. That's not just because of the great bill, but also because of its place in Stones history and the fun one might have had snooping around backstage. In Christopher Sandford's book *The Rolling Stones: Fifty Years*, he quotes Stones insider and chauffeur Tom Keylock as saying that it was at the Colston that Mick Jagger finally got his leg over with Tina Turner ("I tripped over them with their gear round their ankles backstage").

Also present at the show was Marianne Faithfull, who'd been chauffeur driven to Bristol from London at the invitation of Keith Richards and Brian Jones. She was instantly smitten by Jagger's performance, later writing that he was "Dionysus, the dancing god". After the band's second performance (there were two houses that night), she repaired to his Bristol hotel room with sundry Stones and hangers on for several exotic cigarettes and an impromptu screening of Polanski's recently released *Repulsion*. According to Mark Hodkinson's Marianne Faithfull biography *As Years Go By*, she'd hoped to cop off with Richards at the end of the evening, but wound up alone with Jagger and a member of the Ikettes. ("Although never revealed, this was probably P.P. Arnold with whom Jagger had begun a loose association a few weeks earlier at the start of the tour," writes Hodkinson.) To escape the dope smoke that had filled the room, Jagger and Faithfull went for a walk in the dew-soaked hotel grounds, where, Hodkinson reports, the silvery tongued lothario and former convent school girl discussed King Arthur, Stonehenge, Merlin, the Holy Grail and Joseph of Arimathea. As the sun rose, priapic Jagger had his evil way with Faithfull for the first time back in his room, P.P. Arnold presumably having departed by then. All this while he was supposedly blissfully in love with Chrissie Shrimpton (though in reality their relationship was pretty much over by then). The dirty dog. Still, the tryst certainly stimulated his creative juices too. Mick was inspired by his Bristol shagfest to write *Let's Spend the Night Together*.

Although there was never any doubt that this show would sell out, Bristol was enjoying something of a pop glut this month. The Colston Hall also had shows by The Alan Price Set, Dusty Springfield with The Lovin' Spoonful and Eric Burdon and The Animals with the Paul Butterfield Blues Band. The local press suggested that someone was likely to take a bath. After all, it was calculated that teens who attended all of these shows might have to shell out as much as £3.

Roving *WDP* reporter Brian K. Jones managed to blag his way backstage, where he found Keith Richards feigning surprise at the Stones' continuing popularity. "We are all very pleased with the reaction we have been getting on this tour. I must confess we had our doubts - we thought the only people getting this kind of treatment these days was Dave Dee and the rest of the creeps."

The dressing room, Jones reported, was in chaos: "Long John Baldry, compere of the show, was telling stories to Mick Jagger and Brian Jones; Charlie Watts was hidden behind two of Ike Turner's Ikettes; and Bill Wyman was at the point of refusing a Cornish pastie."

Ed Newsom, who went on to become the Granary club's very first DJ, was at the show. "I was blown away by the Ike & Tina Turner Revue," he recalls. "But the Stones were impossible to hear most of the time, because of the screaming fans."

The *Bristol Evening Post*'s recently recruited 22-year-old Pop Correspondent (yes, that was his official job title) James Belsey agreed about the screaming. "The Rolling Stones' second show at the Colston Hall ended in bedlam last night," he reported the following day. "An amiable bouncer stood at the foot of a prancing Mick Jagger. Girls running towards their idol rebounded harmlessly off his ample chest. Then they were led quietly back to their seats... They burst into tears, fainted or just sat dumbly, as if hypnotised. One could distantly hear the numbers and the screams were not quite as deafening as they used to be. I could even pick out individuals and the musicians were playing extremely well."

Like Ed, he was particularly taken with the Ike and Tina Turner Revue, whom he declared to be Bristol's most exciting pop happening in years: "This was pop at its very best. It was a pleasure to watch and listen to their band, girlie singers and star, Tina Turner."

The *WDP*'s Mr. Jones concurred. "For me, the highlight of the evening was the never-to-be-forgotten performance from the Ike and Tina Turner Revue. Words to describe the act come hard. There was a well-drilled professional performance with Tina Turner looking like a fiery tigress and singing with such feeling. Truly knock-out."

Alas, fellow *WDP* hack Maurice Fells described Mick Jagger's dancing as "obscene". This prompted a sharp rebuke from reader Hilda Collins of Fishponds, which was published on the paper's *Teenpage* the following week. "He has the figure to wiggle on stage," she swooned. "If anyone was indecent, it was Tina Turner and her girls. Their dresses were far too tight."

A couple more trivia notes. The recordings of *Lady Jane, Not Fade Away, Have You Seen Your Mother, Baby, Standing in the Shadow?* and *(I Can't Get No) Satisfaction* on the Stones' *Got Live If You Want It!* album released later that year were all taken from these Colston Hall shows.

The incarnation of The Yardbirds playing third on the bill during this tour was the exceedingly short-lived one (little more than four months) featuring both Jimmy Page and Jeff Beck on guitar. You could also have seen them at the Bath Pavilion on July 25, albeit with Page playing bass as he'd just replaced Paul Samwell-Smith. The *WDP*'s busy Mr. Jones had also been there for that one. In his *Long Thin Column* a few days later, he noted a "touch of high drama" among the famously volatile group: "Yardbirds guitarist Jeff Beck was seen to kick vocalist Keith Relf over the footlights into the packed audience. It happened when Keith was kneeling down evading many outstretched arms, and it called for some quick thinking and action from one of the hall stewards to rescue him from the obviously delighted (and very surprised) girls in front." Relf then "picked up the microphone stand and approached Beck looking very unhappy with what had happened." Fortunately the moment passed without fisticuffs. Jones also observed that "the good-looking Paige (sic) is obviously going to be an asset to the group; he was full of action and very talented."

The Who
Bath Pavilion, 10 October 1966

Yes, it's The Who at the Pavilion again. But this was no ordinary gig. The band were being trailed by a US CBS film crew making a documentary about exotic British teenagers. The *Western Daily Press*'s Brian K. Jones was there and reported how punters arriving at the hall were "met by a battery of cameras and arc lamps. A lot of interest centred around two young ladies from Bristol who started queuing at 10 o'clock in the morning. The group rose to the occasion brilliantly as did the stewards in their handing of the hysterical, fainting and trance-like ladies!"

Playing up to the cameras, The Who unleashed the full gear-smashing routine during a climactic *My Generation*. "All very well for the benefit of the screamers, and of course for the film producers, but to members of various local groups present it was sheer sacrilege of expensive equipment," opined Mr. Jones.

Ike and Tina Turner Revue
Bath Pavilion and Bristol Locarno, 17 October 1966

After the Stones tour, Ike and Tina Turner stayed in the UK for a short, gruelling run of headline shows to cash in on the chart success of the Phil Spector production of *River Deep - Mountain High*. This had become a hit in Europe, if not back in the US, and later soul arrangements of rock hits helped to cement their massive crossover appeal as a raunchy rock'n'roll counterpart to the slick, besuited acts rolling off the Motown production line.

And, yes, that's no misprint: they really did play shows in both cities on the same evening, performing in front of a total of 3,000 fans. But only just. The agreement had been they would use borrowed equipment at the Pavilion, beginning their show at 8:20pm and coming off stage at 9pm. That would give the entire Revue just enough time to pile into a van and charge over to Bristol, where their own equipment had been set up, for a 9:40pm start. But when ornery Ike turned up in Bath, he ruined these carefully laid plans by insisting on using their own gear for both shows. This caused such a delay that they finally appeared on the Locarno stage at 10:20pm. Punters were reportedly disgruntled. Until the band started to play...

Our view of them might now be coloured by knowledge of the appalling domestic abuse suffered by Tina behind the scenes. But everyone who attended these gigs was astounded by the experience.

Freddy Bannister had been surprised and not a little relieved to find Ike in good humour, despite those equipment shenanigans, even giving permission for the promoter to film one of the songs from the side of the stage. Needless to say, Freddy chose *River Deep - Mountain High*. "... as you would expect, it was Tina who stole the show," he writes in his autobiography. "Only 25 years old, she was dynamite."

"She was *phenomenal*," confirms Ken Pustelnik. "The energy of the whole show was amazing, with the Ikettes doing this extraordinary vibrating dance. Regardless of what he may have been like as a human being, Ike was a great band leader. I'd never seen anything like this."

The *Western Daily Press*'s Brian K. Jones was at the Pavilion show and reported that he "stood in awe at this brilliant, breathtaking performance - the big sound of the backing group, the guitar work of Ike Turner, the voices of Prince Albert and Jimmy Thomas, the vocal backing and dancing of the Ikettes and, last of all, the superb Tina Turner."

1967

Abbie Hoffman and Allen Ginsberg attempt to levitate the Pentagon in protest against the Vietnam war... The Six-Day War take place between Israel and a coalition of Arab states... Muhammad Ali refuses military service... Harold Wilson announces that the UK will apply for membership of the EEC... The Abortion Act is passed and the Sexual Offences Act partially decriminalises male homosexual relations in England and Wales. Meanwhile, the Marine Broadcast Offences Act makes pirate radio illegal... It's a massive year for music soundtracking the Summer of Love. The Grateful Dead, Pink Floyd, The Doors, Jimi Hendrix Experience and Velvet Underground all release their debut albums. The Beatles release *Sgt Pepper* and perform *All You Need Is Love* to an estimated 400 million viewers in the first international satellite TV broadcast. Procol Harum's *A Whiter Shade of Pale* is the biggest hit single of the year... First issue of *Rolling Stone* magazine published... Cops raid Keith Richards' Redlands abode and bust him and Mick Jagger for possession of drugs. Apocryphal Mars bar story follows Marianne Faithfull for the rest of her days... Monterey Pop, the first great rock festival, is captured for posterity by D.A. Pennebaker... *Hair* musical opens off-Broadway... The Redcliffe Flyover, a structure made of 120,000 tons of steel, is opened to relieve traffic around Temple Meads. This temporary structure remains in place until 1998. Lorry driver Bill Spring is the first person to travel over it. Later, he becomes the last person to travel over it too.

Jimi Hendrix Experience
Locarno, 9 February 1967
This was Hendrix's earliest show round these parts on his debut European tour and the first of three gigs he played in Bristol during 1967. Admission

was a princely six shillings and thruppence (that's about 31p). *Hey Joe* had been a top ten hit back in December, and *Purple Haze* was to follow in March. At the Locarno, the Experience's hour-long set included the former, plus *Wild Thing, Stone Free, Can You See Me, Killing Floor, 3rd Stone From The Sun* and Dylan's *Like a Rolling Stone*.

"I was the DJ at the Heartbeat Club upstairs from the Locarno," Warren Davies told Hendrix fan site *Lifelines*. "The trio came up after their show and stayed 'til we closed at 2am. They came over and complimented me on some of the music I had played – particularly a Booker T set of six tracks. One of the tracks featured Booker T playing piano instead of Hammond, a track they didn't recognise. So we sat cross-legged on the floor talking about Booker T until the manager wanted to lock the place at 3:15am."

Bristol Post reviewer Nicholas Williams reported that Hendrix left the Locarno reeling with his 'way-out guitar': "Backed by a two-man group, he bombarded his audience with an unbelievable wall of sound, which he somehow coaxed from his guitar. He played it in the usual way. He played it under his arm, over his shoulder and between his legs. He scraped it on the stage floor and over the amplifiers – he even plucked the strings with his teeth.

"Something has to snap – and it did. He broke a string at the end of the show.

"But that's nothing unusual. 'I buy several sets a week', Hendrix said."

Two days later, on February 11, the Experience pitched up at the Blue Moon Club in Cheltenham. In the audience was Mark Kidel - then an Oxford University student, but now an award-winning, Bristol-based filmmaker whose CV includes *Becoming Cary Grant* and multiple music documentaries (Elvis Costello, Rod Stewart, Robert Wyatt, Boy George, Ravi Shankar and Tricky being among his subjects).

"I was an immense blues and rock fan in the sixties," he told me. "*Hey Joe* was such a game-changer. We were all Stones and Beatles fans, but this was something different. It was before Led Zeppelin, because they didn't come along until '69. I was editing *Isis*, the weekly magazine in Oxford, at the time, and I saw that he was on tour and playing a tiny club in Cheltenham. Emma Rothschild and I went along. We went backstage and there was Jimi. He was extremely nice. There were only about 80 people in the audience. He did an absolutely incredible set. I'd never seen anything like it. None of us had *heard* anything like it."

Nine days after he played the Blue Moon, Hendrix was back in the west. On February 20, he played the Bath Pavilion as a last-minute replacement for the AWOL Chuck Berry. Promoter Freddy Bannister said the gig didn't really stand out for him. ("Possibly because we used him quite regularly at this time in our other venues and possibly because I was too unaware to recognise his unique talents immediately.") But the show belatedly made headlines in 2022. It emerged that two local girls, aged 15 and 16, had sought autographs at the backstage door before the show. With no paper to hand, obliging Jimi tore a sheet from his notebook and ripped it in half to provide autographs for each of the girls. Noel Redding and Mitch Mitchell also added their signatures. Only later did the young fans realise that Hendrix had written lyrics headed *51st Wedding Anniversary*, which later appeared as *51st Anniversary* on the B side to *Purple Haze*, on the reverse side of the paper he'd torn in half. They subsequently lost touch. Fifty-five years later, one of them approached a memorabilia store with a view to selling her half of what was now considered to be a rare manuscript. Then the hunt was on to track down her former chum. Turned out she still lived in Bath and had also kept her autographs intact, so the two women, who chose to remain annymous, stood to make a tidy five-figure sum between them.

Pink Floyd
Corn Exchange, 28 March 1967

They'd charted with *See Emily Play* and *Arnold Layne*, but debut album *The Piper at the Gates of Dawn* was still some months away when Floyd played their first Bristol gig. "It's the new rage! It's the most talked about group on the scene!" screamed the handbill. Syd Barrett was reportedly already off his face by this stage. The show was billed as the Chinese R&B Jazz Club's Easter Rave and the set list included *Astronomy Domine*, *Interstellar Overdrive*, *Take Up Thy Stethoscope and Walk*, *See Emily Play*, *Bike* and *Chapter 24*. Ken Pustelnik was there for this suitably psychedelic experience: "I remember they had one of the early bubble projectors trained on the roof. I don't know whether Syd was really all there, but that didn't matter to people like me."

The Move

Corn Exchange, 4 April 1967

1967 was a big year for the Brummie beat combo, who'd already played in Bristol twice in the previous four months. They'd been at the Locarno on March 9, less than a month before the Corn Exchange gig, and had created quite a stir when they played the Anson Rooms on January 26, just after the release of their first single, *Night of Fear*.

Later in the year, *Flowers in the Rain* would become the first single played on Radio 1 and they'd be sued by Prime Minister Harold Wilson for using his image to promote the song. The Move had always enjoyed attention-grabbing antics and set out to rival The Who for scenes of destruction. Roy Wood was reportedly quite embarrassed by some of the stuff they got up to, but the rest of the band embraced it, egged on by manager Tony Secunda.

Student paper *Nonesuch News* had published an over-excited preview of the January show, which noted that "at Wesker's Roundhouse Club two girls were incensed enough by their music to strip to the waist". Sure enough, the packed house at the Anson Rooms hoping for scenes of spontaneous female nudity and wanton vandalism were at least partially rewarded. The show had been fairly staid until the end of the second set, the paper's reviewer noted, whereupon: "Frenzied strumming in the midst of dense smoke, illuminated only by spasmodic hell-fire lighting, was a devilish background to the ritualistic smashing of a television set. Not content with the destruction of a TV set, the axe wielder attempted to demolish the Anson Room stage... Mr. Cuthbert, Assistant Permanent Secretary, estimated the damage at £25 to £50. It hasn't yet been decided who will pay."

A more satirical view was offered by *Nonesuch*'s pseudonymous columnist 'Mephistopheles & Son': "The freak-out was the most hilarious part of the evening; we were so impressed that we went home and had one ourselves, using a golf club, a box of matches and a clapped-out typewriter."

Brian K. Jones of the *Western Daily Press* caught The Move's show at Bath Pavilion a few days later on February 6 and was not amused, describing it as 'sick' (and not in the modern slang sense of 'jolly good' or 'awesome'). He thought the show started well, but: "Unfortunately the boys spoilt this for me - and I hope the other sensible, sane people in the audience - with their last number, during which the lead singer chops a television set to bits. Using a mike stand and then a big axe he smashes the set, exploding the tube and showering wood splinters and glass over the kids in front of the stage. For me, this is sheer idiocy… "

But how do you follow smashing up a TV set on stage? Ken Pustelnik was at the Corn Exchange to find out. "You have to remember that The Move were quite heavy duty characters back then," he says. "There was a queue all the way round the market. As we were waiting to file in, this Bedford van drove up to the entrance. There were about twenty of those old, boxy TV sets strapped to the roof, which the roadies carried in. During the show, the roadies brought the TVs onto the stage and the audience all moved back. Carl Wayne then came out with a double-headed axe and proceeded to smash them up. They exploded as he hit them. This was all new at the time. Cliff Richard wasn't doing that kind of thing. We really liked the violence of it."

Cream

Corn Exchange, 18 April 1967

The very first 'supergroup', Cream barely lasted for two years before dissolving in acrimony. Their first recorded Bristol show was at the Anson Rooms in October 1966, shortly after releasing debut album *Fresh Cream*. This Corn Exchange gig came just a month before they departed for the US to record the rather more psychedelic *Disraeli Gears*. By this time they were already performing their best-known song, *Sunshine of Your Love*, prior to its official release on the album in November.

Ken Pustelnik was working with the crew in Bristol and saw the tensions at first hand, particularly between Jack Bruce and Ginger Baker. "I knew they weren't going to last because it was totally obvious that they really didn't like one another. It was like, 'Have you been in the dressing room? *Oooh,*" he grimaces. 'The atmosphere - you could eat it.'

"I loved Jack Bruce's vocals and his bass playing. Me and my mates were a bit iffy about Eric Clapton - but when he did good stuff, on John Mayall's *Beano* album and *Layla*, it was brilliant. Ginger Baker came and spent some time with me, because we'd known each other from London. Everybody said no one gets on with him, but we got along fine - so either we were both bastards or we had something in common."

The Walker Brothers/Englebert Humperdinck/The Jimi Hendrix Experience/Cat Stevens
Colston Hall, 25 April 1967

No, really. Those crazy sixties package tours threw up some bizarre bills. And this was the most peculiar by a wide margin, chucking four very different acts with very different audiences on the same bill. The Walker Brothers had been Big Pop Cheeses in the mid-sixties, with a string of hits to their name, including *The Sun Ain't Gonna Shine Anymore*. And all the girls loved moody Scott. But in truth, their brand of pop was beginning to sound very dated indeed by the Summer of Love, their commercial success was drying up, and internal ructions led to this being billed as their farewell tour. Representing the very old school, future Eurovision shame-bringer Englebert Humperdinck was on board as 'special guest star'. Further down the bill was mellow Cat Stevens, basking in the glory of his *Matthew and Son* hit.

Conventional rock history records that they were all about to be blown away by Hendrix. On the night of the first show of this tour at the Finsbury Park Astoria, Hendrix, his manager Chas Chandler and journalist Keith Altham were having a backstage chinwag about how they could grab some headlines. Altham jokingly suggested that Hendrix could try setting fire to his guitar. "That's not a bad idea," mused Chas...

As Charles Shaar Murray writes in *Crosstown Traffic: Jimi Hendrix and Post-War Pop*: "Around the country audiences went nuts, parents complained and wrote angry letters to newspapers and promoters. The other acts on the bill might as well not have bothered to show up."

Actually, that wasn't quite true. Few people had bought tickets specifically to see Hendrix, and the Experience's set was cut short at early shows after a poor audience response. Gaggles of middle-aged ladies turned up for Englebert, dutifully tut-tutting at the Wild Man of Rock. But with the Experience's latest single *Purple Haze* rapidly ascending the chart, the trio found themselves bumped up the bill to rival the putative main attraction. This was also driven by manufactured rumours about Hendrix being chucked off the tour for being too outrageous. The Walker Brothers, meanwhile, were monumentally pissed off at being upstaged each and every night by their support act on what was supposed to have been their grand swansong.

This was the Brothers' second consecutive miserable experience at the Colston Hall. The previous year, they'd headlined a package that included The Troggs and Dave Dee, Dozy, Beaky, Mick and Tich. But the non-sibling Walkers stomped off in a huff after the house lights were turned on following an outbreak of teenage over-excitement. This prompted a flurry of demands for refunds and irate letters to the local press. "What really makes me mad is the childish way the Walkers acted in refusing to carry on with their set because the house lights were on," wrote a furious Barbara Van Eker ("ex-Walker Brothers fan") of Portishead to the *Western Daily Press*. "Some, like me, paid 15s for a ticket, 4s 6d bus fare, and got thoroughly drenched getting there just to be treated like dirt. The only thing that made my evening worthwhile was seeing The Troggs, who have taken over from the Walker Brothers as my favourite act."

Suitably chastened John Walker had promised the *WDP*'s Brian K. Jones that no such strop would occur on this occasion. "We've aged, man," he said. "Gone are those wild days. We like applause but no longer do we go out of our way to provoke trouble."

"This is a silly little tour," Hendrix told Altham in the *NME*. "I go on and tear up the stage so the audience are jumping up and down and then on comes Englefluff and stops the show dead with *The Last Waltz*, and damn me if that Scott Walker follows that by being even more miserable. He is so pretty and so sad that every time I run into him I want to kiss him and make it feel better."

There were reportedly plenty of high jinks on and offstage too. Whenever the rather aloof Cat Stevens played *I'm Gonna Get Me a Gun* (oddly no longer in his set), Noel Redding and Mitch Mitchell would soak him with water pistols from the back of the stage. Englebert's bass player Jimmy Leverton joined in the fun but claimed he was summarily sacked for hanging out with 'undesirables'. This tour certainly proved memorable for the future Yusuf Islam. He even mentioned it during his performance on the Pyramid stage at Glastonbury 2023.

The compere for the entire tour was a 21-year-old Bristol comedian, impressionist and former insurance salesman named Nick Jones. He'd clearly made up with the *Western Daily Press*, who originally dismissed him as "the poor man's Harry Worth". Jones told the paper that he was "petrified" at the prospect of being the link man on this 31-date tour. The multi-tasking comic's skills as a fire-eater certainly came in handy on the opening night and even earned him a mention in *The Stage* after he dashed from the wings to retrieve Hendrix's burning guitar. In Bristol, Jones was "funny and quick", reckoned the *Post*'s James Belsey.

For Belsey, the slick Walker Brothers were still the main attraction. He was also rather taken with Englebert's "natty 'South of the Border' get-up" and the way in which he bowled over the older members of the audience with his old-school crooning and belting. Alas, Cat Stevens' "tiny voice couldn't be heard" and the Experience were "completely out of place on this particular package show". Nonetheless, he conceded that "Hendrix played well with his guitar behind his back, better with his teeth, and was a maestro playing straight."

Fellow old-schooler Brian K. Jones also enjoyed Englebert's "first-class" performance, calling him the "star of the show". Jones took the opportunity to collar Cat Stevens (who - odd couple alert! - described Englebert as his best friend) and rather bravely read out his damning review of the 18-year-old Stevens' debut local show at the Bath Pavilion on February 13 ("His voice was flat, tuneless and off-key, his movements were dated and his personality non-evident"). Rather than decking the impudent reporter, peace-loving Cat agreed that his showbiz skills left something to be desired and that writing meant more to him than performing.

Freddie Mercury was Queen's resident Hendrix obsessive. He claimed to have followed his mixed-race idol round the UK on those early club tours. There's no suggestion that young Farrokh Bulsara was at the Colston Hall tonight. But future Queen drummer Roger Taylor was. He and a bunch of mates skived off school early to make the pilgrimage from Truro to Bristol. Taylor's bass drum was soon adorned with a painting of Hendrix and his band, The Reaction, incorporated a cover of *Foxy Lady* into their set.

Having enjoyed himself in the Heartbeat Club above the Locarno back in February, Hendrix seems to have made it his regular haunt when in Bristol. It was here, over the road from the Colston Hall, where Jones found the somewhat disconsolate if "wild-looking" guitarist bemoaning his relatively lowly position on the bill and reflecting on the publicity machine: "Showing a badly-scarred hand, he asked who would burn himself for publicity - who indeed?"

Interestingly, James Belsey subtly revised his view of this show in his

1989 book *The Sixties in Bristol*. He now made no mention of the Walker Brothers, choosing instead to reflect on how Hendrix "came on stage immediately after a brief performance by Englebert Humperdinck and played three ear-shattering numbers. Bizarre barely describes the culture clash between *Please Release Me* and *Purple Haze*."

The Who
Locarno, 18 May 1967

Things were getting even crazier than usual in the Who camp in early 1967, which saw them in transition from mod heroes to something much bigger. This was the second of their two shows at the Locarno that year. After the first one on January 26, Brian K. Jones of the Western Daily Press caught them in ebullient mood backstage. "So you've finally made it in the West Country with your cider song," quipped Pete Townshend, referring to Adge Cutler and the Wurzels' debut single *Drink Up Thy Zyder*, which had reached the heady heights of number 45 in the charts. Jones reported that the entire band then broke into a rousing chorus of Adge's career-maker, "as they downed some excellent Scotch".

Derek Jones of Bristol University Student newspaper *Nonesuch News* was also present at the January show to confront Roger Daltrey about why The Who didn't play university venues. The singer replied that "the audiences tend to be too narrow-minded. They refuse to accept us, to let themselves go and as a result our performance is not so good. We'd much prefer to play to an audience like this." In fact, The Who returned to play the Anson Rooms the following year.

Derek Jones reported that 1,000 ticketless punters were turned away and the Locarno was packed with a "swaying, shouting mass of bodies". The Who "started their act only to lose Roger Daltrey to the audience twice in the first number. The second time, he was pushed onto the iron guard rail and took his time to emerge, appearing very shaken." An extended encore of *My Generation* gave Pete Townshend "ample time to whirl his guitar around his head and smash it on his amplifier, wrecking both."

In a bizarre incident backstage in Stevenage the night before this show, bassist John Entwistle had broken a finger while punching a photograph of "a well-known pop singer" hanging on the wall. But The Who still honoured their commitment to play in Bristol. Perhaps more significantly, Pete

Townshend had attended the 14-hour Technicolour Dream at Alexandra Palace a couple of weeks earlier and was becoming positively rapturous about the creative potential of LSD. Meanwhile, *Pictures of Lily* (one of "The Who's wanking songs", according to the ever-droll Entwistle - see also *Mary Anne with the Shaky Hand*) was about to peak at number four in the chart. Later this month, they would start recording *The Who Sell Out*.

Among those turning up to see their heroes was 15-year-old Bristol mod Chris Powell, who contributed a vivid account of the evening to the *Bristol Post* when the paper asked for its readers' gig-going memories. After it opened in late 1966, the Locarno had become the Monday night haunt of Chris and his pals. "Smooth wasn't the word, what with our blue mohair suits (£15 from John Collier in Broadmead) with slant pockets, ticket pocket and rear centre vent (the longer the better), the obligatory Ben Sherman shirt and the thin tie, we were the business - or so we thought. However, real mods drove Lambrettas, not the number 8 from Kingswood."

Naturally, Chris was overjoyed when it was announced that the mod band of the moment were coming to the venue. "The first obstacle was the entrance price of 8s.6d (yes, that's 42p in today's money). However, a plea to my parents raised the readies and I was off. The queue stretched all the way down the steps and halfway up Frogmore Street, and attracted the main 'faces' on the Bristol scene."

Having bagged their seats right in the centre of the balcony, Chris and his mate waited for the band's advertised 8:30pm arrival. And waited. And waited. And waited. A hour-and-a-half later, The Who turned up, somewhat the worse for wear. "They may have been there in body, although I have grave doubts whether they were really there in spirit, as they all wore slightly glazed expressions and seemed to be on another level. I never had that problem with my illicit half of Woodpecker!

"The level of sound that reached what remained of the crowd's eardrums was deafening with the boys going straight into *I Can't Explain*, swiftly followed by *Anyway Anyhow Anywhere* and the mods' favourite, *My Generation*. This was class. This was history in the making.

"Around that time, The Who had a reputation for smashing their equipment and this evening was to be no different. Pete made short work of the loud speakers with his guitar, and Keith demolished his very impressive drum set with a small (?) charge of explosive. After a quick repair/

replacement job, they proceeded onto *I'm a Boy*, *Happy Jack* and their latest hit *Pictures of Lily* - and then they were gone."

It's been suggested that, having tipped her toe into rock with Bob Dylan's performance the previous year, celebrated Bristol novelist and folkie Angela Carter may have attended one of The Who's shows at the Locarno, as well as a performance by the Small Faces at the same venue. The only reference to them in her published writing, however, comes in an article about the sartorial symbolism of 'sixties style' (*Dressing Up and Down*, New Society, 1967) in which she addresses Pete Townshend's appropriation of the Union Jack as an example of the desecration of 'sacrosanct imagery'.

Al Stewart
Troubadour, 7 October 1967

> *And all along the way*
> *Wanderers in overcoats with*
> *Collars on parade*
> *And steaming in the night*
> *The listeners in the Troubadour*
> *Guitar player weaves a willow strain*
> *I took my love to Clifton in the rain*
> **- Clifton in the Rain, Al Stewart, 1970**

To most people, Al Stewart is best known for the platinum-selling 1976 soft rock classic *Year of the Cat*, which was so beautifully produced by Alan Parsons at Abbey Road Studios that it became one of those great hi-fi demo discs of the era, alongside *Dark Side of the Moon*. But back in the late sixties, the Scottish singer-songwriter was a callow, self-effacing youth who spent much of his time in Bristol. One of his favourite venues was tiny folk hangout The Troubadour club at 5 Waterloo Street, which tends to get rather overlooked by those who chart the Bristol music scene. It didn't last long (from 1966-1971) and was so tiddly that it could accommodate no more than 50 punters over two floors. But the Troubadour succeeded in attracting musicians of the calibre of Bert Jansch, The Incredible String Band, John Martyn, Sally Oldfield (then a Bristol Univeristy student who formed a short-lived duo, The Sallyangie, with her brother Mike), Keith

Christmas and Sandy Denny. Stewart would regularly pop in after playing bigger shows elsewhere in town and immortalised the club in the song *Clifton in the Rain* on the 1970 edition of his *Bedsitter Images* album. On this occasion, he was competing with Pink Floyd, who were playing at the Victoria Rooms down the road.

Stewart wasn't the only folkie to be inspired by Bristol in the early 1970s. Lesser-known singer-songwriter, excellent guitarist and luthier Dave Evans composed songs about City Road and St. Agnes Park (titled, er, *City Road* and *St. Agnes Park*) in his Montpelier basement. These can be found on his albums *The Words in Between* (1971) and *Elephantasia* (1972), both released on Ian A. Anderson's Village Thing Records.

Traffic
Colston Hall, 13 October 1967
Headlining the Colston Hall in October was not bad going for a band that only formed in April. Following the Spencer Davis Group's farewell tour in March, young prodigy Steve Winwood wasted little time in "getting it together in the country" - as the parlance of the era would have it - with his new band, Traffic. By the time of this show, they'd notched up three top ten singles (*Paper Sun*, *Here We Go Round the Mulberry Bush* and the atypical *Hole in My Shoe* - later revived by Neil the Hippy) but had yet to release debut album, *Mr. Fantasy*. It was also a rare opportunity to see the founding line-up of Winwood, Dave Mason, Jim Capaldi and Chris Wood, as Mason left the band shortly after the album was released. Traffic were clearly finding their feet at the time, showcasing a modish, sitar-flavoured psychedelic sound on those singles that wasn't to last long.

Indeed, the whole package was a fascinating snapshot of mostly hoary old rhythm and blues musicians swiftly updating their sound and image in imitation of the Fabs' *Sgt. Pepper* makeover and at a time when much cooler US invaders like Jimi Hendrix were capturing the imaginations and pocket money of the nation's youth. Just months earlier, many of these guys would have been wearing matching outfits and bashing out standards. But just as the musical opportunists of a decade later would cut their hair and attempt to disguise their class backgrounds in the hope of hitching a ride on the phlegm-flecked punk gravy train, so the arse end of the Summer of Love saw several future big names coming over all Flower Power - with varying degrees of conviction. Meanwhile, the mostly teenage audience just carried on screaming.

Pity Dave Berry, who played just this one show on the tour. A few years earlier, he'd been a teen idol with a string of chart hits, including the croony *The Crying Game*. Now, despite adopting hippy-era garb, he was old hat. That's showbiz. "God help us," sniffed Dave Bowles in student paper *Nonesuch News* of his appearance on this bill, adding gleefully: "During Dave Berry's act, cries of 'We want Keith' came from the girls around but Mr. Berry, obviously used to cool receptions in this country at any rate, carried on regardless."

The Keith craved by those girls was Keith West, who'd had a solo hit with *Excerpt from 'A Teenage Opera'* and was now briefly a member of Tomorrow. Formerly known as The In Crowd (purveyors of derivative R&B) and Four Plus One (purveyors of derivative soul), this lot recorded the first ever John Peel session less than a month before the Colston Hall show and were best known for their psychedelic debut single *My White Bicycle*, which inspired the title of Joe Boyd's memoir (Boyd was a huge fan. His evocative, justly lauded autobiography begins thusly: "The sixties began in the summer of 1956, ended in October of 1973 and peaked just before dawn on 1 July 1967 during a set by Tomorrow at the UFO Club in London.") Their line-up included the young Steve Howe (later of Yes) and John 'Twink' Alder (later of The Pretty Things and the Pink Fairies). Like his contemporaries Cat Stevens and Richard Thompson, Twink later converted to Islam. He now goes by the name Mohammed Abdullah

Two other acts in transition were billed as part of this package, but it's not clear whether they actually played as they're not mentioned in any of the reviews. Lumpen R&B combo The Ramrods had just reinvented themselves as the groovy Art. Guitarist Luther Grosvenor underwent a further reinvention later in his career as Mott the Hoople's Ariel Bender. Formerly led by Wayne Fontana, beat boom survivors The Mindbenders were also coming over all far-out and experimenting with concept albums. After they split, Graham Gouldman and Eric Stewart went on to form 10cc.

Definitely absent were the billed Vanilla Fudge, playing their first UK tour. It would have been grand to hear their proto-metal versions of the likes of *You Keep Me Hangin' On*, but they actually fucked off home after the first show in London, which was reportedly something of a disaster for them.

And The Flower Pot Men? They were manufactured by Tin Pan Alley veterans John Carter and Ken Lewis, whom we previously met with Jimmy Page at the Co-op hall in 1963. By this time, Carter and Lewis were recruiting session musicians to perform their material, which included cheesy novelty hit *Let's Go to San Francisco*. The fake hippy chancers' shtick was to chuck chrysanthemums at the audience. Shamefully, their ranks included Nick Simper and Jon Lord, who went on form two-fifths of the first Deep Purple line-up. Another fascinating local connection is boasted by singer Tony Burrows, who'd been a member of Bristol vocal harmony quartet The Kestrels alongside Roger Cook and Roger Greenaway - later hugely successful songwriters whose many hits included *I'd Like to Teach the World to Sing (In Perfect Harmony)*. The duo also had a key role in launching the career of the young Elton John. Burrows' chief, if possibly apocryphal, claim to rock'n'roll fame is that he appeared three times on the same edition of *Top of the Pops* in 1970 fronting three different bands. One of these was Edison Lighthouse. Search for their hit *Love Grows (Where My Rosemary Goes)* on YouTube and you'll find Burrows and chums miming like troopers in a promo film shot on the steps of the Victoria Rooms in Clifton.

Bristol Evening Post pop correspondent James Belsey lamented that the teenage audience were screaming at Keith West and 19-year-old Winwood. In his view, they "should have taken time off to listen to the Traffic group playing some of the best pop music the hall has heard for a long time." Brian K. Jones of the *Western Daily Press* also rated the headliners, but objected to their attempts to be heard above the screaming: "… why on earth did the Traffic have to be so loud?… Stevie was using a reputed £2,000-worth of amplification equipment that made the wings look like Cape Canaveral just before countdown! But with the exception of *Paper Sun* and *Hole in My Shoe*, most else from the group went way over the heads of the audience."

Belsey enjoyed the "weird and wonderful noises" produced by Tomorrow, but was also seduced by the comforting ersatz naffness of The Flower Pot Men, who "joined into the spirit of the evening with a touch of the Hippies. Between them they threw several dozen carnations into the audience and won big applause for their flower power."

Fellow old-schooler Brian K. Jones of the *Western Daily Press* agreed.

The Flower Pot Men, he asserted boldly, "have enough talent to survive the dying flower cult".

Student journalist Bowles, who'd begun his review with modish references to beads and kaftans, ignored the fake hippies and lavished praise on the real ones. "Traffic is without doubt the most striking group to appear on the scene in 1967," he wrote, singling out "the great Steve Winwood" as the highlight of the evening.

Jimi Hendrix Experience/Pink Floyd/The Move/The Nice/Amen Corner/Eire Apparent/The Outer Limits
Colston Hall, 24 November 1967

Of all the gigs included here, this must surely be the most incredible: Hendrix and the Floyd, plus The Move with Roy Wood and The Nice with Keith Emerson all on the same bill and each playing two houses.

Very early on the morning of the show, Hendrix and several members of The Move arrived from Cardiff with an unusual request: they wanted to do some filming at Bristol Zoo. The nature of their cinematic project is something of a mystery but they'd hoped to secure the use of some empty cages. The obliging *Western Daily Press* tried to set this up for them, but was thwarted by a raging foot and mouth epidemic.

The compere for the tour was former pirate radio DJ Pete Drummond, who'd become one of the founding disc-spinners on the Beeb's new-fangled Radio 1 a couple of months earlier. Such was his fame that he got £25 a night - more than any of the acts except Hendrix.

Eire Apparent recorded one album with Hendrix guesting and then split up, with guitarist Henry McCullough going on to join Joe Cocker's Grease Band and Paul McCartney's Wings. Together with newcomers The Outer Limits, they opened the show, each being allotted a mere eight minutes to strut their stuff. Amen Corner then got 15 minutes and The Move closed the first half of the show with 30 minutes.

The Nice and Pink Floyd opened the second half. Floyd still weren't that big a deal at the time and played a brief two-song set comprising their hits *See Emily Play* and *Arnold Layne*. According to Trevor Burton of The Move, Syd Barrett was completely away with the fairies by this time. Henry McCullough would stand on the side of the stage playing his parts while Syd gazed off into the distance. Hendrix then got a full 40 minutes for his suitably incendiary performance, receiving 50% of the gate for his troubles. Had you been backstage, you might also have run into his roadie/drug dealer, one Ian Kilmister - yet to be nicknamed Lemmy. Above him in the hierarchy was tour manager Dave Robinson, who also managed fellow Irishmen Eire Apparent and went on to found punk label Stiff Records. Their paths crossed again later when Stiff signed Motörhead.

"I can remember being quite awestruck by Hendrix," recalls Ed Newsom, who was fortunate enough to be there. "Everything else that night paled into insignificance. It was probably the first occasion that I had seen a Marshall stack, and his use of feedback was something completely new to my ears."

Also present at the Colston Hall was a young Hendrix enthusiast named Ken Downing, who later became better known as Judas Priest guitarist K.K. Downing. In his autobiography, *Heavy Duty*, Ken describes how he first caught the tour at the Coventry Theatre: "The whole night was insane because the audience literally went mad... People stormed the stage and I was one of them. They were jumping from balconies, landing on people below. Faced with such aural excitement, it seemed the entirely natural thing to do. Everything about Hendrix was such a turn-on."

Naturally, Ken made a pilgrimage to Bristol when the tour arrived here a fortnight later. This time, he had a very different experience. "That night showed me another side of the Hendrix effect, how he instinctively knew how to turn it on or off at will, as if he controlled the collective emotions of the audience.

"Instead of starting the set with *Foxy Lady*, for which people always just went absolutely fucking crazy, I remember being so disappointed that he opened not with one of his own numbers but with *Sgt. Pepper's Lonely Hearts Club Band*. The reaction was totally different. It just wasn't right and the audience knew it. Looking back, maybe it was his way of curtailing things for the sake of health and safety, but to me it was an anticlimax."

The *Bristol Evening Post* reviewed the show the following day, reporting rowdy scenes: "In the hall, youths hurled abuse at performers, but the trouble died down as officials brought the shouting minority under control. But the incidents did not spoil a triumphant return of Hendrix to the first city to put him into the charts. He paid tribute to Bristol over the microphone and then launched into the wildest, noisiest pop music of all... He received a frenzy of applause."

Hendrix stayed at the Avon Gorge Hotel during his visit. Rather than shagging groupies, puffing reefers and chucking TV sets out of windows, he became addicted to... English afternoon tea. While being interviewed by *Post* pop correspondent James Belsey he talked incessantly about his new discovery. Trouble is, Jimi was none too experienced when it came to recharging his cuppa. At regular intervals, he phoned room service and demanded "More tea!" As a result, the room rapidly filled up with trollies laden down with cakes and other fancies, which were of less interest to the guitar great than our national beverage.

1968

In a year of protest and political unrest around the world, Martin Luther King Jr and Robert F. Kennedy are assassinated, the Prague Spring begins and ends and Enoch Powell makes his notorious 'rivers of blood' speech… Feminist Valerie Solanas shoots Andy Warhol… *Dad's Army* premieres on UK TV… The Beatles unveil Apple Corps. *Hey Jude* is the biggest hit single of the year. Cream play their farewell concert at the Albert Hall. *The Rolling Stones Rock and Roll Circus* is filmed but isn't released until 1996… In Bristol, revolting students occupy Senate House for 10 days. Among their egalitarian demands are that students from the city's smaller colleges should be allowed access to the swanky new Students' Union building on Queens Road, which had opened in 1965… Bristol University student paper *Nonesuch News* publishes an admiring interview with Jimmy Savile conducted prior to his appearance at a local youth festival: "Much of Jimmy's spare time is spent talking at schools, teacher training colleges and the like… Mr Savile especially enjoys his schools round.".… Bristol is struck by a great flood in July following torrential rain. Seven people die and 3,000 properties are flooded.

Robert Plant and His Band of Joy
Corn Exchange, 1 January 1968

Had you survived the New Year's Eve celebrations, you could have stumbled on down to the Corn Exchange on this cold Monday evening to see half of the future Led Zeppelin finally hitting their stride as the Band of Joy played their only Bristol gig. Percy Plant's combo had been through several incarnations, but the Corn Exchange audience got to see the best one, featuring the singer's old chum John Bonham on drums. "With this line-up the Band of Joy gelled at last," writes Paul Rees in his biography *Robert*

Plant: A Life. "Bonham's hulking drums giving them added weight, they were all heft and power, indulging themselves on sprawling instrumental workouts. This was a precursor to all that would soon change the lives of Plant and his hooligan drummer."

The band's roadie was a young man from Walsall named Neville John Holder, who'd performed a similar role for Plant's earlier band the Tennessee Teens. Noddy tells a funny story about how he used to ferry the singer around in his dad's window cleaning van, while Percy was in the back shagging eager young ladies amid all the clanking ladders and buckets. That almost sounds like a pitch for a sitcom. Hell, I'd watch it.

Plant briefly revived the Band of Joy in 2010 and released an eponymous album, which became an international hit.

The Bonzo Dog Doo-Dah Band
Glastonbury Town Hall, 13 January 1968
Back in the sixties, the elderly conservatives of sleepy old Glastonbury were much exercised by weekly pop outrages at their historic Town Hall. The chap responsible was Brian Mapstone of popular local rock'n'rollers The Salvos, whose Street-based Westside Promotions established the venue as the location of 'Somerset's top Saturday dance', drawing teenagers from as far afield as Baltonsborough and West Pennard for shameful scenes of rug-cutting and general merriment. Many of the big rock'n'roll stars of the era played here, from Gene Vincent to Billy J. Kramer. By the end of the decade, louder and hairier performers were sowing the seeds of degeneracy among younger members of the farming community, with acts like John Mayall's Bluesbreakers, Ten Years After, Fleetwood Mac and the suitably agrarian Jethro Tull wending their way down the A361.

So it was that Vivian Stanshall, Neil Innes, 'Legs' Larry Smith, Roger Ruskin Spear and Rodney Slater arrived in this most cosmic of Mendip towns at a key point in their career. Having moved on from their early trad jazz leanings to embrace a more rock-oriented sound, The Bonzos had appeared in The Beatles' *Magical Mystery Tour* film, signed to Liberty Records and released their debut album, *Gorilla*. A new single from it, the Fabs parody *Equestrian Dance*, failed to chart. But something utterly bizarre had started to happen on British children's television. While their older brothers and sisters were having their brains frazzled by mind-altering drugs, the nation's kids were being similarly warped by a surreal TV show titled *Do Not Adjust Your Set*, which started with a Boxing Day special in 1967 and began running every week from the first Thursday in January 1968. These days, the ITV network would never broadcast anything quite so deranged at teatime, but for two series impressionable nippers - and more than a few stoned adults - were subjected to future Pythons Terry Jones, Michael Palin and Eric Idle alongside a very young David Jason and Denise Coffey, plus animations by Terry Gilliam (who'd just arrived in the UK) and regular performances and skits by the Bonzos.

Adding to the unpredictability was the borderline insane decision to broadcast the show live, which proved a particular challenge for eccentric's eccentric Viv Stanshall. Back in 2010, I asked Terry Jones whether Stanshall was as bonkers as his reputation suggests. "I think he was, yes," he replied. "He was very eccentric. A bit like Graham Chapman in a way."

The hectic schedule meant that the Bonzos were charging off between broadcasts to play gigs like this one, for which they were billed as 'Britain's top comedy group'. What's more, for their 8/6 admission fee the Glastonbury audience was treated to material that never made it onto record. In his band biography *Jollity Farm*, Bob Carruthers describes the set list as a 'strange mix': "Stage favourites at the time included *Little Sir Echo*, which had somehow survived the days when it was performed as a duet by Bob Kerr and Sam Spoons, *Mr Hyde in Me*, *Monster Mash*, *Shirt*, *I Want to Be With You*, *Give Booze a Chance*, *We Were Wrong* and *Tragic Magic*, which was later transformed into *Keynsham*."

As for those licentious Saturday Dances at the Town Hall, they carried on until July 19, 1969. Glastonbury's upstanding citizens then congratulated themselves on seeing off the menace of pop music for good.

The Crazy World of Arthur Brown
Anson Rooms, 9 March 1968

"I am the god of hellfire and I bring you... FIRE! FIRE! FIRE!" Arthur Brown's big hit and its accompanying album were three months away at the time of the University of Bristol's End of Rag Ball in 1968. So when he took to the Anson Rooms stage with Vincent Crane (organ), Drachen Theaker (drums) and Nick Underwood (bass), it's likely that not all of the students present would have known what to expect during the big dramatic set-piece in which Crazy Arthur donned his flaming helmet and set off smoke bombs. He'd been performing the improvised stunt since the previous year - with many a mishap, which mostly involved igniting his own hair. On this occasion, however, he succeeded in setting off the hall's fire alarm, causing the venue to be evacuated and bringing the rag revelry to a premature end.

Student newspaper *Nonesuch* observed that Arthur's performance "… made use of vile language, smoke bombs and stink bombs. Most people, in a packed audience, just watched in awe, some raved, others just fainted."

Fire topped the singles chart in August and Arthur's shows were now packed to the rafters. Managers Kit Lambert and Chris Stamp opted to cash in by keeping his Crazy World on the road all year. *Western Daily Press* reporter Jo Bayne offered a vivid description of "the most spectacular act in pop today" when he returned to play the Bath Pavilion on August 26. "Long, lean, mild-looking Arthur transforms himself into a convincing God of Hellfire," she wrote. "With flames shooting from a horned steel helmet, and silver mask covering his face, he explodes onto the stage swirling a vivid multi-coloured cape… The stage is a red glow and the image of hell is considerably heightened by the heat rising from the fan-packed hall. Their screams are midway between adoration and nervous hysteria. The scene as a whole is strangely sinister, and very impressive."

The Jeff Beck Sound
Bath Pavilion, 8 April 1968

In the great game of musical chairs that was sixties rock, moody Jeff Beck had been booted out of The Yardbirds and recorded the atypical novelty hit that he loathed but followed him to his grave (*Hi Ho Silver Lining*) for Mickie Most by the time he got around to forming his own group. Rod Stewart, meanwhile, had worked his way through Steampacket and Shotgun Express, while Ronnie Wood was a veteran of The Birds and (briefly) mod group The Creation. With Ronnie on bass and Mickey Waller on drums, they went into Abbey Road Studios in May 1968 to record the brilliant, hugely influential *Truth*, which is often cited as the first heavy metal album. This was released just months before Led Zeppelin's debut - with which it has a great deal in common. Indeed, both albums included versions of the blues standard *You Shook Me*, and while the authorship of *Beck's Bolero* has been contested there's no doubt that most of Zeppelin play on it. Beck said the album itself is essentially the group's live show at the time, which they'd honed at a series of gigs that included this one in Bath.

The *Western Daily Press*'s *Teenpage* was in a bit of an odd place in 1968, with columnist Brian K. Jones still holding out against the awful menace of psychedelia that was turning the kids' heads.

But to be fair to Jones, he also championed Jeff Beck - though, typically, he was most taken with the syrupy *Love Is Blue* - the last of Beck's pop singles for Mickie Most. Jones reported that "a fair crowd had turned out to see Jeff and his brilliant blues vocalist Rod Stewart," at the Pavilion. Beck "delighted the purists and probably converted a few of the pop fans" with "a non-stop hour of blues highlighted by *Beck's Boogie*."

Backstage, he collared Beck and Stewart to review the week's new pop releases. Beck didn't like The Kinks' *Wonderboy* ("They are trying to be so original and it hasn't worked"), but he and Stewart both raved about *To Love Somebody* by The Mirettes (a bunch of former Ikettes). "Must be a hit," reckoned the guitarist. They were half right: both singles flopped.

Small Faces/Canned Heat/Tim Rose
Colston Hall, 25 September 1968

Mod heroes the Small Faces had released their crowning achievement, the concept album *Ogdens' Nut Gone Flake*, back in May. It went on to top the charts for six weeks over the summer, which meant the quartet were at the peak of their popularity when they arrived at the Colston Hall.

Blues rockers Canned Heat were a year away from their Woodstock triumph and certainly won over the Bristol audience as their set for the second of two houses went on. And on and on and on. Eventually, they delighted Bristol enough and departed. A very, very long interval ensued. The trouble was that the headliners had been enjoying themselves very much indeed. Now barely able to stand, they eventually took to the stage a few minutes before the curfew. Halfway through their number one hit *All or Nothing*, the house lights went up. All hell promptly broke loose.

'Fighting end to pop show' was the headline in the following day's *Post*, over a report that described how the show "exploded into angry violence" after three members of the band stormed offstage when the gig was cut short: "Police arrived as many of the audience of more than 2,000 stood shouting in gangways. And the stage became an arena of struggling officials, fans and stars."

The highlight of the ensuing fracas came when a bouncer picked up keyboard player Ian McLagan and hurled him off the stage into the stalls. This early example of involuntary stage diving wasn't quite as difficult a feat as one might imagine. As the name implies, the Small Faces were characterised by their diminutive stature. The Hall's security, meanwhile, comprised off-duty wrestlers back then, so little Ian barely stood a chance.

Bristol University students had been revolting and were about to occupy Senate House, so there was obviously something in the air that Autumn. Writing in student newspaper *Nonesuch*, Paul Nunn placed the blame for the Colston Hall fracas firmly at the door of old squares: "...the violence and near riots at the finale of the Small Faces-Canned Heat-Tim Rose concert were over the principles of the right of aging, turned-off, don't understand bouncers and managers to spoil the enjoyment of a (largely) teenage audience by ending the show when the main attraction had barely started."

For him, the highlights were Canned Heat ("for their scintillating heights of musical ability and moving presentation") and opener Tim Rose ("... bringing us the original versions of *Hey Joe* and *Morning Dew*... tumultuous audience reaction and deservedly so.").

Inevitably, both the Small Faces and Canned Heat were promptly added to the list of bands who were banned for life from the Colston Hall.

Small Faces trivia fact: Ronnie Lane wrote the lyrics to the band's 1967 hit *Itchycoo Park* while sitting in his Bristol hotel room after a gig and reading a tourist brochure about Oxford that mentioned 'dreaming spires' and the 'bridge of sighs'.

Joe Cocker and the Grease Band
Anson Rooms, 1 October 1968

If there was such a thing as a Woodstock anthem - and it wasn't *Woodstock*, which was, of course, written by someone (i.e. Joni Mitchell) who wasn't there - it would have to be Joe Cocker's extended, impassioned and croaky voiced rendition of The Beatles' *With a Little Help from My Friends*. Contrary to the assumptions of most who've seen the Woodstock film, Cocker always insisted he played the show straight; it was the rest of the Grease Band (including future Wings guitarist Henry McCullough) who'd dropped acid. Cocker released the song as a single shortly after his first Bristol appearance at what was called the Presco Dance as part of freshers' week at the Anson Rooms. According to student newspaper *Nonesuch*, Cocker and the Grease Band "provided a great start to the Union dance programme with a pounding, overpowering presentation of their own brand of music". The uncredited reviewer was rather surprised to find him "soft spoken and unassuming" off stage when he remarked that he was "hoping for big things" with his new record. A month later, *With a Little Help from My Friends* was sitting at number one in the chart. Cocker returned to Bristol to play the Colston Hall on Valentine's Day 1969, six months before Woodstock.

Led Zeppelin
Bristol Boxing Club, 26 October 1968

There's some dispute over whether this gig actually happened and where it took place. In his autobiography, *Give the Anarchist a Cigarette*, the late Mick Farren, of support band The Deviants, swears it was in Exeter, but admits he might be wrong. Others insist it definitely took place in Bristol. But nobody knows where the Bristol Boxing Club is or was. Anyway, it was certainly eventful and was only the second gig to be billed as being by Led Zeppelin. This from an interview with Farren and bandmate Russell Hunter in respected hippy era chronicler Jonathon Green's *Days in the Life: Voices from the English Underground 1961-1971*:

"Hunter recalls: 'We supported Led Zeppelin at one of their first gigs. It was at the local Bristol boxing club and the audience hated us and despised them. Somebody threw a beer glass at the stage and Sid Bishop, our guitarist, unfortunately threw it back and cut somebody's head. When Led Zeppelin came on, they got through a number and a half until the fire extinguishers, buckets, bricks and everything was being thrown at them.'

"Mick Farren: 'All these farm boys in brown suits and haircuts, who had come into town on Saturday night looking to get laid, marched in. Page and Plant were cracking up in the dressing room after we'd come off, saying how terrible we had been. They had got the same treatment because by now it was completely out of hand. We had to huddle inside the van while the farm boys bounced up and down on it and we didn't escape until two in the morning when it was safe to go home.'"

The American Folk Blues Festival 1968
Colston Hall, 29 October 1968

The American Folk Blues Festival tours continued on an annual basis until 1972, but in 1968 a 22-year-old Bristol musician got to experience the veterans' backstage shenanigans at first hand. By this time, the Groundhogs were firmly established as John Lee Hooker's pick-up band of choice whenever he toured the UK - which is rather appropriate given that they took their name from Hooker's *Groundhog's Blues*. The 1968 tour saw Hooker joined by fellow legendary bluesers T-Bone Walker, Big Joe Williams, Jimmy Reed, Curtis Jones and the Eddie Taylor Blues Band for an eight-date jaunt that began at the Hammersmith Odeon on October 24.

Drummer Ken Pustelnik was one of a handful of white musicians on the tour. He describes Hooker as "a heavy-duty, hard man. You wouldn't mess with him. But when he liked people, you're friends for life. And he really liked us. He gave one interview in which he described the Groundhogs as the best blues band in Britain. He refused to travel in the chauffeur-driven limo that the promoter supplied because he preferred to be with the band."

He tells a story about Hooker sitting in his London hotel room and saying, "Hey, Kenny, man. I want to buy a suit." So Ken took him down the King's Road to a mod shop in search of the lightweight tropical apparel he craved.

"The kid behind the counter was looking at him and looking at me - a long-haired hippy musician. Hooker goes in the changing room to try on a suit and the kid says to me: 'Is he famous or something?'

'Yeah, he's John Lee Hooker.'

'Who?'

'One of the top five bluesmen in the world.'

'Is he rich?'

'I would have thought so. He's the first black blues musician to get a number one in America. That's quite a good payday by anyone's standards.'

"So Hooker comes out looking all dapper, rather like Charlie Watts, and agrees the price. The guy says, '...and then there's purchase tax.' Hooker looks at me, looks at the kid, grabs him by the head and smashes it into the counter - Bang! 'Don't give me any - Bang! - fucking purchase tax bullshit - Bang! - when I've agreed a fucking price beforehand.' Bang! I said, 'John, you're black, you're American and you've just assaulted a little white kid. Go out in the street!' I had to pay the kid off to keep his mouth shut."

Then there was Jimmy Reed, already a notorious alcoholic and a generation younger than the older bluesers on the tour, some of whom were Christians who'd worked in the cotton fields.

"He was a terrible drinker," confirms Ken. "Spent his whole time on the tour drinking. On the first night, we're sitting in the foyer and the coach is waiting to take us to the show. Hooker says, 'Where's Jimmy at?' Then the lift doors open and Jimmy Reed falls face forward on the floor. I thought he'd never play. 'Listen man, I know Jimmy,' said Hooker. 'We're going to the gig with him.' When it came to his spot, they lifted him into place and introduced him and he played perfectly. Afterwards I said, 'That was amazing.' 'No, he does that every night,' Hooker replied. 'He gets tanked up and you think he's going to die but then he goes and plays his music.'

Jimmy Reed died of respiratory failure eight years later, just a few days short of his 51st birthday.

The Muddy Waters Blues Band
Granary, 15 November 1968

The Granary on Welsh Back began life as a jazz club under the stewardship of Acker Bilk. Its transition to legendary rock dive was inaugurated in 1968 by great Chicago bluesman Muddy Waters and his band (which at this time included fellow guitarists Luther 'Georgia Boy' Johnson and James 'Pee Wee' Madison, plus pianist Otis Spann). That's rather appropriate given the musical debt owed to McKinley Morganfield (Muddy's real name, fact fans) by many of the acts who played here in subsequent years. Let's not forget too that The Rolling Stones took their name from a Muddy Waters song. The gig was so prestigious that *Blues Unlimited* magazine sent a reviewer. "Few words can really capture the brilliance of Chicago's foremost band as they swung through two outstanding sets of hard driving blues," enthused a rapturous Peter Moody. "Muddy Waters in Bristol… unbelievable!"

In a nod to the venue's past, the interval was filled with a set of trad jazz by the long-running Avon Cities Jazz Band. The only thing that didn't go according to plan that evening was Muddy's entrance. Legend has it that as he emerged from the dressing room to greet the hero-worshipping hordes, he banged his head on the low beam above the door, dislodging his toupee.

The story of the Granary's development to become one of the country's foremost rock clubs begins with a quartet of local musicians - Al Read, Ed Newsom, Mike Tobin and Terry Brace. Between them, they'd played in local bands such as the Franklyn Big Six and prog one-hit-wonders East of Eden. (Al's proud boast was that he'd been the singer in a band whose only hit was an instrumental - 1970's fiddletastic *Jig a Jig*). As promoters, their Plastic Dog nights at the Dug Out club were so popular that they started to look out for a bigger venue and soon claimed the under-attended Monday night at what was then called The Old Granary. The very first official Plastic Dog night at the Granary took place on December 30, 1968. Headliners were Griptight Thynne, fronted by Andy Davis - later of Stackridge and The Korgis. Over the next 20 years, just about every UK rock band of note played at the club, from Yes and King Crimson to Iron Maiden, Def Leppard and Motorhead. The Granary also became Plastic Dog's HQ, from which was spawned Bristol's very own contribution to the 60s and early 70s alternative press: *Dogpress*. This began as a single typewritten page advertising upcoming gigs. But with the arrival of Rodney Matthews (now a renowned fantasy and album cover artist), it began to expand into a playful, irreverent and excellently illustrated journal of the Bristol underground. It was also very much of its time, as the regular Groupie of the Month feature underlines. "These were free-spirited times! Wildly liberating but terribly sexist," wrote Entertainments Manager Al in his book *The Granary Club: The Rock Years 1969 to 1988*, which cannot be recommended highly enough.

"The early days were much more cosmic and far out," Al told me when the book came out. "It was all peace and love. We actually used to stand at the door and dissuade people from coming in. 'Oh you don't want to come in here: it's all noisy and hippy. There's a soul club round the corner.'"

Although his personal favourites were the original proggers ("I was astonished that anyone could play so well. And, of course, you could practically reach out and touch them."), his selection of the most memorable Granary nights was perhaps surprising: Mungo Jerry (of *In the Summertime* drink/drive lyric infamy), who packed the place to the rafters, and white-suited sixties popsters The Tremeloes. The latter begged a sceptical Al to be allowed to play and then came on to perform obscene versions of all their hits, which they apparently despised. "The club was in fits," he guffawed at the memory.

The Beach Boys
Colston Hall, 2 December 1968

The Beach Boys in general and Brian Wilson in particular have undergone something of a critical rehabilitation in recent years. But back in 1968, no one in the US was interested in that anachronistic, clean-cut sun, sea'n'surf shit anymore. The records weren't selling and the concert halls were so empty that the band's self-styled 'Million Dollar Tour' with the Maharishi in April actually wound up costing them $250,000 when it was cancelled after just four dates. At one of these, shortly after Martin Luther King was assassinated, just 800 people turned up to a venue with a capacity of 16,000. "Music fans wanted jambalaya; we were selling vanilla ice cream," confesses Mike Love in his autobiography, inevitably titled *Good Vibrations*. He also complains that culturally tone-deaf Capitol Records were still marketing them as "the nation's number one surf band" and that while they'd finally rid themselves of those ghastly striped shirts they were now being obliged to wear all-white suits.

So, hey, if the Yanks aren't buying this stuff, maybe the Limeys will. Things couldn't get any worse, after all. And at least troubled Dennis had found a nice new friend in the form of a rather intense young man named Charles Manson, with whom he'd just recorded a song. At this time, The Beach Boys were actually enjoying greater chart success in the UK than back home. They'd not got as far as Bristol on their 1966 UK tour, so this was their first gig in the city. Brian was absent, as he was withdrawing from the band to spend more time with his drugs. But Carl and Dennis Wilson were present, along with Mike Love, Al Jardine and Bruce Johnston. They also brought along a horn section, this being the latest fad among hipper acts - notably The Doors, who'd now completely usurped The Beach Boys as America's favourite band and had just returned from their own hugely successful, high profile European tour.

If The Beach Boys thought they'd be getting away from political unrest by travelling to Europe, they were sorely mistaken. In Bristol, the mood was dark and students were in the middle of their occupation of Senate House.

The *Western Daily Press* caught up with a rather whingy Johnston between shows backstage at the Colston. He branded US audiences "unappreciative" and noted gnomically that "teenagers are craving for something intangible that they can't understand".

As for the performances, *Post* pop correspondent James Belsey was overjoyed by their brand of cheerful, old-timey entertainment. He was even delighted by the outfits they loathed. Pronouncing the show "a triumph", Belsey raved: "The five Californians sounded as healthy as they looked and a packed house gave them one of the noisiest receptions of the year. Dressed in natty brilliant white suits, they sang cheerful songs about sun, surf, hot beaches, nice girls back home and love."

The brief, if hit-packed, set included *Barbara Ann, Good Vibrations* and *God Only Knows*. Six days later, their show at the Astoria in London was recorded for an inessential contractual obligation album titled *Live in London*, which was eventually released in 1970. Confusingly, the same recording was also packaged as *Beach Boys '69* (even though it was recorded in 1968).

The Who

Anson Rooms, 7 December 1968

Cementing their reputation as one of the UK's most hard-working and incendiary live acts, The Who pitched up in Bristol once again for this suitably riotous show at the Anson Rooms. Their psychedelic hard rock makeover was in full swing with *Magic Bus* in the chart and Roger Daltrey was sporting his iconic fringed jacket'n'trousers combo, exposing his bare chest. Student Tony Byers took some great photos of the 'oo in action and recalls that this show took place during an 11-day sit-in at Senate House which added to the insurrectionary fever. This gig also featured the public unveiling of Keith Moon's brand spanking new Champagne Silver Premier drum kit, which he was to play up to and including the show recorded for the legendary *Live at Leeds* album. Naturally, the Loon celebrated taking possession of this precision kit by kicking it over at the end of the show.

Just three days later, The Who were in Wembley filming the ill-fated Rolling Stones *Rock'n'Roll Circus* TV special, alongside the likes of John and Yoko, Eric Clapton, Taj Mahal, Jethro Tull and Marianne Faithfull. Alas, so comprehensively did they upstage the lacklustre headliners that the film didn't see the light of day until 1996. A portion of Moon's drum kit was eventually sold at Christie's in 2004 for £120,000 and is now on display at the Rock & Roll Hall of Fame in Cleveland, Ohio. Two of the floor toms are owned by the V&A in London.

1969

Nixon is inaugurated as US President… Neil Armstrong becomes the first man to walk on the moon… Plenty of unrest, including the Stonewall riots and Manson murders… The internet is born as the first message is sent and received across ARPANET…Woodstock Festival marks the culmination of the Hippy Dream. This crashes a few months later when young black man Meredith Hunter is stabbed to death at Altamont - leading commentators to proclaim "the end of the sixties"… Jim Morrison whips out his old fella on stage in Miami. Allegedly… UK news is dominated by 'The Troubles' in Northern Ireland… The Beatles give their last, impromptu public performance on the roof of the Apple building. 'Supergroup' Blind Faith play to 100,000 people in Hyde Park. Bob Dylan headlines the second Isle of Wight festival. Brian Jones drowns in his swimming pool… *Monty Python's Flying Circus* and *Scooby-Doo* make their TV debuts… Chart-topping albums include *Abbey Road*, *Let It Bleed*, Cream's *Goodbye*, Dylan's *Nashville Skyline* and *Stand Up* by Jethro Tull. Other key releases include The Who's *Tommy* and Led Zeppelin's first two albums. Biggest-selling single of the year is *Sugar, Sugar* by cartoon bubblegum pop band The Archies… Ryan Williams (Roni Size) and Adrian Thaws (Tricky) are born in Bristol… Prototype Concorde makes its maiden flight from Filton airfield… Bristol Polytechnic is created on a greenfield site in Frenchay.

The Nice
Anson Rooms, 18 January 1969
A little more than a year after playing the Colston Hall with Pink Floyd and Jimi Hendrix, pioneering proggers The Nice had started to grab headlines, partly because of Keith Emerson's theatrical antics but mainly because of a dramatic reworking of Leonard Bernstein's *America* and their performance

of it at an anti-apartheid show at the Royal Albert Hall the previous July. Stripping away the lyrics, Emerson created what he described as "the first protest instrumental", whose spoken word ending was supplied by P.P. Arnold's three-year-old son. The Albert Hall show featured a bizarre line-up that included Sammy Davis Jr., jazzers Johnny Dankworth and Cleo Lane and, erm, the cast of *Till Death Us Do Part*. At the climax of The Nice's set, Emerson borrowed a lighter from Alf Garnett himself (Warren Mitchell, for it was he) and set fire to the American flag, earning the band a lifetime ban from the venue.

Tony Byers' vivid photographs of the Anson Rooms show depict an animated Emerson attacking his keyboards with his usual gusto - and a prominent knife. Chances are this is one of the two Hitler Youth knives he was given by his roadie Lemmy Kilmister. "At one point, two students went off and got drummer Brian Davison a pint of beer, which they handed up to him," Tony recalls. "No barriers or security guards or strict health and safety rules in those days..."

The student paper's reviewer was ecstatic, describing "unprecedented scenes of audience participation and reaction" at the "sell-out dance". Emerson was singled out for particular praise, albeit unfortunately phrased: "[He] manipulated, pounded and raped his organ, and by careful use of implements and by bodily moving the instrument produced sounds the makers could never have envisaged."

Tyrannosaurus Rex/Fairport Convention/David Bowie
Colston Hall, 23 February 1969

History records that Marc Bolan played the Colston four times. This was his first appearance as Tyrannosaurus Rex, with Steve Peregrin Took on bongos. It was part of the - deep breath - *Lion and the Unicorn in the Forest of Faun* tour, hot from what was practically a residency at Middle Earth in Covent Garden. Bolan was an underground hippy hero at the time, much loved by John Peel, who was present on every night of this tour to introduce the duo (using his posh voice rather than the Liverpudlian accent he affected later in his career) and - chortle! - read poetry. This was all serious, flowery, fey, cross-legged acoustic stuff.

I should perhaps attach a health warning to that mention of Fairport Convention as the main support. They're listed on all the press ads in both the local and student press. But this show doesn't appear to have been reviewed anywhere and those who obsessively compile online Fairport gig histories make no mention of it. That said, it has also been claimed that Fairport headlined the Colston at some point in January 1969, though this show does not appear to have taken place and certainly wasn't advertised locally. Anyway, if they did turn up, this would have been the second and final opportunity to see what many consider to be the classic, Sandy Denny-fronted version of Fairport in Bristol. They'd played at the West of England College of Art at Bower Ashton in July 1968, just after she joined the band. But by the time of this show, Fairport had found their folk-rock feet as they embarked on the most prolific (three albums in one year), creative and justly renowned period of their career. *What We Did on Our Holidays* had just been released and they broke off from working on *Unhalfbricking* for this short run of dates.

Wherever and whenever their Bristol show took place, it was certainly significant. It's worth revisiting producer Joe Boyd's account in his memoir *White Bicycles*: "As the album took shape, I got more and more excited. Sandy's *Autopsy* and Richard's *Genesis Hall* were mature compositions that showed they could fulfil all the ambitions I had for them. During a break in recording, they summoned me to a gig in Bristol to hear two new songs. First, a French version of Dylan's *If You Gotta Go, Go Now* performed cajun-style, then a traditional ballad Sandy had taught them called *A Sailor's Life*. The first became their only hit single, the second turned English folk music on its head. The implications of their version of this old ballad have reverberated far and wide. A member of Los Lobos told a friend of mine that they had just been another rock band from East LA until *A Sailor's Life* challenged them to find something in their own Mexican traditions as rich as Fairport had found in their English ones. Many bands around the world have begun to look back to their own culture when they come up against the limitations of the Anglo-American 'rock' model. The map for such journeys leads back to that night in Bristol."

Beneath Fairport on the bill was sitar player Vytas Serelis. Opening the show was a fella named David Bowie, making his very first appearance in Bristol. But the future Dame David wasn't singing; he was performing two brief mime pieces as the opening act. The rivalry between Bowie and Bolan was already in full swing, and at the time Bolan was by far the biggest star. It wouldn't be long before he was eclipsed, but for the time being his generosity in inviting Bowie to open each night of this short six-date tour (of which the Colston Hall show was the fourth) as a mime artist rather than a singer was actually an act of sadism. That's the view of producer/bassist Tony Visconti, who told David Buckley: "David was open to friendship but Marc was quite cruel about David's as yet unproven musical career."

"I had no idea, from seeing him on the tour, that he had any musical aspirations at all," Serelis is quoted as saying in Nicholas Pegg's impressively exhaustive *The Complete David Bowie*. "I do remember thinking what an old woman he was, because he used to take hours to get his make-up on. He'd go on in a draggy costume with tights and everything, and do this fairly conventional Marcel Marceau-type act."

Incredible String Band
Colston Hall, 1 March 1969

Sixties counterculture heroes and a huge influence on Led Zeppelin (notably *Led Zeppelin III*), the classic String Band line-up of Mike Heron, Robin Williamson, Rose Simpson and Licorice McKechnie hit the Colston Hall just five months before appearing at Woodstock.

Backstage, the suitably chilled ISB were interviewed by Ian Leese of Bristol student newspaper *Nonesuch*. "Man, there are so many nice people here tonight - it's just great," enthused Williamson, who added that the recently departed Clive Palmer "left to go to Afghanistan because he wanted to." Those were the days, eh?

Mike Heron, meanwhile, got heavy when asked to explain the use of religious imagery in the band's songs. "We believe in life, man, rather than being convinced Christians... Everyone has been Jesus at some time in their lives. 'Jesus' means a lot of things but basically it's just faith in life. It doesn't matter whether there's a higher power above us."

They later became Scientologists.

In her autobiography *Muse, Odalisque Handmaiden*, Rose Simpson reveals that after the Colston Hall show the band and their entourage (including manager Joe Boyd, who produced the ISB's early albums) were invited for a meal and impromptu gig at the home of a local vicar. Apparently, this sort of thing was a regular occurrence, thanks to the band's growing army of fanatical enthusiasts - but it wasn't universally welcome.

George Harrison and Ringo Starr at the Colston Hall in 1963. Photograph: Bristol Post

The Beatles (Ringo, George, John and Paul) at the Colston Hall 15 November 1963. Photograph: Bristol Post

The Beatles at the Colston Hall on 15 November 1963. This was their second visit to Bristol.

Photograph: Bristol Post

THE PAVILION - BATH

WHIT MONDAY 3rd JUNE
SORRY NO SESSION

FROM LIVERPOOL THE

MONDAY 10th JUNE
BEATLES
PLUS PLUS
THE COLIN ANTHONY COMBO
and CHET AND THE TRIUMPHS
ADM 6/-

MONDAY 17th JUNE
SHANE FENTON AND THE FENTONES

FROM AMERICA THE GLAMOROUS

MONDAY 24th JUNE
KETTY LESTER
(LOVE LETTERS IN THE SAND ETC)

7.30-10.30 p.m.
ADM. 4/-
(Except the Beatles Night)

TOP POP STARS EVERY MONDAY

BRISTOL WEEK-END
NO 18 WEDNESDAY AUGUST 19 1964 PRICE 6d
THE ROLLING STONES and MIKE JAGGER
PAGES 12 & 13

Handbill for the Bath Pavilion, June 1963, advertising The Beatles' first show in the west. Rock'n'roller Shane Fenton later enjoyed a string of glam rock hits in the early seventies as Alvin Stardust.

Bristol Week-End cashes in on The Rolling Stones Longleat furore in August 1964 with a feeble cover story on 'Mike Jagger' and a string of irate readers' letters.

The Rolling Stones (left to right: Charlie Watts, Keith Richards, Bill Wyman, Mick Jagger, Brian Jones) backstage at the Colston Hall, 1964. Photograph: Bristol Post

THE MOST FAMOUS CLUB IN EUROPE

BRISTOL CHINESE R & B JAZZ CLUB

EVERY TUESDAY AT THE CORN EXCHANGE, CORN ST.

TUESDAY, 9th NOV.   The Raving R & B of

GRAHAM BOND ORGANISATION

TUESDAY, 16th NOV.   From London's Marquee Club

THE VAGABONDS

TUESDAY, 23rd NOV.   "You've Got to Hide Your Love Away"

THE SILKIE

TUESDAY, 30th NOV.   Girls! Girls! Girls!

THE BIRDS

TUESDAY, 7th DEC.   The Greatest Show on Earth

THE STEAM PACKET

LONG JOHN BALDRY   BRIAN AUGER TRINITY
ROD STEWART   JULIE DRISCOLL

Students admitted on Student Cards   Nurses Half-Price
Crocodile Sandwiches   Fly Lice   Chop Chop   Uncal Bonny

THE   EXCHANGE

PUBLIC   DANCE

◄━━ TICKET OFFICE

NO ADMISSION OR RE-ADMISSION AFTER 9·45 P.M.

Left: Bristol Chinese R&B Jazz Club poster for Nov/Dec 1964. Above: The entry sign at the Corn Exchange. Below: The programme for the Jimi Hendrix Experience/Pink Floyd show at the Colston Hall, 24 November 1967.

Jimi HENDRIX Experience

HAROLD DAVISON and TITO BURNS
present

The MOVE

THE PINK FLOYD   THE NICE   THE EIRE APPARENT   THE AMEN CORNER
THE OUTER LIMITS   Compere PETE DRUMMOND

Illustration/design A Litri/Paul Martin & Associates

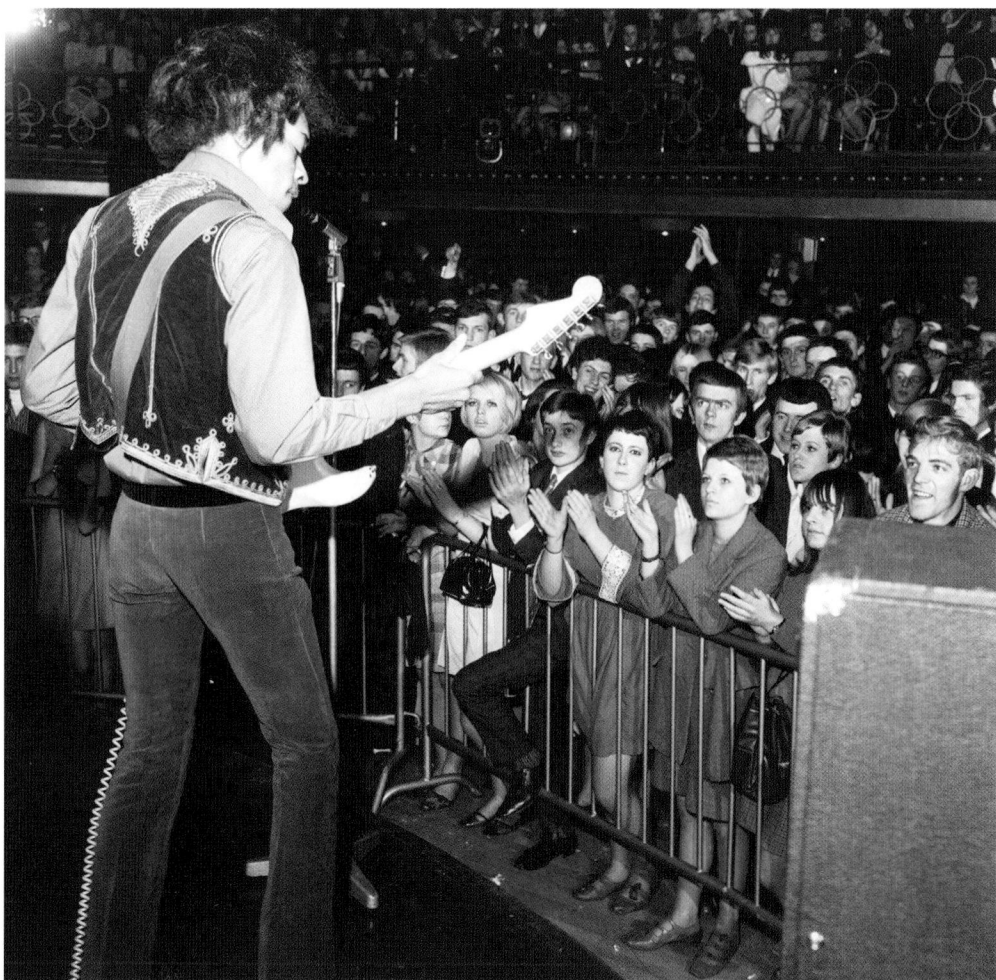

Jimi Hendrix makes his Bristol debut in front of a rather square looking Locarno audience, 9 February 1967. Photograph: Mirrorpix/Alamy

Ginger Baker and Eric Clapton of Cream at the Corn Exchange, 18 April 1967. Photographer unknown

Steve Winwood of Traffic at the Colston Hall, 13 October 1967. Photograph: Bristol Post

Pete Townshend of The Who strikes a familiar pose at the Anson Rooms, 7 December 1968.

Photograph: Tony Byers

Top: Keith Moon kicks over his brand new Champagne Silver Premier drum kit at the end of The Who's performance at the Anson Rooms, 7 December 1968. Bottom: Keith Moon and Pete Townshend at the same show. Photographs: Tony Byers

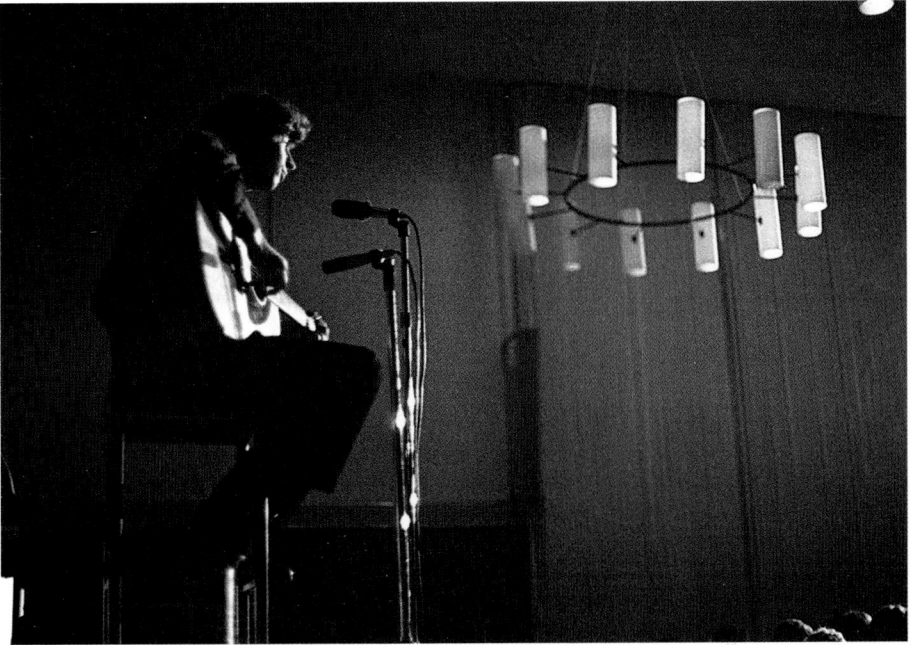

Troubadour Club regular Al Stewart at the Presco Folk Concert, Anson Rooms, October 1968, eight years before he hit the big time with the platinum-selling 'Year of the Cat'.
Photograph: Tony Byers

Joe Cocker at the Anson Rooms, 1 October 1968, just before the release of the career-making 'With a Little Help from My Friends'. Photograph: Tony Byers

George Harrison backstage at the Colston Hall with Delaney and Bonnie Bramlett and friends (including Eric Clapton, seated front), 2 December 1969. Harrison was so alarmed at the press interest in what would have been his first post-Beatles show that he refused to perform, hiding backstage while the audience rioted in the hall. Photograph: Mirrorpix/Alamy

Guitar great Peter Green of the original Fleetwood Mac on stage at the Anson Rooms, 5 March 1969. Note his natty Sgt. Pepper badge. Photograph: Tony Byers

Marsha Hunt, allegedly the subject of the Stones' 'Brown Sugar', on stage at the Anson Rooms, 31 October 1969. Photograph: Tony Byers

Top: Roger Waters gets over-excited during a 'happening' at the Victoria Rooms, 2 March 1969.
Bottom: Pink Floyd (Left to right: Richard Wright, Nick Mason, Roger Waters, David Gilmour) at the same show. Both photographs: Tony Byers

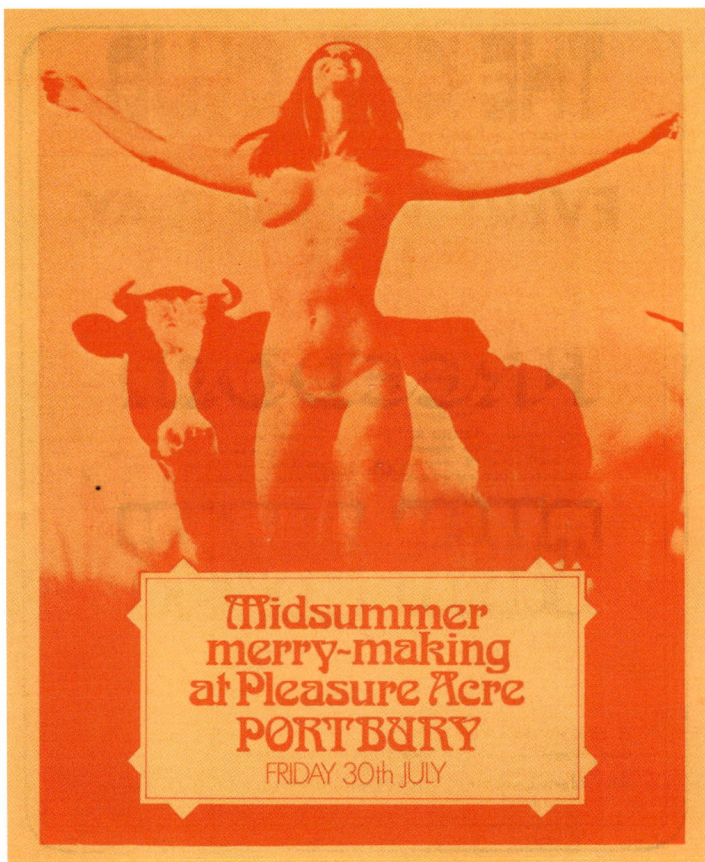

Top left: Free admission for the ladies at the Granary in the late 1960s. Top right: Granary gig poster for July 1969. Bottom: Careful ma'am! Poster for the ill-fated Midsummer Merry-Making event of 1971. All images from the Granary archive, courtesy of Ed Newsom.

Top: Granary gig poster for August 1969. Bottom: A selection of covers of Dogpress, the Bristol alternative music magazine, 1969-1971. All images from the Granary archive, courtesy of Ed Newsom.

The Granary souvenir T-shirt design. Now a sought-after collectors' item.

Image from the Granary archive, courtesy of Ed Newsom.

"It was a mystery to me why we turned up at some of the houses we visited after gigs," she writes. "We had to eat, and if it was at someone's home, I assumed it was one of Robin's unpredictable fancies. Mike and I went along with them and tried to avoid conflict... The vicar's house in Bristol was one of those imposed visits. Luckily, we were not exhausted at this point or the outcome might have been very different. Kind people had clearly made a great effort, and we usually tried to respond - but that evening Joe was not pleased at having to be polite to strangers, while Mike and I wanted to get back to the hotel. He had a song to work on and I didn't want to meet anyone else that night.

"But Robin and Licorice insisted, and were willing to answer the questions we had been asked a million times: 'Do you all live together?', 'When did you meet?', 'Did you learn to play sitar in India?' As Mike and I were about to make excuses and go, copious wine saved the evening, smoothing ruffled feathers and relaxing strained nerves. As the bottles drained, they all became lovely people, Licorice was adorable, Robin an inspiration, Mike a delight and Joe our guardian angel. We ended up singing in harmony for our supper, but this was a rare conclusion to such an evening mid-tour."

(In the tiny subsection of autobiography that is the Sixties Hippy Chick Musician Memoir, this is by far the most insightful, truthful and self-aware, revealing much about ISB dynamics and Rose's secret love of uncool hard rock.)

Today, Heron and Williamson continue to record and perform. In 1994, Rose Simpson became the Lady Mayoress of Aberystwyth. Christina 'Licorice' McKechnie set out to hitchhike across the Arizona desert in 1987. She was never seen again.

Pink Floyd/Principal Edwards Magic Theatre
Victoria Rooms, 3 March 1969

Things you wouldn't see today, part 94: a 10:30pm torchlight procession up Park Street from Colston Street to the Victoria Rooms where Bristol University's Rag Queen ("blonde-haired Alison Clout") is crowned. Then it's time for what's billed as "a happening" from 11pm-1am (admission 7/6).

First to happen were the Principal Edwards Magic Theatre, who were either a ground-breaking, multi-media performance art collective or a pretentious load of old bollocks, according to taste. They certainly impressed John Peel after he saw them at Exeter University, becoming the first act to sign to his Dandelion Records. They also had local connections, since vocalist Martin Stellman was, at the time, a second year Drama and English student at Bristol University.

Stellman ("who says his Jimi Hendrix hair is natural") told new *Western Daily Press Teenpage* editor Penny Weston that they "prefer to think of ourselves as musical theatre rather than a group. Our music is often incorporated with dancing and poetry." She wasn't won over, describing the Principals as sounding "like a combination of medieval dirge and a piano smashing contest".

With Syd Barrett now departed and about to restart work on his aborted *Madcap Laughs* solo record, the four-piece Pink Floyd were taking a break from recording the *More* soundtrack and early tinkering on what would become their solo studio contributions to *Ummagumma* for a quick romp round the nation's student venues. The set they were playing at this time didn't change much from gig to gig and would have included *Astronomy Domine, Interstellar Overdrive, Set the Controls for the Heart of the Sun, Pow R. Toc H., Let There Be More Light, Flaming* and *Careful With That Axe, Eugene*.

Penny Weston managed to collar drummer Nick Mason backstage, where he mysteriously claimed that the band were working on an invention that would revolutionise music. Alas, he couldn't elaborate much as they hadn't got around to patenting their device, which cost £7,000 and included more than a mile of cables. "Basically it's a machine which can amplify and distort noise, concentrating the sound on one area of a room." This new, upgraded surround sound system was unveiled at London's Royal Festival Hall the following month.

She also asked David Gilmour why Floyd had stopped playing dance halls. Turns out people kept chucking stuff. "We find that we just don't go down well with teeny-bopper audiences any more," he explained. "In the past at dance halls bottles and glass have been thrown at us. So we play safe and go to gigs at colleges, universities and clubs, where the audiences want to listen to the music."

The uncredited reviewer for student paper *Nonesuch* was clearly ODing on good vibes, or possibly something stronger, describing the show as "mind-blasting" and "one of the best yet seen in Bristol. John Peel wandered around talking to incredibly nice people and generally had an incredibly beautiful time."

Trivia note: Martin Stellman subsequently dropped out of Bristol University and later forged a successful career in the film industry. He got off to a flying start with a co-writing credit on *Quadrophenia* (1979). Next up was Franco Rosso's incendiary *Babylon*, which he also co-wrote. Starring Aswad's Brinsley Forde as a young man battling racism and police brutality as he pursues his musical ambitions in Thatcher-era London, this has been rightly acclaimed as one of the key films in black British cinema. It certainly had a profound effect on audiences. When it was premiered in Bristol in 1980, punters were reported to have torn up the seats. In the US, *Babylon* was considered so controversial that it didn't get a cinema release until 2019.

Stellman also wrote the political thriller *Defence of the Realm* (1986) and co-wrote and directed *For Queen and Country* (1988), starring Denzel Washington. Later, he created the Sean Penn/Nicole Kidman thriller *The Interpreter* (2005) and, most recently, collaborated with Idris Elba on the latter's directorial debut, *Yardie* (2018).

BB King/Fleetwood Mac
Colston Hall, 27 April 1969

Imagine the young Peter Green's joy: opening every night for his dapper hero BB King. Actually, the admiration was mutual. Green went on to play on King's 1971 album *B.B. King in London*.

Comprising Green, Mick Fleetwood, John McVie, Jeremy Spencer and Danny Kirwan, Fleetwood Mac were coming to the end of their run as a pure blues band at this time. Christine Perfect, who'd already married McVie, had contributed keyboards and vocals to the band's second album, *Mr. Perfect*, but was not by then a full member of Fleetwood Mac. *Albatross* had topped the UK singles chart back in January and was the final song in their covers-dominated set at the Colston. With Green yet to discover the dubious joys of vast quantities of LSD, this would have been the perfect opportunity to see Fleetwood Mac's first incarnation at their peak. As for the headliner, the great bluesman was on his very first tour of the UK. It had opened at the Albert Hall a few days earlier to rave reviews. As usual, there were two houses for this show, at 5:30pm and 7:45pm. King went on to land the opening slot on The Rolling Stones' 1969 US tour, which exposed him to a whole new audience in his homeland. Despite his hard-touring reputation, he wouldn't return to the Colston Hall until the 1980s.

A grumpy David Harrison reviewed the show for the *Bristol Evening Post*. He was a fan of King, whom he reckoned "typifies the ultimate development of the blues". But he was less pleased by what he described as "more than 20 minutes of boring, inane and ingratiating comic monologues and homespun cottonfield philosophy". Harrison also disliked the amplification, which he described as "harsh and overpowering". But if he found King disappointing, he was positively appalled by the groovy youngsters of Fleetwod Mac: "… an overamplified and overrated pop group whose songs were unsubtle and electronically ear shattering." He didn't even give Green a namecheck as his 'dad watching *Top of the Pops*' rant continued. "B.B. King was noisy but this was ridiculous," he concluded.

Ten Years After/Jethro Tull/Clouds
Colston Hall, 9 May 1969
There's no shortage of 'Best Woodstock Performances' lists on the internet. But each and every one of them includes the epic, high-energy rendition of *I'm Going Home* by Brit blues-rock trio Ten Years After, featuring the lightning fretboard skills of Alvin Lee. But what if you could have seen Lee and chums giving an equally thrilling performance that same year in a nice cosy English concert hall, without all the rain, mud and bad acid? In retrospect, 1969 was TYA's peak year. It began relatively quietly with a show at Glastonbury Town Hall on January 4. By February, *Stonedhenge* had become the first in a run of hit albums. Later in the year, they would play the Bath Festival (billed above Led Zeppelin), enjoy the distinction of being one of the first rock acts to perform at the Newport Jazz Festival and pitch up at Mr. Yasgur's farm. But before all that, they were sharing the bill with Jethro Tull at the Colston Hall.

This was Tull's very first Bristol show, though they'd headlined club gigs at Glastonbury Town Hall on November 9, 1968 and the Bath Pavilion on January 7, 1969. At this stage, they'd got just one album under Mr. Anderson's bulging codpiece - what would prove to be an atypical blues-rock collection prophetically entitled *This Was*, with guitarist Mick

Abrahams' influence very much to the fore. But Abrahams had just left the band to found Blodwyn Pig and had been replaced by Martin Barre.

So on paper, TYA were the natural headliners. But Tull were buoyed by a rapturous, career-making reception from the 50,000-strong crowd at Reading Festival precursor the National Jazz and Blues Festival at Sunbury-on-Thames the previous August. What's more, they'd just released *Living in the Past* as a single, which eventually rose to number three in the charts, backed by a memorable *Top of the Pops* performance in which Anderson gave it the full boggle-eyed unipedal flautist. As a consequence, when this tour kicked off the two bands found themselves on an equal footing in the popularity stakes, leading to plenty of backstage ructions that spurred each on to upstage the other.

"TYA were the big kids on the block and suddenly Jethro were as big as them and the rivalry - and resentment - between them showed itself very obviously on the Spring 1969 UK tour... especially in fighting over the headline spot," writes Billy Ritchie of support act Clouds in the sleeve notes to the 50th anniversary reissue of *This Was*. "If you look at the tour posters, they vaguely suggest equal billing, but it's noticeable that Jethro's name is first. Jethro were the headliners more times than TYA. We just tried to keep the peace. At the Newcastle Town Hall, TYA were the stars and it was the best I'd ever heard them play and at the Bristol Colston Hall Jethro brought the house down."

The *Bristol Evening Post*'s uncredited reviewer was astonished to find that the Colston Hall was packed to the rafters for these 'underground' acts, praising TYA's "wild bluesy set" and the "outstanding" range and versatility of Tull: "Their brand of pop was built around the antics of Ian Anderson on flute - funny, subtle and more in key with jazz than pop."

Western Daily Press Teenpage editor Penny Weston challenged Anderson to define exactly what this new-fangled 'underground' music was all about. "It's not a commercial tag for a type of pop music," he explained. "It's a sincere sound produced by musicians who believe in what they're playing."

Anderson added that *Living in the Past* was the first composition he was actually satisfied with. "I often get depressed with the music I write. Sometimes the end product is not as good as I expected it to be."

As for the absence of screaming, which had rendered the likes of the Fabs and Stones inaudible just a few years earlier: "I really appreciate it when audiences bother to listen. Teenagers today have a different concept of pop music. They don't go to a concert to watch someone wiggle their hips, or to see a pretty face. They go to hear the music."

Later in 1969, Jethro Tull were voted Best New Group by readers of the *NME*. In the *Melody Maker* poll, they came second in the Best Group category, behind The Beatles but ahead of The Rolling Stones.

Tull returned to the Colston Hall to play to another capacity crowd on October 4, 1970, on the *Benefit* tour (supported by Procol Harum and Tír na nÓg), two months after their career-enhancing performance at the Isle of Wight Festival. This show was reviewed by Bristol-based sports journalist and historian David Foot, who wrote for *The Guardian* for the next four decades. Foot enthused about "the frenzied brilliance of Jethro Tull" and noted that: "… the night inevitably belonged to Ian Anderson, whose all-embracing tour de force kept an admiring audience mesmerised. It is not simply his reserves of energy and his limitless extrovert traits. There are his changes of mood: his sensitive flautist moments, his disciplined singing, his confidential jokes and asides… if there was ever the faintest hint of boredom - and faint it was - it came with the length of the instrumental solos."

Frank Zappa and the Mothers of Invention
Colston Hall, 3 June 1969

Frank's only Bristol show, promoting the 'difficult' *Uncle Meat* album, which also formed part of the Mothers' first run of UK gigs outside London. Oddly, the *Western Daily Press* really went to town on this. In a telephone interview in advance of the tour, a serious-sounding Frank told Brian K. Jones what to expect at the Colston Hall: "The programme will include concerto type music, songs from the fifties, some ballet and we will improvise a lot using the audience as part of the orchestra. I will be conducting the audience applause making it go back and forth in giving it a stereo sound."

As it turned out, there wasn't much audience to conduct. According to one report, so few people turned up to see the Mothers that Frank asked everyone to come forward to the front of the hall. Further excitement occurred when a stink bomb was thrown on stage.

Teenpage's Penny Weston grabbed a word with Zappa in his dressing room after the show, challenging him to concede that 'America's most freakish group' was indeed 'weird'. "Audiences never know what to expect when we appear on stage," he mused. "The American and British public look upon us as a novelty. I'm sorry to say that they don't appreciate us as much musically as they do visually. I suppose we are very much a mixed bag. Some of the members of the group are old enough to be grandfathers."

Bristol Evening Post pop correspondent James Belsey was a tad disappointed to find that the event was neither a 'freak-out' nor a 'happening' and seemed most fascinated by the tonsorial display. "The long-haired audience were certainly put to shame by the back-length tresses of this group," he observed.

Fortunately for Uncle Frank, Belsey's disappointment did not extend to the music. "Under the direction of guitarist and conductor Frank Zappa, The Mothers played two sets of imaginative, blockbusting music... Zappa danced and pranced around at the centre of The Mothers and he admitted later: 'I train these guys. Players leave The Mothers to join other groups - they don't leave other groups to join The Mothers."

After the Colston Hall gig, the Mothers decamped to the Granary until closing time and went on to party all night with members of the Plastic Dog collective, publishers of Bristol's sixties alternative magazine, *Dogpress*.

"We were all fans of Zappa and the Mothers and somehow managed to talk our way backstage after the Colston Hall show," recalls Mike Tobin, by then a member of Plastic Dog. "Zappa himself travelled on his own, so had already left for London, but the rest of his outfit were obviously keen to party. We took them to The Old Granary where it was a jazz night and Bristol's very own Avon Cities were playing. The Mothers were both amused and bemused to hear music played that they claimed they never witnessed back in the USA. Laden with crates of beer and bottles of wine, we all adjourned to Ed Newsom's flat in Clifton for more partying. Unable to locate a corkscrew, one of the (very American) roadies assured us that if you banged the base of a bottle against the wall, pressure would build and the cork would pop out. Sadly this did not work, the bottle smashed and wine cascaded down the wall and on to the carpet. I was sat on the floor next to drummer Jimmy Carl Black ('the Indian of the group') eager to chat with him. He rolled the biggest joint I had ever seen, took a few drags then passed it to me. I took one toke, passed out and fell asleep. When I woke up at dawn, everybody had vanished and the Mothers entourage had gone back to London."

There's an intriguing footnote to this story. Frank and the Mothers very nearly played a second show in Bristol. They'd been booked to appear at the Anson Rooms on December 13, 1971, which was quite a coup for the Students' Union Ents as this was the only university date on the band's entire, gruelling European tour. Alas, these proved to be the most eventful couple of weeks of Frank's life. On December 4, the Mothers arrived in Montreux to play to an audience of 3,000 at the Casino. During the encore, an over-excited fan fired a flare gun into the ceiling, setting fire to the building. As Deep Purple's Roger Glover observed to his great financial advantage, this produced a considerable amount of smoke on the water of Lake Geneva. (Purple were in the audience as they'd recently arrived in Montreux to record their *Machine Head* album.) As Zappa surveyed the wreckage of his band's gear the following morning, he held a vote on whether to continue the tour. The musicians voted in favour. So although the French and Belgian legs were pulled, the Mothers proceeded to London for a couple of shows at the Rainbow Theatre. At the end of the first one on December 11, just two days before they were due to play Bristol, a young man leapt on stage and pushed Frank violently into the orchestra pit - a drop of ten feet. He suffered a broken rib, paralysed wrist and fractured ankle. The rest of the tour was cancelled immediately.

The Bath Festival of Blues
Bath Pavilion Recreation Ground, 28 June 1969

There were two Bath festivals, the first being the only one to actually take place in Bath. Freddy Bannister had been approached by the posho Bath Festival Society, who'd decided to do something about the stinging accusation that they were too elitist. They'd noticed his success at the Pavilion and asked whether he would consider putting on a groovy pop show for young people at the Recreation Ground. The rental charge for the venue was £40, and the biggest cost was Led Zeppelin's £200 fee.

This was Zep's first ever outdoor show (they'd played the Colston Hall a week earlier on June 21) and they performed in the middle of the afternoon, fourth on the bill behind Fleetwood Mac (Peter Green incarnation), John Mayall and Ten Years After. Not bad for a ticket price of eighteen shillings and sixpence. Jimmy Page deployed his violin-bow technique on *Dazed and*

Confused and their show earned a standing ovation from the 30,000-strong crowd. "Nobody had coerced the youth of England into becoming Zep fans, but there they were cheering Page, Jones, Bonham and Plant, as the drums thundered and the guitars roared," reported *Melody Maker*'s Chris Welch. He wasn't wrong about that lack of coercion. Regardless of what the revisionists may tell you, Welch and, perhaps unexpectedly, feminist Germaine Greer were the only people championing Zeppelin in the press during the late sixties and early seventies.

History records that a young Methodist dairy farmer from Somerset named Michael Eavis snuck in to this first Bath Festival under the fence. "It's true," he confirms. "I'd just met and fallen in love with [his late wife] Jean. We went to chapel in the morning and travelled on to the festival in the afternoon. It was such an incredible experience. The whole place was full of loved-up people just like us. I don't really remember any of the music. The Moody Blues were probably my favourite band back then, but they didn't get to play even though they were there. I do remember thinking, 'I can do this'. And I did…

"Freddy Bannister and his wife actually came to visit us at the farm a few years later. He drove down the narrow Somerset lanes in his Rolls Royce. I remember him saying to me, 'What you've got here, Michael, is the future of music festivals,' which I thought was rather nice. He was quite right too."

One of the earliest outdoor rock festivals staged in the UK, the trouble-free Bath Festival "drew one of the biggest mass pop audiences ever seen outside London," reported the *Western Daily Press*. The paper grabbed a few of the peaceable hairy punters for vox pops. Tony, "who could have been mistaken for an Indian warrior if it hadn't been for the paisley bedspread which partly covered his otherwise bare chest," was a biology student from Oxford. "I haven't dressed up for the occasion", he insisted. "Such a big crowd gives you a nice secure feeling. I shall stay for the night just for the fun of sleeping out in the open with a lot of others."

It had taken more than a day for Cornish student couple Margaret Rotherham and Craig Harrison to hitch their way to Bath. "Drivers mistrust you if you don't look conventional," said Margaret. "We ended up walking half of the way, but it was worth it just to be here."

The good vibes were stoked by John Peel, who introduced the bands and compared the Festival favourably with Blind Faith's massive free Hyde Park show three weeks earlier. "Must confess, I've never been a John Peel admirer - until Saturday, that is," wrote Brian K. Jones the following week. "He knows how to handle the multitudes perfectly, his approach is like a gospel, they sit up and listen to him." Overall, Jones considered it "a great day, enjoyed by all".

The only sour note was sounded by the city's retired colonel contingent who vented their fury on the letters page of the *Bath and Wilts Evening Chronicle*. "If we must have this kind of deplorable event, may I suggest we ask the noble Marquis to accommodate it at Longleat?" demanded a particularly splenetic correspondent. "No doubt the lions would clean up some of the leftovers…"

To the city's eternal shame, these views seem to have swayed local councillors, who narrowly voted in favour of banning the festival from the Recreation Ground.

King Crimson
Granary, 30 June 1969

Al Read's definitive book *The Granary Club: The Rock Years 1969 to 1988* records that the short-lived first line-up of King Crimson (Robert Fripp, Greg Lake, Ian McDonald, Mike Giles and Pete Sinfield) played the Granary just six weeks after they formed and days before they appeared on stage at The Rolling Stones' free Hyde Park gig. Yes, they did play *21st Century Schizoid Man*. "The King Crimson gig at the Granary was a real coup for Al Read, and *21st Century Schizoid Man* was unlike anything we had heard before," recalls Ed Newsom. "It really was spine-tingling. I felt sorry for the roadies back then. There was no lift at the Granary to begin with, and all the gear had to be heaved up the stairs to the first floor. King Crimson used a Mellotron, which was designed as a studio instrument and was never really meant to be taken on the road. It weighed over 50kgs."

Yes
Granary, 28 July 1969

Ace proggers Yes hadn't even released their debut album when they appeared at the Granary with a line-up that featured Jon Anderson, Chris Squire, Peter Banks, Tony Kaye and Bill Bruford.

Plastic Dog's Mike Tobin was suitably astonished by the super-talented quintet. "We were all gobsmacked at the brilliance of the original line up of Yes. As we booked them again for other gigs and they became frequent visitors to my flat in Clifton, often when passing through to engagements further down the road in Devon and Cornwall, I developed a friendship with them - in particular with singer Jon Anderson. Thus when I moved to London in early 1970 to take a job as a booker with a leading Soho-based agency, it was Jon who found me a flat, sharing with guitarist Pete Banks and drummer Bill Bruford. Also it was Jon's influence that gained slots for Bristol's Stackridge (who I managed), supporting Yes at such London venues as The Rainbow. Sadly, over the years I lost touch with Jon, but thanks to the internet I did reconnect with Pete Banks shortly before he tragically died a few years ago."

Humble Pie/David Bowie
Colston Hall, 13 October 1969

On paper, this might seem like an odd combination. And indeed it is, with Steve Marriott's hard-rockin' post-Small Faces act supported by the still rather fey, curly-haired David Bowie. But backstage it was a reuniting of old mates. Fresh from The Herd, Humble Pie guitarist Peter Frampton was a childhood friend who'd known Bowie since 1962, when they went to Bromley Tech together. What's more, Frampton's art teacher father Owen was a huge influence on the young Bowie. Marriott also hailed from Bromley and Bowie had always been somewhat in awe of him. Humble Pie were very much the band of the moment, having just had their first chart hit with *Natural Born Bugie*. Bowie, meanwhile, had also enjoyed his first success with *Space Oddity*, but was about to enter an odd period of his career in which he was widely considered to be a washed-up one hit wonder. Dubbed the *Changes '69* tour, this 10-date UK jaunt saw Bowie as the opening act of a three band bill, which also included Welsh band Love Sculpture, formed by the young Dave Edmunds. Humble Pie manager Andrew Loog Oldham wanted Bowie to do his mime routine again, but he'd had enough of that shit on the Tyrannosaurus Rex tour and refused. Oldham relented, so young David took to the stage each night with his battered 12-string acoustic guitar for a 20 minute, six song set that included *Wild Eyed Boy from Freecloud* and, inevitably, *Space Oddity*.

Bristol Evening Post reviewer Geoffrey Simms lamented the poor turnout for this show but was overjoyed by "Peter Frampton's superb guitar work and [Steve] Marriott's dynamism." And Bowie? On his second appearance in Bristol, the poor fella was heckled by a section of the audience who'd come to rock. That said, "he won almost the biggest cheer of the night when he performed his present Top Ten hit, *Space Oddity*."

"We weren't thinking that Bowie was going to be one of the all-time greats," writes Peter Frampton in his autobiography *Do You Feel Like I Do?* "I just thought that he was mesmerising on stage, even then - he was special. I had no idea he would go on to do what he did. I'm sure he had it in his mind, like I did, but none of us knew what was coming."

Within a few short years, things would be very different for the former David Jones, both musically and sartorially. Peter Frampton, meanwhile, would later play on Bowie's *Never Let Me Down* album and join his backing band for the accompanying *Glass Spider* tour in 1987.

Marsha Hunt/Eclection
Anson Rooms, 31 October 1969

An iconic sixties figure (that's her with the giant afro on the poster for the UK production of *Hair*) and allegedly the subject of the Stones' *Brown Sugar*, Marsha Hunt was a huge star but enjoyed only a brief and modest musical career that peaked in 1969 with a minor hit single in the form of a cover of Dr. John's *Walk on Gilded Splinters* (with the young Rick Wakeman on piano). She pitched up at the Anson Rooms with Pleasure, the same trio who'd backed her at that year's Isle of Wight Festival, for the student union's Halloween Ball. Photographer Tony Byers recalls her taunting the assembled students for their appearance and dress. This from an artist who'd scandalised the easily scandalised for appearing in a musical best remembered for members of its cast wearing no clothes at all.

Indeed, Marsha had made her Bristol debut at the Locarno back in July with her earlier band White Trash, shortly after allegedly shocking the nation with what would today be termed a 'wardrobe malfunction' on *Top of the Pops*. Naturally, the *Western Daily Press*'s Brian K. Jones had been at this show by the woman he described, somewhat imaginatively, as "a female Arthur Brown" and couldn't resist quizzing her backstage about this unfortunate career-boosting incident. "It was absurd - I didn't intend to do it," she insisted. "But why all the fuss? People take no notice of the top of a woman's breast showing, yet there is uproar when I showed the bottom of my breasts… They had a lot of letters saying it was wrong for children to see such a thing."

Support at the Anson Rooms came from intriguing, short-lived, Peel-approved prog-folkies Eclection, who became one of the few British acts - alongside the Incredible String Band - to sign to Jac Holzman's hip US label Elektra, which released their sole, self-titled album.

Deep Purple
Mayfair Suite, 1 November 1969

Deep Purple have played many a weird show, but their first appearance in Bristol must count as one of the weirdest. The occasion was the *Western Daily Press*'s Teenpage Ball, which was a glorified beauty contest with a few pop acts. The 1968 Ball had been held in Clifton's Grand Spa Ballroom. This latest one was shifted to the swanky Mayfair Suite in the New Bristol Centre - the same building in which common or garden pop shows were staged at the more downmarket Locarno. And for the first time, they decided to book a major headlining act. "There were plenty of other groups we could have chosen, playing more conventional pop. But we picked Deep Purple because they are excitingly different," trumpeted the paper, describing Purple as a a "avant garde British pop group who received a Beatle-type reception in America and on the continent."

Readers were encouraged to vote for their favourite local groups in what was billed as the *WDP*'s own *Top of the Pops* contest, with the three winners getting support slots at the show. As for the beauty contest, the paper was looking for "the West's personality girl of the year", with a cash prize on offer (£35, with £10 and £5 prizes for the runners-up) - plus the even more coveted title of Miss Western Daily Press 1969. There was also a go-go dancing contest, first prize being a blonde wig from Wig Inn of Bristol.

For Purple fans, this would have been a fascinating opportunity to see the definitive Mark II line-up (Ian Gillan, Ritchie Blackmore, Ian Paice, Jon Lord, Roger Glover) in embryonic form. They'd just started work on the classic *In Rock* album that would spend more than a year in the UK album chart from June 1970 onwards.

Starting in September, the paper indulged in two solid months of relentless Deep Purple hype. Readers were reminded that Blackmore was a local lad, hailing from Weston-super-Mare. Brian K. Jones was dispatched to review the performance of Jon Lord's *Concerto for Group and Orchestra* at the Albert Hall on September 24. "Deep Purple were fantastic," he raved. "There isn't a weak line anywhere." Indeed, he was so enthused that he interviewed Jon Lord twice.

Inevitably, the Teenpage Ball was judged to be an unqualified success - mainly by the *WDP*, which published a pull-out souvenir supplement the following Monday. The Dipps were the winners of the local band contest, with Papa Weslie and Lot 39 as runners-up. As has become traditional for Bristol acts down the decades, all three can now be found in the 'Where Are They Now?' file.

Madeleine Stevens won the Miss Western Daily Press title and said she'd put her £35 swag towards the cost of a car. "I would like to travel the world to see how the other half lives," announced the 22-year-old Horfield garage receptionist, reading from the beauty contest script. Some 600 girls auditioned for the go-go dancing contest, with 60 of them performing on the night. Walking away with the wig was 18-year-old Corinne Comer of Pound Lane, Fishponds.

Even the paper's fashion editor was on hand to pronounce on what the event said about the 'in-gear' for 1970 and beyond. The answer? Trousers, "and it wasn't only the boys who were wearing them". Fortunately, some proprieties were still being observed: "… although the fashion scene at the ball was monopolised by trousered girls, don't get the wrong idea - there was no question of unisex."

Brian K. Jones described Purple's headline performance as "shattering". What the besuited *WDP* executives (including editor Eric Price) and their spouses, local businesspeople and sundry civic dignitaries present made of the hard-rockin' likes of *Speed King* and *Child in Time*, both of which were already in the band's set by this time, is not recorded.

Naturally, the paper sought to follow this with an even bigger and better Teenpage Ball. Late in October 1970, the breathless announcement came: "For months we've been waiting for the right group," read the teaser. "It had to be the right name, the name worthy of the tradition of the Teenpage Ball, the name that could follow Deep Purple, the fabulously successful stars of last year's ball."

Yes, yes... the name? Black Sabbath, "the heavy, brilliantly progressive group." They were to headline the Ball at the Top Rank, which had just undergone a £40,000 refit, on January 9, 1971.

Now before you get too excited about the delicious prospect of WDP executives headbanging to *Paranoid* and Ozzy urinating drunkenly over the Miss Western Daily Press contestants, Sabbath didn't actually turn up for the Teenpage Ball. Such was their rocketing popularity that they played the Colston Hall on the same night instead, the official excuse being that they'd recently changed agents. Given the riotous scenes that they were starting to attract, that was probably just as well. No matter, a new headliner was swiftly found: Yes ("the top progressive group name for 1971"). Two days after the announcement, they cancelled too.

So the 1971 Teenpage Ball was headlined by, erm, Mungo Jerry and Shakin' Stevens. (Trivia note: the first Bristol show by former Cardiff milkman Shaky - real name: Michael Barratt - with his band The Sunsets took place at Bishopston Parish Hall on October 3, 1970, shortly after the release of their debut single for Parlophone, *Spirit of Woodstock*. It was presented by the Eddie Cochran Memorial Society.)

Once again, there was a Top of the Pops contest. This time it was won by Dorset heavy rockers Crimson Earth. That wouldn't be worth mentioning but for the fact that one of the team of journalists assigned to produce the paper's pull-out Teenpage Ball supplement the following Monday was a young reporter who'd recently joined the paper. So it was that Crimson Earth were interviewed by 'Terence Pratchet' [*sic*]. Terry seemed particularly taken with their wooden mascot Wormold Gruntfuttock, which sounds uncannily like a Discworld character name. Crimson Earth never really succeeded in making waves nationally, but they did set a local record, becoming the band who notched up the most appearances at the Granary Club (sixteen in total from 1971 to 1974). As for Terry Pratchett, he was about to publish his first novel, *The Carpet People*. Nobody noticed or reviewed it.

While we're on the subject of the late, great Terry, here's an anecdote that was previously thought unverifiable, but has now been confirmed by retired *WDP* Deputy Editor Peter Gibbs, who witnessed it. Legend has it that *WDP* editor Eric Price was something of a sweary, intimidating figure, of whom the young Pratchett lived in fear.

One day, Price stormed into the newsroom holding up some of Terry's copy and yelling, "Who wrote this fucking rubbish?!"

Our hero was so terrified that he fell to the floor in a dead faint. Price just stepped over him, saying, "Oh bollocks, who's going to re-write this story now?"

There's another great anecdote attached to the late Mr. Price. Between 1960 and 1963, ACH Smith (Bristol playwright and author) and Tom Stoppard were in charge of the *WDP*'s arts page. Price didn't like them, or the idea of an arts page, but he went along with it. That, however, didn't stop him loudly posing the vital question: "What cunt reads this fucking shit?"

Mott the Hoople
Granary, 24 November 1969

Mott's eponymous debut album for Island had been released a few days before their first Bristol show, which meant most of the audience were familiar only with the single *Rock and Roll Queen* when the band pitched up at the Granary as a last-minute replacement for Blossom Toes (who'd been in a car accident). Despite this inauspicious start, they went down a treat with the Granary hordes. So much so that they were promptly re-booked for the next available date (January 29, 1970).

The *Western Daily Press*'s Penny Weston was present to see this "new electrifying progressive pop band" who "whipped up a storm of brilliant sounds". Alas, Penny seemed to be under the impression that they were called Mott the Hopple and their frontman was a chap named Ian Huntz. "Our music isn't exactly hard progressive," Hunter told her. "It is sometimes Dylanesque. We don't really mind if we are never recognised as a top group. It isn't important to us to make it big as long as we feel we are achieving something musically."

Those early Granary gigs certainly made an impression on Hunter and the audience. He reminisced fondly about them when he played a solo show at the Bierkeller in 2002, receiving a huge round of applause.

Delaney and Bonnie and Friends
Colston Hall, 2 December 1969

Delaney and Bonnie Bramlett had so impressed the post-Cream Eric

Clapton when they supported Blind Faith that he jumped at the chance to join them as one of their 'friends' on this short, seven-date UK tour. The Bristol show was the second one, after the band's Albert Hall debut. This had been postponed because the Bramletts' relationship carried unfortunate echoes of Ike and Tina Turner's. Delaney had beaten Bonnie so badly after the couple's arrival in Britain that their debut had to wait until her face had healed.

For months, rumours had circulated that another of D&B's friends at the Colston Hall would be Clapton's chum and - it later emerged - love rival George Harrison, playing what could be his very first post-Beatles gig. But an excellent, soundboard-derived bootleg, recorded for Atlantic Records and imaginatively titled *Delaney and Bonnie and Friends, Colston Hall, 1969*, tells a different story. The show opens with an extended jam (yes, this was the late 1960s) and ends with *I Don't Want to Discuss It*. D&B's classy 11-piece band includes Bobby Whitlock on keyboards, Rita Coolidge on backing vocals and Bobby Keys on saxophone. But no Beatle George. After the final song, Dave Mason deals with crowd heckles demanding the appearance of the soon-to-be-former Fab by announcing that Harrison is not even in the building. The promoter then pitches up and threatens the disgruntled audience with arrest if they don't all bugger off before the second house.

So that's a Great Rock Myth firmly put to bed. Or is it? There's an inconvenient set of photographs purporting to show the long-haired Beatle posing with D&B and their band backstage at the Colston Hall. So are these mislabelled pix from another show? They are not. It turns out that Mason was being a tad economical with the truth. Harrison was there all along, but he hid in the dressing room for three hours, where he could presumably hear the audience rioting out in the hall. On their way to Bristol, the band had made a detour to his Esher mansion and dragged the slumbering Harrison from his bedchamber to join them on the tour. But why the no-show?

Brian K. Jones of the *Western Daily Press* was backstage that night, where he found a deeply unhappy Harrison surrounded by the media. "Beatle George hunched his shoulders against the relentless posse of press and TV men and stared unhappily into his cup of coffee," Jones wrote.

"It's always the the same," Harrison complained over a buffet. "They see one Beatle by himself and straight away they are making suggestions that

The Beatles are splitting up."

Harrison said he was fed up with being followed everywhere he went and just wanted to be left alone. "I'm not billed to appear - they shouldn't be chasing me. It's Delaney and Bonnie and, of course, Eric Clapton that people have come to see. I've just come along for the ride on the bus."

Jones noted that Harrison had actually spent some time rehearsing backstage with the band, and at one point Delaney even asked him what guitar he'd be playing. But his mood had changed abruptly when the press pitched up. Despite the reporter's pleading, he refused to budge. "I am sure that deep down he did very much want to appear," Jones wrote. "Regrettably, 11pm came around, the show was drawing to an end and for the last 45 minutes George had been sat backstage listening to the recording."

So the Quiet One was more than usually quiet that night. Paul McCartney announced The Beatles split the following April.

Harrison relented later in the tour and can be heard on the Delaney and Bonnie album *On Tour with Eric Clapton*, which was released in March 1970 and became the duo's biggest seller. Beatle George appears under the pseudonym L'Angelo Misterioso in a show that was recorded at the Fairfield Halls, Croydon. In 2010, the Atlantic Records recording of the Colston Hall show finally got an official release as part of a deluxe four-disc CD verison of *On Tour...* This added the complete Albert Hall debut and extracts from the Colston Hall performance.

The Who
Hippodrome, 4 December 1969

Arguably the most important year in The Who's career, 1969 saw them release Pete Townshend's rock opera *Tommy* (factual note: it's not actually an opera), which proved to be their first major US hit. They previewed the album at Ronnie Scott's in May and then performed the whole thing pretty much in its entirety on the lengthy subsequent *Tommy* tour. This reached the Bath Pavilion on August 4, but between that show and this one they'd made their mark with extraordinary performances at two of the world's most legendary rock festivals: Woodstock and the second Isle of Wight Fest. Following a three week break, the fourth leg of the tour kicked off in front of a capacity audience at the Bristol Hippodrome. The show opened with a selection of hits (*I Can't Explain, Substitute, Happy Jack, I'm a Boy*) before unleashing the full *Tommy* experience. Some would say they had now hit their peak as a live act. This is borne out by a widely available bootleg of the Bristol gig, a fairly grotty audience recording oddly titled *Love, Cry Want Light By Us*, which misses the first part of the show, cutting in with *The Acid Queen* and ending with the encore of *My Generation*. "The Who are now the band against which the rest of rock must be judged," proclaimed *Melody Maker*.

Bristol Post reviewer Geoffrey Sims agreed. "Give The Who any superlative that comes to mind and it would have fitted amply for this wonderful two-hour concert," he swooned. Of the *Tommy* section, he remarked: "Townshend on guitar was magnificent and Daltrey, living the part throughout, gave an often haunting performance. At the end, the crowd rose for a huge ovation."

According to a fan review on The Who Concert Guide website: "There were a group of hippies in one of the boxes stage right and towards the end one threw a smoke bomb onto the stage. At that point management thought it a good idea to shine the spotlight on them as various attendants converged to eject them. The lad immediately stood up turned round and mooned at everyone before they were hustled out. Pete apologised ("we don't do smoke bombs anymore but did you see the pimples?"). A memorable night."

Brian K. Jones of the *WDP* caught up with Daltrey backstage after the show to discuss, er, mammon - or, more specifically, why The Who and many other UK bands were spending so much time in the US. "You've got to go to America to earn the big money," admitted Daltrey frankly. "A thousand pounds a night is nothing over there, much more than we can pick up in this country... America is positively hungry for British sounds and we played to packed houses wherever we went."

But things never went smoothly in the Who camp. Exactly one month later, Keith Moon ran over and killed his chauffeur.

The Moody Blues
Colston Hall, 11 December 1969

Michael Eavis's favourite band returned to Bristol after a long absence on the tour to promote *To Our Children's Children's Children*, which had just peaked at number 2 in the UK album chart - although the set was dominated by its predecessor, *On the Threshold of a Dream*. The show was sold out and Brian K. Jones of the *Western Daily Press* swooned that "their performance was faultless, their sounds superb."

Aping the Fabs' Apple, the Moodies had just established their own Threshold label and brought along two of their newly signed acts. Timon (real name: Stephen John Murray) went on to enjoy an eclectic career as Tymon Dogg, collaborating with The Clash and joining Joe Strummer's final band, The Mescaleros. The excellent Trapeze achieved comparatively little commercial success but proved hugely influential and served as an incubator for several musicians who went on to much bigger things. Bassist/vocalist Glenn Hughes joined Deep Purple, drummer Dave Holland wound up in Judas Priest and guitarist Mel Galley was briefly a member of Whitesnake.

1970

A pollo 13 lunar mission is aborted but catastrophe is averted… Four student protesters are shot dead by the National Guard at Kent State University. This inspires Neil Young to write one of the all-time great protest songs, *Ohio*… The first Earth Day is commemorated with a huge march in New York City… Miss World pageant at the Royal Albert Hall is disrupted by feminists… Jimi Hendrix and Janis Joplin die… 600,000 people turn up to the third Isle of Wight festival… Often depicted as a comedown year after the tumultuous events of the late 1960s, 1970 is in fact "… a pivotal, transitional - and under-documented - year that was as important as the much-studied 1968 and 1969," argues David Browne in his book *Fire and Rain: The Beatles, Simon & Garfunkel, James Taylor, CSNY and the Lost Story of 1970*… The UK's biggest selling album of the year is *Bridge Over Troubled Water* by Simon & Garfunkel. Other chart-toppers include *Paranoid* by Black Sabbath, *Led Zeppelin II* and *III*, The Beatles' *Abbey Road* and *Let It Be* and *Atom Heart Mother* by Pink Floyd. Biggest selling single of the year: *In the Summertime* by Mungo Jerry… Terry Pratchett joins the *Western Daily Press* as a general reporter. During his stint at the paper, he also writes two serials for the paper's kids' page: *Prod Ye A-Diddle Oh* and *Albert Caveman*… Bristol University's Rag Week programme promises a Drink Crockers Dry event (2d a pint), a pram race from Westbury to the Centre and a 'old age pensioners show' at the Victoria Rooms ("girl helpers required")… Maverick director Ken Russell comes to Bath to shoot scenes for his ripe Tchaikovsky biopic *The Music Lovers*, which he describes as "the story of a marriage between a homosexual and a nymphomaniac". The Pump Room doubles for the Moscow Conservatoire… The rusting SS Great Britain returns to Bristol from the Falkland Islands… BBC Radio Bristol is launched. Initial presenters include Michael Buerk and Kate Adie.

Led Zeppelin
Colston Hall, 8 January 1970

The auspices weren't too good for Led Zep's second headline appearance at the Colston Hall (they'd played here a week before the Bath Festival in 1969, with Blodwyn Pig and poetry collective The Liverpool Scene). It was freezing cold, heavy snow had been falling all day and the show began an hour late because Robert Plant and John Bonham were battling their way through snowstorms and breakdowns. That left Jimmy Page tuning his guitar backstage, which gave the *WDP*'s Brian K. Jones the perfect opportunity to grab a chat. Jones seemed particularly impressed that 24-year-old Page was on his way to being a millionaire as a result of Zeppelin topping both the albums and singles charts in the US, despite being relatively unknown over here. "Maybe it's because we won't appear on television, and of course Radio One is a bit of a joke," mused the guitarist. "Television people don't know how to present a group properly, particularly from the point of view of getting the right sound. If we can't be seen and heard at our best then we would rather do without television."

Asked to define Zeppelin's music, Page replied: "Progressive rock is what we play... Underground has been exploited so much that it is now overground. Progressive rock seems to be the sanest title until someone finds something better."

After Plant and Bonham finally arrived, the gig turned out to be an absolute cracker. We know this because of the existence of a bootleg recording entitled *Out of the Bristol Tale*. This was the second night of a seven date UK tour to promote *Led Zeppelin II*, which meant future staples *Thank You* and *Heartbreaker* were being introduced to audiences for the first time. The shows also opened with a high-energy take on Ben E. King's *We're Gonna Groove*, a recording of which eventually turned up on the *Coda* compilation. Zeppelin history was made when they played *Since I've Been Loving You* for the very first time at this gig. They didn't get round to recording it for another four months. Those with stopwatches to hand will be gratified to learn that *Dazed and Confused* clocks in at a full 16 minutes. Oh, and after the John Bonham showcase *Moby Dick*, Robert Plant attempts a joke: "There was the Lone Ranger and Tonto. Tonto turned into a door and the Lone Ranger shot his knob off!" I guess you had to be there...

John Mulally of Bristol student newspaper *Nonesuch* was suitably impressed. 'Led Zeppelin Are Heavy' read the indisputable headline on his review. He reported that the Hall management played "Mantovani or somesuch" in an attempt to soothe the restless audience. But finally the long wait was over and the triumphant show began. "Page makes great efforts in the progressive idiom - sometimes in complicated solo guitar numbers, sometimes in call-and-answer with Plant's vocals - but not always successfully; although his guitar playing with a bow is quite a joy." He was particularly taken with new song *Since I've Been Longing For You* [sic], "featuring John Paul Jones on a churchy organ backing and Plant screaming pitifully into the microphone: a number that left the audience breathless."

But no concessions were made for that late start as the old squares put the kibosh on the kids' fun once again. "During the second encore, genius management moved in to close the show - to great boos - at 11 o'clock. It's a regular confrontation here that might come to a nasty head."

Ralph McTell
Troubadour, 17 January 1970
Another of those packed Saturday nights at the tiny Troubadour club, punching well above its weight as usual. Ralph McTell had actually written and recorded his signature song *Streets of London* back in 1968, but this didn't become a big hit until it was released as a single in 1974. So despite being championed by John Peel, McTell was primarily a fixture on the folk scene in 1970. Reviewing this show for student newspaper *Nonesuch*, D. Satterthwaite noted that: "He sings with great sensitivity about problems not usually thought worthy of any attention". Also on the bill were locals and Troubadour regulars Ian A. (not that one) Anderson ("His music distinguished by his use of open tuning and various contrasting finger styles, coupled with his distinctive voice, show why he is becoming increasingly well known on the folk scene") and Keith Christmas (who "got a really good, well-deserved reception"). Christmas was already playing that stoner fave *Robin Head*, which appeared on his *Brighter Day* album in 1974. He also performed alongside a dizzying number of rock greats in the 1970s, was signed to ELP's Manticore label, and famously contributed acoustic guitar to Bowie's *Space Oddity* album.

Oh, there was actually another local musician playing that night: "Wizz Langham, a first year Bristol student, played four of his incredible songs, in which he has put his own poetry to highly original music - I hope we will hear a lot more of him in Bristol."

Whatever happened to Wizz Langham? Well, his real name was Chris Langham. After dropping out of university, he went on to achieve fame as a comedian and actor (notably playing cabinet minister Hugh Abbot in *The Thick of It*). In 2007, he was jailed for downloading child pornography.

John Martyn
Troubadour, 7 February 1970

John Martyn was fond of a drink. He was also fond of large numbers of drinks. The slurred voice was part of his shtick, but on occasion his alcohol intake was so great that it impaired his ability to perform. And at this notorious Bristol show, he became so belligerent that he was chucked out and packed off back to London before playing a note. Nobody complained. *Folk Roots* editor Ian A. Anderson contributed a vivid description of this memorable evening to J.P. Bean's book *Singing from the Floor: A History of British Folk Clubs*.

"John Martyn threw a big wobbler. He was very drunk or stoned and effing and blinding at the top of his voice. The whole audience could hear it and the manager said, 'This won't do. Tell him we don't need him to play. We'll give him his money, we'll get him a taxi to the station. He's not playing.'

"I drew the short straw 'cos I was standing there. I wasn't happy, but I did it. I then got up on stage and said to the audience, 'Well we have a little local problem as you may have noticed ... John Martyn is unable to play tonight. However in the audience we have Keith Christmas, Shelagh McDonald, Dave Evans, Steve Tilston, Fred Wedlock, all of whom will get up and do a couple of songs. If any of you want your money back, ask now. It's not a problem.' Not a single person asked – because every one of those people had an album out on a national label.

"I poured him into his cab and sent him off. Somebody told me the next day that he'd gone up to Cousins [London folk club Les Cousins] and he'd got up on stage, still effing and blinding and he said 'Fucking Bristol – that Ian Anderson, I knocked him out and I left him lying in the street.'"

Pink Floyd
Colston Hall, 7 March 1970

Floyd returned to Bristol as part of the University of Bristol's Timespace Arts Festival to promote the transitional *Ummagumma* album. Syd Barrett-era songs still formed part of the set, but the quartet were also playing around with a composition known as *The Amazing Pudding* that would later surface in revamped form on the chart-topping *Atom Heart Mother* album. In addition, the band were keen to show off their latest toy, as Ed Newsom recalls: "They were very proud of their new quadraphonic PA system. It was used to full effect on some of their numbers, with speaker stacks in all four corners of the auditorium. I kid you not: they set up a primus stove on stage and fed the sound of an egg being fried, or a kettle being boiled, through the system. Using a joystick control, the sound could be made to swirl around the hall."

Bristol Evening Post's pop correspondent James Belsey seems to have found the whole experience quite alarming - possibly because it started at 3pm (The Who played the evening show), interrupting his afternoon nap. "Tea-time at the weekend isn't exactly the right time to suffer the violence and intensity of a Floyd concert," he objected. "The volume on a couple of their disturbing, destructive numbers was quite terrifying, enough to make you physically ill."

Nonetheless, he conceded that "...in their melancholy numbers - particularly the main theme from *More* - they created a sumptuous atmosphere of sadness and regret."

Fotheringay
Colston Hall, 22 March 1970

Fotheringay was a very short-lived British folk-rock group founded by Sandy Denny with former members of Eclection after her departure from Fairport Convention. Alas, they didn't last long, possibly because they were hampered with the 'Folk Rock Supergroup' tag on posters for this tour. But we're primarily concerned with the support act here. Not the main support, The Humblebums, although they too are interesting, being a folk duo comprising Billy Connolly (yes, *that* Billy Connolly) and pre-Stealer's Wheel Gerry Rafferty.

Billed as the opening act was a fella named Nick Drake. These days, his is the name to drop among that terrible plague of strum'n'whine merchants who hope to acquire cool by association and lump him in with the great romantic poets, pretending that he committed suicide because he was too sensitive to live (Drake died of an accidental overdose of prescription drugs). But he can hardly be blamed for this grotesque phenomenon. During his lifetime, the now legendary guitarist and songwriter was mostly ignored, his three albums selling few copies and receiving poor reviews. Drake played only around ten gigs, his most substantial bout of touring being this five date trek with Fotheringay. Just as there's no film of him, and he only ever gave one (short, unrevealing) interview to a journalist, there's always been doubt about whether he actually played many of these shows - though Connolly has told stories about the tour and the *International Times* carried a review of the final London date ("It seemed he felt a little uncertain as to whether or not he wanted to make public performances, there being little or no communication with the audience"). Copies of the programme, which include a rare photo of Drake, go for a small fortune on eBay. The Colston Hall show would have been his penultimate live performance. But, alas, Richard Morton Jack, who wrote the definitive biography of Drake, reckons that he definitely didn't turn up in Bristol.

Traffic
Anson Rooms, 25 April 1970

Connoisseurs tend to agree that peak Traffic was achieved between 1970 and 1971. Fortunately for those who were around at the time, they headed west twice in that period. Naked and stoned punters got to enjoy the band at the second Glastonbury Festival in 1971. But this earlier gig at the Anson Rooms came just after Traffic reformed following Steve Winwood's brief foray into supergroup territory with Blind Faith. In the spring of 1970, they'd been reduced to a trio comprising Winwood, Jim Capaldi and Chris Wood and had almost completed recording their greatest album, *John Barleycorn Must Die*, when they arrived at the Anson Rooms. Chances are the student audience got to hear most, if not all, of it for the first time. How can we be so sure? Five days later, Traffic recorded a spectacularly good BBC In Concert performance in London, during which *John Barleycorn...* was played in its entirety.

"I do remember Traffic being a somewhat intense evening, with concentration on the music as the group played close together under stark spotlights cutting through the darkness," says Tony Byers. "I think they must have used it as a sort of rehearsal for the BBC performance as I seem to remember the music differed from some of the familiar pop hits Steve Winwood was known for. They left the staging simple, avoiding the whirling coloured oil blob light shows so common at the end of the '60s."

They didn't return to Bristol until a Colston Hall show in 1974, when things had got excessively noodly and jazzy. Traffic split later that year.

The Aquae Sulis Incident
Twerton Park, Bath, 23 May 1970

Back in 1970, Bath City FC decided to address its financial woes by grabbing some of the lucrative hippy pop festival action with an event of its own, taking the Latin part of its name from the city's motto. Unfortunately, this proved to be a commercial disaster. 'Pop flop forces crisis on ailing football club' was the *Western Daily Press*'s headline the following Monday. It was reported that the event cost £6,000 to stage and had been expected to draw 15,000 punters. On the day, only 4,500 turned up. Disconsolate festival chairman and former club director Ken Ollis admitted afterwards: "It's a loss. It is just a question now of how much. I am very disappointed that so few people came. This year has been a hard luck story all round for the club."

One theory for the tumbleweed blowing through the terraces was that punters were saving their pennies for next month's second Bath Festival, which had a much stronger line-up. But had you paid your £1.20 (£1 advance) and pitched up on this warm and sunny spring day, you'd have been able to savour a fine line-up dominated by British blues acts and compered by the ubiquitous Pete Drummond. The young Wishbone Ash, who'd just released their debut album, were the hit of the day for many. Further up the bill were psychedelic/raga rock festival stalwarts Quintessense, Juicy Lucy, Stan Webb's Chicken Shack, Matthews Southern Comfort and headliners Fleetwood Mac, playing what proved to be their last show with the now totally acid-fried Peter Green.

The *WDP*'s intrepid Brian K. Jones actually managed to exchange a few words with Green in the bar. Jones offered to buy him a pint but he'd only accept a glass of water. "I have nothing to say other than what has already been said," grumped the guitar great, whose abrupt mental decline had been sparked by taking LSD in Munich a couple of months earlier. "I just want to spend some time by myself and play my guitar. I want to be completely free to do what I like."

Local journalist Dave Massey was there. "Wishbone Ash were totally unknown at the time but were brilliant, from the twin guitar attack to the snazzy drumming along with some great songs. Juicy Lucy (who replaced the originally billed Soft Machine), with the amazing steel guitar of Glen Campbell (not *that* one), had or were about to have their only hit with *Who Do You Love?* and the singer was the only black person performing at the event. Matthews Southern Comfort had the *Woodstock* hit, but were pretty ordinary. Quintessence were the usual Ladbroke Grove hippy jazzy noodlers. Chicken Shack at that time had Christine Perfect [the future Christine McVie] in their line-up so you have the rock family tree element..."

Also in the audience that day was 18-year-old guitarist Bernie Marsden, who would go on to compose Whitesnake's multi-million selling hit *Here I Go Again*. In his autobiography *Where's My Guitar?*, Bernie cites Fleetwood Mac's performance in Bath as one of the nine seminal moments in his musical education - though he seems slightly confused between this show and the previous year's Bath Festival, at which Fleetwood Mac also played. Maybe he attended both. "I was on the pitch in the centre of Bath football ground for the one-day festival," he writes. "It had been publicised that Peter was leaving the group and so the gig was very emotional. I shed a few tears as I watched and listened to him."

In true 1970s festival style, everything ran late so Fleetwood Mac didn't appear until long after their 10pm slot. Dave Massey remembers them playing all their big songs, from *Albatross* to *The Green Manalishi (With the Two Prong Crown)*, which had just been released as a single. When they went past the midnight curfew, the power to the stage was cut. But Mick Fleetwood carried on playing an extended drum solo, while punters joined in by bashing empty beer cans and anything else that came to hand. The Powers That Be then switched on the floodlights to encourage the now rebellious hordes to go home, but the impromptu jam continued as campfires were lit from discarded rubbish. Result: Hippies 1, The Man 0.

Edgar Broughton Band/Third Ear Band/Kevin Ayers and the Whole World

Locarno, 7 June 1970

"Out Demons, Out!" Yep, those hairy, rabble-rousing Notting Hill free festival psych/prog faves the Edgar Broughton Band were out on tour to promote their second and, as it turned out, most commercially successful album, *Sing Brother Sing*. They'd also just released a single which offered their considered commentary on this month's General Election: *Up Yours!* ("My mother voted Tory/Daddy voted Red/Now they all want me to be liberal/But we're all dropping out instead").

This was the second in what was billed as a new series of weekly progressive rock shows at the Locarno. Excitingly, the usual dress code had been dropped and audience members were permitted to wear whatever they wanted. Despite this, the first gig was a disaster. Just 200 people turned up to see Family, who were so pissed off that they refused to play. Instead, they reportedly sat in their car outside the venue and sulked. Edgar and chums were made of sterner stuff, despite attracting only 50 more punters. But everyone clearly enjoyed themselves. Nobody sloped off early from this five-hour marathon which finished after 1am.

The show was an eclectic touring package of artists from the fledgling Harvest record label who were managed by Pink Floyd's Blackhill Enterprises. It was opened by Americana act Formerly Fat Harry (featuring former members of Country Joe and the Fish), who were followed by singer-songwriter Michael Chapman. The main support was the Third Ear Band, who specialised in improvisational music and are best known for their soundtrack to Polanski's *Macbeth*.

But who's this third on the bill? Having left Soft Machine and taken time out to recover from touring the US with Jimi Hendrix, Kevin Ayers had recorded his magnificent debut album, *Joy of a Toy*. Now it was time to tour the bloody thing, so he needed a band to play it live. Not just any old band, as it turned out. The Whole World featured ace saxophonist Lol Coxhill, composer and arranger David Bedford on keyboards and a young chap named Mike Oldfield on bass.

The following month, most of the package wound up playing a free concert in Hyde Park alongside Pink Floyd, in front of an estimated 200,000 people. By this time, Robert Wyatt had joined the Whole World.

Soft Machine
Colston Hall, 17 June 1970

Having failed to show up as advertised for the Aquae Sulis Incident, Soft Machine headed west less than a month later for this final show on a brief six date summer tour. This was in support of their *Third* double album, which had been released on June 6 and remains their best seller. For many, this represented Soft Machine at their finest, straddling the worlds of prog and jazz fusion - which was later to swallow them whole. And what a line-up: Elton Dean (from whom Elton John nicked half of his stage name), Hugh Hopper, Mike Ratledge and Robert Wyatt - multi-tasking on drums, Hammond organ and Mellotron. In August, they became the first rock band to play at the Proms in the Royal Albert Hall.

Reviewing the show for the *Post*, James Belsey pronounced himself puzzled. Indeed, such was his puzzlement that he mentioned this twice. "Their concert last night was puzzling, but really very, very good," he wrote, hedging his bets. Belsey praised the band as "a breath of fresh air" and for being "inventive and creative" but seemed confused by their musical evolution: "… today they owe much more to modern American jazz than the mainstream of British progressive pop."

Stray/Stackridge
Victoria Rooms, 20 June 1970

Frequent touring partners of the Groundhogs and much loved by Iron Maiden, London hard rockers Stray were once managed by Charlie Kray. A version of the band continues to this day, still fronted by Del Bromham. This was their very first show in Bristol, hard on the heels of the release of their debut album on hip folk label Transatlantic Records. But we're more concerned with their support act here.

Our local contribution to the first wave of wonderful world of progressive rock was, er, pretty measly. The late jazz pianist Keith Tippett had a wider hinterland than most jazzers, forming the vast 50-member prog act Centipede (see below), collaborating with various Soft Machine members (notably Elton Dean) and working regularly with Robert Fripp. Back in 1973, Supertramp convened at Southcombe Farm just outside Yeovil to conceive their masterpiece *Crime of the Century* (see below too). Bristol's sole, modestly successful prog act was the suitably eccentric

Stackridge, who were referred to as the West Country Beatles and even, on one occasion, "the thinking man's Slade". How eccentric, exactly? Well, their fans (the 'Rhubarb Thrashers') used to show up at gigs with dustbin lids to bash and sticks of rhubarb for, er, thrashing one another.

Those crazy seventies, huh? These foolish young art student types must have all been on drugs, what with their flagellating fans, jumble sale chic attire and lengthy, idiosyncratic, unfailingly mellifluous prog workouts whose witty, literate, whimsical lyrics were often peculiarly animal-related when they weren't about *Purple Spaceships Over Yatton*. Except that the pleasingly irreverent Stackridge were never great enthusiasts for the rock'n'roll lifestyle. "It was partially a drugs culture back then," violinist Mike Evans told me back in 1999, when Stackridge reformed at the behest of his daughter, Ruth. "There were the bands that did and the bands that didn't. And we were one of the bands that didn't. We were, and still are, defiantly anti-fashion. Billy the drummer was the nearest we got to the rock and roll image, with his long hair and tight jeans. He looked like he ought to be in a real pop group, instead of with Stackridge. The rest of us were, shall we say, more individually attired."

Groupies, then? "Well, yes. We'd go home with some 15- or 16-year-old girls who'd become friends. Mum would cut the sandwiches and make the tea while dad was diplomatically mowing the lawn or washing the car."

That's more like it. What happened next? "We'd sit in the front room at 4:45pm when the teleprinter got going, waiting for the Leeds United score, sipping cups of tea and talking about what people were doing for their O levels."

"We were all a bit shy and introverted in those days, despite some of the wacky goings-on onstage," added guitarist James Warren, apologetically.

It all kicked off for Stackridge with this Victoria Rooms gig. Having tired of the slog of a residency at the Dug Out club with their blues band Gryptight Thynne, Warren and bricklaying bassist Crun Walter formed the act that would become Stackridge Lemon. Once the Lemon had been wisely squeezed from their name, manager and local music scene veteran Mike Tobin lured MCA's David Howells to Bristol, where he was impressed enough to sign up the band to record their imaginatively titled debut, *Stackridge*. Three months after the Victoria Rooms show, they played the very first Pilton Pop Festival. Stackridge went on to realise a dream by working with Beatles producer George Martin on their 1973 album, *The Man in the Bowler Hat*. This became their biggest 'hit', charting at number 23.

Despite this lack of commercial success, Stackridge's status as cult heroes was assured. Such was their leftfield nature that even when they undertook one of the era's grand prog productions it was a budget affair unlikely to threaten the Rick Wakeman hegemony. "We did King Arthur on ice, but it wasn't King Arthur and it wasn't quite on ice," Evans told me. "We had some dry ice, which was the nearest we got. It was a *Treasure Island* pantomime written by the Pigsty Hill Light Orchestra - Bristol folkies and jazzers - starring themselves and us. We toured it in November and December 1972 and it was quite a success. John Peel nearly got roped in as the parrot."

After Stackridge, James Warren and co-founder Andy Cresswell-Davis formed The Korgis, whose *Everybody's Got to Learn Sometime* was such a huge global hit that writer Warren didn't really need to work again. Crun Walter returned to bricklaying.

But the Stackridge story didn't end there. In 2006, the band reformed yet again, with founder members Andrew Cresswell Davis and Mutter Slater on board with James Warren and 'Crun' Walter. In 2009, they released a new album, *A Victory For Common Sense*, produced by Chris Hughes (of Tears for Fears fame). Six years later, the Final Bow tour was announced, including dates all over the UK and a trip to Japan for two performances in Tokyo. Fittingly, Stackridge's very last gig was back home in Bristol at the Fiddlers Club, Bedminster, on December 19, 2015.

The Bath Festival of Blues and Progressive Music
Shepton Mallet Showground, 27 & 28 June 1970

Having been banned from the Bath Recreation Ground, Freddy Bannister took his second and final local outdoor festival to Shepton Mallet and added 'Progressive Music' to the title. The ticket price had rocketed to a whopping fifty shillings (£2.50) and Led Zeppelin were headlining a bill that has been described as the strongest ever assembled for a festival in this country, pulling an estimated 150,000 punters. This time Led Zep's fee had rocketed to £60,000. The mouth-watering list of supporting acts included Pink Floyd (premiering *Atom Heart Mother*), Jefferson Airplane, The Byrds, Santana, Frank Zappa and the Mothers of Invention, The Moody Blues, Dr. John,

Steppenwolf and Fairport Convention. In what was to become a great UK rock festival tradition, repeated more famously at the Isle of Wight fest that August, Hawkwind pitched up and played for free on the back of a truck outside the fence, where they were joined by the Pink Fairies.

Little wonder Jimmy Page dressed up in what appeared to be an amusing 'yokel' outfit in celebration. Indeed, all four members of Zeppelin were sporting beards on this occasion.

Zeppelin's devoted and formidable manager Peter Grant had turned down a $200,000 offer to play two shows in New York that weekend, correctly surmising that his band's profile would be better served by headlining the closing night of Freddy Bannister's event. But he left nothing to chance. Grant worked out where the stage was to be constructed and contacted the Met Office to find out the time of sunset. He then told Bannister that Zeppelin would appear at precisely 8pm on Sunday evening, so the stage lights could be brought up for dramatic effect just as the sun went down. But at 7:50pm, Chicago jazz-rockers The Flock were still noodling away. Grant personally went on stage to inform them in no uncertain terms that they were no longer welcome. His cunning plan worked a treat. "Bath was a turning point," he's quoted as saying in Mark Blake's entertaining biography *Bring It On Home*, which also reveals that the intimidating manager was already alert to the nefarious activities of bootleggers: "While Led Zeppelin were thundering through *Whole Lotta Love* at the Bath Festival, Grant had been beneath the stage. He had spotted bootleggers recording the show and had grabbed the nearest thing at hand. 'I threw a bucket of water over the equipment,' he recalled, 'and then waded in with a fire axe, chopping everything up.'"

Zeppelin's set opened in style with the first public performance of the mighty *Immigrant Song*, which would appear on *Led Zeppelin III* later that year. Another first was chalked up that day when *That's the Way* became the first song they ever performed acoustically in a live setting. The band's set lasted for three hours and included four encores. But as Chris Salewicz notes in *Jimmy Page: The Definitive Biography*, Zeppelin remained resolutely unpopular with hacks and members of the too-cool-for-school tosspot community: "The show was an utter triumph. With The Beatles having announced that they were breaking up two months previously, Led Zeppelin became the kings of British rock music. Yet even so, there were 'freaks' who basked in the snobbish cool of informing you that they had left the festival site before Led Zeppelin had come onstage; among 'intelligent' fans of rock there were still many who were utterly dismissive of Page's group."

During the afternoon, Page had met future collaborator Roy Harper, who didn't have the faintest idea who he was. Suitably impressed by Harper's non-conformity, Page later wrote *Hats Off to (Roy) Harper* - an idiosyncratic reworking of Bukka White's *Shake 'Em on Down* - which also turned up on *Led Zeppelin III*.

Back in 2003, I got the opportunity to quiz Robert Plant about his memories of the event. "It certainly was extraordinary," he told me. "I don't remember what was going on out front. I just remember the bonding backstage. We'd already played the Fillmore West in San Francisco and the Fillmore East, so we'd crossed paths with quite a few of the artists who were there. For me, I was very proud and probably quite emotional at the idea of being in the position to play alongside people who I had such great respect for… to play alongside those people was such a great honour because they were coming from the right side of music. It wasn't just blues-based English rock. The whole American culture was going somewhere else… There was a message out there which was more than just dissatisfaction with social circumstances. There was something going on that I was really, really keen to associate myself with. So when I was at that festival, I was with a number of people who were standard bearers for a new time. And for me as a kid - which I was, I think I was 21 - my eyes were really rolling. The Airplane were really something special. I also saw Janis [Joplin] that day, who became sort of my big sister until she went… upstairs."

For Freddy Bannister, however, the second Bath Festival was an utterly miserable experience. "We were a little too idealistic, I think," he told me. "We decided to go for a chain link fence around the perimeter rather than putting up these big corrugated iron fences, which I hated then and hate now. It felt like you were building a fortification and treating the kids as the enemy. But people sneaked in without paying and we got ripped off terribly by everybody. It was a very steep learning curve. It was not one jot enjoyable."

As for Pink Floyd's unveiling of *Atom Heart Mother*, co-composer and orchestrator Ron Geesin offered a robust opinion when I interviewed him in 2016 while he was promoting the entertaining documentary about his work, *An Improvised Life*. "The live performances were a disgrace," he told me. "They were uncoordinated… The actual EMI session had to come out reasonably, otherwise the album wouldn't have been issued at all. One section was recorded a beat out, but that worked out all right. My best phrase for the whole thing is that it was 'a good piece of crafting'. Because I had to craft art and new melodies given an existing framework which was the backing tape. That was all they could get together. I mean, they left me with a tape and fucked off to America. In a lot of ways that was fortunate, because I was able to get on with it without being titted about."

At Shepton Mallet, *Atom Heart Mother* was introduced under its original title, *The Amazing Pudding*. Floyd were joined on stage by The John Aldiss Choir and The Philip Jones Brass Ensemble. One of the brass players later recalled spilling a pint of beer into his tuba before the performance. Hey - it was 1970. Stranger things happened.

Ed Newsom remembers it well. "I do recall quite vividly waking to the strains of *Atom Heart Mother* with the arrival of the dawn," he says. "The scheduling of the acts had gone tits-up by then."

Indeed, there had been massive traffic jams in the narrow country lanes all around the festival site, which led to huge delays in the arrival of bands and their gear. These problems were compounded by regular heavy downpours on Saturday. It was quickly decided to make the festival a 24-hour event, ending at 6am on the Monday morning.

In his autobiography, *Beeswing*, Fairport Convention guitarist Richard Thompson describes missing all the main acts because Fairport were stuck in the tailback: "The single-track country lanes were jammed solid, and the only access in and out for band and gear was on the back of a Hells Angel motorcycle. A greaser who looked like Baby Face Nelson insisted I wear his leather jacket on stage, and I didn't want to disappoint him in any way."

Western Daily Press journalist Peter Gibbs was also there, but managed to dodge the traffic jam hell on account of having to go home early because his wife was heavily pregnant. "I remember being in the VIP area in front of the stage watching Santana," he recalls. "That was a lovely sunny day."

Jefferson Airplane had to cut their set short in order to race for a train back to London from Castle Cary station. During the anxious wait for bands to struggle through the traffic jams on Sunday, Donovan was drafted in to play an impromptu greatest hits set. Heroically, he managed to spin this out for a couple of hours. But spare a thought for the poor Moody Blues and Dr. John. The Moodies achieved the distinction of becoming the only advertised band to make it to the site and not actually play. The lashing rain was deemed to be too hazardous to Mike Pinder's Mellotron, presenting a severe risk of electrocution. The festival's final public announcement first thing on Monday morning was: "That's it. It's all over. The Moodies have gone home..."

The Moodies' spot was taken by the latest incarnation of The Byrds, who decided to take no risks by playing an acoustic set. As if to rub it in, this was later acclaimed by some reviewers as the festival's absolute highlight.

Dr. John, meanwhile, had planned an attention-grabbing stunt. The idea was that for his 3:20pm Sunday afternoon slot, the former Mac Rebennack would ascend gracefully in a hot air balloon to serenade the crowd from above. At the same time, 2,000 smaller balloons attached to Dr. John posters were to be released from the ground. Beautiful, huh? As it turned out, the poor fella actually became the festival's last performer. He finally slid onto the soggy stage during the early hours of Monday morning in the pissing rain and was forced to play an acoustic song instead. Reports suggest he went down rather well with bedraggled punters who were still on site and awake.

The event was largely free of trouble, with a local police spokesman describing the crowd as "a peaceful lot" and the *Western Daily Press* swooning that "the West does a Woodstock". Even the Hells Angels were said to have done a good job guarding the backstage area - though it should perhaps be noted that these were nice British Hells Angels and not the nasty American ones who'd ruined Altamont.

One of a handful of criminal incidents reported involved a trio of young men from Hull who were arrested after breaking into an RAC phone box to steal the coins inside. "After the festival, we were walking home and went for a drink," one of the repentant youths told the magistrates court in mitigation. "We misjudged the strength of the local cider."

Elsewhere, local traders were overjoyed as pubs were drunk dry and shop shelves stripped by hungry and thirsty hippies. Even the local carpet store succeeded in flogging a lovely blue Wilton to a well-heeled, comfort-seeking reveller for £23. Farmers were less pleased with the litter, trespassing and public urination (and worse), prompting the NFU to demand £3,500 in compensation.

An intriguing footnote: that 1970 festival was one of the first to use a large projection screen, and it seems that an enterprising individual thought to copy the whole thing onto videotape. Where is it now? Nobody seems to know.

Skid Row
Granary, 13 July 1970

This isn't the sweary, hairy 1980s Skid Row with Sebastian Bach, obviously. It is, in fact, the original Irish trio with a little kid on guitar, playing one of their very first gigs in this country. At just 16 years of age, the precocious lad wasn't allowed to be served at the bar. Hell, as far as the law was concerned he wasn't even permitted to enter the venue. But the statute of limitations on that one has probably run out. His name? Gary Moore. As soon as he picked up his guitar, jaws hit the floor. In *The Granary Club: The Rock Years 1969-1988*, Al Read recalls: "I remember that when I arrived at the club to set up the disco, Gary was already on stage with a practice amp reeling off some incredible guitar licks. When the club started to fill up, I asked Gary if he could stop so that the records could start. Gary just turned down and jammed perfectly with every disc that was put on. Then Skid Row went on and played several hours of the finest rock the club had heard for ages. When I went backstage to pay the band at the end of the night, Gary was in the corner of the dressing room, still playing."

Al rated this night as showcasing the Granary at its best. Little wonder Skid Row were invited back multiple times, playing here a further three times in 1971 and once in 1972. After leaving Skid Row, Gary also played the Granary with his own band twice in 1972 and once in 1973, before going on to hit the big time with Thin Lizzy and as a solo act.

The Pilton Pop Festival
Worthy Farm, 19 & 20 September 1970

Permit me a moment of self-indulgence here with one of the most vivid memories of my childhood. Having fled Nazi Gemany in 1935, my grandparents took over a dairy farm in a small village not far from Pilton. Like the Eavises, the family were nonconformists (Quakers rather than

Methodists, and chums of the Morlands and Clarks), though I have no reason to believe they ever met. As a snot-nosed kid in short trousers, the absolute highlight of my year was the long summer spent on the farm. One of my duties was to help farmhands Cecil and Edmund to herd the cows up the road to one of their fields after morning milking. These father and son farm workers were proper-job villagers for whom Shepton Mallet was the teeming metropolis and Wells was Babylon itself. They also had impenetrable Somerset accents that even I struggled to understand, so if any cars should turn up behind us I'd be dispatched to explain that we'd only be a few minutes. One morning - it might have been 1970 or 1971 - a psychedelic Mini driven by Austin Powers himself pitched up. Edmund tapped his forehead to suggest the driver was some kind of nutter, but I was transfixed. This was the first actual hippy I'd ever seen in the flesh. "That's fine, man," he beamed at me after I explained what was going on. "Everything's groovy." Today I like to imagine that he was one of the posh hippies behind the original Glastonbury festivals - maybe Andrew Kerr or someone like that.

Later, when I worked as a volunteer in the Green Field during the early 1980s, I was able to sneak off for a surreptitious bath every so often - thus becoming the cleanest person on site who wasn't actually named Eavis.

Like so many of his generation, farmer Eavis had become obsessed with pop music while listening to Radio Luxembourg. The clandestine nature of the experience added to the fun - until he was caught. "I was a boarder at Wells Cathedral School and got whacked on the bottom for listening to my radio under the sheets," he told me. "I don't know whether the master enjoyed it. He probably did. They generally do…"

Before The Beatles and the Stones there was… Al Martino. Eavis saw the Italian-American pop crooner at the Colston Hall at the age of 14 and still rates this as one of the best shows he ever went to. He'll even sing you a snatch of *Here in My Heart* (the UK's first official number one hit single) if you ask nicely. By 1970, however, tastes had changed and this was reflected in the line-up of the very first Glastonbury Festival. Nobody called it 'Glasto' (or - *shudder* - 'Glasters') back then.

So much has already been written about this ramshackle inaugural event - 2,500 punters, £1 entry including free milk, Marc Bolan and Tyrannosaurus Rex, financial loss of £1,500 etc - that it's difficult to find anything new to say. But the significant involvement of artists and expertise from Bristol has often been overlooked. Al Read recalled how the offices of the Plastic Dog collective received a panicked phone call from Michael Eavis on the first day of the festival. Some bands, notably The Kinks, hadn't turned up, while others were refusing to co-operate with his running order. At the time, Plastic Dog was busy with an ELP show in Malvern, but Mike Tobin was dispatched to lend a helping hand.

"Some details are a bit hazy, such as how and when I got there," he confesses. "Oddly I had already 'sold' Stackridge, Steamhammer and the First Light Lightshow to Eavis so knew of his festival. Next thing I remember is actually being at Pilton and somehow getting roped into being stage manager. I didn't get any sleep until the next afternoon, when I ended up on the stone floor of his cottage wrapped in a sheepskin coat and a young lady."

Bristol's very own Stackridge earned the distinction of being the first band ever to play the first Glastonbury Festival. Fellow Bristolians Squidd pitched up at the farm too. These flamboyant proggers were Granary regulars who had a stage act that included exploding toilet pans and a flaming drum kit. Their drummer, Rodney Matthews, later became a renowned fantasy artist whose work was famously used on the jackets of Michael Moorcock's Elric series and the covers of many an album by artists ranging from Nazareth to Magnum. Squidd also merit a footnote in rock history on account of their keyboard player, Steve Swindells, being openly - nay, flamoyantly - gay at a time when this was unusual, especially in prog (The Enid's Robert John Godfrey was the only other example). Described by Matthews as "a clean yet rather pimply little boy from Saltford who ate eucalyptus sweets at an alarming rate," Swindells secured Squidd slots on a couple of Gay Liberation Front benefits in London in 1971 and 1972 (the first of which was described, with rare restraint, as "an off-beat booking" by the Western Daily Press).

He also had no fear of the dressing-up box. In Darryl W. Bullock's excellent book Pride, Pop and Politics, he elaborates: "I had already appeared on television back in Bristol with Squidd, wearing fishnet tights, sequinned knickers, an Afro, football boots and my Moroccan cape! Rodney went on to become really successful as an illustrator, but when he was with Squidd he used to look like Frank Zappa and would smash toilet bowls on stage and burn effigies of skinheads... It was all very provocative! We knew what we were doing was political, but we were also having fun. The media was relentlessly evil when it came to gay people… If they were short of news it would be the pervy vicar stories or ridiculous stories connecting gay people to paedophiles, so what I was doing was deliberate: it was gender-confusing. It wasn't traditional drag: there was no make-up involved, I just liked the idea of challenging people's assumptions."

Swindells went on to release a couple of solo albums, write songs for Roger Daltrey and join Hawkwind spin-off project Hawklords for their excellent 1978 album *25 Years On*.

Also on the bill at this first festival were local folky proggers Marsupilami, whose flautist Jessica Stanley-Clarke is now better known as organic herbalist Jessica 'Jekka' McVicar. She was awarded the Victoria Medal of Honour for services to horticulture in 2017.

The night before Pilton Pop, Al Stewart had played Bristol's Troubadour club, supported by Keith Christmas. Al crashed at Ian A. Anderson's flat after the show, and the following morning all three of them made their way to Glastonbury. Good job they did. Michael Eavis would later credit Ian with saving the festival after headliner Marc Bolan failed to turn up on time: "He knew I couldn't pay him, but he played a great set that got everybody in the right mood."

So while it's true that Stackridge were the first *band* to play Glastonbury, the first *musicians* on stage were a ramshackle Troubadour Club jam collective comprising Stewart, Anderson an off-his-tits-on-acid Christmas and chums, who delighted the stoned hippy crowd with a hastily cobbled together set that included a rendition of Country Joe McDonald's *I Feel Like I'm Fixin' to Die Rag*. Anderson later described this, perhaps a tad self-deprecatingly, as "a sad attempt to drum up Woodstock spirit in the jaws of immense apathy".

"Jimi Hendrix had died the night before," recalls Eavis. "So there were a lot of tributes to him. It was all enormous fun. But, of course, we lost money…"

Derek and the Dominos
Colston Hall, 27 Sept 1970

These days *Layla and Other Assorted Love Songs* is rightly seen as the crowning achievement of Eric Clapton's career. On release in 1970, however, the sole album by the pseudonymous Derek and the Dominos (their spelling) was a critical and commercial flop, failing to chart in the UK. It didn't help that Clapton resolutely refused to promote the Dominos and flew into a rage if his name was used in publicity. A UK club tour in August had seen Clapton, Bobby Whitlock, Carl Radle and Jim Gordon play to as few as sixty punters a night. After travelling to the US to record the Layla sessions in Miami, the Dominos returned for a slightly larger jaunt, including this date at the Colston Hall. At Clapton's insistence, the highest ticket price was pegged at one English pound. But there still wasn't much interest, especially as the album wasn't due to be released for another couple of months, although this show drew a near-capacity crowd. What's more, God himself was reportedly in a bad way, wolfing down huge quantities of cocaine and heroin with the rest of the band. The death of his chum Jimi Hendrix on September 18 had also hit Clapton hard.

'Cacophony and cliches - that's Clapton' was the headline on *Post* pop correspondent James Belsey's harsh verdict. After a couple of paragraphs complaining about the 'din', he sniffed that for most of the adoring audience this was a 'pilgrimage' rather than a gig and they "weren't too bothered about the content".

Still, it must have been some consolation for Eric that he was squiring both the sixteen-year-old Hon. Alice Magdalen Sarah Ormsby-Gore (youngest daughter of the 5th Baron Harlech) and nineteen-year-old Paula Boyd while simultaneously pining for Paula's older sister Patti Harrison (wife of Beatle George), who had, of course, inspired the title track of the *Layla* album.

Emerson, Lake and Palmer
Colston Hall, 19 October 1970

Their debut album hadn't even been released (it came out in November) but ELP's literally explosive performance at the Isle of Wight Festival in August grabbed headlines around the world. This launched the first prog supergroup on their debut national tour. Every date sold out, including this one at the Colston. Interestingly, the music press had yet to decide that ELP were to be despised and most of the reviews were rapturous.

Brian K. Jones of the *Western Daily Press* wangled his way backstage after this show by "one of the brightest hopes for many a year". He grilled Emerson about his £4,000 Moog synthesiser ("It has been criticised as being a gimmick by some people but I think that it has a valid place in today's music in producing new sounds") and found he had no misgivings about leaving The Nice. "The future looks very bright really, it is pretty well planned out - we know what we're doing on our second album, although the first isn't released until next month."

That debut album reached number four in the chart. Its follow-up, *Tarkus*, went to number one. Despite the venom of irate music journalists, ELP then romped into the world's stadiums and eventually imploded in 1979. They didn't return to the Colston Hall until their reformation tour in 1992.

Dawn Records Penny Tour
Colston Hall, 6 November 1970

Following the success of the Harvest and Vertigo labels, Pye Records decided to grab a slice of the progressive rock action and inaugurated their own Dawn label. To promote their signings, they sent four bands off on a national tour for which admission was pegged at just one old penny (that's half a modern penny, kids). The bargain line-up was Demon Fuzz, Titus Groan, Heron and Comus. None of these acts achieved great success in their time. But pagan folk-rockers Comus in particular are now lauded by everyone from metalheads (Mikael Akefeldt of Opeth is a huge fan) to hipsters. Heron is the band pictured on the cover of the first edition of Rob Young's scholarly tome *Electric Eden: Unearthing Britain's Visionary Music*.

The *NME* covered the tour and, unsurprisingly, reported that Comus upstaged the other three bands: "Comus scored an immense hit on the first night of the Penny Concert tour at Brighton and at each successive date has received rapturous applause from pleasantly surprised audiences… On stage, the group is nothing short of phenomenal."

The *WDP*'s Brian K. Jones was at the Colston Hall show and applauded the notion of the cheapo package. "Comus, I was told, are the brightest hope," he wrote afterwards, "but on the night Heron came over better."

T. Rex
Colston Hall, 9 November 1970

This was Marc Bolan's second show at the Colston. By the time of his third gig here, on May 24 1971, glam rock in general and Bolanmania in particular were in full swing and the diminutive electric warrior was playing all the hits. Six years later, on March 14 1977, it had all turned to shit. Bolan's 15 minutes had expired and the hits had dried up. To be fair, he wasn't afraid to take out The Damned as his support act. (Amusing trivia note: for all their punk rock posturing, The Damned were closet progheads. Captain Sensible and Rat Scabies were such fanatical fans of Soft Machine that they practically stalked the Canterbury band on tour.) A few months later, the bopping elf was dead, aged 29. So why choose this 1970 show? Well, Tyrannosaurus Rex had just mutated into T. Rex and the career-changing *Ride a White Swan* single was enjoying a slow climb up the charts, eventually peaking at number two. By now, Took had been replaced by Mickey Finn in the expanded line-up that headlined the very first Glastonbury Festival (then named the Pilton Pop Festival) back in September. Shrewdly, a decision was now taken to cash in on Bolan's newfound teen appeal by capping ticket prices at a pocket money-friendly ten bob (50p). Result: the original hippy audience turned up expecting mellow vibes and songs about doves, unicorns and beards of stars, only to find themselves surrounded by squealing teenage girls as Bolan reached for his electric guitar. Bummer, man.

1971

I di Amin becomes president of Uganda… Mariner 9 is the first spacecraft to enter Mars orbit successfully… The UK and Ireland switch to decimal currency… Jim Morrison dies in Paris… Described as "the most febrile and creative time in the entire history of popular music" by David Hepworth in his book *1971: Never a Dull Moment*, this is the year of the first Reading Festival of 'jazz and progressive music' and the first broadcast of *The Old Grey Whistle Test* on BBC2, with a session by America. Check it out on YouTube - it's great. The UK's biggest selling album of the year is *Bridge Over Troubled Water* by Simon & Garfunkel. Again. So is Hepworth right? Judge for yourself - here's a selection from his list: *The Man Who Sold the World* and *Hunky Dory* (David Bowie), *Led Zeppelin IV* (Led Zeppelin), *The Yes Album* and *Fragile* (Yes), *Sticky Fingers* (The Rolling Stones), *Tago Mago* (Can), *Aqualung* (Jethro Tull), *Four Way Street* (CSNY), *Tarkus* (ELP), *LA Woman* (The Doors), *Split* (the Groundhogs), *Blue* (Joni Michell), *Fireball* (Deep Purple), *Who's Next* (The Who) *Electric Warrior* (T. Rex), *Master of Reality* (Black Sabbath), *Teaser and the Firecat* (Cat Stevens) *Nursery Cryme* (Genesis), *Fog on the Tyne* (Lindisfarne), *Madman Across the Water* (Elton John), *Meddle* (Pink Floyd) and *Cahoots* (The Band). The biggest selling single of the year is George Harrsion's *My Sweet Lord*… Portishead's Geoff Barrow is born in Somerset… Terry Pratchett's first novel, *The Carpet People*, is published by Colin Smythe… Hugh Cornwell graduates from Bristol University with a degree in biochemistry. In addition to his studies, the future Strangler writes many theatre reviews for student paper *Nonesuch* and performs his first solo gigs in Keith Floyd's restaurants.

Black Sabbath
Colston Hall, 9 January 1971

Sabbath's Bristol debut was rather late, but at least local audiences got to see them on the *Paranoid* tour. They'd been booked to play the Granary in 1970, but never turned up. "They said they were busy in the studio and we were terribly nice about it," former Granary DJ Al Read told me. "But after that they were too big to play here." Sabbath weren't lying. After their debut album became an unexpected chart hit on release in February 1970, they were sent back to the studio to record a follow-up just four months later. Released three months after that, in September 1970, *Paranoid* topped the UK album chart. This tour was supposed to kick off at the Royal Festival Hall on January 5, but the Hall's authorities promptly banned the Brummie metal pioneers, fearing that their violent, Satan-worshipping audience would destroy all the historic building's fixtures and fittings. Support at the Colston Hall was Curved Air, six months away from their sole top ten hit, *Back Street Luv*. Contemporary reports suggest that they even blew away the headliners on some nights. Incidentally, if you've ever wondered how much concert promoters paid to hire the Colston Hall in 1971, recently unearthed documents reveal that the standard fee was £84.

David Bedford's Garden of Love
Victoria Rooms, 14 January 1971

The early seventies was a bumper era for rock/classical crossover ventures, what with Jon Lord's *Concerto for Group and Orchestra* and ELP rocking Mussorgsky's *Pictures at an Exhibition*. But this lesser-known entry in the genre is an intriguing one and the Bristol show seems to have been the only public performance outside London. Later in the seventies, such ambition would be greeted with a reflexive sneer. More respect was accorded in 1971, when *Garden of Love* was billed in the Arnolfini Arts Centre's January 1971 programme as 'The major Arnolfini Music event of the 1970/71 season', with a sophisticated, new-fangled wine bar open throughout the evening.

The first part opened with music by Terry Riley and William Ganz, followed by poetry and music with David Bedford and John Tilbury. In a fabulous display of elitism, the 'fini's pseudy programme noted that: "Terry Riley is now something of a cult figure, and those of us who have played his music for years have mixed feelings about this."

The meat of the programme came in part two, with Bedford's avant-garde musical theatre interpretation of William Blake's poem. Composer and musician Bedford had long been equally comfortable in the worlds of classical and rock music and wrote the two-part, 20 minute piece specifically to be performed by Kevin Ayers and the Whole World, of whom he was a member, alongside an orchestra; the Whole World on this occasion comprising himself on keyboards, Ayers (who sang the poem), Robert Wyatt (drums), Mike Oldfield (guitar) and Lol Coxhill (saxophone). The of-its-time theatrical element required the cavorting participation of "six beautiful girls".

Premiered at the Queen Elizabeth Hall in September 1970, the piece was warmly received by contemporary critics, with much attention focused on what the Arnolfini's programme describes as "'imitation games' in which one player improvises a phrase, and another player has to attempt an immediate imitation, so far as his memory and instrument will allow him to. It is then his turn to improvise a phrase for the first player to imitate, and so on. Most of these games are between one of the group and one of the 'straight' instrumentalists, which gives an element of competition."

But - hey! - that's quite enough avant-gardery. The show concluded with the orchestra leaving the stage for the Whole World to romp through two of Ayers' own compositions: *Did It Again* and *Why Are We Sleeping?*

Genesis/Lindisfarne/Van Der Graaf Generator
Colston Hall, 26 January 1971

The brainchild of Charisma Records boss Tony Stratton-Smith, this pre-decimalisation *Six Bob Tour* (that's 30p in new money) turned out to be one of the most successful packages of the era. Stratton-Smith told the music press that he expected to make a heavy loss by putting a trio of 'club bands' in front of the widest possible audience at a bargain price. But every single one of the nine shows sold out, with as many as 500 people being turned away each night. The *NME* reported scenes of "almost unparalleled hysteria". From today's perspective, Genesis are clearly the main attraction, but in 1971 they were still unknown. Most of the band members had yet to reach the age of 21, and *Nursery Cryme*, the ground-breaking follow-up to *Trespass*, was still on the distant horizon. But this would have been an opportunity to see a very early incarnation of the classic Genesis line-up

(Steve Hackett and Phil Collins had just joined). Van Der Graaf Generator were riding high on the success of their *H to He, Who Am the Only One* album. But the main attraction was Lindisfarne, who'd just released their brilliant debut, *Nicely Out of Tune*. Peter Gabriel has estimated that they were responsible for 90% of tickets sold. Despite this, the headline act revolved each night. By the time the tour reached Bristol, Genesis were closing the show.

Tight budgeting meant that all three contrasting bands had to share a bus. In his autobiography, *A Genesis in My Bed*, Genesis guitarist Steve Hackett describes the scene: "The friendly down-to-earth Lindisfarne guys sprawled out in the back, beer drinking and singing songs... Genesis sat in the middle in an insular bubble, either reading books or doing the *Times* crossword. In the front, observing the open road ahead, the Van Der Graaf Generator chaps would chat away about anything, from the price of bedsheets to the meaning of life and the secrets of the universe."

Trivia note: had you been at the pictures around this time, you might have caught Phil Collins' final blink-and-you'll miss it big screen role before he devoted himself to music until 1988's *Buster*. It's also the best film he ever appeared in. Shot in 1969 and finally released in November 1970, *I Start Counting*, which starred Jenny Agutter, enjoyed a very brief cinema run, was broadcast twice by the BBC, and then disappeared for decades. Finally restored in 2K and released on blu-ray by the BFI in 2021, it's now rightly acclaimed as one of the era's key British thrillers. If you're looking out for him, Phil plays the ice cream seller. He doesn't get a single line, just a grunt.

Deep Purple
Colston Hall, 13 February 1971
The classic Mk II Deep Purple line-up (Blackmore, Gillan, Glover, Lord, Paice) performing their breakthrough album *In Rock* - one of the founding masterpieces of heavy metal. What's not to love? Overjoyed *Bristol Post* reviewer Tim Davey couldn't think of anything. "Deep Purple are the sound of now," he raved.

"Powerful rock, almost hymnal keyboard sets, funky guitars, an enterprising drum solo and some tremendous ear-shattering climaxes, their concert included them all.

"For two hours, this outstanding five-man British group held the hall's capacity audience spellbound, running faultlessly through heavy numbers like their renowned *Speed King*, slowing down for the moving *Child in Time* and finishing, inevitably, with their world-wide smash, *Black Night*.

"Each number played received a standing ovation and Purple deserved it."

The album was still in the charts eight months after its release, and non-album single *Black Night* reached number two. That didn't stop the busy band recording and releasing their more proggy *Fireball* later that year and returning to the Colston on September 30. Just a year after that, on September 16 1972, they were back again with yet another great album: *Machine Head*. But watching them surf this first peak of popularity would have been the Purple experience to savour.

Free/Amazing Blondel
Colston Hall, 19 February 1971

Catch 'em while you can! Free's breakthrough *Fire and Water* album had been released the previous June, yielding the global hit *All Right Now*. This led to an acclaimed performance in front of hundreds of thousands of people on the closing day of the 1970 Isle of Wight Festival, on a bill that included Jimi Hendrix shortly before his death. By April of 1971, Free were no more. Sure, they reformed in 1972 but by this time guitarist Paul Kossoff was in the grip of the heroin addiction that was to claim his life at the age of 25 - two years shy of meeting the admission requirement for membership of the fabled '27 Club'. So this was a rare chance to see the classic Free line-up of Kossoff, Paul Rodgers, Andy Fraser and Simon Kirke. Incredibly, the oldest member of the band (drummer Simon Kirke) was just 21-years-old at the time. Support came from 'progressive folk' labelmates Amazing Blondel. Their brand of self-styled "pseudo-Elizabethan/Classical acoustic music sung with British accents" might seem an odd fit with the blues-rock of the headliners, but Free were great supporters of Amazing Blondel and had introduced them to Island Records boss Chris Blackwell. The band's penchant for relating bawdy anecdotes between songs also helped endear them to rock audiences.

Black Widow
Bristol Poly, Unity Street, 20 February 1971

Britain, the late sixties and early seventies. The occult is everywhere. Ingrid Pitt is unleashing her ample bosom in Hammer horror movies; Dennis Wheatley is back on the bestseller lists, inspiring hordes of inferior imitators; and the tabloids are filled with stories of covens and devil worship in suburbia, happily involving the ritual cavorting of many a naked lady. Much of this is stoked by self-styled 'King of the Witches' Alex Sanders and his much younger 'High Priestess' wife Maxine. Enter a modestly successful Leicester soul band with the decidedly non-Satanic name of Pesky Gee! (their exclamation mark). The Peskies decided to grab a slice of the tabloid-baiting action by becoming one of the very first occult rock bands.

They changed their name to Black Widow and in 1970 released the quite brilliant *Sacrifice* album. It's not metal, as you might have expected, but an unsettling and accomplished collection of jazz-prog-folk songs with an occasional *Wicker Man* vibe, the best known of which is the single *Come to the Sabbat* with its catchy chanted chorus: "Come, come, come to the Sabbat/Come to the Sabbat - Satan's there!"

In his sleeve notes to the 2001 CD reissue, veteran music journalist Chris Welch writes: "I seem to remember covens of crazed rock journalists chanting this over pints of lager in various London pubs as they celebrated the end of a day's work."

Needless to say, the tabloids obliged with confected outrage - especially as the Black Widow stage show had been put together by Alex and Maxine Sanders (but actually choreographed by the Leicester Phoenix Theatre), with plenty of female nudity. 'Don't Let Your Kids See This Act!' screamed the headlines. Guess what the kids did?

Sadly, even Beelzebub himself couldn't avert Black Widow's subsequent run of bad luck. The album entered the chart at number 32 and was expected to go higher, but every vinyl pressing plant in the country was churning out *Bridge Over Troubled Water*. The resultant shortage benefited Black Sabbath, to whose debut kids asking for "that Satanic album" were referred. Then an American tour was pulled because promoters felt that it was probably unwise to put an overtly occult rock band on the road in the wake of the Manson murders.

Black Widow returned to Bristol to play the Granary three times. Sadly, it appears that they'd expunged much of the headline-grabbing theatrical ritual by this point and their audience swiftly vanished along with the naked ladies. Unimprovably named Antiguan drummer Romeo Challenger wound up in Showaddywaddy. Today, *Sacrifice* is rightly revered by young black metal and occult bands around the world (Tobias Forge of Ghost is a huge fan), sparking tribute albums and covers. A German TV recording of the original ritual performance was released on DVD in 2007.

Support at the Poly came from Sweet Slag (don'tcha just *love* early seventies band names?): one of the era's glut of psych/prog/jazz acts, whose debut - and indeed only - album *Tracking with Close-Ups* was released on the President Records label. It's now highly collectable with original vinyl copies going for more than £100.

Genesis
Granary, 22 February 1971
Genesis made a swift return to Bristol after the Six Bob Tour for their one and only club date at the Granary. Records show that they were paid £50. Al Read recalls that Peter Gabriel had already started to raid the fancy dress box.

The Kinks
Colston Hall, 28 February 1971
The relentless hit machine that was Ray Davies had been pumping out classic after classic since the early sixties, but The Kinks spent a lot of time in the US after their touring ban was lifted in 1969. When they finally returned to Bristol, it was on the back of their biggest commercial success in years: the *Lola Versus Powerman and the Moneygoround, Part One* concept album and its accompanying hit singles (*Lola* and *Apeman*). The audience was rewarded with a to-die-for mostly hard rockin' set list that opened with *Till the End of the Day*, took in *Sunny Afternoon* and *Lola*, dipped into *The Kinks Are The Village Green Preservation Society* and *Big Sky*, and concluded, inevitably, with the songs that launched heavy metal: *You Really Got Me* and *All Day and All of the Night*.

Writing in the *Post*, James Belsey hailed this "really welcome comeback", asserting that: "They put over loud music which was entirely today. Ray Davies, the lead singer, somehow managed to lose the old image as he led the group through a series of heavy numbers".

He also lavished praise on the under-appreciated support act: rock's great nearly man Terry Reid, who "won a lot of applause. And he deserved it."

The *WDP*'s Brian K. Jones was also impressed by Reid ("very good indeed") but bemused by the rapturous applause that followed every song by the headliners: "Personally I thought they were pretty grim." Conceding that Davies was on good form and the set was packed with hits, he was nonetheless disdainful of "what presumably was their contribution to the heavy scene, which was no more than a lot of noise."

Centipede
Colston Hall, 7 March 1971

If you're going to go big, why not go bloody enormous? I mean, how can the likes of Cream and ELP qualify as 'supergroups' when there are only three of the buggers? Fifty musicians on stage at the Colston Hall? That's more like it. Yes, this is one of those "only in the seventies" stories of musical hubris.

Southmead-born jazz pianist and composer Keith Tippett had a pretty wide musical hinterland and is best known to proggers for his contributions to the King Crimson albums *In the Wake of Poseidon*, *Lizard* and *Islands*. He also collaborated with Arthur Brown on the God of Hellfire's *Dance* album. In 1971, he came up with the frankly bonkers idea of bringing together the cream of the UK's young musicians to record an album (*Septober Energy* - a double, naturally, comprising four 'suites', which proved to be a huge influence on the young Mike Oldfield) and then take everybody on the road for a massively expensive four date tour. Even more incredibly, RCA agreed to bankroll the whole crazy endeavour, even though Tippett was just 24-years-old and had only one jazz quartet album to his credit.

Among those squeezed on to the Colston Hall's stage as part of the unwieldy jazz-prog ensemble that night were the then-current King Crimson line-up (including future Foreigner co-founder Ian McDonald and Bad Company bassist Boz Burrell), Soft Machine (including Robert Wyatt), Nucleus with Ian Carr (who also played an opening set), Tippett's wife Julie (best known for her version of *This Wheel's On Fire* with Brian Auger and the Trinity), Zoot Money, future Spooky Tooth vocalist Mike

Patto, members of psychedelic popsters Blossom Toes... the list goes on. To make things even more challenging for the audience, *Septober Energy* had yet to be released so nobody had heard a note of it before the show. Nonetheless, Centipede attracted a capacity audience.

Sadly, Keith Tippett died in 2020, but local journalist Tony Benjamin interviewed him for a planned retrospective feature for *Jazzwise* that never got published. "He confirmed that, after a highly successful debut at the Lyceum in London, the band played the Albert Hall, Bordeaux and Bristol," Tony recalls. "RCA records' largesse extended to chartering an airliner to take the 50 musicians and gear between gigs. Keith said (with no trace of irony): 'The idea was very simple - a 50-piece band with amplified classical strings, both rock and jazz drummers, double bass and bass guitars ... Nobody had tried to amplify a string section before and of course that meant a 5-6 hour soundcheck ... It was all held together by hard work, love and friendship.'"

Tony also coaxed out some backstage gossip. "Apparently the plane journeys were a flying jam session obscured by reefer smoke. Happily, when the French authorities saw the mountain of musical gear and a dishevelled crowd of bleary beat hippies on the tarmac they decided not to bother with customs formalities, thus missing large quantities of weed cached in saxophone bells, etc."

"I was there, and it was an astonishing gig," says Ed Newsom, who confirms that it took place at the Colston Hall rather than the Anson Rooms, as some sources suggest (the show was promoted by Plastic Dog for rag week, which may have led to the confusion). "It was a real tour de force for Keith, who I knew very well back then. I know that he was immensely proud of his achievement."

Tony Fennell was one of Centipede's three drummers. The main thing he remembers about the Centipede gigs was how long the performances were. With that many musicians, and Keith's fondness for improvisation, there were many opportunities for solos - and the soloists never knew quite when to finish.

The *Western Daily Press* sent along its jazz correspondent Harry Davidson, who was suitably impressed. "Being back in Bristol to play his composition obviously meant a lot to Keith and his enthusiasm was justified by the performance," he wrote. "Using progressive musicians like

Bob Fripp from King Crimson and jazz artists like Alan Skidmore together with students from the Royal College of Music is really taking a chance. But it comes off."

Another fascinating piece of trivia is that the multimedia experience was enhanced by First Light ("probably the best light show in the country," wrote Davidson), who worked regularly at the Granary and went on to secure a residency at London's Roundhouse. This was formed by Rod Bell, his brother Nick and a certain Dave Borthwick, who later found fame as an animator, co-founding Bristol studio the bolexbrothers with his chum Dave Alex Riddett (now a lighting cameraman at Aardman). They were best known for the brilliantly surreal, award-winning feature *The Secret Adventures of Tom Thumb*.

The Rolling Stones/The Groundhogs
Colston Hall, 9 March 1971

To say audiences were excited by the prospect of this show would be a major understatement. Many Stones fans had camped outside the Colston Hall box office as soon as tickets went on sale in February. Local TV news footage depicts queues snaking all the way up Colston Street in the driving snow as punters hoped to get their hands on the 75p tickets. Hundreds were turned away empty handed, even though there were two shows that night. Why such eagerness? This short nine-date jaunt was the Stones' first UK tour since 1966 and also marked the band's first live gigs since the Altamont debacle in December 1969 - largely, it seems, because Mick Jagger still feared retribution from the Hells Angels, who had chapters all over the world.

Everyone knew too that this was the last chance to see Stones before they scarpered into tax exile in the south of France to avoid the start of the new financial year. The signs of what was to come were already evident. Keith Richards was habitually late for the gigs and had brought along an entourage that included Anita Pallenberg and his perpetually loaded drug buddy Gram Parsons. Mick Jagger was travelling with the pregnant Bianca Pérez-Mora Macías, who would become his wife in May. Anita and Bianca were not exactly bosom buddies, which led to rising tensions.

For the duration of the tour, the band had been expanded to an eight-piece that included Nicky Hopkins on piano, plus the horn section of Bobby

Keys and Jim Price. The setlist took in *Jumpin' Jack Flash*, *Midnight Rambler*, *Honky Tonk Women*, *Street Fighting Man* and the inevitable *(I Can't Get No) Satisfaction*. They also played *Brown Sugar*, though nobody recognised it because it wasn't released for another month, a week before the *Sticky Fingers* album. So what were they like? Critical opinions seem to differ. "The Stones were so-so in Bristol, sloppy in Leeds, late in Liverpool," writes Stephen Davis in *Old Gods Almost Dead: the 40-Year Odyssey of The Rolling Stones*. It certainly seems to be true that the Bristol show was better than the Liverpool one three days later. And that's straight from the proverbial horse's mouth. Bill Wyman was openly upset that the Stones had been playing so badly. "I just want everyone to say it *was* shit," he was quoted as saying. In his autobiography *Every Night's a Saturday Night*, Bobby Keys describes an incident on the tour when they'd tried to play an under-rehearsed *Can't You Hear Me Knocking*: "...it kept on goin' downhill until it just died out onstage. It literally just died. It's the only time I've ever been onstage with The Rolling Stones when the wheels just *completely* came off."

1971 was also something of a banner year for great British blues-rock trio the Groundhogs. Released this very month, *Split* became their biggest hit album, going gold and reaching number five in the charts. On April 15, they even made an unlikely appearance on *Top of the Pops* (the same edition on which the Stones did *Brown Sugar*) performing *Cherry Red* - the single from which the record label took its name. Alas, in one of the Beeb's many acts of cultural vandalism from that era, the Groundhogs' performance has been wiped while the Stones one survives.

The Groundhogs had been personally recruited by Mick Jagger for the tour. But there's a story behind this, as drummer Ken Pustelnik explains: "We'd been touring with John Lee Hooker and had done two shows in Boston, Lincolnshire, before playing an all-nighter at the Roundhouse the same day. I think we went on at about 4am. Unbeknown to us, Mick Jagger was there to see a British Black Panther band called Noir, who'd been telling him: 'We've had enough of you white guys stealing our music. We want you to put us on with you.' Unfortunately, Mick thought they were crap."

But Jagger had noticed the Groundhogs and was impressed by what he saw. Two days later, Ken found himself summoned to the London offices of the band's label Liberty Records (later United Artists) and was bemused to receive spontaneous applause as he walked down the corridor to the Chief Executive's office on the top floor of the building. It turned out the Groundhogs were the last to know about their good fortune. "Who's gonna pay the buy-on?" demanded an unconvinced Ken, who knew that big acts like the Stones generally required their support bands to pay for the exposure such a tour would give them.

"Mick's actually paying *you*," he was told. "£100 each per gig."

"Where do I sign up?" was Ken's only remaining question.

Having a ringside seat at the Stones circus every night allowed Ken to form his own considered view of the state the band were in. "They were terrible," he confirms. "Mick was wearing this studded belt, which he would take off during *Midnight Rambler*. He'd come to the front of the stage, kneel down and sing 'Did you hear about the…' and then bang it down for '… midnight rambler'. The rest of the band, including the horn section, would then all come in at different times."

The Groundhogs got on best with Bill Wyman and Charlie Watts, who they'd known for years on the live music circuit. Then there was Keef. "Keith Richards was a mess," says Ken. He tells a story about the Leeds University show (the same venue at which The Who recorded *Live at Leeds* the previous year). There was a communal backstage area downstairs from main hall, where a huge spread had been laid out for the headliners ("There was enough food to feed Ethiopia, which the Stones ignored"). The Groundhogs were in their dressing room when there was a knock at the door. They opened it, and in fell a monstrously wasted Keith Richards. Ken does a pretty accurate impersonation of the guitarist's stoned drawl: "I can't get into my dressing room, man," he whined. "It's locked!" The Groundhogs dispatched a roadie to take the lock apart for him and thought no more about it.

Fifteen minutes later, there was another knock at the door. It was Keith again, full of gratitude. "Look, man, I haven't got anything to give you for your kindness, but I got you this," he bumbled. From behind his back, he produced an enormous cut glass bowl which was full to the brim with liquorice allsorts.

Further shenanigans ensued backstage at the Colston Hall. Guitarist Tony McPhee had gone downstairs to the Green Room before the show. He pushed at the door, but it wouldn't give. He finally gave it a big shove and it burst open. Alas, it turned out that Mr. Jagger and the future Mrs Jagger had been enjoying an intimate moment up against the other side of the door and were sent sprawling across the floor. Tony made his apologies and went back upstairs. "I just flattened Mick and Bianca," he told his bandmates.

One undeniably great thing came out of the Colston Hall shows: a series of iconic live photographs by David Redfern portraying the Stones in their pomp. The band wouldn't return to Bristol for another 11 years, when they played Ashton Gate stadium.

As for the Groundhogs, the Stones tour proved a great success. "We were a hard-working band," says Ken. "When we arrived at the Colston Hall, the *Bristol Evening Post* took a photograph of us at the backstage door. Just look at our eyes in that picture! But we were pretty hot at the time. We didn't amend our set or compromise in any way for the Stones audience and went down well every night. Some people even said we blew them off."

Alas, the trio's success was to be short-lived. It all fell apart when associates of the Kray twins decided they were going to 'manage' the band. But that, as they say, is another story…

Led Zeppelin
Bath Pavilion, 13 March 1971

"A ticket for Led Zeppelin, sir or madam? Certainly. That'll be fifty of those new-fangled pence please."

No misprint here. These days, the cynical response to bands playing 'back to the clubs' tours is that this is a fig leaf to disguise increasingly selective appeal. Back in the 1970s, it was genuinely a thing as musicians tired of playing increasingly enormous gigs and yearned to get a proper whiff of an audience at close quarters once again. Everyone from Genesis to post-Beatles Paul McCartney was doing it. Indeed, for Macca's first tour with Wings in 1972, he'd just turn up and play university venues unannounced. (Despite what the internet may tell you, this did not include Bristol University.)

Zeppelin took the idea so seriously that in addition to pegging the tickets at 1968 club prices, they also accepted the same fee that they were paid for their first gigs. So it was that for Freddy Bannister's massively over-subscribed penultimate show at the Pavilion, he got them for £75 rather than the £60,000 he'd paid them to headline the previous year's Bath Festival. Zeppelin were the biggest band in the world at this point, so Freddy was forced to break with one long-standing tradition. For the first time, he put tickets on sale in advance rather than on the door only.

They might have been playing in smaller venues than usual, but Zeppelin brought along their standard sound rig, which meant that their two-and-a-half hour show was very loud indeed. Opening with *Immigrant Song*, it drew from all three of their albums to date. Significantly, the band also took the opportunity to road test four songs from their upcoming fourth album. These were *Black Dog*, *Rock and Roll*, *Going to California* and an epic that the *NME* thought was "called something like *Stairways to Heaven*". The Pavilion gig marked the sixth occasion on which these were performed live.

The *WDP*'s Brian K. Jones interviewed Jimmy Page after the show. The guitarist explained that the tour had been planned as a release from the frustration of recording, revealed that the upcoming fourth album could be a double (it wasn't) and advanced a fairly utopian view on the future of festivals: "Maybe they should be for free - with all the bands getting together and working it out between themselves. The only out of pocket expenses would be in building a stage. If we all put our PAs together we would have a sound system for a festival."

And the Pavilion gig? "Tremendous - a marvellous audience. They listened to our new material without giving us a bad time for the old tunes. Their reaction tonight really answers why we came."

Trivia note: Robert Plant always had a penchant for these smaller gigs. On May 19, 1981, he played the Granary club with his low-key first post-Zeppelin band The Honeydrippers (also featuring guitarist Robbie Blunt). Inevitably, the invitation-only show was packed to the rafters. Before changing into his stage gear (a silver lamé suit, fact fans), Percy enjoyed a pre-gig pint in the Old Duke over the road. Over the years, Plant has also racked up shows at the Corn Exchange, Fiddlers, Anson Rooms, Ashton Court Festival, Colston Hall and St. George's. It's a safe bet that no other musician of his stature has played so many Bristol venues.

Stomu Yamash'ta
Arnolfini, 16 March 1971

Before he blotted his copybook by coming over all prog and appealing to the vulgar masses with his own band East Wind and the supergroup Go (fellow members: Steve Winwood, Klaus Schulze, Al Di Meola and Michael Shrieve), Japanese master percussionist Stomu Yamash'ta was the toast of the snooty modern music scene. He was best known back in the early 1970s for his collaborations with Peter Maxwell Davis and for bringing his Red Buddha Theatre Company to Europe in 1972. But a year before that, the 23-year-old Yamash'ta pitched up in Bristol for this suitably bizarre show which concluded Arnolfini Music's first season. The day before the gig - uh, sorry, 'recital' - he'd embarked on a tour of Bristol's scrapyards in search of anything that could be repurposed as a percussion instrument. He then proceeded to startle the assembled beard-strokers by battering the crap out of these finds in his familiar athletic style, "which enables him to leap from one end of his array of ironmongery to the other, landing on the split second to deal a blow at a gong before sprinting off to devastate a pair of xylophones," as the Arnolfini's programme put it. If this seems rather too avant-garde, you wouldn't have had to wait too long for Prog Yamash'ta. He returned to Bristol with East Wind on February 19, 1974, playing the Victoria Rooms with Hatfield and the North in support.

Gentle Giant
Granary, 22 March 1971
One of the all-time-great prog acts, whose reputation continues to grow with each passing year. This show came just before the release of their second album, *Acquiring the Taste*, on which they really found their feet. They were paid £30. Amazing Gentle Giant trivia note: it's a little bit funny, but a certain Reginald Dwight was really, really keen to join the band as their vocalist, having played briefly with psychedelic-era precursor act Simon Dupree and the Big Sound. During his audition, he unveiled his latest composition, *Your Song*. The founding multi-instrumentalist Shulman brothers decided that he wasn't a good fit for their brand of prog. So off he went to forge a solo career, which proved rather successful. Another big fan was producer Tony Visconti, who ranks working with GG as one of his career highlights ("I was in heaven working on their concept album," he writes in his autobiography *Bowie, Bolan and the Brooklyn Boy*). High praise indeed from the chap who produced all the best David Bowie albums.

Caravan/Barclay James Harvest/Gringo
Colston Hall, 23 April 1971

A cracking prog package with a cunning idea at its core. Canterbury's Caravan were big down south while Oldham's BJH were big oop north. So bunging them together on the same bill allowed each to make incursions into the other's territory.

Both headliners were at key moments in their careers. The greatest of all the Canterbury scene bands, Caravan were touring their masterpiece, *In the Land of Grey and Pink*, which was released the following month. This blended the trademark English whimsy of *Golf Girl* with the epic, jazz-prog wizardry of *Nine Feet Underground*, which occupied the whole of what we used to refer to as side two. Like just about everything ever released by Caravan, this enjoyed not the slightest whiff of chart action on release. But it has remained a steady seller over the years, with multiple reissues as new generations discover the band's music. The best of these is the revelatory 40th anniversary 5.1 remix by 21st century prog hero Steven Wilson, which was released in 2011. As recently as 2015, Rolling Stone ranked *In the Land of Grey and Pink* at number 34 in their list of the 50 Greatest Prog Albums of All Time.

BJH had just released their second album, *Once Again*, and spent the early part of 1971 touring with their own orchestra under the musical directorship of Robert John Godfrey, who went on to found The Enid. They played much of the magnificent, mellotron-heavy album on this tour, including the song that would remain in their set, well, forever: *Mockingbird*.

Gringo were a short-lived Somerset prog band formerly known as Toast (no, really), who released just the one album on Decca. Singer Annette Casey firmly resisted leering attempts to market her as a sex object. After Gringo were, you know, toast, she went by the name Casey Synge and joined an all-girl trio named, ahem, Thunder Thighs, who earned a place in rock history for supplying the backing vocals to Lou Reed's *Walk on the Wild Side*.

The *Post*'s James Belsey clearly hadn't got the memo about Ms. Casey, describing Gringo lip-smackingly as "a fairly immature band with an extremely attractive girl singer." But he recovered his composure sufficiently to form the view that BJH upstaged the headliners. "Their music was moody, musical and compulsive," he enthused.

The Byrds
Colston Hall, 3 May 1971

As we have seen, the Byrds' 1965 performance in Bristol was widely panned. But it was literally all change when they returned to the Colston Hall in 1971. Roger McGuinn was the only remaining member of the line-up that played the Corn Exchange six years earlier. Ace bluegrass/country guitarist Clarence White had joined, but the band's recorded works had gone seriously downhill. Indeed, they were about to release the worst album of their career, *Byrdmaniax*. That said, this incarnation of the Byrds had acquired an impressive reputation on stage and they'd triumphed in the rain at the previous year's Bath Festival.

As this was the first date on a European tour, the inkies (*Disc*, *NME*, *Melody Maker*) were out in force to review the Colston show and all agreed that it was outstanding. "Bristol not only saw one performance," wrote Ray Hollingworth in *MM*, "but an encore that stretched way over half-an-hour. The serenity of the sunny day had fed The Byrds. They couldn't stop playing. The splendidly warm audience didn't want them to stop, and, darn it, this group didn't want to stop either. And this was the first gig in a country that in the past has proved rather unfortunate for this cowboy unit."

Their set at the Colston Hall included *So You Want to Be a Rock'n'Roll Star*, *Truck Stop Girl*, new-ish single *Chestnut Mare* and a 20-minute version of *Eight Miles High*. Inevitably, they also played *Mr. Tambourine Man*. But it wasn't the version everyone was expecting. "Yes, Tambourine Man was different," Roger McGuinn told the *WDP*'s Brian K. Jones after the show. "It was the Dylan version, the way he would have liked to have done it but CBS wouldn't let him get away with it. We do it just for fun. Sure, some of the fans will prefer to hear the original but we hope they liked this version. They were a great audience, excellent. They started off applauding loudly. We didn't know how long we would be wanted to do, but in the end there was no question."

Fascinating trivia note: The Byrds arrived hideously early for the show, so they decided to amuse themselves by heading up to Ashton Court Estate for a traction engine rally they'd seen advertised. Clarence White was so impressed that he penned *Bristol Steam Convention Blues*, which was released on the *Farther Along* album.

The Bristol Free Festival
Clifton Downs, 9 May 1971

Live music on the Downs these days means corporate, branded and ticketed affairs. But back in 1971, Bristol had its very own free festival - one of the earliest to take place in the UK. A vivid account by Gordon Strong of Bristol band Flash Gordon on the UK Festivals website reveals that it was organised by the Dwarf Party's Dave 'Basil' Hayes (dwarf in this context referring to anarchists rather than persons of restricted growth). The generator was supplied by the West Coast chapter of the Hells Angels, who rejoiced in such names as Tank and Pete the Pervert. All the city's heads pitched up for performances by three local bands, who played in the centre of the crowd. The hairy hordes responded with outbreaks of authentic idiot dancing when they weren't recumbent and spliffed-up. Search for 'Bristol Free Festival 1971' on YouTube and you'll find a fascinating short film of the event, which includes rare - possibly unique - footage of a Hells Angel playing the bongos.

The acts were Wisper, Flash Gordon and the city's biggest and best band of the era: Magic Muscle. In keeping with the spirit of the times, these psychedelic hard rockers lived together in a commune at 49 Cotham Road, toured in an old Cadbury's bus, and often shared bills with Hawkwind and the Pink Fairies. The name? That came from Captain Beefheart's term for the male member. Their self-styled 'guru' was guitarist/vocalist 'Rustic' Rod Goodway.

"We used to play on acid all the time," Rod told me when the band reformed in 1988 for a tour that included a local show at the Thekla. "Lots of bands talked about doing that, but it was only us and the Grateful Dead that actually *planned* it."

The Muscle went on to play at the Pilton Pop Festival (as did Flash Gordon) a couple of months after the Bristol Free Festival. But the big time was to elude them. On the night that Chris Blackwell was due to see Magic Muscle with a view to signing them to Island, he flew to Jamaica and signed Bob Marley instead. Rod went on to live in a Dorset commune with Arthur Brown and Viv Stanshall until things got just too fucking weird. "Once they woke me up at five in the morning to try a special vocal effect," he recalled. "What this actually meant was that I had to stick my head in a bucket of water and try to sing. Needless to say, it didn't work."

The commune was at Ilsington Farmhouse - an 11-room manor near Puddletown, which had served as an inspiration to Thomas Hardy when he wrote *Tess of the D'Urbervilles*, and is now a holiday rental business. Arthur rented it for a mere £15 a week in 1969 and set up the Jabberwocky recording studio on the premises. Led Zeppelin recorded some demos here. Most famously, America used it to record their hit *A Horse With No Name*. Arthur's hippy madness on the lawn was once interrupted by a BBC crew filming a documentary entitled *In the Footsteps of Tess*.

Magic Muscle Violinist Simon House joined Hawkwind for the *Hall of the Mountain Grill* album and stayed for four years, returning to the band later in his career. In 1978, he joined David Bowie's band, appearing on the *Stage* and *Lodger* albums. Bassist Adrian Shaw also joined Hawkwind and then worked on the London buses for several years. Guitarist Hugh Gower teamed up with Graham Parker and former New York Doll David Johansen before becoming a producer.

Meanwhile, back at the Bristol Free Festival, the pigs eventually showed up. Did they crack heads and ruin the mellow vibe? Er, not exactly. According to Gordon Strong, there were two bobbies in a Morris Minor. They surveyed the scene in a leisurely fashion and went away again.

As for Bristol Dwarf anarchist Dave Hayles, he stood for election to the city council in the Cabot ward during the 1971 local government election, describing himself as "educated at Bristol University. Has not done national service. Unmarried. Acid head. Interested in cannabis, rock and roll, balling and bicycles." His brief manifesto asserted that: "We feel that local government needs a fucking good shake up at all levels." Interested parties were invited to contact him "through your friendly neighbourhood hippy." He polled 161 votes, coming third. In 1978, Hayles founded the Bristol-based ornamental plastering company Hayles & Howe in Picton Street, Montpelier, which subsequently moved to larger premises in Templegate. It has also expanded internationally and now boasts an office in New York State, where he is currently based. Despite working for many a toff - as well as making repairs to Buckingham Palace, the Capitol Building in Washington DC and the Royal Opera House - Hayles makes no secret of his radical, disreputable past. In 2016, he published his autobiography, *Confessions of an Ornamental Plasterer*, which told of his years as a "pot-smoking hippy".

Glastonbury Fayre
Worthy Farm, 20-24 June 1971

Think of the early seventies Glastonbury festivals and you're likely to picture cavorting naked hippies. That's because of Nic Roeg's impressionistic *Glastonbury Fayre* film. Roeg didn't have the rights to film the main musical performers - including headliner David Bowie, who went on at 4am. There's also an equally misleading if collectable triple album, again titled *Glastonbury Fayre*, which includes artists who didn't actually play there in 1971 (The Grateful Dead, Pete Townshend, Marc Bolan), performances by artists who did play there that were actually recorded elsewhere (Hawkwind) and studio demos rather than live recordings (Bowie, Bolan).

This time round, Michael Eavis ceded control of his festival to a bunch of hippy toffs, chiefly Andrew Kerr (Randolph Churchill's former private secretary), Arabella Churchill (Winston's granddaughter) and great British eccentric John Michell. The author of *The View Over Atlantis*, Michell was a UFOlogist, Earth mysteries enthusiast and 'alternative archaeologist' who also denied evolution and embraced some fairly right-wing views. Eavis liked him. "John Michell was a lovely bloke," he told me. "I got on really well with him. He had a great sense of fun and he said everything with a wink. I didn't even know what a ley line was when I met him..."

The date was shifted to midsummer and Bill Harkin's pyramid stage (constructed at a cost of £1,100 on a ley line between Glastonbury and Stonehenge, obviously) was the focal point. Headliner David Bowie turned up three days early with long hair and sporting a rather fetching cape/flares/wide-brimmed hat combo that suggested he was perhaps unaccustomed to farmyard living. He'd arrived by train at Castle Cary Station with wife Angie in tow. The couple then attempted to walk the six miles to the festival site in their impractical yet indisputibly groovy attire. Yokel chortling may well have occurred along the route.

Bowie had been on *Top of the Pops* the previous week, miming the piano part to Peter Noone's cover of his *Oh! You Pretty Things* and had just unveiled his new band (Mick Ronson, Woody Woodmansey, Trevor Bolder) who were yet to be named the Spiders From Mars. Stoned hippies who managed to prop their eyelids open to watch his pre-dawn set were treated to much of the material that would eventually wind up on *Hunky Dory* (*Kooks, Changes, Song for Bob Dylan*, etc), which he'd already started recording, performed as a duo with Ronson.

The rest of the thoroughly hippyish line-up playing over what, after initial downpours, eventually became a gloriously sunny weekend included Hawkwind, Traffic, Daevid Allen and Gong, Family, Fairport Convention, Melanie, Joan Baez, The Pink Fairies and the Edgar Broughton Band.

The most theatrical and controversial performance was by that great showman Arthur Brown with his new band Kindgom Come. "When we went on, we did our very heavy *Galactic Zoo* act featuring burning crosses," Arthur told Polly Marshall for her biography *The God of Hellfire: The Crazy Life and Times of Arthur Brown*. "After the performance the darkness was all-encompassing. It all felt rather heavy for Glastonbury. I took in the world as it is. I felt it was quite apposite. The festival was a little more new agey, love and peace. One review said we mind-trashed the whole county of Somerset."

Arthur wasn't invited back to the festival for another three decades.

For Eavis himself, the best performances weren't the obvious ones. "Terry Reid and Linda Lewis were the highlight for me. They were really something special. I'd say those were among the very best performances we've ever had at the festival."

Don't take Michael's word for it: judge for yourself. Terry Reid and Linda Lewis are the opening musical sequence in Roeg's film. Hugely enjoyable though it is, *Glastonbury Fayre* has no captions. So here are some handy viewing notes. The posh chap with the long luxuriant hair and equally luxuriant beard is Andrew Kerr. The balding posh chap with the beard is Bill Harkin. The older geezer talking about ley lines is - surprise! - John Michell. Arabella Churchill can be seen briefly standing next to Andrew Kerr at the side of the stage. The drummer with Terry Reid and Linda Lewis, who's seen taking a huge toke on a joint before their performance, is Alan White. He played on John Lennon's *Imagine* and spent the next 50 years in Yes following Bill Bruford's departure. The drumming procession is led by members of the Pink Fairies. It's claimed that Hawkwind's Robert Calvert is in there too. The tuneless chap with his willy hanging out is Michael Cousins - aka Magic Michael - a Ladbroke Grove fixture and general eccentric, who went on to record a single with members of The Damned. The fella standing next to him on stage is William Jellett, aka 'Jesus', aka "the naked hippy dancer", who turned up at every UK festival in the 1970s and could still be seen strutting his stuff, albeit fully clothed by then, at prog shows well into the 1980s. If there had been an internet back then and Magic Michael and Jesus espoused fashionable causes, they'd both have enjoyed a gazillion followers on social media.

Despite the fun had by everyone on drugs, the second festival was a miserable experience for the only person not on drugs (Farmer Eavis, for it was he), not least because all the hippies fucked off leaving him with a big pile of debt. As a clean-living soul who's outlived all of the younger key organisers of the 1971 festival, he'd been alarmed by all the scarfing down of psychoactive chemicals. "They were all taking lots of LSD and jumping out of trees and things, which I found rather scary," he confesses.

Little wonder there wouldn't be another official event until 1979. But does he look back more fondly on those early, more radical and bohemian festivals with the passage of time? "I think I do, yeah. Of course, it turned out that the hippies were absolutely right - even though they looked a bit strange. They were talking about things like rising sea levels back in the 1970s. The green thing is still a very important element of the festival and although my daughter's now in charge I remain very hands-on."

These days, the freshly knighted Sir Michael Eavis is universally hailed as a National Treasure. But this wasn't always the case. The *Western Daily Press* in particular proved a thorn in his side all the way into the 1990s. Initially, the paper didn't seem to know what to make of the Glastonbury Fayre. The first mention came on January 21 in its *Mr. West's Diary* section, which was primarily concerned with the doings of West Country toffs, especially those involved in hunting. Andrew Kerr's posho credentials triggered the forelock-tugging reflex, despite Mr. West's misgivings about vulgar pop music. "What we are trying to do is organise a spiritual gathering of people of all sorts," Kerr said soothingly. "It is true that the occasion will include music as a means of spiritual expression."

Once the 12,000 filthy hippies started to turn up, however, the paper knew exactly who to blame: "bearded 35-year-old farmer Michael Eavis" (yes, even his follicles gave offence), who, the *WDP* claimed, was making £3,000 from the event and already planning to accumulate more swag from "yet another hippy invasion next year".

Pearl-clutching readers were aghast at news that all police leave in Somerset had been cancelled, Pilton was sealed off with residents given special passes, and "heavy rain has turned the farm into a quagmire… As more hippies arrive each hour, others, rain-soaked, leave for home." To underline the depravity of the event, multiple references to hippy nudity were made. "Last night, some of the dancers who gathered round the giant steel pyramid stripped stark naked," read one suitably horrified report. "And in amongst the hippy pilgrims stood curious villagers, who might not have brought their children along if they had realised the nature of the show."

Tory MP for Wells Robert Boscawen pitched up on a 'fact-finding mission' and observed: "I thought the toilets were rather crude, especially for women."

Drugs? Well, as Eavis noted, there was plenty of bad acid on site, but also no shortage of con artists. A press release reported that suede cleaner was being sold as cannabis and junior aspirin dyed with beetroot passed off as LSD. Bummer, man. Even more shamefully, the *WDP* revealed that the festival's PA was being used to warn tokers of advancing pigs. "One such warning given yesterday was: 'There are plain clothes police at the top tents busting them for stuff. If you see any of them, cool it and get stoned when they go.'"

As the event progressed, the paper grew ever more apoplectic. 'It's village war on the hippies' screamed a headline on a story that claimed Pilton residents were forming a vigilante group. No mention was made of pitchforks and burning torches. Instead, it seems local businesses were finding creative ways to profit from the invaders while expressing their disgust. The postmaster banned "long-haired youths" from his shop and was serving them in an adjacent shed instead, while the licensee of the Crown Inn would only dish out beer to hippies from a side entrance: "They left so much filth behind we could not stand it any longer."

At least the hippies were given the chance to have their say in a couple of vox pops. "What a scene, man, it's so peaceful," raved blissed-out Alan Stevenson, 21, from Worcester. "If the sun keeps shining, I'll stay forever."

He's probably still there.

Midsummer Merry-Making

Biddisham, 30 July 1971

1971 sure was Peak Hippy Festival. Little wonder Bristol's Plastic Dog decided to stage an event of their own. Trouble was that by late summer the phrase 'hippy festival' was becoming a major cause for concern to the straights. Plastic Dog announced their 'Midsummer Merry-Making at Pleasure Acre' on the back page of their magazine *Dogpress,* with a photograph of an ecstatic naked lady standing in a field in front of a curious bull. Don't try this at home, kids.

No one seems to have noticed that July 30 isn't actually midsummer, but the residents and local cops certainly noticed that the event was planned for a field in Portbury. Organisers Al Read and Terry Brace had cunningly attempted to disguise their plans by calling it a 'show' rather than a festival. ("It seems that any open-air event that includes a pop group or two is automatically termed a pop festival by local authorities, residents' associations and the straight press, and is tarred by the same brush as all previous festivals," they told the local press.) But the Port of Bristol Authority, which had a claim on the land, saw through their ruse and turfed them off with just days to go.

After a frantic search, they eventually found a new site thanks to a kindly farmer: a field off the A38, 30 minutes from Bristol, between the villages of Biddisham and Rooks Bridge. Result! Well, not exactly. Loads of local bands pitched up to play, including Stackridge, Birth, Spring and Squidd. There was even an out-of-town headliner: The Climax Chicago Blues Band. The local press was generally supportive and took photographs of some fruity 17-year-old pop girls frolicking in the sun. But there were only 850 people on site. Then the weather turned abruptly, with a violent thunderstorm erupting during Spring's set.

"The weather was dramatically memorable for the amazing lightning that upstaged the light show and the sweeping rain that drenched the few people who had been able to find the location," wrote Al Read in his book on the Granary Club. Climax Chicago refused to play for fear of being electrocuted and the event almost bankrupted Plastic Dog. "We've certainly learned one or two things," Al told the *Western Daily Press* afterwards. The al fresco experiment was not to be repeated.

Edgar Broughton Band
Greenway School, Bristol, 6 August 1971

It's another of those 'only in the seventies' yarns. Back in the summer of 1971, Bristol City Council backed a scheme to entertain the kids of Southmead and keep them from turning to delinquency during the summer holidays. Presumably at the behest of a groovy teacher, they chose the Edgar Broughton Band to perform this service. This wasn't a first for the free festival counter-culture heroes, as they'd recently played the Free and Parochial School in Hackney, which was judged to be a great success. Other shows on the eventful tour had proven rather more controversial. The previous week, Edgar appeared in court in Redcar accused of behaviour likely to cause a breach of the peace.

The Broughtons played a Friday matinee show at Greenway School in Doncaster Road, Southmead, starting at 2pm. They'd promised to tone down their usual heavy rock and perform songs with big choruses for the nippers to join in. Whether they concluded with *Out Schoolkids, Out!* is not recorded. There were no subsequent press reports of trouble, so presumably the school's one and only experiment with hairy agit-prop rock passed off peacefully.

Yes
Colston Hall, 12 October 1971

One thing that's really striking about early seventies tour schedules is just how hard bands were working. Two albums a year, each supported by a national tour, was not an unusual pattern. Sometimes the quality suffered; often it didn't. Yes are a case in point, releasing three of their key albums in the space of little more than 18 months, and playing the Colston Hall to promote each one of them. What's more, they managed to lose/gain a keyboard player and drummer in this period (Rick Wakeman replacing Tony Kaye and Alan White taking the place of Bill Bruford, who buggered off to join King Crimson).

They'd played the Colston on the *Yes Album* tour on January 17, with Iron Butterfly supporting.

But this was Bristol's first opportunity to see caped crusader Wakeman on keyboards with Bruford still on drums. Yes were touring the *Fragile* album and playing for the first time many of the songs that remain in their set to this day, including *Roundabout, South Side of the Sky, Long Distance Runaround, Heart of the Sunrise*, and the Steve Howe acoustic showcase *Clap*. Then they returned to the Colston on January 30 the following year to do it all again. Just eight months after that, they were back on the *Close to the Edge* tour (September 9, 1972) - this time with Alan White on drums.

Despite labouring under the impression that the band's guitarist was named Steve Lowe, the *Post*'s James Belsey was highly impressed, pronouncing this "an exciting, original event".

"It's always good to see a group on the way up - and Yes are certainly that," he enthused. Belsey was particularly impressed by Jon Anderson's "extraordinary voice... with immense range and texture" and the instrumental prowess on display: "Throughout the show there were regular contrasts from acoustic guitar solos by Lowe (sic) to a five minute virtuoso by keyboard player Rick Wakeman, who played piano, mellatron (sic) and organ, one after the other."

Trivia note: This show came just a couple of months after busy Mr. Wakeman had popped into London's Trident studios on the last day of David Bowie's *Hunky Dory* sessions to record his brilliant piano contribution to *Life on Mars*?

The Faces/Thin Lizzy
Bath Pavilion, 13 November 1971

Picture the debauchery! Legendary boozers Rod Stewart, Ron Wood, Ian McLagan, Ronnie Lane and Kenney Jones join forces with the hard working (they'd played the Granary twice already) yet equally hard partying Lizzy before they'd even released first single *Whiskey in the Jar*. Tickets were 75p. From this distance, it's easy to overlook just how rapid the Faces' ascent was. Their first two albums, *First Step* and *Long Player*, had done bugger-all. But Rod Stewart's solo album *Every Picture Tells a Story* was a huge hit and its single *Maggie May* was enjoying a five-week run at the top of the UK singles chart in November 1971. Four days after this show, the Faces' album *A Nod Is as Good as a Wink... to a Blind Horse* was released, also becoming a massive hit, bolstered by Rod's success. By early 1972, they were playing huge stadiums in the US. Success took rather longer to arrive for Lizzy and they never cracked the US, thanks in equal parts to tomfoolery and misfortune.

1972

Watergate scandal begins as five White House operatives are arrested for burgling the offices of the Democratic National Committee... Eleven Israeli athletes are murdered by Black September terrorists at the 1972 Summer Olympics in Munich... Survivors of Andes plane crash are rescued after 72 days, having scoffed the bodies of fellow passengers to stay alive... British Army kills 14 unarmed civil rights marchers in Derry in what becomes known as Bloody Sunday. Paul McCartney's *Give Ireland Back to the Irish* is banned by the BBC... *M*A*S*H** makes its TV debut... Atari's *Pong*, the first successful arcade game, is released... Loads of great singles in the charts, with *Telegram Sam* (T. Rex), *School's Out* (Alice Cooper) and *You Wear It Well* (Rod Stewart) all hitting number one. But the biggest seller is *Amazing Grace* by The Pipes and Drums and the Military Band of the Royal Scots Dragoon Guards, while the biggest selling album is K-Tel's *20 Dynamic Hits* - the first in a plague of chart-dominating compilations. Key album releases: *Harvest* (Neil Young), *Machine Head* (Deep Purple), *Argus* (Wishbone Ash), *Exile on Main St* (Rolling Stones), *The Rise and Fall of Ziggy Stardust and the Spiders From Mars* (David Bowie), *Transformer* (Lou Reed), *Close to the Edge* (Yes), *Octopus* (Gentle Giant), *Can't Buy a Thrill* (Steely Dan)... A shocking report in the *Western Daily Press* reveals the depth of Bristol's latest crisis. A surfeit of buyers and shortage of properties has caused house prices to rocket. In areas of Redland, Clifton, Stoke Bishop and Sneyd Park, new four-bedroom detached houses are now touching the £20,000 mark. Even dilapidated properties in a good area can fetch up to £5,000... The first Bristol Powerboat Race takes place in the city docks. After seven deaths, the carnage is finally ended in 1990... At the cinema, you could see Peter Medak's *A Day in the Death of Joe Egg*, starring Alan Bates and Janet Suzman. This was shot in Bristol back in1970.

Pink Floyd

Colston Hall, 5 February 1972

Back in those glorious days before the advent of file-sharing, the only hazard faced by musicians eager not to be ripped off was presented by a small but dedicated band of bootleggers and tape sharers. This meant that bands were able to road-test material before release. Pink Floyd were great enthusiasts for this process, which is why Bristol audiences got to hear the whole of *Dark Side of the Moon* played in its entirety, in sequence, for only the eighth time - a full year before its official release. Briefly titled *Eclipse (A Piece for Assorted Lunatics)*, it was very much a work in progress. Recording eventually began at Abbey Road Studios in June and there was quite a bit at this show that we wouldn't recognise from the version that went on to become the fourth biggest selling album of all time. The synthesisers were absent, as were Clare Torry's stunning vocals on *The Great Gig in the Sky* (audiences were instead treated to, erm, tape loops of readings from the Bible and a ranty speech by Malcolm Muggeridge). Being there for this one must have been rather like watching Led Zeppelin performing *Stairway to Heaven* for the first time, since no one present was familiar with any of what would later be hailed as one of the greatest albums of all time. To add to the sense of occasion, the *Bristol Post* reported that tickets for this show were the most sought-after since The Rolling Stones played the Colston a year earlier.

Floyd certainly pushed the boat out on the sound and lighting front. They turned up at the Colston with nine tons of equipment, having insisted that the venue be available from 8am. Their elaborate lightshow and surround sound system took six hours to set up and a further four hours to take down again. A guarantee was demanded that the stage would be able to take the weight of all their gear and 16 local roadies were recruited to help haul it out of the trucks. This tour also marked the first time that Floyd worked with lighting designer Arthur Max, whom they'd lured across the Atlantic from Bill Graham's Filmore East. Max went on to create the innovative light shows for all of Floyd's early 1970s tours before moving into the film industry, where he became a renowned production designer. He's been nominated for Academy Awards for his work on *Gladiator*, *American Gangster* and *The Martian*.

Ian Gregory was 17 at the time and recalls this lengthy piece of new music being received in reverential silence. "It was mesmerising," he says. "Obviously, at the time no one realised the significance of what they were hearing, but I do remember the audience being quite stunned."

Having recovered from his disagreeable previous encounter with Floyd at the Colston, *Post* reviewer James Belsey was in a much better mood for this gig. He noted that Floyd caused a minor traffic jam round the back of the Hall with their truckloads of gear, but all this was put to good purpose: "There wasn't a single moment when their battery of tapes, multi-channel stereo systems and robot-like banks of rock music technology failed to act as mere servants of the four players' talents"

Belsey was, perhaps understandingly, a bit vague about *Dark Side of the Moon* itself, describing the piece merely as "slightly less ethereal music than they have been composing recently."

After unveiling their new masterpiece in full, Floyd then rewarded the patient audience by cherry-picking both *Echoes* and *One of These Days* from *Meddle*, rescuing *Careful with That Axe, Eugene* from *Relics*, and even nipping back to the Syd Barrett era with *Set the Controls for the Heart of the Sun*. All killer, no filler - as the more recent saying goes. Belsey was completely won over by this half of the show, especially the "extraordinary climax as blinding fireworks burst into clouds of smoke".

Two years later, Floyd returned to Bristol for the last time, playing a two-night stand at the Hippodrome on December 13 and 14, 1974. By then, they'd become a huge draw on the back of the success of *Dark Side of the Moon* and tickets sold out instantly. This time, the Bristol audience got to hear the final version of the album in its entirety. But Floyd continued to develop new music on stage too. The Hippodrome shows opened with early versions of *Shine On You Crazy Diamond* (later recorded for *Wish You Were Here*) and *Sheep* and *Dogs* from the subsequent *Animals* album.

Black Sabbath
Colston Hall, 7 February 1972

"What the heck was all that reaction about?" Not for the last time, poor old *Bristol Evening Post* pop correspondent James Belsey found himself stuck in a Colston Hall full of teenage heavy metal fans, and he didn't like the pandemonium one little bit. There were, he wrote, "nasty moments", principally when "some hysterical kids clambered on the lip of the circle and looked in danger of plunging down and later when the bouncers formed an on-stage wall between audience and stars."

Sabbath were on a roll in early 1972. They'd just released *Master of Reality*, the third of their four successive great founding contributions to modern heavy metal, just six months after *Paranoid*. The press hated it, obviously, but audiences lapped it up and the album went top ten on both sides of the Atlantic. They'd also been touring relentlessly and had yet to succumb to the cocaine snowstorm that would impair future performances. Ozzy was battling against flu during this show, which perhaps explains why the two subsequent gigs on the tour were cancelled. But Belsey acknowledged that "They used deafening, slicing riffs to create an atmosphere of pretty obvious tension and the audience rose to the band's instructions like an orchestra to the conductor." Nonetheless, he concluded his review by sniffing: "If you wanted to hear good rock music… their gig wasn't much fun." One suspects 2,000 punters would beg to differ.

Jethro Tull
Colston Hall, 5 March 1972

Many Tull fans didn't get the joke when the band released their parody of a concept album, *Thick as a Brick*. But this rather rebounded on smirking Ian Anderson after it was acclaimed as one of the all-time-great progressive rock records. With the 21st century resurgence in popularity of prog, *Thick as a Brick* remains a key part of his live repertoire today. But one long, continuous piece of new music spanned over two sides of vinyl was a lot for punters to digest. Matters were complicated further by production difficulties stemming from the miners' strike. The album was supposed to have been released in February, but didn't actually reach the shops until five days after this Colston Hall gig.

Tull performed an extended version of the entire album to open the show, with drum and flute solos plus all kinds of added funny bits. It began with a bunch of blokes in capes coming on to sweep the stage and even included a 'news and weather' interlude at half-time. Only then did they deliver audience favourites *Cross-Eyed Mary*, *A New Day Yesterday*, *Aqualung*, and *Locomotive Breath*.

Sounds like a self-indulgent recipe for disaster? Not according to the *Post*'s James Belsey, who considered it an absolute triumph, with the famously abstemious Anderson giving it the full deranged, wild-eyed loon and leaving the audience "stunned [and] silenced".

"Their performance was so exaggerated, deliberate and ferocious that they wore the audience out," he continued. "The grimacing, cavorting - but always weirdly graceful - Anderson was the sinister genius who pushed the concert way beyond the limits of standard rock extremism."

Supertramp/Judas Priest
Granary, 16 March 1972

Bizarre double-bill alert! This must have been a fascinating opportunity to see two very different bands before they hit their strides. Supertramp already had chief songwriters Roger Hodgson and Richard Davies on board, but were struggling badly. *Crime of the Century* was two years away. For this show, they were joined by guest guitarist Mickey Moody, whose band Juicy Lucy had just split. In his highly enjoyable autobiography *Snakes and Ladders*, Mickey describes sharing spliffs with the band en route to Bristol in a large American car: "A totally unknown commodity and a few years away from stardom, they were loose enough musically to invite me on stage to play a few songs with them. As people were wont to say: 'Nice one, man.'"

As for Judas Priest, this was long before their world-conquering days with leather-clad Rob Halford. In March 1972, they were fronted by a chap named Al Atkins and their debut album, *Rocka Rolla*, wasn't out for another 18 months.

Captain Beefheart and the Magic Band
Colston Hall, 24 March 1972

The Spotlight Kid was arguably Don Van Vliet's most accessible album, as he sought to widen his appeal and make a little loot for a change. You can't eat critical acclaim, after all. But 'accessible' is a relative term in Beefheartland, so this European tour in support of the album, which marked the Magic Band's first visit to the Colston Hall, was never going to be a conventional affair. For a start, the opening act was a ballerina. Followed by a belly-dancer. Then, for reasons best known to himself, drummer John French, aka Drumbo, performed with a pair of brightly coloured women's knickers atop his bonce for the entire show. Fellow *Trout Mask Replica* survivors

Zoot Horn Rollo (guitar) and Rockette Morton (bass) were also in the touring band. The career-spanning set list was dominated by the current album, but also took in a couple of tracks from *Trout Mask* (*Hobo Chang Ba*, *Steal Softly Thru Snow*) and a cover of John Lee Hooker's *Black Snake*. The Captain himself was reportedly on fine form, dryly observing of the notorious Colston Hall acoustics that "this place is coming back at me".

Wishbone Ash/Renaissance/Fumble
Locarno, 14 May 1972

They'd played the Colston Hall back in January on the *Pilgrimage* tour and would return there in November, but this was Wishbone Ash's first Bristol show since the release of their career-defining *Argus* album one week earlier. This peaked at number three in the UK chart and was voted Album of the Year by *Sounds* readers and named Best British Album by *Melody Maker*. Every single band who used melodic twin lead guitars after that, from Thin Lizzy to Iron Maiden and Judas Priest, owe Wishbone Ash in general and *Argus* in particular a huge (generally acknowledged) debt. Andy Powell and Ted Turner were positively on fire at the time. We know this because the *BBC Radio 1 Live in Concert* album was recorded 11 days later on the same tour and is prized by many aficionados as being the band's best live release. Right down the front at this show was young Wishbone Ash fan Steve Street, who later became a key part of the Bristol music scene as a producer (The Pop Group, Glaxo Babies, etc), engineer and bassist. He remembers it not just for the great music. "A PA cabinet fell off and bounced off my head. I momentarily passed out, but recovered to see the end of the set."

No doubt because they were also managed by Miles Copeland, Brit proggers Renaissance were the support act, showcasing vocalist Annie Haslam's magnificent five-octave range. They were still finding their feet at this point and it would be another six years until they had a UK chart hit.

Opening the show was the biggest band from Weston-super-Mare: Fumble. These guys had started out in the rock'n'roll era as The Iveys. By the early 1970s, they'd changed their name to the rather uninspiring Balloons and were playing covers in clubs around the UK. A final name change to Fumble came in September 1971. As a rock band now playing original material, they bagged the support to Slade at the Granary on October 26, 1971 and returned to play headline shows at the club on a further six occasions. They also appeared on *The Old Grey Whistle Test* twice (1972 and 1975) and recorded a session for John Peel in 1972.

Celebrated art design agency Hipgnosis created the covers for Fumble's self-titled debut album (EMI-Sovereign, 1972) and its follow-up *Poetry in Lotion* (RCA, 1974). It was the former that attracted the attention of David Bowie, who was so impressed by their music that he booked the band to support him on the US leg of his Ziggy Stardust tour in 1973. Keyboard player Sean Mayes was later recruited to play in Bowie's band on the 1978 *Heroes* world tour. He can also be heard on the albums *Lodger* and *Stage*. Mayes subsequently toured and recorded with Tom Robinson.

There is, however, a sad footnote to Mayes' story. By 1995, he had contracted AIDS. In February of that year, the Cambridge philosophy graduate made national headlines after walking into a police station in Paddington to reveal all about the death of his brother back in April 1972. It turned out that their mother, Joy, had murdered his junkie sibling Roderick while Sean was on tour with Fumble in Switzerland because she feared he'd wind up in an asylum. She'd laced the young man's cocoa with poison, bashed in his skull with a metal footscraper and slit his throat. Upon Sean's return from tour, she solicited his help in burying the body in the back garden of the family home in Weston-super-Mare. This terrible family secret was kept for 23 years. Sean's motivation in coming forward was to ensure his brother received a proper burial before his own imminent death. No action was taken against him, despite his role in covering up the murder. He died in May 1995, at the age of 49. His book about his experiences with Bowie, *We Can Be Heroes: Life on Tour with David Bowie*, was published five years later by Independent Music Press.

In 2020, Cherry Red Records released a 4CD box set entitled *Fumble: Not Fade Away - The Complete Recordings 1964-1982*. This was billed as "the definitive career anthology of a criminally underrated band."

Budgie

Granary, 15 June 1972

One of the key bands in the development of heavy metal, great Welsh trio Budgie also came up with some of the most amusing song titles in any genre: *Nude Disintegrating Parachute Woman*, *Hot as a Docker's Armpit*, *I'm Compressing the Comb on a Cockerel's Head*, etc. It's quite possible that they would have been playing their best-known track, *Breadfan*, at this, their second gig at the Granary, as they tended to work songs up some time before recording them (it eventually appeared on the following year's *Never Turn Your Back on a Friend*). Budgie never enjoyed anything approaching what might be described as a hit, but proved to be hugely influential on a younger generation of musicians. It helped their bank balances considerably to have songs covered by Iron Maiden, Soundgarden and, especially, Metallica, who perform *Breadfan* regularly to this day.

Hawkwind/Roxy Music
Locarno, 9 July 1972

The first of two bizarre double bills headlined by Hawkwind at the Locarno in 1972, this one is particularly odd because none of the tomes or multiple websites devoted to either Roxy or the Hawks mention that they ever played together. But it definitely happened, because several reliable eyewitnesses were there. This was part of a short run of Electric Mecca gigs at the venue offering two acts for less than a quid. Indeed, for 90p the audience also got to see Hookfoot - a band made up of DJM session musos who'd backed the likes of Elton John - and a screening of the *Jimi Hendrix Plays Berkeley* movie.

In truth, the two bands weren't quite as far apart as one might suppose. Brian Eno, in particular, was chums with Robert Calvert, playing on his first solo album *Captain Lockheed and the Starfighters* and producing the second one, *Lucky Leif and the Longships*. And, of course, Simon House played on Eno's *Here Come the Warm Jets*. The question of why Roxy Music appealed so much to pseudy cultural commentators who treated Hawkwind with disdain is addressed by Joe Banks in his excellent book *Hawkwind: Days of the Underground*: "Roxy's own mutability gave them the air of sci-fi dilettantes indulging in cosplay on the holodeck, as opposed to the proletariat grease monkeys of Hawkwind in the engine room."

Among those who witnessed this up close on the night was Steve Street. "Brian Eno certainly made an impression with the costume and feathers," he recalls. "They all looked the part as a glam rock outfit. I think it was a tough ask supporting Hawkwind, and I, like most of the audience, was rather bemused by Roxy Music. They were undoubtedly ahead of their time, but certainly not a rock band. A lukewarm response probably sums it up.

If the gig had been at the Colston Hall, the bar would have been rammed. But the layout at the Locarno was better for support bands in that respect.

"Hawkwind were almost completely the opposite to Roxy Music in looks and approach - rough and ready, almost a grunge band. The place took off when *Silver Machine* started up and a semi-naked Stacia, gyrating at the front of the stage, was the icing on the cake for many in the crowd, leaving little to the imagination."

David Bowie/Thin Lizzy/Gnidrolog
Locarno, 27 August 1972

It's Lizzy again - and this time they're supporting Dame David! Punters wouldn't necessarily have known this in advance, mind, as the £1.25 ticket billed Bowie with "supporting acts + film". This was the third Bristol date on the Ziggy Stardust tour with the brilliant Spiders From Mars line-up of Mick Ronson, Trevor Bolder and Woody Woodmansey. They'd already played the Anson Rooms (supporting Focus) and the Colston Hall. But this was the first Bristol show since the oft-repeated homoerotic *Top of the Pops* performance of *Starman* in July that sent Ziggy stratospheric. Naturally, the Bristol audience was treated to the full guitar fellatio routine that was captured in Mick Rock's iconic photographs, though how many of the teens present would have recognised the two Velvet Underground covers (*I'm Waiting for the Man* and *White Light/White Heat*) is open to question.

The show was staged by Frome-based Fi-Sounds Entertainments - a promotion/management company that ran concerts throughout the region, including the regular Electric Village nights at the Locarno. One of its employees was Adrian Copley, who also worked as a DJ at the Granary. "Bowie did the whole Spiders from Mars thing during the warm-up session, although no one was allowed in the auditorium except his crew," he recalls. "Everyone - band members, crew, promoters, et al - then trooped off to the Bali Hai bar."

Yes, that's right. If you'd been in the vicinity of the Locarno in the early evening of 27 August 1972, you could have caught the astonishing sight of David Bowie in full Ziggy regalia, platinum-haired Mick Ronson, lavishly sideburned Trevor Bolder and their entourage sitting round on bamboo chairs, surrounded by plastic palm trees and fake 'totem poles', being served cocktails by Bristolian-accented waitresses wearing grass skirts in a naff

Polynesian-themed bar adjacent to the venue.

Fascinating Bowie footnote: Al Read at the Granary ranked turning down Bowie on the grounds that he was "too folky" as his worst ever decision. "I remember looking at the album cover [that'll be *The Man Who Sold the World*] and saying, 'I'm not having a man in a dress at the club," he groaned at the memory.

Status Quo

Boobs, 15 November 1972

Yep, this regular Wednesday live rock night really was called Boobs. Just in case you didn't geddit, their press ads featured a silhouette of an unfortunate naked lady visibly feeling the effects of the cold. The sign above the entrance read "Through these doors pass the world's most beautiful women - our patrons" and the décor was, um, plastic palm trees. You can almost taste the Watney's Red Barrel, can't you? The venue was Tiffany's at the top of Blackboy Hill (now the Spire private hospital), whose later legendary Tuesday rock nights with DJ Andy Fox lasted well into the 1980s.

Boobs was run by Frome's busy Fi-Sounds Entertainments and billed as an attempt to bridge the gap between the Granary and the Colston Hall. Their booking policy was certainly eclectic. The night began on March 1, 1972, with local heroes Stackridge. The following week brought a performance by Bath's Natural Theatre Company. As we shall see, Boobs later booked avant garde artists and the first Bristol show by Bob Marley and the Wailers. Other notable Boobs shows included Geordie (fronted by future AC/DC singer Brian Johnson) on April 25, 1973, and an early incarnation of Manfred Mann's Earthband (coincidentally including future AC/DC drummer Chris Slade) on September 26 of the same year.

Had you paid your 50p to get in on this occasion, you'd have caught the mighty Quo finding their twelve-bar feet after that rather uncomfortable psychedelic period, performing the likes of *Gerdundula* and an early version of *Big Fat Mama*.

The busy Frantic Four actually played Bristol three times in 1972 on this *Dog of Two Head* tour, appearing at the Granary on April 20 and the Anson Rooms (supported by local heroes Magic Muscle) on October 13. But five days before this show, which was advertised as "by public demand", they'd released their first single on Vertigo: the two minutes and 52 seconds of heads-down perfection that was *Paper Plane*, which peaked at number eight in the UK singles chart. The breakthrough *Piledriver* album followed in December. Oh, and if you hadn't blown all your loot on Watney's Red Barrel at this gig, you could have come back the following week to see Nazareth at Boobs. As for Quo, within 18 months they'd be playing multiple nights at the Colston Hall and, indeed, the Empire Pool, Wembley (now better known as Wembley Arena).

Hawkwind/Fred Wedlock
Locarno, 19 November 1972

Their only top ten hit, *Silver Machine*, had reached number three in the charts by the time Lemmy-era Hawkwind arrived in Bristol for the third time in 1972 on their legendary *Space Ritual* tour. Trouble was, support band Fat Mattress (founded by Jimi Hendrix Experience bassist Noel Redding) didn't turn up. Enter brave local folkie Fred Wedlock, nine years before his novelty hit *The Oldest Swinger in Town*, to entertain the stoned hippies before they had their brains fried by the Hawks. Being a Hawkwind support act is a thankless task at the best of times, but Fred deserved a medal for agreeing to this unlikely pairing.

A blogger who goes by the name of Bhagpuss remembers it well as this was his first gig. "With just an acoustic guitar, a laid-back stand-up comedian's polished patter and a set filled with genuinely funny and catchy songs, he went down a lot better than Fat Mattress ever would have," he writes. "I bought his album the following week and it still amuses me on the odd occasion I remember I have it."

"Fred had a few support spots due to last minute cancellations by bands," recalls Adrian Copley, who worked for the promoter. "He was always reliable and would turn up after a quick phone call. It started in September 1972 when Family were about three hours late for their Locarno gig. He also became a good friend, as well as one of my college lecturers."

King Crimson
Top Rank, 28 November 1972

KC obsessives, of whom there are many, will notice that this was a rare chance to catch the band's relatively short-lived Mark 3 version featuring founder Robert Fripp, violinist/keyboard player David Cross, bassist/

vocalist John Wetton, drummer Bill Bruford and colourful, soon-to-depart percussionist Jamie Muir. Admission was 75p.

For many, this *Larks' Tongues in Aspic* tour marked the start of Crimson's artistic peak. For local journalist Tony Benjamin, it also marked the beginning and end of his ignominious foray into the world of bootlegging. "Thanks to friends who worked at the Top Rank, we managed to smuggle in a reel-to-reel tape deck and set it up on the balcony with a view to bootlegging the gig. We left my mate's girlfriend in charge of the recording process - she didn't like the music and was coming down with a bit of a cold - while we went down in the stalls. It was, predictably, larky (sic!) with mad percussionist Jamie Muir performing one solo section that included throwing sticks at cymbals from about twelve feet away. The music was great - Fripp brilliant, especially, and Bill Bruford's drumming definitely added energy to the sound - so we were really keen to hear it again once we'd sneaked the tape deck home. Unfortunately, however, the otherwise flawless recording was marred by Shirley coughing repeatedly at five or six second intervals throughout. Thus ended our career as bootleggers."

Slade/Thin Lizzy/Suzi Quatro
Colston Hall, 5 December 1972

Slade were proper rockers who could actually play their instruments and had been swept willingly along on the glam wave (or were "brickies in make-up", according to sneering art-rockers) after a brief, unsuccessful and unconvincing attempt to pretend to be skinheads. Although they'd been denied a third consecutive number one after *Goodbye T'Jane* was kept at bay by Chuck Berry's shameful *My Ding-A-Ling*, *Slayed* was at the top of the album charts and the preposterously attired quartet were officially, if briefly, the biggest band since The Beatles when they arrived in Bristol on their second full UK tour. In his autobiography *So Here It Is*, guitarist Dave Hill ascribes Slade's imperial period from 1972-73 in part to the wide availability of new-fangled colour TV sets at a time of social unrest, bringing joy to a beleaguered nation by permitting teenage fans to marvel at his increasingly absurd outfits (Exhibit A: the 'metal nun') on *Top of the Pops* while dads gained equal pleasure from venting their loud disapproval. But this was a pre-Christmas Slade show in which *Merry Xmas Everybody* wasn't played, mainly because they hadn't written it yet.

In his autobiography, *Who's Crazee Now?*, Noddy Holder describes this as "probably the most riotous tour we ever played. It was madness from start to finish." Pity the other two acts on the bill, though. The Colston Hall show was the last night of a lengthy jaunt, during which they'd been booed by audiences who only wanted to see the headliners. Detroit rocker Suzi Quatro was already playing her future number one hit *Can the Can*, but it had yet to be released as a single. The hostile reaction to her band's 20 minute opening set reportedly reduced her to tears on occasion. But it wasn't all bad news for Suzi. At the previous show in Plymouth, she got it together with her recently recruited guitarist Len Tuckey. They later married and were together for 20 years.

Thin Lizzy (in trio from, with Eric Bell on guitar) were still very much in embryonic form as performers, while playing on the biggest stages of their career. Phil Lynott, in particular, was rather shy and introverted. So much so, in fact, that Slade's manager Chas Chandler threatened to throw Lizzy off the tour for being too boring. But watching Noddy Holder in his mirrored top hat every night gave Lynott the idea for what became his signature pose. He went out and bought a budgie mirror from a pet shop and mounted it on his bass guitar to shine in the eyes of young ladies in the audience who attracted his attention.

Slade were nearly a man down at this show, as Dave Hill had just broken his foot. Indeed, the interestingly coiffured guitarist was pictured backstage by the *Bristol Post* displaying his cast while surrounded by adoring dolly birds. But in a move that was later to be emulated by the likes of Axl Rose and Dave Grohl, he chose to make a feature of this pedal impediment by plonking himself upon his own private podium. In fact, he had a little silver mini-stage and wore an extravagant gold outfit. Classy, huh?

The *Post*'s James Belsey didn't seem to notice any of the other acts but was in raptures over Slade, describing them as "the natural successors to The Rolling Stones". This may seem rather excessive from today's perspective, but Belsey had actually reviewed the Stones so is entitled to his opinion. "They turned everything on full force last night to get a reaction that even the much-adored T. Rex couldn't equal here," he continued. "The whole show pivoted on the maniacal voice of Noddy Holder. He whipped the audience into a frenzy for more than an hour and had hands clapping, feet stomping and voices singing with the slightest gesture."

1973

War breaks out again between Israel and Arab states, including Egypt, Syria and others. Israeli victory leads to worldwide economic problems stemming from the resulting oil embargo led by Saudi Arabia and other oil exporters... In Roe vs Wade, the US Supreme Court rules that abortion is a constitutional right... Three-day week introduced in the UK... TV Sitcom *Last of the Summer Wine* begins. It carries on forever... Two of the biggest selling albums of all time are released: Pink Floyd's *Dark Side of the Moon* and Elton John's *Goodbye Yellow Brick Road*. This is certainly Elton's year, as *Don't Shoot Me, I'm Only the Piano Player* becomes the biggest selling album. Other chart toppers include Status Quo's *Hello!*, Roxy Music's *Stranded* and, in a banner year for glam rock, Slade's *Slayed* and *Sladest*. Biggest selling single is, groan, *Tie a Yellow Ribbon Round the Old Oak Tree* by Tony Orlando and Dawn. At least Bowie has three of his greatest hits: *The Jean Genie, Drive-In Saturday* and *Life On Mars*... Bristol celebrates 600 years as a city and county in what has since become a rather familiar orgy of civic self-congratulation, which persists in the clickbait-era 'Bristol - whoo!' school of uncritical journalism. Local author Derek Robinson is so incensed that he's inspired to write his classic *A Darker History of Bristol: Swindles, Scandals and Skulduggery*. An outraged ratepayer writes to the *Western Daily Press* calling for this to be burned in the gutters... Arguments rage over the fate of Bristol's City Docks, which have closed to shipping and some say should be filled in/covered over to make space for, among other things, a huge road system... Stanley Kubrick comes west to shoot scenes for his stately *Barry Lyndon*, which is released in 1975. Locations include Corsham Court, Longleat and Wilton House... Banksy is born in Yate. Possibly.

Uriah Heep
Colston Hall, 13 January 1973

Adored by fans and reviled by contemporary music hacks, Heep have as good a claim as anyone on being the progenitors of progressive metal. That means they've undergone something of a critical reappraisal in recent years, as younger people discover their music. But let's not exaggerate: for most of those who write about music for a living, Heep remain beyond the pale.

Those of us who love 'em, on the other hand, know that there are multiple peaks and troughs in their lengthy story. And in January 1973, they'd hit the first peak. Heep had followed the brilliant *Demons and Wizards* album barely six months later with the relatively inconsistent *The Magician's Birthday*, but were a magnificent live act. We know this because their top 30 double album, imaginatively titled *Uriah Heep Live*, was recorded at Birmingham Town Hall just 13 days after this Colston Hall show. You couldn't ask for a better Uriah Heep set list, showcasing those trademark multi-part vocal harmonies that would prove such an influence on Queen: *Sunrise*, the hit single *Easy Livin'*, *July Morning* (the song that inspired an annual Bulgarian festival - no kidding, Google it)…

Sadly, this line-up wasn't to last. The following year, bassist Gary Thain died of a heroin overdose. Flamboyant and charismatic vocalist David Byron succumbed to alcoholism and was chucked out of the band in 1976. Despite almost continuous touring, it would take years for Heep to find their feet again creatively. Today, indefatigable founder Mick Box remains the only surviving (literally - all the others are dead) member of the band that played this show.

Focus
Hippodrome, 28 January 1973

'Going viral' was a tad more challenging in the pre-internet era and could only be achieved through the medium of television. David Bowie's career-making performance of *Starman* on *Top of the Pops* in July 1972 is the most widely cited example. But Dutch proggers Focus's *Old Grey Whistle Test* session a couple of months earlier, in which they played *Hocus Pocus* and part of *Eruption*, proved equally momentous and seemed to provoke two responses in quick succession: (1) "Hey, look at that crazy yodelling Dutchman!" and (2) "Actually, this is really fucking great!" The following day, record shops across the land were stripped of Focus albums and the band's career took off in the UK.

A few months earlier, they'd been at the Anson Rooms supported by - crazy seventies double-bill alert! - a glum David Bowie, who feared his career was over after *Space Oddity* appeared to be a one-off novelty hit. On November 2, they played the Granary (for which they were paid £125, according to Al Read's meticulous record keeping). But after further *OGWT* and *TOTP* appearances, the band notched up two top 20 singles (*Sylvia*, *Hocus Pocus*) in early 1973. This Bristol Hippodrome show caught the attention of the local press, who, in those not-exactly-cosmopolitan times, considered Focus to be some kind of exotic novelty. In a long, mostly admiring preview, the *Western Daily Press* billed them as "Holland's contribution to Common Market pop".

The Hippodrome gig found the quartet at their unlikely commercial peak, as teens and progheads alike flocked to hear the lengthy, classical-influenced compositions showcased on their double album *Focus III*. This reached number six in the UK, spending a total of 16 weeks on the chart.

The Ladybirds
Granary, 22 March 1973

To leaf through old local newspapers from the late 1960s and early 1970s is to open a window on a repressed Blighty where the exciting sight of a well-turned ankle or shapely naked breast is a highly saleable commodity. At the time of this show, for example, cinemas were full of 'continental films' (code phrase for nudity) and there were multiple ads for 'striptease shows' and 'exotic dancers' at venues which were mostly located in the Clifton area of Bristol. Some tried to pass themselves off as sophisticated gentlemen's clubs. Others didn't bother. One of the most striking ads was for Globetrotters on Whiteladies Road ("opposite the BBC" it read helpfully, either to remind Beeb staffers of the sauciness available on their doorstep or to provide a convenient landmark for out-of-towners eager to sample its services). For an annual membership fee of £2, punters were promised "shocking strip", "dreadful films" and "beautiful bare boob barmaids" from 7pm nightly. Alas, Globetrotters' owners later fell foul of the law and in 1974 were convicted of 'keeping a disorderly house' after a trial at Bristol Crown Court. In the judge's summing-up, he expressed particular disapproval of their screening of a porn version of *Snow White and the Seven Dwarfs*.

Much mostly female nudity was also to be found in the era's alternative press, notably Bristol's *Dogpress*, which was produced by the Plastic Dog collective at the Granary. In a hangover from the 'free love' era, this was presented as being liberated and fun.

It was against this backdrop that The Ladybirds came to the west country. There have been multiple all-female bands with this name over the years. Remarkably, two of them were topless. The American topless Ladybirds were mostly brunettes. The Swedish topless Ladybirds were mostly blonde. And it was the Swedes who embarked on this UK tour in the nippy early spring of 1973. Their first local show took place the night before the Granary gig at the Keel Club in Bathampton, Bath (today the Bathampton Mill Pub and Restaurant). This was Bath's first disco and had recently branched out into live music by booking the young Thin Lizzy. (Some sources erroneously claim this was Lizzy's first show on English soil and took place in 1967, which would have been quite an achievement for a band that didn't form until 1969.)

Grainy YouTube footage reveals that the Stockholm quartet, who'd been plying their trade since 1968, were actually quite competent if unexceptional musicians. But, as Peter Patston observed in his excited *Western Daily Press* preview ('Now, topless of the pops'): "Yes, they do play instruments, electric guitars and the like. And yes, they do sing all the trendy hits. But it is the girls' topless routine that makes them the tops."

Patston revealed that a group of outraged citizens had formed a vigilante group to drive the unwanted semi-naked Scandinavian lovelies out of Plymouth. But they were used to provoking extreme reactions. In Indonesia, for example, they needed a 24-hour police guard. And several over-eager fans were shot after clambering over barricades around their (un)dressing room.

At a time when most bands at the Granary were being paid £40-£100, Al Read shelled out a whopping £200 for The Ladybirds. "Being musically capable of playing half an hour of average pop songs would not normally be enough to earn yourself a well paid gig at the Granary," he later admitted, "but performing topless tipped the balance."

He said the band enjoyed the show, "probably because the audience was younger and hippier than their usual middle-aged cabaret audience" and won much applause: "So much so that at the end of their set one of the girls, who was wearing nothing more than a white leather bikini bottom, treated the lads at the front to a brief full frontal when she whipped off the last remaining item."

Alas, one club member promptly nicked the young lady's bikini bottom as a trophy, which presented her with a problem as the group were due to appear at the Webbington Hotel and Country Club (more of which later) on the outskirts of Weston-super-Mare the following night. Practical Al came up with a solution. "Using the sewing skills I had picked up over the years in the clothing trade and some white leather taken from an old jacket, I made a new costume overnight. The girl was so pleased she thanked me profusely, promising return bookings at much reduced fees. The Ladybirds never returned but the memory lingers."

Rod Stewart and the Faces
Hippodrome, 8 April 1973

1973 was the Faces' year. Their final - and best - release *Ooh La La* topped the UK chart in March, becoming the first Faces album to do so. And their relentless touring schedule brought them to the Bristol Hippodrome twice. But dissent in the ranks was already beginning to show, as signalled by that frequent change in billing to Rod Stewart and the Faces. The rest of the band, notably Ronnie Lane, were increasingly pissed off at being effectively described as a support act to distracted Rodney, whose solo career had really taken off. It didn't help that Rod loudly slagged off *Ooh La La*, which was largely Lane's creation. By the time the band returned to Bristol in December, Lane was gone. His replacement was former Free bassist Tetsu Yamauchi.

When tickets for this show went on sale in March, the Hippodrome box office queue snaked halfway round the centre. If those members of the band not named Rod Stewart had read James Belsey's review of the show in the following day's *Evening Post*, their fears about being sidelined would have been justified. Beneath a large snap of Rod in a familiar flamboyant, chest-exposing pose, Belsey waxed lyrical: "Rock superstar Rod Stewart turned in a performance that you really cannot fault. He's got what is openly admitted to be the strongest and most sensitive voice in rock today, and he used it superbly... In between the vocal action, he danced, zoomed around the stage, fluffed his hair and did more than enough to reduce girls to near hysteria."

The other Faces? They got a quick mention in the final couple of paragraphs for providing "a powerful boogie backdrop for Stewart's vocals." Oh, and Ron Wood's guitar work was "inventive".

Belsey was also present for the "boozy, clowning and completely deafening" December show. Once again, for him there was just the one star: "Rod Stewart put in enough work to prevent any goose-pimples on his half-naked chest. He raced around the stage, tossing his microphone stand into the air, falling to his knees and even collapsing in a heap on his back."

Tellingly, the set list included his solo hits *Maggie May* and *You Wear It Well* as well as the cover of Hendrix's *Angel*, all of which appeared on his *Never a Dull Moment* album. The rest of the band "played their part, strutting around in the hard rock tradition" with Wood doing "a non-stop double act with the singer, sometimes fighting for space to share his mike during a chorus."

One year later, the Faces undertook what turned out to be their final UK tour. It also proved to be the highest grossing tour of 1974. Oddly, the only west country dates were a two-night stand at the Taunton Odeon on December 3 & 4. "It is unlikely whether Taunton has ever seen such an astounding display of rock excitement," observed *Post* reviewer Dave Newman, who reported that the increasingly showbiz Stewart was now sporting a mauve silk jumpsuit. A few weeks later, Ron Wood felt obliged to issue a statement asserting that, contrary to a widely circulated rumour, he would not be joining The Rolling Stones. Three months after that, he joined The Rolling Stones and started recording *Black and Blue*.

Roxy Music
Colston Hall, 14 April 1973

What the hell were Roxy Music? A glam rock band? A prog rock band? An art-rock band? None of the above? Fronted by an old-school lounge lizard, with a teddy boy on sax, a guitar hero in outsize specs, a painted boffin twiddling knobs and a rhythm section who looked as though they'd wandered in from the pub circuit and been assigned silly costumes after losing a bet, they certainly confused many. Notoriously, these included Whispering Bob Harris, who pronounced them a triumph of style over substance prior to their *Old Grey Whistle Test* performance in 1972. Bob was generally a reliable guide to the bearded denim-clad man-rock of the early 1970s, but he got it badly wrong on this occasion. Mind you, he wasn't alone. Granary Entertainments manager Al Read declined to pay £45 to book them because he disliked their clothes and haircuts.

If you wanted to see Roxy in their early experimental pomp, the 1973 *For Your Pleasure* tour was the one to catch, as the primped and prancing Brian Eno left shortly afterwards. Non-album track *Pyjamarama* was still in the singles chart as they arrived at the Colston Hall for a typically flamboyant show.

For 11-year-old Bristol schoolboy Martin Thomas, it proved a major formative experience. "In August 1972, a performance on *Top of the Pops* changed my whole approach to listening to - and loving -music," he recalls. "The band was Roxy Music, who were performing their single *Virginia Plain*. I bought the single as soon as I could get my dad to take me to a record shop.

"When my 12th birthday arrived in March 1973, I wanted two presents: the new Roxy album *For Your Pleasure* and a ticket to see them at the Bristol Colston Hall in April of that year - my very first concert. From memory, I think the ticket cost eighty pence.

"At 6pm on the day, I set off on the bus with two mates from school, who I had convinced to come along even though they were into Slade. I was dressed in my best denim jacket. After joining the Roxy Music fan club, I had a Roxy Music badge to cover the embroidered flower print.

"First impression walking into the Colston Hall was: this place is enormous and there are so many people here already. The second thought was smelling the cigarette smoke wafting throughout the hall. I'm thinking, why does the smoke smell different (and nicer) to the smoke that comes out of the my dad's cigarettes? I was fairly innocent in those days…

"The crowd all looked so much older than me. I saw a sea of denim-clad 20 to 30-year-old men and women. One thing that surprised me was there were not many people dressed like Roxy Music, although possibly the image they promoted would not be tolerated by the beer and football crowds that dominated the dress code of the early 1970s. I do remember being called a 'poof' at school for liking Roxy Music, even though I was playing in the football team at the time. That didn't matter, as I knew I was into the best band around.

"We were in a little box to the left of the stage (as you look at it) - literally right above the musicians, with a great view not hampered by any taller people. When Roxy Music arrived on stage, the crowd was so loud. I clapped and cheered along. To see the band only a few feet away from me literally took my breath away for a few moments. They started with *Do the Strand*, which was delivered at great pace.

"Bryan Ferry was dressed in a black glittery suit with big silver buttons – maybe the same one that he wears on the album cover. Andy Mackay was to his left in what seemed to be a '50s sci-fi outfit that had come off of the set of the TV programme *Lost In Space*. Phil Manzanera was on guitar in a black jump suit covered in glitter and wearing his trademark 'fly' sunglasses. Paul Thompson, who I rate as one of the best drummers ever, was dressed in his usual caveman leopard print singlet. The bass player stood almost out of sight to the left of Paul's drum kit – dressed in denim. I think it was John Porter (although it may have been John Gustafson) but it definitely was not Rik Kenton, who played on Roxy's *Top of the Pops* TV performance I had seen the year before.

"I leave Eno to last because he is the member of Roxy I remember most from the night. Because we were in the box to the side of the stage, I was right above Eno and his vast array of synths, knobs and wires. When I stood up from the seat I thought I could almost touch him as I was really that close. He was slightly bald with long blond hair and dressed in a silver shiny top with silver feathers coming out of his shoulder pads. He kept looking towards the other guys in the band, then would twist some knob or device, and the music went into a different direction – much like the reprise of the track *In Every Dream Home a Heartache* on the second album. One thing I remember vividly is that he came back for the encore in a black tiny top with black feathers on the shoulders – again, I think this was the outfit he wears on the album sleeve. I didn't see any evidence of the falling out between him and Ferry which was going on behind the scenes, though.

"Being nearly half a century ago, my memory is a bit hazy on the tracks played. Other than *Do the Strand* the standout track for me was *Editions of You* which is still one of my favourites from the album. My overriding memory of Bryan Ferry that night was when, during the middle of that song, he cupped his hand to ear as he sang the words "I heard the slinky sirens wail whoo!" *Pyjamarama* was the other track I remember – probably because it was their latest single and it starts with a wall of guitar sound from Phil Manazanera with a treatment by Eno.

"It finished all too quickly. I knew at the time I had witnessed something special and I still really cherish the memories of my first gig by a band that still are important to me now. First four albums only, though!

"Nearly 50 years later, I went back to the Colston Hall to see Bryan Ferry. My seat was about 30 feet from where I'd been for Roxy Music in 1973. I was hoping Ferry would play some Roxy tracks, and to my great pleasure (no pun intended) he performed quite a few of my favourites from the first two albums. When his band started playing the opening bars to *In Every Dream Home a Heartache* I genuinely got tingles up the back of my neck. I turned to my wife to say (rather too loudly for the ladies sat in the row in front of us): 'Fuck me - I've waited nearly 50 years to see him play this one'. My night was complete."

Geordie
Boobs, 25 April 1973

Hard rockers from - where else? - Newcastle upon Tyne, Geordie were at the peak of their short-lived fame in April 1973 when they achieved their one and only top ten hit with the splendid *All Because of You*. These days, they're remembered chiefly for the fact that their singer was Brian Johnson, who went on to join AC/DC after the death of Bon Scott. Cue spooky music: the support act on the early dates of this tour was a little-known band called Fang, who'd recently changed their name from Fraternity. Their frontman was... Bon Scott. That's right: two AC/DC singers on the same tour, before either of them joined AC/DC.

Bon later recalled being hugely impressed by Johnson when they played Torquay Town Hall two days before this Boobs show. The Geordie frontman had been rolling around the stage, screaming his head off and doing what Scott described as the best Little Richard impersonation he'd ever seen. What he didn't realise was that Johnson had been in excruciating pain. Immediately after the show, he was carted off to hospital suffering from appendicitis.

Bob Marley and the Wailers
Boobs, 9 May 1973

Bob Marley played Bristol three times in his short career - twice on the 1973 *Catch a Fire* tour, with what many consider to be the definitive Wailers line-up featuring Peter Tosh and Bunny Wailer. The tour was divided equally between rock venues and Jamaican clubs, reflecting Chris Blackwell's desire to make the band a crossover success. A four-night run at London's Speakeasy attracted the curious Beautiful People of the time. But the regional shows pulled fewer punters and went virtually unnoticed. The Wailers' first Bristol gig took place just a week after recording their legendary *Old Grey Whistle Test* appearance. This was at Boobs - the Wednesday rock night at Tiffany's. Picture, if you can, Rasta Bob and chums performing amid the club's legendary plastic palm trees. Two weeks later, on May 26, they returned to play the Bamboo Club in St. Pauls, run by future hapless capsizer and national treasure Tony Bullimore. In 1977, the Bamboo Club burned down in mysterious circumstances, a few days before the Sex Pistols were due to play there.

Faust
Boobs, 11 June 1973

"Where do you want this cement mixer put, guv?"

There are two things that everyone of a certain age knows about Faust. Firstly, they were one of the first signings to Virgin Records, who chucked out odds'n'sods collection *The Faust Tapes* for the price of a single (49p back in 1973). Richard Branson was jolly pleased to find that it shifted 100,000 copies. What he didn't realise was that most purchasers exclaimed "What the fuck's this shit?" and chucked it away. Those of the Julian Cope persuasion (a tiny minority) loved every minute. Branson promptly whisked these most avant-garde of Krautrockers to the UK and set them up in his Manor studio in Oxfordshire to record the follow-up: the full-price *Faust IV*, which nobody bought.

While they were here, Branson also sent his reluctant new signings out on tour, though some of them (notably Hans Joachim Irmler and Rudolf Sosna) refused to go. That leads us to the second thing that everyone of a certain age knows about Faust: their later, proto-industrial stage shows incorporated such novel 'instruments' as angle grinders, pneumatic drills and, famously, a cement mixer.

Mind-bogglingly, their only Bristol show was at Tiffany's regular Wednesday rock night, Boobs. (Some fan sites assert that Faust played the Colston Hall with Henry Cow the following year, but this does not seem to have happened. The Bournemouth Symphony Orchestra were at the Colston on the date stated, and even the most inattentive audience member would have been able to tell the difference.) At Boobs, they were billed, with admirable understatement, as "possibly Germany's most interesting band" and tickets were 60p. The night before, they'd played London's Rainbow Theatre and we can get a flavour of what the Boobs crowd faced from a review of that show by *Melody Maker*'s Karl Dallas.

They played in semi-darkness with four TV sets in each corner of the stage, pointing inwards at the musicians with the sound turned down. At one point the TV sound was turned up to produce what Dallas described as "a random, John Cage-style element to the proceedings". They also chatted to one another over the PA. As for the music: " ...it ranges over the entire spectrum of modern music, taking what it needs from any and all, the resulting mix can very from gentle, acoustic sounds to the hard-driving near-mesmeric rock of *It's a Rainy Day, Sunshine Baby*."

David Bowie
Colston Hall, 18 June 1973

The gruelling Ziggy Stardust tour was on its third UK leg when Bowie pitched up at the Colston Hall for his final performances at the venue. The hard rockin' *Aladdin Sane* had just been released, becoming his first album to top the UK charts. This was preceded by those brilliant hit singles *The Jean Genie* and *Drive-In Saturday*.

Bowie played two shows at the Colston, with no support act, beginning at 6:15pm and 8:30pm. All the tickets sold out within two hours of going on sale three weeks earlier, which is hardly surprising given that he now ranked as the UK's biggest rock star. Anticipating teen hysteria, Colston Hall boss Ray Muir hired 40 bouncers for the two shows.

Naturally, the local press was out in force, though their requests for interviews were thwarted. According to his tour manager, Bowie needed two hours in make-up before the shows so didn't have time to speak to the hacks. He also successfully dodged the hordes of waiting fans by sneaking in through the Hall's rear entrance. To add to the sense of occasion, many punters had raided the dressing-up box, including a party from Cardiff who, the *Western Daily Press* reported, "arrived in glittering outfits with their faces painted in Bowie-style".

The *Post*'s James Belsey was delighted by the sartorial display in a Colston Hall that "quickly became a steambath". Bowie, he wrote, had now fully inhabited the role of superstar. "His face was carefully sculptured by make up and his brow spangled with silver. His clothes changed constantly, from huge billowing Japanese robes to a brief ballet dancer's catsuit. A diamond earring hung from one ear."

Yes, James, but what about the music? "I think he has fared badly since his early successes on the path to becoming an international star."

How so? "... audiences want their music heavy, and Bowie has leapt into heavy rock head first. The audience left numbed by the volume and attack of the music."

The *WDP*'s uncredited reviewer described this show as "the most glittering and outrageous the city has seen".

"Beautiful, and that's the only way to describe him, Bowie was resplendent in rouge and ear-rings throughout the non-stop show," the reviewer swooned. "Strange hooded men ran on from the sides to rip off his costumes to reveal another below. And as the show got on, the outfits became more daring, plunging ever nearer to the point that would have brought the house down."

Ooo-err! At least the music was more to this writer's taste ("like nothing pop music has heard before... the sound balance was perfect and so was the musicianship") But "the most appropriate moment of the evening came when one of the thousands of hysterical fans handed over a bouquet of flowers. A fitting tribute to the man who has been dubbed the queen of rock."

D'ya see what they did there?

Just two weeks later Bowie dramatically retired Ziggy at the Hammersmith Odeon in front of D.A. Pennebaker's cameras, much to the surprise of the Spiders.

Roy Wood, Carl Wayne and Trevor Burton of the incendiary The Move on stage at the Anson Rooms, 1 February 1969. Photograph: Tony Byers

The Who (left to right: Roger Daltrey, John Entwistle, Pete Townshend, Keith Moon) at the Bristol Hippodrome, where they performed 'Tommy', 4 December 1969. Photograph: Bristol Post

Bristol University student Martin Stellman performing with John Peel favourites Principal Edwards Magic Theatre at Pink Floyd's 'happening' in the Victoria Rooms, 2 March 1969. Stellman later forged a successful career in the film industry, most recently collaborating with Idris Elba on the latter's directorial debut, 'Yardie' (2018). Photograph: Tony Byers

Crowds gather for the Bath Festival of Blues at the city's Recreation Ground, 28 June 1969.

Photograph: Tony Byers

The Incredible String Band (left to right: Robin Williamson, Rose Simpson, Mike Heron) hold court backstage at the Colston Hall, 1 March 1969. Photograph: Tony Byers

Keith Emerson rocks out with The Nice at the Anson Rooms, 18 January 1969. Photograph: Tony Byers

A student hands a pint to Brian Davison, drummer with proggers The Nice, at the Anson Rooms, 18 January 1969. No barriers or walls of bouncers back then, kids. Photograph: Tony Byers

Freaking out at the Bath Festival of Blues and Progressive Music, Shepton Mallet Showground, 27-28 June 1970. Photograph: Tony Byers

Promotional posters for the two Bath Festivals of Blues (and Progressive Music).

Steve Winwood with Traffic at the Anson Rooms, 25 April 1970. Photograph: Tony Byers

Frank Zappa and the Mothers of Invention at the Bath Festival of Blues and Progressive Music, Shepton Mallet Showground, 28 June 1970. Photograph: Odile Noel/Lebrecht Music & Arts/Alamy

The beardy Led Zeppelin (left to right: Robert Plant, Jimmy Page, John Paul Jones, John Bonham) at the Bath Festival of Blues and Progressive Music, Shepton Mallet Showground, 28 June 1970.

Photograph: Michael Putland/Getty

Punters gather for the first Pilton Pop Festival, 19 September 1970. Photograph: Bristol Post

"Bearded farmer" Michael Eavis announces plans for a pop festival on his land in 1970.

Photograph: Bristol Post

Top: Bill Harkin's original pyramid stage, constructed on a ley line (obviously) for the 1971 Glastonbury Fayre. Photograph: Bristol Post. Bottom: The original press ad for the first Pilton Pop Festival. Send nice Mr. Eavis a quid and you'll get admission to the festival, free milk, food at 'fair prices' and a show by The Kinks. (Note: offer no longer applies.)

Hippies worship the dawn of the solstice at the Glastonbury Fayre, June 1971. Photograph: Bristol Post.

Top: Nick Mason and Roger Waters of Pink Floyd at the Colston Hall, unveiling what was to become 'Atom Heart Mother' as part of the University of Bristol's Timespace Arts Festival, 7 March 1970. Photograph: Bristol Post. Bottom: The press advertisement for the event.

Mick Jagger and Mick Taylor of The Rolling Stones at the Colston Hall, 9 March 1971.

Photograph: David Redfern/Getty.

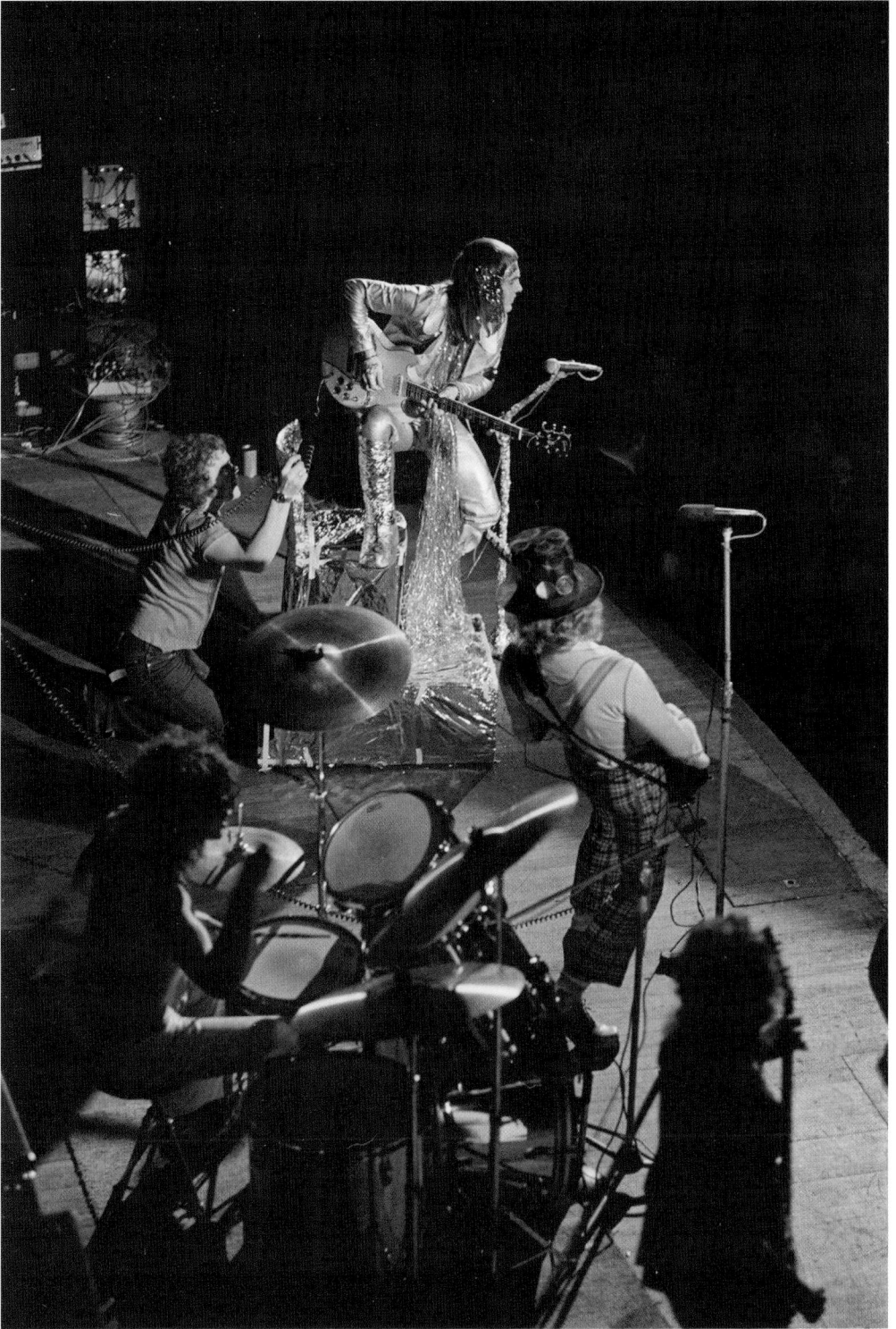

Slade (left to right: Don Powell, unknown roadie, Dave Hill on his throne, Noddy Holder, Jim Lea) at the Colston Hall, 5 December 1972. Photograph: Bristol Post.

Deep Purple (left to right: Jon Lord, Glenn Hughes, David Coverdale) at the Colston Hall, 20 May 1974. Photograph: Bristol Post.

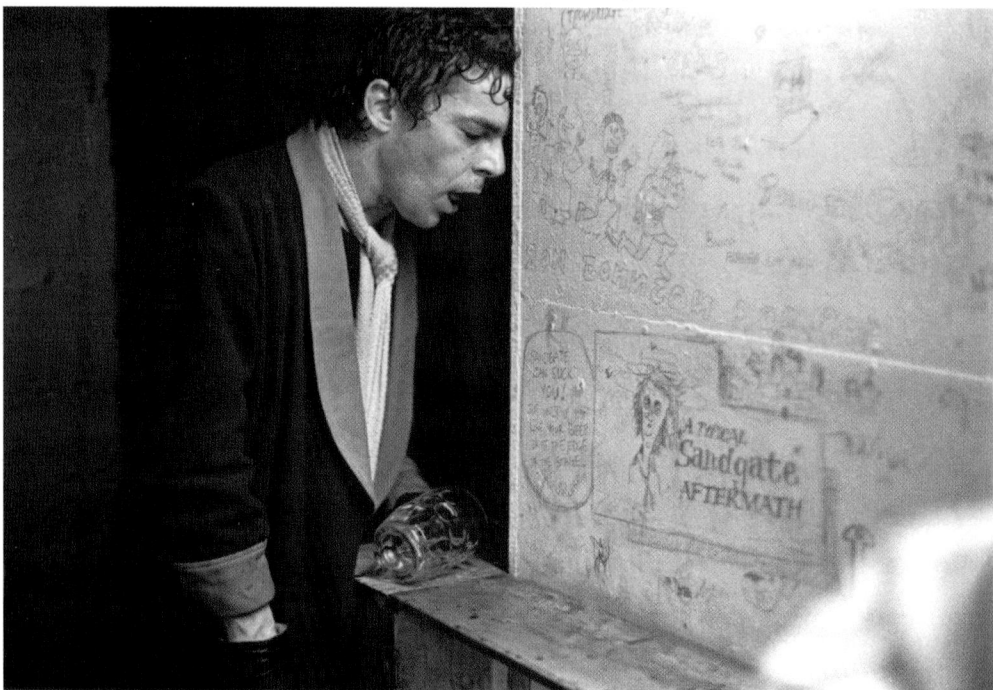

An exhausted Ian Dury after his show with Kilburn and the High Roads at the Granary, 4 July 1974.

Photograph: Alain Le Kim.

Queen (left to right: Freddie Mercury, John Deacon, Brian May, Roger Taylor) at the Colston Hall, 17 November 1975. Photograph: Bristol Post.

Thin Lizzy (left to right: Brian Robertson, Phil Lynott, Scott Gorham) at the Colston Hall, 22 October 1976. Photograph: Erica Echenberg/Getty

Bob Dylan returns to the Colston Hall in 1986, 20 years after his only gig here, to shoot concert scenes for the crappy 'Hearts of Fire' movie. Photograph: Justin Quinnell

JOHNSON HALL YEOVIL
THURS 18th SEPT
FOLLOWING THE SUCCESS OF
'AUTOBAHN'
KRAFTWERK
IN CONCERT WITH
A.J.WEBBER
DOORS OPEN 8PM. LICENSED BAR. ADVANCE·
TICKETS £1·20 FROM ACORN RECORD SHOP, RADIO·
HOUSE, MINNS MUSIC CENTRE. AT DOOR ON NIGHT

Yes, Kraftwerk really did play in Yeovil, with a Bristol folk singer as their support act.

Mahavishnu Orchestra
Colston Hall, 21 June 1973

Back in the early seventies, English guitarist John McLaughlin's intense, ferociously talented, multi-national instrumental jazz/prog/fusion combo seem to have alienated purists of all stripes as they won huge audiences. Bristol got to see the original line-up (McLaughlin, drummer Billy Cobham, keyboard player Jan Hammer, violinist Jerry Goodman and bassist Rick Laird) on the tour to promote their astonishing second album, *Birds of Fire*, which also became their greatest commercial success. Tickets were priced from a mere 50p to £1.25. The promoter was our old friend Freddy Bannister, who subsequently booked the Mahavishnu Orchestra for his very first Knebworth Festival the following year, where they appeared behind Van Morrison and the Doobie Brothers on a bill headlined by the Allman Brothers.

The packed Colston Hall audience included the *Post*'s James Belsey, who was clearly entranced by what he described as "music which shone with much guts and boundless inspiration".

Fascinating trivia fact: acts ranging from Opeth to Bristol's very own Massive Attack have been inspired by the Mahvishnu Orchestra. But the latter went a little overboard with the samples on their *Blue Lines* album. Ralphe Armstrong, who joined Mahavishnu in 1974, sued them for lifting parts of his composition *Planetary Citizen* on *Unfinished Sympathy*. The case was settled out of court, Armstrong reportedly walking away with more loot than he'd ever earned from being in the Mahavishnu Orchestra.

Genesis
Colston Hall, 16 October 1973

The greatest Genesis line-up playing one of their finest albums. The epic *Selling England by the Pound* tour comprised 112 dates over eight months in four legs, visiting Bristol twice as it looped round the globe. The first UK leg sold out well in advance and audiences were rewarded with an epic, theatrical two-hour multi-media show with multiple costume changes for Mr. Gabriel (bat wings for *Watcher of the Skies*, a thug with a stocking on his head for *The Battle of Epping Forest*, Britannia for *Dancing with the Moonlit Knight*, an old geezer mask for *The Musical Box* and, inevitably, a flower for *Supper's Ready*). One of the most dramatic effects came at the end of *Supper's Ready*, when a powerful magnesium flare temporarily blinded the audience while Gabriel whipped off his black cape to reveal a white suit. This probably wouldn't be permitted today under 'elf'n'safety regulations, and before audiences knew what to expect they reportedly dived for cover fearing an IRA attack. (That was a real threat in 1973 as republican paramilitaries had unleashed a bombing campaign on the English mainland. Earlier in the year, these events had forced Hawkwind to withdraw their single *Urban Guerilla*.)

Behind the scenes, Messrs. Rutherford, Hackett, Collins and - especially - Banks were becoming increasingly irritated by their frontman grabbing all the attention with his antics, but this was yet to become a problem given the huge success of the tour. A more immediate challenge was the potential for the complex show to go horribly wrong. Indeed, the first UK date on the tour in Glasgow had to be cancelled for technical reasons. This wouldn't have been so bad, but for the fact that the venue was packed and the support act had finished their set when the announcement was made. Things were going much more smoothly when Genesis arrived at the Colston Hall a week later. An ebullient Gabriel even told punters they were "the best audience of the whole tour".

Reviewing the show for the *Post*, an ecstatic David Newman praised "a set which, for sheer musical and visual tension, eclipsed a *Tarkus* stage performance by the mighty ELP I saw at the Kennington Oval." He also noticed that there were other members of the band apart from Peter Gabriel, even the humble drummer, which must have gone down well. "Although it is unfair to single out a particular highspot, a special mention must surely be deserved by Collins for his efforts in *Supper's Ready* - a number he clearly enjoys."

The *Western Daily Press*'s Michael Macklin agreed: "Superlatives are easy to use but could never convey the sheer power and might of the Genesis concert at the Colston Hall," he wrote. "The concert was musical dynamite, both in presentation and musical ability."

Six days later, Macklin returned to "the most exciting and dynamic live show I have ever seen" in an article praising the increasing theatricality of rock. "When it works, the act is great," Tony Banks told him. "There are teething problems at the moment, but it's early days."

Two weeks after the Colston Hall show, Genesis decamped to

Shepperton Studios where they staged the entire performance and filmed it on 16mm. This has never been officially released, but a bunch of fans managed to get hold of it, painstakingly restored the whole thing in HD, and made it available for free download. You'll find it at the unofficial online Genesis Museum.

The official online Genesis Archive contains a letter to the Colston Hall from promoter Tony Smith requesting the provision of an upright or 6ft Bechstein grand piano tuned to concert pitch. They were charged £5 for this service. Let's hope it didn't have Elton John's footprints all over it (see below).

10cc
Stirling Suite, Yate, 20 October 1973
Arty prog-popsters 10cc had enjoyed hits with *Donna*, *The Dean and I* and the chart-topping *Rubber Bullets*, and were halfway through recording their second album *Sheet Music*, when manager and subsequently convicted paedo Jonathan King dispatched Lol Creme, Kevin Godley, Eric Stewart, Graham Gouldman and touring drummer Paul Burgess off on their first UK tour. Along the way, they pitched up in Yate for the most significant rock show staged in the Stirling Suite. The chice of venue isn't quite as unlikely as it might at first appear. Back in the early seventies, the Yate/Sodbury area had expanded hugely and was a New Town in all but name, with full employment, huge factories and - according to a lurid 1971 *Western Daily Press* expose - a thriving wife-swapping scene. It was also the site of an attempt to create a Southern Soul counterpart to the more famous Northern Soul scene centred on Wigan Casino. Opened in the late sixties, the Stirling Suite was in the shopping centre known locally as Four Seasons Square. Admission was to the 10cc show was £1.25. Exactly one year later (October 20 1974), the band was headlining the Colston Hall.

John Martyn
Anson Rooms, 27 October 1973
The John Martyn sweet spot came after his early folkie period and before those slick divorce albums with Phil Collins (imagine being a fly on the wall at *those* sessions). 1973 was the annus mirabilis of the first white artist to sign to Island Records, bookended by the release of his greatest album,

the Nick Drake-inspired *Solid Air*, in January and the somewhat more jazz-oriented *Inside Out*, which was recorded in July and released in October. He also toured extensively as a duo with Danny Thompson on acoustic upright bass. Their relationship was somewhat fractious, often leading to fisticuffs. Martyn alleged that on one occasion back in March an exasperated Thompson had even nailed him to a hotel room floor so he could go and eat his breakfast in peace.

A little more than a week before this Anson Rooms show, the Beeb broadcast the duo's *Old Grey Whistle Test* session. This gives a flavour of the likely set list (*Make No Mistake, Outside In, May You Never*, the Celtic instrumental *Eibhli Ghail Chiuin Ni Chearbhaill*, etc) and shows Martyn giving it the full echoplex as he explored the outer limits of sounds he could coax from electric and acoustic guitars.

Perhaps continuing to feel sore about being chucked out of the Troubadour all those years ago, he still seemed to have it in for Bristol. In an interview with *Guitar* magazine published in November 1973, Martyn remarked unprompted: "There was a strange thing in the West Country a few years ago – they tried to manufacture Bristol as the centre of something or other. In fact, it was just a load of pretentious young people who caught on to the tail-end of the Davy Graham, Renbourn syndrome and never really got off the train."

Neil Young/The Eagles
Bristol Hippodrome, 4 November 1973
These days, you'd need a second mortgage to buy an Eagles ticket. Back in 1973, you could have caught Don Henley, Glenn Frey, Bernie Leadon and Randy Meisner touring the *Desperado* album at the Bristol Hippodrome. And they weren't even the headline act. That was Neil Young, who was in a particularly ornery mood as he flogged his downbeat, junkie-themed *Tonight's the Night* album.

A *Western Daily Press* preview of this second sold-out show on Young's brief seven-date UK tour had suggested the omens were not good. "When he flies in on Friday afternoon, he will refuse to speak to anyone. He is restricting his public appearances to the stage only... Fans hoping to hear his best-known songs may be disappointed, for he has dropped *Heart of Gold* from his concert repertoire and has threatened to scrap other numbers."

Indeed, Young later wrote that *Heart of Gold* had put him firmly in the middle of the road: "Travelling there soon became a bore, so I headed for the ditch." The ditch, it turned out, was located in the Bristol Hippodrome on this early November evening. Still, at least he made some effort at theatrical presentation, dressing the stage with the fake palm tree that had been swiped from S.I.R. Studios while recording *Tonight's the Night* earlier in 1973.

Here's what Jimmy McDonough has to say about the show in his Young biog, *Shakey*: "Things spun totally out of control at the Bristol Hippodrome, the second English show...The impatient crowd grew more and more rowdy, until Young got so perturbed that he stormed off at the beginning of his acoustic set, vowing not to return. The audience went nuts, and [Elliot] Roberts had to plead with Young to finish the set before a riot started. Young angrily returned to the stage, and by the end of the show - *Tonight's the Night*, of course - the band was going berserk. 'Neil was freaking out on piano, just banging away,' recalled [Nils] Lofgren, 'The intensity was outrageous. All this for an audience that was hoping this was a bad dream and any minute we'd do *Cinnamon Girl*.'

"On a chaotic audience tape you can hear the crowd - what's left of it - getting more and more intense. 'Piss off!' someone screams. Young plays on, unconcerned. 'Elvis has left the arena, ladies and gentlemen,' he drawls, tinkling away at the piano."

Bristol's student newspaper *Bacus* described the performance as a "debacle". Its reviewer remarked that he hoped never to hear any music from Neil Young again.

James Belsey of the *Post* was also present for this one and the paper even sent a photographer along for what turned out to be Young's one and only Bristol show - though they needn't have bothered as he was rocking exactly the same hairy/beardy/shades look as on the cover of the album. Belsey was rather forgiving ("some of the most breathtaking music we're likely to hear in months"), though he did concede that the gig "ended sadly". He also had a different take on the mid-set acoustic section: "His microphones collapsed as the first number began, he took seven minutes chatting and strumming to recover his composure, and when someone finally yelled 'Get on with it', he shoved aside the acoustic guitar and went back to electric."

Belsey was rather taken with the support band, though, remarking that:

"Ever since The Byrds broke up, the Eagles must rate as America's finest country rock band."

The *WDP*'s Michael Macklin agreed, describing the Eagles as "excellent". Oddly, he didn't appear to have noticed any of the later ructions. "Neil Young showed that though time fades away he does not," he enthused.

Santana
Colston Hall, 13 November 1973

The local press were too busy swooning over the Royal Wedding (Anne and Mark, if you're interested) to bother reviewing the first date on Santana's European tour to promote the *Welcome* album. Although they'd played at the Bath Festival in 1970, this was also the first date on the band's first ever full UK tour and proved to be the only time they played in Bristol. To celebrate, they brought along a giant curved mirror as a stage prop.

Welcome was Santana's fifth album and continued the detour into jazz-fusion that began with *Caravanserai*, alienating a proportion of their audience. Alas, Carlos had also just fallen under the spell of guru Sri Chinmoy and had taken to calling himself Devadip, lending a more than usually spiritual air to the proceedings. Most of the original band had left by this stage, with Gregg Rolie and Neal Schon going off to form Journey. That left only drummer Michael Shrieve in an ever-changing line-up, alongside recently recruited keyboard player Tom Coster, who was to become a long-serving Santana sidekick. Shrieve was joined by three percussionists on this tour, so at least there would have been no complaints in the rhythm department. Unpromising though the foregoing may seem, reviews of the tour were mostly positive. As reflected by the career-spanning set list, the band seem to have achieved a balance between latin, rock and jazz styles. And, hey, at least Bristol didn't have to endure Carlos during his full guru-worship/commercial suicide free jazz period that kicked in the following year.

Roy Harper
Colston Hall, 20 November 1973

He never achieved the commercial success of his superstar mates in Pink Floyd and Led Zeppelin, but Roy Harper has maintained his cult status down the generations and is now venerated by the likes of Fleet Foxes and

Joanna Newsom. Back in 1973, busy Roy played the Colston twice. The first show took place on February 11, when he was supported by Judee Sill. In an extraordinary preview by Peter Patston of the *Western Daily Press* ('The Sad Prayer of Roy Harper') he was portrayed as being at death's door. Harper, Patston wrote, was a "sick man" who divides his time "scuttling between his Hampstead hill-top home and St. Thomas's Hospital in Westminster". Not for nothing did his new album *Lifemask* include a side-long version of The Lord's Prayer. He'd recently been diagnosed with the little-known genetic disorder HHT and *Lifemask* was expected to be his swansong. Among those queuing up to sing the ailing songsmith's praises was Ian A. Anderson, who was quoted as saying: "Roy Harper wipes the floor with all your James Taylors, Gordon Lightfoots, Dylans."

By November, Harper had perked up a bit and was working on the more cheerful *Valentine* album that was to be released on Valentine's Day 1974. Appearing solo in the centre of the Colston Hall stage, the lonely looking troubadour had authorised no expense in the lighting depratment. A red spotlight was trained on him from one side and a blue one from the other. Peter Rickwood reviewed the show for the *Post* and, like many a non-initiate, seemed rather nonplussed by the occasionally rambling Roy Harper live experience. "Mr. Harper had a dose of the living room blues, a malaise of self-indulgence, an overdose of telly," he wrote. "He played a little, talked a little, sang a bit more - and so it went." While Rickwood conceded that Harper was a "smashing bloke", his performance left something to be desired: "Apart from a few numbers when everything meshed the mood was either fluffy or strained."

Western Daily Press reviewer David Naylor described Harper as both "very good" and "disturbing". "We walked into the street silent and pensive," he wrote, "liking Roy Harper and concerned about the despair he feels from what goes on around him." Rock'n'roll, eh?

For that authentic 1973 Roy Harper live experience, look no further than the *Flashes from the Archives of Oblivion* album. Frustratingly, this gives no details of where it was recorded, beyond the info that it came from "various concerts in England at one time or another."

Harper somehow survived his serial misfortunes and his belated return to the Colston in October 2013 kicked off with *Highway Blues* from *Lifemask*. It was a brilliant show, albeit with a slightly odd atmosphere. He acknowledged the applause for encore *When an Old Cricketer Leaves the Crease* by saying: "I'd love to do this again, but I'm not going to. Have a nice life…"

It later transpired that he'd been charged with multiple counts of alleged historic child abuse. Those of us who were familiar with *Forbidden Fruit* from *Valentine* feared the worst, as the unwise lyrics might be characterised by the prosecution as a written confession. But in 2015, he was unanimously acquitted by a jury on two counts and the remaining charges were dropped. The case nearly bankrupted him.

Elton John
Colston Hall, 27 November 1973

After naughty young Reg played here in November 1971 on the *Madman Across the Water* tour, he was summoned for a stern dressing down by the starchy suits in charge of the Colston Hall. His crime? Concluding his show by performing a jig on the Hall's grand piano. Fortunately, they stopped short of handing down one of their bans, despite the provocation of the bright red dungarees he was sporting at the time. But when he showed up again in March 1973 on the ironically named *Don't Shoot Me I'm Only the Piano Player* tour, he was issued with a warning before his performance: put one foot on our municipal piano, chummy, and your show will come to a premature end. With security watching him like a hawk, this was an unusually restrained Elton John gig.

By November, he had become established as the world's unlikeliest glam rock star and Eltonmania was in full swing. He was also making a few bob by then and could afford a 'Fuck you!' gesture. That's right: Elton turned up in Bristol for this sold-out show with his own concert grand piano, presumably thumbing his nose at the management as his long-suffering roadies wrangled it into the auditorium. "He can have a bath in it for all we care," sniffed a Colston Hall official.

Elton had just released his finest album, *Goodbye Yellow Brick Road*, which yielded a string of top ten hits, spent eight weeks at the top of the album chart and went on sell 30 million copies. Bristol was the opening night of the UK tour and such was his fame that anything he did was considered newsworthy. So it was that a *Bristol Evening Post* reporter and photographer were backstage at the Colston Hall when Elton was presented with an unusual gift by a trio of Bristol schoolgirls: a three-and-a-half foot long chromium-plated arrow engraved with their names. "We all think he's the greatest, so this time we decided that if we were going to meet him we would have to give him a special present," said 16-year-old Valerie Mallett.

Elton assured the girls that their gift - an oblique reference to *Don't Shoot Me...* - would have pride of place in the sports room of his luxury home.

The *Western Daily Press*'s excited reviewer was full of praise for his "zany antics" and "frantic keyboard playing"

In a somewhat more in-depth review for the *Post*, James Belsey reported that "the biggest thing to hit piano playing since Liberace" initially suffered an attack of first-night nerves at the start of this two-hour show. "But it was obvious he was going to find his level before the end of the show, and he did. He closed down with *Crocodile Rock*, after lengthy diving into new material, and he tore the place apart."

Indeed, the rockier material provoked "scenes of mania as teenage girls hurled themselves at the nearest bit of him to be grabbed."

Imagine their subsequent disappointment.

Mott the Hoople/Queen
Colston Hall, 29 November 1973

David Bowie had famously saved Mott the Hoople's ailing career in 1972 by donating *All the Young Dudes*, which became their biggest hit. By the following year, it was time to stand on their own feet and capitalise on this good fortune with some compositions of their own. They came up trumps with *Mott*, which proved to be their biggest selling album, peaking at number seven in the UK chart. Rock'n'roll hits *Honalochee Boogie* and *All the Way from Memphis* rubbed shoulders with audience favourite *Violence* and achingly sad break-up song *I Wish I Was Your Mother*. By the time the tour reached Bristol, *Roll Away the Stone* had just been released as a single (it would subsequently appear on 1974's *The Hoople* album). But the intra-band ructions that would eventually lead to the departure of Ian Hunter were already being felt, with keyboard player Verden Allen and guitarist Mick Ralphs both leaving the band earlier in the year - the latter forming Bad Company and being replaced by Luther Grosvenor, aka Ariel Bender.

A bonus would have been to catch their support act - a promising young band called Queen. Beause Mott were such hot shit at the time, it cost Queen's management £3,000 to buy them onto this tour. They'd just released *Queen I* and we're still padding out their set with rock'n'roll covers, but the likes of *Keep Yourself Alive*, *Ogre Battle* and *Liar* were already winning over audiences.

The Colston Hall show was certainly better for them than the one that took place two days earlier at Birmingham Town Hall. Legend has it things got off to a poor start when Freddie's cheery "Hello, Birmingham!" elicited a somewhat less cheery "Fuck off, ya cunt!" from a heckler. Alas, things got worse when he slipped and landed on his arse during *Keep Yourself Alive*. He carried on singing, pretending that this was just part of the show. During the final song, *Jailhouse Rock*, a half-eaten hot dog was hurled from the crowd with impressive accuracy, hitting poor Freddie smack in the face and covering him with frankfurter and ketchup.

In one of those reviews that might be described as 'damning with faint praise' (*Dancing to the decibel dudes*), the *Post*'s Peter Rickwood reckoned Mott owed more to Slade than Bowie, which was, apparently, a bad thing. "Mott belted it out like a bunch of navvies knocking down the Bank of England to get at the safe… Brash, heavy, expensive and successful. But, sadly, humourless."

He also noticed the support act, but didn't seem to think much of them either. "It was interesting that Queen, who preceded Mott, got their biggest cheer for a 20-year-old number, *Jailhouse Rock*. But this young and promising group failed to find their form."

In the *Western Daily Press* on the day of the show, David Naylor suggested that "Mott the Hoople had better be good to outshine their touring partners" and described Queen's debut album as "a winner". Oddly, his review, published the following day, didn't even mention Queen. But although he also compared Mott to Slade, he was much more enthusiastic than his *Post* counterpart, writing that "Mott the Hoople drove a crowd of youngsters to near hysteria… The crowd yelled, danced, swayed and hurled paper around the hall as the wild, wailing Mott music drowned them out."

Those hysterical, paper-hurling teens were also treated to a "hypnotic light show" and plenty of theatrics, "like lead singer Ian Hunter's mock outbursts of violence against the other musicians, and the solo he sang to a girl in the front row as he knelt at the front of the stage and held her hands."

Present at this one was future *Bristol Evening Post* Music Editor Richard Jones, who now runs Tangent Books. "Queen were magnificent and Mott were even better," he recalls. "The gig was also notable for the fact that we smuggled in a Watney's Party 7 underneath an RAF greatcoat which exploded over the girls in the row in front of us as we struck it with blunt instruments, having forgotten to bring an opener."

Intriguingly, there's a possibility that half of Queen played in Bristol much earlier than this. Granary Entertainments Manager Al Read remembered designing a poster for Smile - the Led Zep and Yes-influenced Queen precursor trio that included Brian May and Roger Taylor, who were frequently accompanied on tour by young fan Freddie Bulsara. This is quite possible given that they often played in Cornwall, where Taylor lived, during 1969. But there's no record of the Granary show ever having taken place.

Country Joe McDonald
Anson Rooms, 8 December 1973

"Gimme an F . . !" The Fish were long gone by the time Country Joe arrived in town for this Bristol University/Poly Ents co-promotion. But while the Woodstock Nation may have fallen apart, Joe remained committed to radical politics and was frequently way ahead of his time in the causes he supported (he came back to Bristol in 1983 for an animal rights benefit show at the Granary). For this brief UK tour, he brought along the short-lived All Star Band who'd played on his 1972 *Paris Sessions*. Although the songs were written by Joe himself, this has been hailed as one of the first feminist-themed albums and most of the band were women (Tucki Bailey, Dorothy Miskowitz, Anna Rizzo) alongside Peter Albin and David Getz from Big Brother and the Holding Company. In-yer-face anthems like *Sexist Pig* reportedly didn't go down too well with unreconstructed sections of the US audience, who objected loudly to both the politics and the notion of 'chicks' playing rock music. One trusts the Bristol audience was more receptive, especially as student paper *Bacus* published an extensive preview lauding Joe and all his works. That said, 'striptease' was still being advertised as an attraction at the following year's Rag Ball (headlined by Roy Wood's Wizzard, fact fans). Support at the Anson Rooms came from free festival favourites the Global Village Trucking Company and tickets were a princely

99p. Something of a staple on the seventies University circuit, Joe returned to play Bristol Poly on October 4, 1974. This was billed as a co-headliner with Sonja Kristina, who was taking a brief break from fronting Curved Air.

1974

Nixon resigns following the Watergate scandal... Muhammad Ali wallops George Foreman in the Rumble in the Jungle... IRA bombing campaign on UK mainland includes pub bombings in Birmingham and Guildford... Lord Lucan scarpers, never to be seen again... *Bagpuss* makes his TV debut... ABBA's *Waterloo* wins the Eurovision Song Contest. The Allman Brothers headline the first Knebworth festival. Plenty of prog chart toppers, including Rick Wakeman's *Journey to the Centre of the Earth*, *Tales from Topographic Oceans* by Yes and both *Tubular Bells* and *Hergest Ridge* by Mike Oldfield. But the biggest selling album is that MORfest *The Singles 1969-1973* by The Carpenters. And it's not exactly a vintage year for singles, the biggest seller being *Tiger Feet* by Mud... Down at Longleat, filming takes place on *Blue Blood,* a minor horror film adapted from the novel *The Carry-Cot* by the then Lord Bath's son, Alexander Thynn, AKA Viscount Weymouth. The cast includes Oliver Reed (as a satanic butler with a funny accent), Derek Jacobi (as the lord of the manor), and Thynn's missus Anna Gaël (as his lordship's mistress). Reviews of this occult re-working of *The Servant* are unkind. In his definitive *Nightmare Movies*, horror expert Kim Newman calls it "insufferably pretentious"... Bristol and Bath become part of the County of Avon... WD & HO Wills opens Europe's largest fag factory in Hartcliffe... Stephen Merchant is born in Bristol... Terry Wogan opens Bristol's first branch of Primark... *Bristol Evening Post* and *Western Daily Press* move from their old offices on Silver Street to their snazzy new purpose-built fortress of news on Temple Way...While still a member of Genesis, Peter Gabriel moves to the Woolley Valley, just outside Bath. He often goes for walks up nearby Little Solsbury Hill, which proves something of an inspiration. Later, he opens the renowned Real World Studios in Box.

Eno and the Winkies
Colston Hall, 17 February 1974

Yep, that's *Brian* Eno. Beginning in the early 1970s, before he came over all ambient, Eno began recording a quartet of fab post-Roxy Music solo albums that were either prog or 'art-rock', according to taste and/or prejudice. He also undertook his one and only solo tour, in between *Here Come the Warm Jets* and *Taking Tiger Mountain (by Strategy)*. It lasted for just five dates, of which the Colston Hall show was the fourth, before being abandoned. The Winkies were an unlikely bunch of pub rockers who were personally recruited by Eno as his backing band. Their best-known member was Canadian guitarist Philip Rambow, who went on to co-write *There's a Guy Works Down the Chip Shop Swears He's Elvis* with Kirsty MacColl. So what would you have got for your loot if you'd been lucky enough to catch this show on the brief, historic, notoriously ill-fated tour? "The Winkies favoured elaborate stage costumes that owed more to The Sweet than to the greasy denims of Brinsley Schwartz, Eggs Over Easy and their ilk," reveals David Sheppard in *On Some Faraway Beach: The Life and Times of Brian Eno*. "As the Winkies essayed sturdy facsimiles of the *Warm Jets* sound, Eno occupied stage-front - a fabulously gaunt, iridescent figurehead. While most fans would have been content to ogle his rouged cheekbones and gaze in awe as he dabbed at his VCS3 and AKS synthesisers, many were impressed with his surprisingly confident singing," Sheppard continues.

Alas, Brian Peter George St John le Baptiste de la Salle Eno swiftly came to realise that he wasn't really cut out for the business of slogging round the nation's medium-sized venues with a bunch of hairy blokes in a Ford Transit. He also had other things on his mind, principally shagging. "Indeed, he indulged so mercilessly that it was alleged he'd gone through six bedmates within the first thirty-six hours of the tour," reports Sheppard. Having pleasured the eager ladies of Bristol, the priapic preener was overcome with excruciating chest pains during the next show - possibly "thanks to the sheer intensity of his bedroom callisthenics," speculates his biographer - and the entire tour was promptly called off. He later received treatment for a collapsed lung. That was the end of Eno's career as a touring artist. One suspects that his career as a legover artiste continued unabated.

Ronnie Lane's Passing Show
Lambridge House Showground, Bath, March 7 & 8, 1974

One of the great rock follies of the 1970s, Ronnie 'Plonk' Lane's Passing Show must have been quite an experience. Trouble was, few people chose to experience it.

Having tired of the traditional concert hall touring circuit, the diminutive former Small Faces bassist thought it might be a grand and, indeed, romantic idea to travel the land in a Romany caravan convoy, pitching his big top in fields on the outskirts of towns to entertain the locals. In addition to his own band, the rather fine Slim Chance, this old-school travelling circus promised jugglers, fire-eaters, "dancing girls" and what Lane himself described as "the world's unfunniest clowns". For some reason, it was thought that Vivian Stanshall would make the perfect ringmaster. Until, that is, volatile Viv inevitably disgraced himself (among many misdemeanours, he was said to have attempted to defecate in the fiddler's wardrobe) and was "asked to leave" after a few shows.

It wasn't just misbehaving former Bonzos that did for the ramshackle Passing Show. The crappy generators kept breaking down, council permissions proved bureaucratic and hard to come by and advertising was virtually non-existent. "I don't know if magicians formed part of the Passing Show," writes Ronnie's former Small Faces bandmate, drummer Kenney Jones, in his autobiography *Let the Good Times Roll*, "but if they did they performed a brilliant disappearing act. With Ronnie's money!"

The main problem was that nobody turned up. The tour was supposed to continue until the autumn. But bankrupted Ronnie threw in the towel after a run of shows on Newcastle Town Moor in July, which attracted a grand total of 30 paying punters. So what happened when the Passing Show pitched up in a field outside Bath? Local gig goer Jack Gibbons was there for both nights. He recalls tumbleweed blowing through the big top during the first show. But it was packed on the Friday, which must have been a rare evening of good cheer for perennially unlucky Plonk.

Status Quo
Colston Hall, May 6 & 7 1974

Later in their career, it all went a bit *Marguerita Time* for Quo, which rather tarnished their reputation - as Francis Rossi readily acknowledges in his self-lacerating autobiography, *I Talk Too Much*. But back in the 1970s, these lovable merchants of no-nonsense, heads-down mindless boogie were seemingly unstoppable. For those of us who were just kids back then, the depressing sea of shite of *Top of the Pops* was regularly punctuated by the joy of the new Quo single. It always sounded the same as the last Quo single. And it was always brilliant. At least until 1979-ish.

The UK didn't have a regional arena circuit back in the early 1970s. Apart from occasional festival and football ground shows, the only option for bands surfing huge waves of popularity was to play multiple dates at city hall venues outside London (where the Empire Pool, Wembley, and cavernous, acoustically challenging Earls Court were available to those in the big league). So it was that Quo opened their Quo tour to promote the *Quo* album with this two-night stand at the Colston Hall. The double-denim hordes were out in force for what was the Frantic Four's heaviest album. This sustained boogie fury was thanks largely to the songwriting input of bassist Alan Lancaster - who later cited rock's all-time greatest reason for falling out with bandmates. No namby-pamby 'musical differences' for Alan. After Live Aid, he objected that their music was no longer 'manly' enough.

There were no such complaints at this gig, during which Quo delivered a relentless 12-bar barrage powered by their legendary 'Wall of Death' backline. Oddly, the set list included only two songs from the record they'd released three days earlier (album openers *Backwater* and *Just Take Me*). The encore kicked off with *Caroline*. Obviously. Support came from Montrose - hyped as "America's answer to Led Zeppelin" - featuring ace guitarist Ronnie Montrose and the young Sammy Hagar on vocals. The show was opened by funky rockers Snafu, who boasted future Whitesnake guitarist Mickey Moody.

Quo fan Jack Gibbons was there for both nights. "I met some people on the train who only came over for Montrose," he recalls. "The band threw flexi discs over the balcony, so the second night we grabbed a hand full and sold them to schoolfriends for their dinner money. Nice little earner!"

Fellow punter Ian Gregory reports that it was a riotous experience. "If I'm not mistaken, Quo weren't allowed to perform at the Colston Hall for many years after those gigs as there was damage caused to the seating."

Writing in the *Post* ('*An orgy of rock from Quo*'), James Belsey seems to have enjoyed himself. "Sheer exuberant pandemonium reigned supreme for more than an hour as they whipped through tough raunchy rock number after number and even if it was heavy on the eardrums, it was fun."

He was mightily impressed by Ronnie Montrose: "The audience were completely stunned then slowly fascinated by the breadth of his playing and the band won a well-deserved encore - practically unknown for total newcomers opening a big-name show."

Amusingly, Quo became the subject of huge controversy at Bristol University the following year. Not because anyone objected to their amiable brand of foot-stomping 12-bar blues, but because of the £3,000 fee they demanded to headline that year's Rag Ball. This was considered excessive, especially as Exeter University had been offered them for £2,000. What's more, student paper *Bacus* reported that Rag could have had Mud for just £1,000 - though everyone involved in the heated debate conceded that Les Gray's mob were actually a bit crap.

Steely Dan
Hippodrome, 19 May 1974

No, really. Steely Dan did play Bristol on their *Pretzel Logic* tour. It was a close run thing, mind. The UK leg was abandoned after just four shows when Donald Fagen fell ill. As you might expect of the exacting Fagen and Walter Becker, the expanded eight-piece touring band comprised some superlative session musicians, including future Doobie Brothers Jeff 'Skunk' Baxter and old smoothy-chops Michael McDonald - plus Jeff Porcaro, who went on to found Toto with fellow Dan refugee David Paich. Two months after this gig, Steely Dan announced they were to stop touring permanently - which they did until that 1990s reformation. "Al Read and I were both at the Steely Dan gig," recalls Ed Newsom. "It was musicianship of the highest order - we were dead impressed. Later we were to realise how lucky we had been to see them, when Donald Fagen contracted a severe throat infection and the tour was called off."

Bristol Post reviewer Tim Davey described the show as "sensational". "Together the eight of them produced a flawless set, including numbers like *Boston Rag, Do It Again* and *Showbiz Kids*," he wrote. "Becker, on bass, kept out of the limelight, but Fagen was the maestro of the whole gig. Not forgetting two extraordinarily good guitarists - Denny Dias and Jeff Baxter."

Fascinating rock trivia note: technologically-minded Baxter, who subsequently dropped the 'Skunk' but retained the long hair and luxuriant moustache, went on to pursue a parallel career as a military advisor to the US government, specialising in missile defence.

Deep Purple/Elf
Colston Hall, 20 May 1974

The *Burn* album was another commercial and artistic triumph for Deep Purple, but it was all change in the ranks for what's become known as Mark III of the band. Out went Ian Gillan and Roger Glover; in came the phenomenal Glenn Hughes and the unknown David Coverdale (whose previous career highpoint, lest we forget, had been working in a boutique in Redcar). But behind the scenes, Ritchie Blackmore was expressing increasing disgruntlement. He was not happy with the soul and funk influences brought in primarily by Hughes, which he described dismissively as "shoeshine music". And on this tour he was paying particularly close attention to aptly named American support band Elf - the most diminutive act to play the Colston Hall since the Small Faces. After his departure from Purple the following year, he would recruit most of them, including vocalist Ronnie James Dio, for his new band Rainbow.

Ian Gregory was at the back of the stalls. "There was no obvious sign then of the tensions," he recalls. "Purple were on fire. The first half of the set was almost all of Side A (in old money) of the *Burn* album: *Burn, Might Just Take Your Life, Lay Down, Stay Down*. Ritchie teased *Lazy* before they played *Mistreated* and then went on the Mark II stuff. The interplay between Glenn Hughes and David Coverdale was electric. The people around me were in awe."

Western Daily Press reviewer David Naylor may have been one of them, writing that "the loudest rock group in the world produced the ultimate in visual and musical magnificence in the Colston Hall." The packed crowd "was driven to near hysteria . . and they earned the loudest and longest encore I have ever heard."

The *Bristol Post*'s Tim Davey took a very different view. While he'd been rapturous about Purple's performance here in 1971, he now considered that they had "sold out for sound and not quality, which is a sad thing and all the more amazing when they rank as one of the world's top rock bands... The act was tight and the presentation slickly done, with some magnificent stage and lighting effects - but the music was blurred and unimpressive." Nonetheless, he conceded that Purple "could not fail with a sell-out crowd of faithful fans."

There's another local footnote to the story of *Burn*. The album was recorded in Montreux in November 1973, but two months earlier the new line-up of Purple had convened at Clearwell Castle in Gloucestershire for rehearsals. At the time, the Grade II listed castle boasted a recording studio in its basement, which became especially popular with rockers, including Led Zeppelin, Bad Company, Peter Frampton and Queen. Tony Iommi of Black Sabbath claimed to have seen a ghost there while recording *Sabbath Bloody Sabbath*. Eventually, the band managed to spook themselves so much that they refused to stay overnight. "I thought, fucking hell: we got this place in the middle of nowhere so we could start writing, and everybody has terrified themselves that much that they're driving home at night!" writes Iommi in his autobiography, *Iron Man*.

Purple were made of sterner stuff, though that didn't stop notorious prankster Ritchie Blackmore attempting to terrify fellow members of the band - especially the new recruits. "Ritchie got there first," writes Glenn Hughes in his autobiography. "I arrived second and got a good choice of bedroom, unaware that he had wired my room up and put speakers in the closet, and of course at three o'clock in the morning there were these ghostly wails. Blackmore had waited up to do it. When you're in a 700-year-old castle and you hear that, it's pretty spooky."

During their stay, the national and local press were summoned for photo shoots and interviews with the new line-up, attended by servants in mediaeval garb. In the *Western Daily Press* ('Deep Purple, Rock Kings of the Castle'), it was noted that the whole experience proved rather overwhelming for 22-year-old Coverdale: "three weeks ago he was selling shirts".

Clearwell's then-owner Mrs. Alice Yeats remarked that Purple were "very nice people. Very human. They came to wind down and I think they enjoyed their stay. They weren't all that noisy. They were in the basement and it's sound-proof."

The tradition of bands scaring themselves, and one another, at Clearwell Castle continued well into the late seventies. In his autobiography *Where's My Guitar?*, Whitesnake guitarist Bernie Marsden tells of prankstering producer Martin Birch spooking the band by filtering creepy sounds into their headphones while they were recording the *Lovehunter* album in May 1979. He also offers a potential alternative explanation for the supposedly haunted studio's reputation: "I thought it was all in my head and resolved to try not to get quite so stoned."

These days, Clearwell Castle is a wedding venue. Amusingly, the former studio is now known as the Quiet Room.

Steeleye Span/Gryphon
Colston Hall, 24 May 1974

"See: Pitched Battles, Maidens Deflowered, Medieval Exorcism, Miracles... all plus Steeleye Span's bag of musical tricks featuring elves, maidens, sooth sayers, magicians, witches, kings, queens, knaves and jokers."

Really, how could anybody resist? 1974 was folk-rockers Steeleye Span's breakthrough year with the *Now We Are Six* album, which reached number 13 in the chart. Ian Anderson produced, David Bowie played alto sax and folk purists were displeased - as folk purists are wont to be. Theatrical rock was a big deal at the time (Rick Wakeman had recently recorded his *Journey to the Centre of the Earth* production at the Royal Festival Hall), so no one batted an eyelid when Steeleye celebrated their newfound commercial success with a two-night extravaganza at the Royal Albert Hall attended by their unlikeliest fan, Prime Minister Ted Heath. They then took the dressing-up box on the road for a tour that pitched up at the Colston three days later. Demand for tickets was high and this was the first date to sell out.

As the press blurb promised, for the centrepiece of the show Steeleye donned masks and costumes to perform a full ten-minute mummers play. Written by multi-instrumentalist Tim Hart, this has St. George taking on an 'infidel'. Plastic swordplay ensues.

Writing in the *Bristol Evening Post*, David Harrison was overjoyed at what he described as the finest performance Steeleye had ever given in Bristol, which was a great improvement on what he considered to be a rather insipid previous show. "Simple, beautiful and incomparable updated folk music of the highest standard," he rhapsodised. The set list for this "magnificent and unforgettable" show included crowd favourites *Gaudete* and *Thomas the Rhymer*. Even the mumming play delighted Harrison, who noted that it was "hilarious, if less than faithful".

No strangers themselves to the lure of the dressing-up box, splendid mediaeval/Renaissance prog-folkers Gryphon unleashed their krumhorn and bassoon wig-outs in the support slot, having just released their excellent *Midnight Mushrumps* album. David Harrison was impressed with them too, prasing their "inventive and most effective set - highly unusual and thoughtful."

Lou Reed
Colston Hall, 28 May 1974

For those of us who take the minority view that the Velvet Underground were awful, solo Lou Reed was always a more interesting proposition. The VU cool was gone when the bleached blond Reed pitched up in Bristol on this first date of his 1974 UK tour. Now he wanted to rock, which left many of his scenester admirers aghast. They'd disliked his concept album *Berlin*, for which producer Bob Ezrin teamed him up with guitarists Dick Wagner and Steve Hunter, both of whom went on to work with Alice Cooper. And they'd positively loathed the hard-rockin' reworkings of Velvets songs on his recently released live album *Rock'n'Roll Animal*, which the *NME*'s Paul Morley dismissed as "cliché ridden hack heavy metal mutations".

Shades firmly in place throughout, Reed rocked his way through *Sweet Jane, Heroin, I'm Waiting for the Man* and *Walk on the Wild Side*. It was "brash, noisy and violent", reckoned *Post* reviewer James Belsey. "Reed danced like an atomic-powered butterfly," claimed the reviewer, mysteriously, "nice action and heavy with it". Belsey couldn't seem to make up his mind whether or not he enjoyed all this ("… last night's concert may have been one of the most exciting rock concerts I've seen. I'm still not sure.") and reckoned the audience were similarly nonplussed: "The audience weren't sure whether to bop along or listen to the almost suicidal vocals, but Reed gave them their cue with some rocking songs to close the show - notably the classic *White Light/White Heat*."

After the Bristol show, the eventful tour continued to trundle across the UK. Three nights later, there was a riot at the Manchester Free Trade Hall after mercurial Reed refused to play an encore.

Cockney Rebel
Boobs, 24 & 25 June 1974

Motormouth Steve Harley and chums pitched up in Bristol on a tour to promote their second album *The Psychomodo*, just after *Judy Teen* had become a top five single. The shows at club venues had been booked weeks earlier and demand for tickets was huge, so many were moved to larger halls. Consequently, there appears to be some confusion over where and when the Bristol shows took place, but the two-night-stand at Boobs was previewed in the *Western Daily Press* on June 6. They'd definitely played a pre-fame gig at the Anson Rooms on January 12. Despite the band's rocketing popularity, the June tour was reportedly not a happy experience, as a creative gulf had opened up between Harley and his fellow Rebels. Less than a month later, everybody departed apart from drummer Stuart Elliott. Harley promptly got his revenge by writing a new song. Pitched at his erstwhile bandmates, the arrogant, vituperative and hugely catchy *Make Me Smile (Come Up and See Me)* was the first single released as Steve Harley and Cockney Rebel, becoming a massive worldwide hit in 1975. Support on this tour came from a new band named Be-Bop Deluxe, fronted by Bill Nelson. They'd just released their debut album, *Axe Victim*.

Magma
Colston Hall, 27 June 1974

Although the Colston was only one-third full, minds must have been blown at this one and only Bristol show by a band from another planet. No, really: French drummer Christian Vander's bonkers yet brilliant jazz-proggers beamed down from Kobaïa to share their lengthy compositions about impending ecological catastrophe with suitably fried Earthlings. The only act ever to invent their own language (Kobaïan) and genre (Zeuhl) and to have tours promoted by superfan/snooker legend Steve Davis, Magma were hot from the release of arguably their best album, 1973's *Mekanïk Destruktïw Kommandöh*, when they arrived in town with what many would consider the band's key line-up (Jannick Top on bass, Klaus Blasquiz on vocals, Claude Olmos on guitar). Interestingly, the Colston Hall show is one of two UK dates that have subsequently popped up on low-quality bootlegs, so we know that they were previewing the lengthy title track(s) of their upcoming *Köhntarkösz* album in their 30 minute entirety.

One might have expected the mainstream press to respond with ridicule and/or bafflement, but *Bristol Post* reviewer Jennifer Hodgkinson opted to go with the flow, describing the "dramatic" performance as a "good spirited concert that delighted the audience". She conceded that "even if you heard the words you couldn't understand them. However, the fine operatic voice of Klaus Blasquiz rode magnificently through the somewhat lengthy numbers."

Intriguingly, there may have been another Magma gig in Bristol earlier in the year. The student press carries an ad for Magma with Nico (of Velvet Underground fame) at the Anson Rooms on Monday 25 February. No records survive to confirm that the show actually happened, but this isn't as unlikely a pairing as it might appear. Nico seems to have had a thing for European avant-garde acts at the time and there are photographs in existence of her hanging out with the hairy Magma fellas backstage at the 1973 Reading Festival.

These days, Magma are cited as influences by everyone from too-cool-for-school hipster avant-gardists to aging punks (John Lydon), metalheads (Opeth's Mikael Åkerfeldt , Ulver's Kristoffer Rygg) and proggers (Steven Wilson).

Sparks

Victoria Rooms, 3 July 1974

As Edgar Wright's imaginative and enjoyable documentary *The Sparks Brothers* reminds us, Sparks have gone through many incarnations in their long career. But they were a pop-rock act, albeit an extremely quirky one, piggybacking on glam when they came to the Victoria Rooms for their first official gig in Bristol, which was part of the *Kimono My House* tour. *This Town Ain't Big Enough for the Both of Us* had been released in April, reaching number two in the charts thanks to that eccentric *Top of the Pops* performance.

Sally Wild was there, though her memory is a tad hazy. "I seem to remember a lot of screaming girls. Didn't Russell get upset by this and walk off about halfway through as he felt the music was not able to be heard properly over it? They were very much tarred with the 'novelty single' brush at the time."

Little had changed on the screaming teen front when Sparks returned to play the Hippodrome on November 4 on the *Propaganda* tour. "I remember a gang of girls chasing Ron down the alley behind the theatre," recalls gig-goer Chad Gibbons. They were late for the show because they'd been in London recording the mellotron-driven ballad *Never Turn Your Back on Mother Earth* for broadcast on the November 7 edition of *Top of the Pops*. A puncture on the way to Bristol delayed them by a further hour. But the uncredited reviewer for Bristol student paper *Bacus* reckoned this much-delayed performance was far superior to the earlier Victoria Rooms one: "… when the unsmiling moustache was finally poised over the keyboards and the vibrant falsetto spotlighted, they burst into such a rendering of *Talent is an Asset* that the long wait seemed worthwhile. A selection from *Kimono My House* and the new album *Propaganda* followed to thrill the surprisingly large audience."

But had Ron and Russell Mael played here earlier? Tony Benjamin swears they did. Not only that, but he says a group of student friends promoted them at the Granary. The show doesn't appear in any history of Sparks or in the Granary archives, but that doesn't mean Tony is mistaken. In *Talent is an Asset: The Story of Sparks*, Daryl Easlea describes how Sparks were mooching around in London, having relocated from the US late in 1972: "Without a definite touring schedule, the band would be ready at the drop of a hat to go wherever the work took them."

The best guess is that the Granary show would have taken place in December 1972, just after Sparks' first *Old Grey Whistle Test* performance and before they played the Marquee, with Queen opening the show (Sparks famously tried to poach Brian May three years later). Apparently, that *OGWT* appearance prompted a small trickle of bookings at such glamorous venues as the Growling Budgie Club in Ilford. No records of these seem to have been kept.

Tony says nobody turned up for the Granary gig and the only way they could prevent the event becoming a complete embarrassment was by luring in drunken sailors from a nearby pub. "It was a freezing, windswept rainy winter's night and the publicity had been crap," he recalls. "The creepy thing was that Ron, the one with the Chaplin moustache, never came out of character - maybe he really was a stone-faced, impassive automaton. They did a bloody good set, though…"

Kilburn and the High Roads
Granary, 4 July 1974

Kilburn and the High Roads were, of course, the band formed by Ian Dury in 1970. Their music was very much of the 'pub rock' variety, though they were retrospectively claimed as punk pioneers. Their debut album, *Handsome*, was still a year away when they pitched up to play this gig at Bristol's home of rock, for which they were paid a princely £75. Stage front was Peter Blake. Yep, the future Sir Peter Blake, best known for designing The Beatles' *Sgt Pepper's Lonely Hearts Club Band* album cover. Blake had been Dury's art college tutor and had lived just outside Bath since 1969. He was reportedly mesmerised by his former pupil's performance. "Ian would wind people up," he later recalled. "At one point he tried to get the other Kilburns to throw the man who ran the Granary club off the balcony." The show certainly took it out of Dury. There's a great photograph in Will Birch's *Ian Dury: The Definitive Biography* which shows the utterly exhausted future Blockhead leaning against one of the club's pillars just after coming offstage.

Incidentally, this was Kilburn and the High Roads' second gig in Bristol during 1974. Had you been at Bristol University on March 5, you could have seen them for a princely 25p. That's right: Ian Dury plus a couple of subsidised student pints and you'd probably still have change from a quid.

Ashton Court Festival
Ashton Court, 21 July-11 August 1974

According to Richard Jones's lively official history *Court in the Act: Ashton Court Festival, Bristol, 1974-1992*, the identity of the young couple who came up with the idea for what became the city's biggest and longest-running festival is lost in the mists of time. In fact, they were student Tony Mitchell and teacher Bernice Germann of Redland. So let's give them their belated due, even though they dropped out at an early stage and passed the daunting organisational work to idealistic free festival enthusiast, former RAF technician and motorcycle designer Royce Creasey of Greenbank.

Royce and his band of self-styled Hippy Deviants managed to find themselves some respectable attire and trotted along to Bristol City Council to seek permission to hold their festival in Ashton Court Estate on four successive Sundays in July and August 1974, with events scheduled to run from 2-8pm. Naturally, they were astonished when the Parks Committee not only approved their request but also awarded them a grant of a princely £50. That said, Hengrove Labour councillor Bert Adams sounded a note of caution, warning that the festival could prove a magnet for undesirables. "I hope we will not get them swinging on trees and climbing up the front of the house."

A thousand punters turned up on the sunny first day. The blissed-out audience enjoyed themselves, there was no trouble at all, the council was pleased and the local press approved. Remarkably, it only pissed with rain on one of the Sundays, so the inaugural Ashton Court Free Festival was judged to be a great success. A collection and raffle raised £30 towards the costs of the next year's festival.

A diverse cross-section of the Bristol music scene turned up to play, including folkies Steve Tilston and the ubiquitous Fred Wedlock, as well as the Pigsty Hill Light Orchestra. There was also a Strawbs-influenced, all-female trio called Pussy, who were inevitably compared to Fanny (a pioneering American female rock group, m'lud). They were student teachers from Redland whose band name, they informed the press, derived from their "close affinity to cats". Amusingly, the official Ashton Court history drops a comma, conflating the names of two completely different bands to produce the even ruder Pussy Spasm.

But the biggest hit of that first festival were Calne hard rockers Ale House. This short-lived act featured two guitarists: Rod Goodway of Magic Muscle and a young fella named Dave Gregory. Ale House came to nothing, but Gregory went on to join XTC - the biggest band ever to come out of Swindon. In the next millennium, he burnished his prog credentials as a member of Big Big Train.

Ashton Court wasn't just about music. Street theatre played its part too. Bristol's very own bizarre Crystal Theatre of the Saint, led by the eccentric Paul B. Davies, were regular performers at the early festivals. On one memorable occasion, they alarmed the stoned hordes by storming the stage in a military Land Rover. Among the prankstering Crystals were Dave Borthwick and Dave Alex Riddett, whom we met earlier in the entry for Centipede at the Colston Hall. Davies went on to forge a successful career as an actor and writer, whose credits include work for *Spitting Image*, Jasper Carrot, Rory Bremner, Jeremy Hardy and BBC Radio 4's *Midweek*.

Procol Harum
Colston Hall, 20 September 1974

They'd had The Hit way back in 1967, but Procol Harum opted to spend much of their career cultivating US audiences. By 1974, they'd broadened their sound from sixties psychedelia to become one of the great early symphonic rock bands. Non-performing lyricist Keith Reid was in the audience for this Colston Hall show on the *Exotic Birds and Fruit* tour, which came towards the end of the band's classic era. That meant Bristol punters got to hear everything from *A Whiter Shade of Pale* and *Conquistador* to the title tracks from *A Salty Dog* (their prog masterpiece) and *Grand Hotel* - the song that inspired Douglas Adams' *The Restaurant at the End of the Universe*.

The *Bristol Post* sent along reviewer David Lister. If that name seems familiar, it's probably because Lister went on to become one of the founders of the *Independent* newspaper, where he served as Arts Editor, and is now a Fellow of the Royal Society of Arts. Unsurprisingly, his rock reviews for the *Post* were somewhat more perceptive than those of his colleagues. Lister observed that "the band's real weakness is that Gary Brooker's voice is just not a rock voice and too often gets lost" though he concluded that Procol Harum were "one of the musically more sophisticated bands around".

Gong
Colston Hall, 25 September 1974

"Virgin Records and Gull Records, in association with a one-legged water diviner and a very nice pork pie, is proud to present the very unique and unspeakably je ne sais quoi Giant Tour of Great Britian featuring Gong with Isotope". So read the press ads, with rather forced quirkiness.

Gong played the Colston twice in 1974. Their first appearance was on April 30 on the *Angel's Egg* tour with Hatfield and the North. In one of those Virgin Records gimmicks of the time, this was billed as a Crisis Concert, with admission pegged at just 44p. "We planned the concert to coincide with the national power crisis," a rueful Virgin spokeswoman told the press. "That's why it's so cheap. But the country solved its problems quicker than we thought. Anyway, we didn't bother changing the name or the price." Strangely enough, that packed show was reviewed by the *Western Daily Press*, whose uncredited critic was impressed by Gong's "strange mixture of musical styles and weird visual effects... They brought in a wide range of instruments, including human gurgling and howling, to produce their sound, which varied from gentle to frenzied."

The September tour saw Gong (first Daevid Allen iteration) at their most accomplished, leavening the occasionally rather trying Pothead Pixie/ Flying Teapot whimsy with stunning musicianship from the likes of Steve Hillage, Tim Blake, Didier Malherbe and Pierre Moerlen (who would go on to produce a string of albums with the very different French incarnation of Gong). *You*, the concluding and greatest album in the *Radio Gnome Invisible* trilogy, was released the following month. By 1975, it had all gone wrong for Gong, leading to the departure of most of the key players amid acrimony prompted by personality clashes and our old chum 'musical differences'. In 2015, *Rolling Stone* cited *You* as one of the 50 greatest progressive rock albums of all time.

Queen
Colston Hall, 12 November 1974

A year on from their support slot with Mott the Hoople, the ascendant Queen returned to the Colston on the opening leg of their first world tour. *The Sheer Heart Attack* album had just hit the shops and double A-side single *Killer Queen/Flick of the Wrist* was released to accompany the tour. With more loot in the kitty, Queen were also able to splash out on lighting, pyro and costumes. A week after the Colston Hall show, the tour arrived at London's Rainbow Theatre for two nights. Both of these were filmed and a truncated 30 minute version was shown in cinemas. Forty years on, the entire show was released on CD/DVD/blu-ray so we can finally see what it was like.

Andy Fox has been at the centre of Bristol's rock scene for decades as a club/radio DJ and the Bierkeller's Entertainments Manager who was responsible for bringing the likes of Nirvana and Soundgarden to town. Back in 1974, he was a 15-year-old schoolboy up from his home in Devon at the start of what was to become a lifelong obsession with Queen. To this day, he can pinpoint the exact moment at which he was hooked. "We were down the front in the stalls. During *Now I'm Here*, Freddie was on the right-hand side of the stage. He then appeared to jump to the left-hand side before reappearing in the middle. Obviously, I now know that it's a simple illusionist's trick. But to a 15-year-old kid, it was like 'Wow!' I just loved the theatricality of the whole show. Freddie absolutely captivated me.

"The other thing that sticks in my mind is Brian May playing a banjo during *Bring Back That Leroy Brown*. It was only for a few seconds, but I just thought, wow, someone's playing a banjo at a rock concert. How cool is that?"

Golden Earring/Lynyrd Skynyrd
Colston Hall, 29 November 1974

Dutch rockers Golden Earring would be remembered as one-hit wonders with 1973's *Radar Love* had it not been for the fact that they enjoyed a belated second hit nine years later with *Twilight Zone*. Of greater historical significance was the other half of what was billed as "the best double bill this year!!" (the promoter's own exclamation marks). You might be forgiven for thinking that the headliners would be completely outclassed and blown away by their support act. And you'd be right.

1974 was a year of traumatic culture shock for great southern rockers Lynyrd Skynyrd. Before that November, they'd never left the US. Hell, they'd spent very little time outside the Florida bar circuit. Officially this was titled the *Nuthin' Fancy* tour after the difficult third album they'd get around to recording in a brief break from the road the following January. But internally they referred to it as the Torture Tour. *Sweet Home Alabama* from *Second Helping* had been released back in June and Europe was eager for Skynyrd. Skynyrd, by contrast, simply could not wrap their heads around Europeland and responded with an orgy of fightin', drinkin', druggin' and destruction. It was all too much for drummer Bob Burns, who literally went bonkers and left the band. He was replaced by former US Marine Artimus Pyle as soon as they got back to the US. A wedge was also driven between self-styled 'Southern California hippy' guitarist/*Sweet Home Alabama* co-writer Ed King and the street-fighting redneck contingent. King left the band a few weeks after Burns, the final straw being when volatile frontman Ronnie Van Zant had to be sprung from jail just minutes before a gig.

Interestingly, Skynyrd's hippy/redneck dichotomy was exacerbated in later years. Despite his military background, Pyle turned out to be a bigger hippy than King, describing himself as a left-wing liberal, supporting gun control (as indeed did Ronnie Van Zant), and - this was the mindfuck of a clincher - being a vegetarian (check his T-shirt on the cover of the *Street*

Survivors album). Future backing singer Cassie Gaines, meanwhile, was a full-on New Ager.

The Colston Hall show came as tensions were rising but just before the big bust-ups. No set list survives, but it's likely that they opened with *Whiskey Rock-A-Roller* and ended with both *Sweet Home Alabama* and the original three-guitar (King, Allen Collins, Gary Rossington) onslaught of *Freebird*. The *Old Grey Whistle Test* performance that catapulted them to fame in the UK was a year away, so only hardcore fans were present to enjoy this. Steve Street had gone specifically to see Skynyrd. "They obviously didn't disappoint and were clearly going to be a tough act to follow," he recalls. "A fact about this gig that I remember to this day is Golden Earring are the loudest band I've ever heard. Maybe sitting in the stalls underneath the circle intensified the sound but god was it loud. Clearly they were feeling threatened by Skynyrd, and their only response was to turn it up to 11."

Post reviewer David Lister enjoyed Golden Earring's stunts, especially the "startling visual climax in which drummer Cesar Zuiderwijk leapt over his drums, which appeared to explode in a flash behind him." But he found their music "instantly forgettable". He went on to note presciently that they could learn much from Skynyrd, "a group in the Allman Brothers mould who delighted the audience with their unpretentious rock'n'roll. We could be hearing more of them. But somehow I doubt many will remember Golden Earring one year from now."

Tangerine Dream
Colston Hall, 30 November 1974

Although John Peel named *Atem* his album of the year in 1973, for some time back in the eighties it seemed as though Tangerine Dream were being denied their rightful Krautrock kudos - probably because they didn't invent modern dance music or pretend to be robots. But their critical stock has risen again of late as younger audiences discover their work, especially those many film soundtracks. And even the most surly, vigorously expectorating punk rock outfit cannot claim to have achieved the distinction of being excommunicated by the Pope, as TD were just a fortnight after this Colston Hall show.

That came about because the electronic music pioneers played at Reims Cathedral on December 13, supported by Nico, formerly of the

Velvet Underground. So had there been wild scenes of Satanic ritual? Not exactly. Some 7,000 punters turned up to a venue that seated just 2,000. The shameful desecration of this ancient gothic building took place largely because of the lack of toilet facilities. Your imagination can supply the details. Pope Paul VI promptly issued a bull of excommunication, banning Tangerine Dream from performing again in any Catholic church anywhere in the world. The Church of England proved rather more accommodating, however. TD played Coventry Cathedral, Liverpool Cathedral and York Minster the following year.

The Colston Hall show came towards the end of the trio's first tour of the UK. As usual, Edgar Froese, Peter Baumann and Chris Franke performed virtually motionless in semi-darkness, their synthesisers sprouting a spaghetti forest of cables, rather like avant-garde telephone operators. Although they'd just signed to Virgin and released the hugely influential *Phaedra* album, which introduced the rhythmic sequencer-driven sound that was to dominate their music for years to come, there's no point looking for a setlist. TD preferred to use their new toy to drive Mellotron/Moog improvisations.

Reviewing the show for the *Bristol Post*, David Harrison observed that TD have "taken electronic rock presumably to its ultimate, rejecting standard instruments completely for synthesisers and a veritable power plant of special effects. And they produce a weird hypnotic effect which tends to mesmerise the critical faculty."

Although he thought the first half of the show had "long stretches with little happening between the interesting bits," the second set "with some beautiful, captivating light pattern projection was much better, with the group using their machinery to produce a galaxy of weird and wonderful sounds."

Teenage gig-goer Martin Jones was ill-prepared for the solemnity of the occasion, which, Papal disapproval notwithstanding, was rather like being in church. "I liked prog but they were not a band I was particularly fond of, so I didn't have a ticket. As with many gigs that were not sold out, we 'knocked in' using the ticket stub trick or maybe just sneaking past the bouncers (they were not real bouncers and I am sure that they let us be when there were spare seats). Anyway, we were into loud kick-ass rock'n'roll bands, so when TD came on stage we cheered raucously. Most other people there just clapped politely. This just made us worse. We were shouting out stuff and making complete fools of ourselves. It then went silent and one of us would shout again. This went on for a while and the band did not play a note. Then a guy from behind leaned over and said to me, 'They won't play unless you cunts shut up. If you don't like the band, fuck off!' We shut up and only when total silence fell did Tangerine Dream begin to play."

Bad Company
Colston Hall, 8 December 1974

The first act signed to Led Zeppelin's Swansong label, Paul Rodgers and Simon Kirke's hard-rockin' successor to Free was an instant hit on both sides of the Atlantic and one of the most succesful of the era's supergroups. Boasting former Mott the Hoople guitarist Mick Ralphs and ex-King Crimson bassist Boz Burrell, Bad Company had played a low-key debut show at the Colston back in April. But by December, their self-titled debut album had spent 16 weeks on the UK chart, peaking at number three. It also reached number one on the US Billboard chart and was eventually certified five times platinum, becoming one of the biggest selling records of the 1970s.

By the time of this second Colston Hall show, Bad Company were already playing songs from the forthcoming follow-up, *Straight Shooter*, which proved to be just as popular. But the *Post*'s James Belsey was not impressed, despite "the enthusiasm of a packed, adoring audience". He considered the new material to be "short of excitement" and complained that Rodgers "sounded tired and hoarse at times".

After this tour, Bad Company headed off for the enormodomes of the USA. They never played Bristol again, though Rodgers eventually returned as a solo artist.

Rory Gallagher
Colston Hall, 13 December 1974

Choosing a particular Rory Gallagher show is something of a challenge as he toured so frequently and was so consistent. But this was part of the jaunt to promote arguably his best album, *Tattoo*, which came hard on the heels of the magnificent *Irish Tour* live album and accompanying film directed by Tony Palmer, which had been recorded back in January and showcased

Gallagher's band on peak form.

The Colston Hall gig was on the same night as Pink Floyd's last visit to Bristol down the road at the Hippodrome. Writing in the *Post*, David Lister was hugely impressed by Gallagher, describing the two-hour show as 'sensational' and 'explosively exciting'.

"Before the rousing opener *Messin' with the Kid* was finished, the former Taste guitarist from Ulster proved that his many followers, who came in coach loads to Bristol, are right in rating him the top blues-rock guitarist in the world," he enthused.

Gallagher's rider, submitted in writing to the Colston Hall from Derek Block Concert Promotions, reveals that his tastes were as straightforward and unpretentious as his music: "one case Guinness, one case lager, one bottle of Irish whiskey (plus suitable mixers)." Mixers, Rory? You big jessie…

1975

Vietnam War ends with the fall of Saigon... Bill Gates and Paul Allen found Microsoft... It's International Women's Year... Margaret Thatcher becomes leader of the Conservative Party... Birmingham Six are wrongfully sentenced to life in prison... A bungled attempt to shoot Rinka, a dog belonging to male model Norman Scott, leads eventually to the revelation of Scott's relationship with Liberal Party leader Jeremy Thorpe... The world's Jehovah's Witnesses await their prophesied Armageddon (spoiler alert: they're still waiting.)... *Jaws* inaugurates the summer blockbuster... The first series of *Fawlty Towers* is broadcast on BBC2... *The Best of the Stylistics* is the UK's biggest-selling album in a year dominated by old crooners (Englebert Humperdinck, Perry Como, etc). Rock chart-toppers are Status Quo's *On the Level*, Led Zeppelin's *Physical Graffiti*, Pink Floyd's *Wish You Were Here* and Queen's *A Night at the Opera*. The biggest selling single is *Bye, Bye Baby (Baby Goodbye)* by the Bay City Rollers. In November, Queen's *Bohemian Rhapsody* is released. This tops this charts in both 1975 and 1976, eventually becoming the third biggest-selling single of all time... Locally, there's rejoicing in the streets (er, possibly) as the M32 is finally completed... Arnolfini art gallery moves from Queen Square to its new premises at Bush House.

Supertramp
Colston Hall, 9 February 1975
After years of slog, it suddenly all went right for Supertramp with a new line-up and their breakthrough album, *Crime of the Century* (written, lest we forget, in a 17th century Somerset farmhouse). This was sitting at number 10 in the album chart when they arrived in Bristol for their first Colston Hall show and went on to peak at number four on March 9. Early

birds who'd picked up on the slowburning album when it was released could have seen them perform the whole thing at the Victoria Rooms on December, 12, 1974, accompanied by Mike Oldfield's *Tubular Bells* film. Admission? 80p.

The 2014 'deluxe' CD reissue of the album includes a full show from the Hammersmith Odeon, recorded a month after the Colston Hall show. This reveals that they were now bookending the full *Crime of the Century* performance with new songs from the upcoming *Crisis? What Crisis?* album (plus a throwaway cover of 'A' You're Adorable, as popularised by Perry Como). Side A opened the show and Side B closed it.

The *Post*'s James Belsey hailed Supertramp as "one of the fastest rising star acts in the country", noting that "last night they showed what all the fuss was about with a faultlessly staged, intelligent concert which saw them explore their material in depth."

Belsey added that they were joined for a "vocal spot" by both support acts: Gallagher and Lyle and an unknown who opened both this show and the previous one at the Victoria Rooms. Said new face was a fella named Chris de Burgh, who "made a great many new friends with his offbeat and attractive numbers". It would be another eleven years before de Burgh succeeded in making his fortune and tormenting the entire planet with mawkish wedding staple mega-hit *The Lady in Red*.

Supertramp, meanwhile made a swift return to the Colston on the *Crisis? What Crisis?* tour in November 1975, with Joan Armatrading in support.

Robin Trower
Colston Hall, 18 February 1975

With Hendrix long gone, a vacancy had arisen in the languid stoner guitar hero department. Enter former Procol Harum string-bender Robin Trower with a tone to die for and a remarkable repertoire of gurning. Trower was at his commercial peak when his trio arrived in Bristol on the tour to promote the recently released, hugely successful *For Earth Below* album, which became a top five hit in the US.

Trower was by no means a household name but the Hall was packed, which the *Post*'s James Belsey attributed to "that underground jungle drum system which signals the arrival of something interesting."

But he was disappointed by the lack of showmanship on display ("He raised a knee from time to time, flashed the occasional grin to the band and then returned, head down, to concentrate on chords") and couldn't help but be reminded - and remind readers - of the fact that he saw Hendrix himself at this very venue years earlier: "When Hendrix played Colston Hall concerts, he attacked the place like a tiger and chewed the audience to pieces. It's unfair, unrealistic and over-nostalgic to compare last night with seven years ago, but I couldn't help it."

Genesis
Colston Hall, 29 & 30 April 1975

Peter Gabriel's penultimate UK gigs with Genesis came towards the end of the long (104 shows) and reportedly fractious *The Lamb Lies Down on Broadway* Tour. By this time, Gabriel had told his increasingly irritated bandmates he would be leaving at the end of the tour, though no public statement was made. A grand spectacle involving plenty of theatrics, projections and costume changes, this was at the time the most ambitious rock production ever staged. Alas, it was also prone to multiple Spinal Tap-esque technical glitches. With the new double album played in its entirety, the show focused attention almost entirely on Gabriel - hardly surprising given that one of the costumes he sprung from his mammoth dressing-up box was the Bollockman... er, Slipperman, whose inflatable genitalia provoked much mirth. Anyone who was unfamiliar with his sprawling concept had to wait a full 90 minutes before Genesis relented with old favourites *Watcher of the Skies* and *The Musical Box*.

The *Post*'s James Belsey was impressed to see how the Colston stage had been transformed into a theatre, with an arch of steel girders, triple back-projection screens and raised stages for the musicians. Unfortunately, "the heavily-produced event occasionally belly-flopped with a thud," he continued, whereupon the frontman "began boring, irritating monologues, wisecracking with the crowd." That said, when it worked Gabriel was "outstanding in his many roles, arrogant, totally involved, always convincing." The other members of Genesis got a brief mention at the end of his review.

Can

Victoria Rooms, 15 May 1975

Cult reputations don't often fill concert halls. When great German experimentalists Can played the Colston Hall on September 30, 1974, just 300 people turned up. It was, reckoned the *Post*'s James Belsey, "uncomfortably empty", though he praised their "interesting, clever performance". This was, in fact, Can's second show in Bristol. They'd played the Top Rank on March 18, 1973, shortly after the release of *Ege Bamyasi*.

Eight months after the Colston Hall gig, they returned to play the more appropriately sized Victoria Rooms. During this period, they were a band in transition. Damo Suzuki had left and Can continued to tour the mostly instrumental *Soon Over Babaluma* album - their last for United Artists - as a vocalist-free quartet comprising the core team of Michael Karoli, Irmin Schmidt, Jaki Liebezeit and Holger Czukay. Their somewhat more conventional Virgin debut *Landed* was still to come, but for now they were enjoying themselves with lengthy wig-out jams. Many, including the band themselves, reckon this was the apogee of Can. A bootleg from the tour, *Can Live in Stuttgart*, finally got an official release in 2021. Quizzed about the tour by *Mojo*, Schmidt commented: "The only shows I remember are when something very, very special happened. One of the few shows that I remember was in Bristol... One day I might find the tape from that concert." Let's hope so...

Footnote: Can's foremost local fan was the proprietor of Bristol's most snobbish, elitist and unwelcoming independent record shop, Revolver Records on the Triangle, who was notorious for abusing customers for failing to share his niche tastes. Picture, if you will, a more sour and misanthropic *High Fidelity*. As a punter, I enjoyed their Krautrock section and managed to dodge any tongue-lashings. But, perhaps wisely, after buying something obscure on the Ohr or Brain label, I never let on that I was then off to the store's conspicuously more popular and successful rivals, Rayners and Rival Records, to check out the latest metal releases. Eventually, Revolver's customers tired of being berated by the owner and his sneering musky entourage and stopped turning up for their ritual abuse, leading to the shop's slow demise and eventual closure. The whole, frequently hilarious story is told by former Revolver employee Richard King in his book *Original Rockers*.

The Sensational Alex Harvey Band
Colston Hall, 23 May 1975

Like Grace Slick and Bill Wyman, Alex Harvey was part of an older generation than the freaks and hippies who venerated them. All three were born in the 1930s, but Harvey was the oldest. Indeed, he was born in 1935 - the same year as Elvis Presley. His background was in skiffle and Dixieland jazz, and his big beat combo had even supported a very early incarnation of The Beatles. A complicated chap, he adopted a Gorbals hardman persona but was actually a pacifist and registered conscientious objector. By the time of this Colston Hall performance, Harvey was an unimaginably ancient 40-years-old. After a 20 year slog, he was also at the peak of what proved to be his short-lived fame, following SAHB's only top ten album *Tomorrow Belongs To Me* and the novelty hit cover of Tom Jones's *Delilah*.

SAHB were another of those seventies acts that didn't sit easily in any pigeonhole. The band were formerly members of proggers Tear Gas. Their costumes and theatrics saw them lumped in with glam rock, though their often dark lyrical themes sat uneasily alongside the oeuvre of Slade or The Sweet. While SAHB could perform alongside any of the hard rock acts of the era, none of the others drew on vaudeville or musicals like Alex did. And, yes, inevitably some have claimed them as "the original punk band".

They'd played the Colston a year earlier, on May 30, 1974. The hall had been half full on that occasion, but David Naylor of *The Western Daily Press* was suitably impressed by the theatrical production. "It was not only great rock and roll, but a complete visual and musical spectacular," he wrote a few days later, marvelling at Harvey's nimble transition from the tailcoated song'n'dance routine of *Sergeant Fury* to the tenement delinquency of *Hot City Symphony*. "Never seen anything like it. Incredible..." one of the hall's stewards remarked.

A year later, the *Post*'s veteran pop correspondent James Belsey seemed a tad unsettled when he took his usual seat for this second, even more elaborate and now packed-out Colston Hall show. Acknowledging that SAHB were "rapturously received" by their genuinely fanatical following, he found them "confusing [and] uneven".

With disapproval set to stun, Belsey objected that Harvey "did various unpleasant things, like emptying a bottle of beer over his head and writing four-letter words on a blackboard."

Imagine! But the reviewer also conceded that "he sang quite beautifully, with a sharp, tense voice in contrast to his scruffy, stumbling antics."

Teenage gig-goer Martin Jones saw it somewhat differently. "It was a lovely summer night and the temperature in the Hall and the bar was way up. I got served by a barman who probably knew I was under-age but took pity. I drank my pint fairly quickly, but one or two of my mates were struggling with theirs. Then a bouncer appeared and said, 'You lot ain't old enough to drink, get out of here'. My mate protested that he hadn't finished his beer, but this just made the bouncer more angry. He said, 'I'm confiscating these drinks. Get out now or I'll confiscate your tickets.' We soon moved!

"It was a packed house and SAHB were amazing. I remember the Adonis-like Chris Glenn, complete with tights and posing pouch, with his foot up on the monitor. Zal Cleminson played as well as any guitarist I ever saw (and I saw a few good 'uns - Page, Blackmore and more over the years). Alex was a fantastic frontman and raconteur. He had the crowd in the palm of his hand and it was pure rock'n'roll theatre. The one thing I remember him saying in his thick Glaswegian accent was: 'I am going to give you some very good advice for life...' He paused, the suspense growing. 'Whatever you do, don't piss in your water supply.' It may not sound very funny now. But at the time, to a tipsy teenager high on rock'n'roll and fun, it was great."

Harvey and his band made an equally strong impression on fellow teen Peter Nunez. "I first heard SAHB on Alan Freeman's show in summer 1974 – he played *The Faith Healer* from their second album *Next* and it just knocked me out.

"Some friends from school also picked up on them and when they announced a UK tour we sent off for tickets at the Colston Hall. The gig was the day before the Hammersmith Odeon show that was captured on the *Live* album released later that summer.

"The lights dimmed, the fanfare started, and Alex strode onto the stage, alone, before introducing his band. Gradually the other members joined him, whilst the throbbing intro of *The Faith Healer* went on behind them.

"Alex prowled around the stage during the set – he was so captivating that you couldn't keep your eyes off him - while Chris Glenn and Zal Cleminson flanked him in their glam costumes. I suppose SAHB were sort of a Scottish version of Slade – glam but a bit 'rough around the edges'; of course, they supported Slade earlier in their career.

"This was only the second gig I ever attended and it was fantastic. Alex held a large book open with his foot on the monitor to recite the story whilst they played *The Tale of the Giant Stoneater*. And of course, *Delilah* was marvellous, with Chris and Zal's routine during the instrumental section. Finally, during *Framed*, Alex burst through a polystyrene wall before asking 'Do you believe me? I was Framed!'

"Many years ago I acquired a bootleg CD of the whole Hammersmith Odeon show (the live album only covers about half the set) and I was able to see what other songs would have been played in Bristol.

"In May 1976 I saw them again at the Colston Hall – they played two shows and I went to both nights. The support act, Pat Travers, was also really good.

"Unfortunately, the second night was marred somewhat by a friend, who was a little worse the wear for drink and started shouting throughout Zal's mime routine, and basically ruined it. Something else I recall was that Hugh McKenna came down to the stalls where I was seated to scrounge cigarettes from the punters."

Less than six years later, Alex Harvey was dead. His commercial decline was as abrupt as his rise to stardom had been achingly slow. By 1980, he was fronting the jazzy New Band, who struggled to pull more than a few hundred punters to their shows, one of which was at Leyhill open prison in South Gloucestershire. In John Neil Munro's biography *The Sensational Alex Harvey*, New Band guitarist Matthew Cang describes the show as "… different. Songs like *Framed* and *Delilah* have a different intensity in front of an audience like that - you did feel that some members of the audience had a certain empathy with the subject matter!"

The Leyhill gig was not exactly one to stand alongside Johnny Cash at San Quentin in music legend. It had been organised by Ray Conn, a friend and contemporary of Harvey from the 1960s Glasgow music scene. "We came inside the prison gates in a van and the governor came out and said 'where is this famous pop star?'" he told Munro. "So we opened the van door and… Alex was actually drunk and unconscious in the back of the van… We said, 'Oh, he's just asleep' - but in fact he was totally out of it."

I had the misfortune to see what may have been his last UK show, which took place at the Granary on November 5, 1981. He came on at

1am, two hours late, looking like death warmed up, and shambled his way through a mostly half-hearted set - though things were livened up a bit by his deranged, axe-wielding drummer. He died on the road in Belgium on February 4, 1982, one day before his 47th birthday.

Neil Innes with Fatso
Granary, 17 June 1975

In his later years, former Bonzo and semi-detached Python Neil Innes became a stalwart of Bristol's great Slapstick Festival of silent and classic comedy. Back in 1975, he supplied the music for Eric Idle's BBC2 comedy series *Rutland Weekend Television* with his band Fatso (which included guitarist Billy Bremner and drummer John Halsey). Their most successful sketch spawned that brilliant Beatles parody act The Rutles, whose 1978 mockumentary *All You Need is Cash* remains rock satire of a Spinal Tap standard. This rare local show was promoted by *Let It Rock* magazine. Al Read recalled that Innes brought the house down with his spot-on send-ups of The Shadows, Roy Orbison, Bob Dylan and others. "They were simply brilliant," he enthused.

Wings
Hippodrome, 10 September 1975

Paul McCartney's post-Fabs venture was slow to get off the ground. They played the Hippodrome twice. The first performance was on May 11, 1973, which was also the debut show on the first major Wings tour to accompany the release of the fairly uninspiring *Red Rose Speedway* album. "If all Bristol doesn't go out and buy this LP, we will both cry," Linda McCartney told the *Western Daily Press*'s Michael Bath in a brief interview.

The show "did not see a return to the Beatlemania of ten years ago," noted Bath. Part of the problem was the Hippodrome security. When McCartney urged the seated audience to "Get rockin'!" they were quick to comply. "Several tried to get into the aisles and were moved back by a man who didn't seem nearly as nice as Mr. McCartney." Still, Wings did debut a new song that wouldn't be released until June of that year: the James Bond theme *Live and Let Die*.

By 1975 they'd got their shit together with the release of the *Venus and Mars* album. McCartney now insisted upon Wings being promoted as a band in their own right and was eager to play down his role as the main attraction. It is not recorded what he made of the giant sign on the front of the Hippdrome advertising this show as 'Paul McCartney and Wings'.

Ever since the dissolution of The Beatles, he'd also been reluctant to play his former band's songs. But he relented for this epic *Wings Over the World* tour which stretched into 1976. And since the two-hour Hippodrome gig was the second show on that tour, Bristol audiences were among the first to hear Beatles songs performed live by McCartney for the first time in nearly a decade - without all the screaming. The set list included *Yesterday*, *Blackbird* and *The Long and Winding Road*.

Wings and Beatles fan Ian Gregory was in heaven. "There I was in the middle of the Hippodrome - a wee 20-year-old listening to Paul McCartney belt out *Lady Madonna*," he marvels. "My word, *Band On The Run* was a hell of an album too."

The *Post*'s James Belsey reported that the best music came from the new album and "McCartney himself was faultless". What's more, "Linda McCartney's keyboards were proof that she's not just a pretty face riding on her old man's bandwagon" although her vocals were, he conceded diplomatically, "slightly inaccurate at times".

Western Daily Press critic Leonie Walther praised "old pro" McCartney for structuring his show beautifully, "kicking off with the rockers, sliding into quieter acoustic songs like *Bluebird* and *Long and Winding Road*, and keeping the audience with him all the way".

In *Man on the Run: Paul McCartney in the 1970s*, Tom Doyle records that Wings stayed overnight in Bristol after the show and gave a press conference at the Post House Hotel the following morning before heading off to the next date in Cardiff. Most of the questions were the usual boring ones about when The Beatles were going to get back together. But when one cheeky hack enquired "Just what keeps you going?" the former lovable moptop replied "Drugs!" Two months later, he was refused entry to Japan following an earlier marijuana conviction.

In 1980, the concert film *Rockshow* was finally unveiled in cinemas, becoming the first feature released by Miramax - the company founded by, oh dear, Bob and Harvey Weinstein. This had been shot in several enormodomes on the American leg of the tour in 1976, but the set list hadn't changed much so it's a fairly good representation of what the Bristol audience would have seen - albeit on a much more intimate scale. This being the post-punk era, UK reviews were naturally sniffy ("An interminable experience" - *Time Out*), but the film was more warmly received when it was remastered for a blu-ray release in 2013, accompanied by a BAFTA premiere.

Kraftwerk
Johnson Hall, Yeovil, 18 September 1975

That's right: Kraftwerk really did play in Yeovil. The tour reached the Colston Hall four days later on September 22. But it would have been much more fun to see those crazy Teutonic robots in Wurzel Country. Admission was £1.20. The Johnson Hall, in case you're wondering, was intended to bring culture to Yeovil. But the brand spanking new £266,000 venue got off to a rocky start when it opened in July 1974 on account of the fact that Yeovil didn't seem terribly interested in culture. Indeed, the first four events lost more than £1,000 because of low attendance. It was later renamed the Octagon Theatre and is now rather more successful.

Kraftwerk in Yeovil not surreal enough for you? Consider this. You're promoting the first UK tour by one of the great pioneers of electronic music and you need a support act. Who ya gonna call? Why, a folk singer from Bristol, obviously. Singer/songwriter Adrienne Webber, who went by the stage name A.J. Webber, started her career at the city's Troubadour Club but soon acquired a reputation as an artist who could appeal to any audience. She supported acts as diverse as Frank Zappa, Neil Young and Moody Blues offshoot the Blue Jays. A.J. also attracted some top-notch musical collaborators with whom she toured and recorded, notably two members of Heads Hands & Feet: Grammy winner Albert Lee (later of Emmylou Harris's Hot Band) and Chas Hodges (later of Chas and Dave).

"I got a lot of work over my career with a lot of big names, mainly as I could have a good banter with the audience and make them laugh," she says. "I also had a couple of funny songs up my sleeve. Most importantly, I only needed two microphones which meant there were no big changeovers for the road crew."

She can't recall exactly how she landed the 15 date Kraftwerk tour, but agrees "it does seem like an unlikely pairing and I do remember they were difficult, maybe arrogant. But that could have been the language barrier."

Fortunately, they warmed to each other as the tour went on. But her favourite touring partner in the 1970s was Uncle Frank. "Frank Zappa was an unlikely pairing too, but we got on really well and I remember going down very well with his audiences."

Do Kraftwerk really belong in this book? Well, yes they do. Decades would pass before they were claimed as the godfathers of dance music. Back in the 1970s, they were classed as Krautrock, which, to most punters, was simply a German outpost of prog. Hell, their self-titled debut album (of which I have a first pressing on vinyl, now worth a small fortune) was full-on experimental rock featuring organ, flute and violin. Despite being hated by those self-styled tastemakers at the *NME* ("For simple minds only"), 1974's international hit *Autobahn* provided their breakthrough. Founders Ralf Hütter and Florian Schneider had been joined by percussionist Wolfgang Flür to showcase their new signature streamlined sound, though this still featured organic instruments (the following year's *Radio-Activity* was their first full electronic album).

Astonishingly, despite *Autobahn*'s huge success, Vertigo declined to stump up the cash for Kraftwerk's first full international tour, so they financed it themselves. The set they played throughout the UK leg drew heavily on the band's three previous albums, including *Ruck-Zuck*, whose rockiness might surprise younger fans. An epic rendition of *Autobahn* itself was, of course, the centrepiece - the album from which it came having peaked at number four in the UK back in July. The expanded quartet (with additional musician Karl Bartos) were already experimenting with what was to become their robot image. But, as Wolfgang Flür reveals in his entertaining autobiography *I Was a Robot*, the technology wasn't always playing along. On the first night of this UK tour, his illuminated 'percussion chamber' failed completely and the Liverpool audience was greeted by the sight of Flür waving his arms furiously in complete silence.

Trivia note: Consult all-knowing Mr. Google and you'll find someone is selling designer T-shirts featuring a stylish poster design for Kraftwerk's Yeovil gig. Be warned that these are eye-wateringly expensive.

Utopia
Colston Hall, 3 October 1975

Much to the disappointment of fans of his early solo work, such as the great *Something/Anything?* and *The Ballad of Todd Rundgren* albums, Todd Rundgren tended to ignore this side of the pond in the early 1970s. As fish-out-of-water in-house producer and star artist at Bearsville Records, he was busy infuriating label boss Albert Grossman with his genre-hopping career self-sabotage.

So when he pitched up in 1975 for his first full UK tour with Utopia, those who preferred Rundgren's delicate, sensitive balladeering were aghast to find that their hero had reacted against pigeonholing by going Full Prog, with scintillating, complex, critic-infuriating music influenced by Zappa, Yes and the jazz-fusion of the Mahavishnu Orchestra. This Colston Hall show was Utopia's second European date and came just six days before the Hammersmith Odeon performance that was broadcast by the BBC and subsequently released on CD. The slimmed-down line-up playing those convoluted, bombastic epics on this tour included Roger Powell and Willie Wilcox, who would remain with Utopia for much of their career. Their set included a mix of band compositions and solo Rundgren staples, running for more than two-and-a-half hours - including three encores. *Bristol Post* reviewer Nigel Bunyan pronounced himself exhilarated and exhausted. "High energy would be an understatement for their frenzied attack," he swooned. "Only for *The Wheel*, for me their best song, was the pace allowed to slacken. But it was soon back to the synthesisers and searing guitar work of Rundgren, who acted his way through most of the vocal parts."

Fascinating trivia fact: one of Utopia's two backing singers on this tour was future soul star Luther Vandross.

Fascinating trivia fact 2: Many bands claim to have inspired *This Is Spinal Tap*. In fact, the primary inspiration was Saxon. But one of the funniest scenes in the film was taken from Utopia's first US tour in 1973. In Philadelphia, rhythm guitarist Jean-Yves Labat found himself trapped inside a perspex geodisc dome that stubbornly refused to open.

Queen

Colston Hall, 17 & 18 November 1975

By 1975, the nation's sub-editors were unable to resist the temptation of the 'reign supreme' cliché as Queen were, quite literally, in their pomp. The band's third and final visit to the Colston Hall was a two-night stand that permitted them to party in between. And they had much to party about. These were the third and fourth dates on the sold-out *A Night at the Opera* tour (tickets from £2.50 to £1), the album was at the top of the chart and *Bohemian Rhapsody* had taken up residence at number one in the singles chart, where it would remain for nine weeks - becoming the Christmas number one and selling more than a million copies. Naturally, the inkies were out in force for these two Bristol shows.

The *NME*'s Julie Webb joined the band the previous night in Coventry and travelled to Bristol in their luxury coach, of which she marvelled: "It has its own loo, changing room (with bed) and tables (with lamps)". She was mostly taken with Steven, the band's twentysomething full-time on-the-road masseur, whose previous clients included Rudolf Nureyev and who came personally recommended ("Well you can imagine what sort of replies they'd get advertising for a masseur for Queen"). One of Steven's many tasks is removing the thorns from the roses that Freddie throws to his adoring audience during the encore of *Big Spender*. Another is finding a new sash for the singer's kimono after a wardrobe mishap the previous night ("I mean, you try scoring a silk sash in downtown Bristol").

As for the performance, she reports that the band are more polished than in Coventry. The rock section of *Bohemian Rhapsody* opens the show, "with Mercury in his disgusting cat suit reaching every high note possible and launching into the 'Scaramouche, thunderbolts and lightning' part. Brian May comes into his own during *Son and Daughter* with a fine six-minute guitar solo. But the real new Queen highlight is *The Prophet Song*, where they feature vocal echo repeats."

Over in *Record Mirror and Disc* ('It's Bristol Queen, Cheri!'), Ray Fox-Cumming finds Freddie in a slightly disconsolate mood at the post-show backstage party, where he sits alone in a separate room.

He moans that lack of time for preparation means the show is under-rehearsed. "The show is thrown together, my dears," he says theatrically. "*Thrown together.*" *The Prophet Song*, in particular, he insists, is "but a mere skeleton of what it should be." Thrown together it might have been, reckons the reporter but "it was done so marvellously well. Visually it was stunning, largely because it was the best lit concert I have ever seen." There were plenty of effects including "magnesium flares", a "twirling prism" and "enough dry ice to engulf three-quarters of the auditorium and obliterate the band completely". ("Well, it's not really worked yet, that I will say," concedes Brian May in the *NME* of this dry ice overkill.)

Nonetheless, Freddie gives it his all during the show "…amid frequent enquiries as to the well-being of 'my lovelies in the balcony'."

Locally, even the *Post*'s James Belsey - no fan of heavy rock he - seems to have almost enjoyed himself despite complaining about the volume, as usual. The performance was, Belsey wrote, "beautifully staged" with "delicious light changes and glinting with electronic effects", though he sniffed that "the slower stuff has never been their chosen style". His conclusion? "It's a flash show, but heavy rock bands rarely come as well-packaged as Queen. They deserved the massive reception they won."

Queen convert Andy Fox was there for both shows, with a front row seat for one of them. "It's true about the dry ice. They used to pump it out from everywhere during the closing song *In the Lap of the Gods*, so the band would disappear at the end. The trouble was that everybody else disappeared too. But the whole show was up a level. I can remember everything, from the Kenny Everett intro to what I was wearing on the night. That tour changed my life."

Queen returned to Bristol one last time the following year for two shows at the Hippodrome on the *A Day at the Races* tour (May 23 & 24). In his book *Pride, Pop and Politics*, Darryl W. Bullock reveals that the still semi-closeted singer dragged the rest of Queen to the Oasis gay club on Park Row for an aftershow party, where "his nervous bandmates occupied a corner booth while Freddie took to the dancefloor."

Gentle Giant
Colston Hall, 11 December 1975

Things were looking (slightly) up for the most under-rated band of all time in 1975. These great British proggers were such talented multi-instrumentalists that they could tour with just about anyone. So that's exactly what they'd been doing in Europe and the US. Although their cerebral brand of progressive rock had proven somewhat, ahem, unpopular with Black Sabbath audiences in the early years, GG were now playing alongside everyone from Frank Zappa to Return to Forever and Yes to Ted Nugent and Kiss. At one time, they even had Dr. Feelgood out as their support act. The band had just signed to Chrysalis and the brilliant *Free Hand* became their most commercially successful release (though this isn't saying much - number 48 in the US, didn't chart in the UK) as they began the tour in which they finally got to headline at the Colston Hall. In retrospect, however, this was GG's last great album, as they were about to embark upon a slow creative decline. But the subsequent *Playing the Fool* live album, recorded in 1976, underlines that they really could pull off everything in concert, from those intricate vocals to the delicate mediaeval instrumentals. In 2021, *Free Hand* was superbly remixed in Dolby Atmos by Steven Wilson and has gone on to win over another small army of fans who weren't even born when the album was first released.

1976

Apple is founded by Steve Jobs and Steve Wozniak... A lengthy heat wave and drought hits the UK. Prime Minister James Callaghan responds to the crisis by appointing Dennis Howell 'Minister for Drought'. Torrential downpours follow days later... *The Muppet Show* premieres on ITV... The Sex Pistols get sweary on Bill Grundy's TV show... Some insist that 1976 is the worst-ever year for music in the UK. Perhaps not coincidentally, it's also the year in which The Wurzels top the charts with *The Combine Harvester (Brand New Key)*. This is to be the west country's greatest pop success until those trip-hoppers come along. The Brotherhood of Man win the Eurovision Song Contest with *Save Your Kisses For Me*, which becomes the year's biggest selling single. The album charts are stuffed with TV-advertised compilations (Slim Whitman, Glen Campbell, The Beach Boys, etc). Great rock releases include *Rainbow Rising* and Aerosmith's *Rocks* - plus, of course, an album that goes on to become one of the biggest sellers of all time: *Hotel California* by the Eagles... A pissed Eric Clapton calls on his Birmingham Odeon audience to support Enoch Powell and succeeds in inspiring the foundation of Rock Against Racism... David Sproxton and Peter Lord move to Bristol, where they establish Aardman Animations and unleash their first creation: Morph... Bristol City win promotion to the First Division.

Electric Light Orchestra
Colston Hall, 15 June 1976

Regular visitors to the Colston in the early 1970s, ELO were a year away from that huge commercial breakthrough with *Out of the Blue* when they returned on the *Face the Music* tour to play their final show in Bristol. They'd just come back from a lengthy, triumphant romp around arenas in the US, where the album had made the top ten. Bristol was the first UK date, but the air of eager anticipation was punctured somewhat when support act the Steve Gibbons Band managed to blow the Colston Hall's fuses. The grumbling janitor was dispatched into the bowels of the building and eventually sorted the problem in time for Jeff Lynne and chums to play their headlining set.

The *Post*'s James Belsey was impressed, describing the show as a "well-conceived exploration of the dynamics which can spark between amplified strings and electric rock, always interesting, often moving."

Bob Marley and the Wailers
Colston Hall, 23 June 1976

From today's perspective, it's easy to make the mistake of assuming that Bob Marley had always been a global icon. In fact, despite all the critical acclaim and Chris Blackwell's cunning plan to make reggae palatable to white audiences by incorporating rock guitar, Marley's records sold poorly in his lifetime. *Catch a Fire* shifted just 14,000 copies on release in the UK. His biggest seller, *Exodus*, managed only 189,000. Marley's commercial breakthrough came in 1984, three years after his death, with the brilliantly marketed, multi-platinum selling compilation album *Legend*, which made him a, you know, legend.

The 1976 album *Rastaman Vibration* provided a breakthrough of sorts. Marley's first release to feature synthesizers, it became his debut top ten hit in the US Billboard chart (number 15 in the UK). Two months after its release, he played his final show in Bristol. The Hall Formerly Known as Colston likes to trumpet this gig, as it chimes so well with the current management's eagerness to move the conversation on from slavery and celebrate the big group hug of diversity and inclusivity. But on this hot and sweaty midsummer night there was a heavy police presence and an atmosphere that *Bristol Post* reviewer James Belsey described as "edgy". The official explanation was that significant numbers of Bob's fans declined to pay for tickets to see him. But you may wish to speculate that Hall officials were unnerved by such a large number of black youths turning up for a show in a year when racial tensions were rising, mainly because of the controversial 'sus' law. Two months later, these exploded with a riot at the Notting Hill Carnival.

Original Wailers Peter Tosh and and Bunny Wailer were long gone by this point, with Marley's band now including Earl 'Chinna' Smith on guitar alongside the long-serving rhythm section of siblings Aston (bass) and Carlton Barrett (drums). They certainly played a great set, including *No Woman, No Cry* and *I Shot the Sheriff*, while set closer *Get Up Stand Up* had the desired effect of bringing the audience to their feet. "He's an extraordinary man who has crystallised the growing talent of West Indian music," noted skanking Mr. Belsey. Although he seemed to struggle a little with the "monotonous rhythms of reggae", Belsey described Marley's voice as having a "neat touch of furious strangulation" and hailed the songs as "all beauties".

AC/DC/Motorhead
Bath Pavilion, 18 August 1976

On their first tour of the UK, AC/DC experienced something of a culture shock when they found themselves lumped in with punk because of their high-energy shows. In fact, Chuck Berry-worshipping Angus and Malcolm Young despised punk and loathed the bands' ineptitude. In his book *AC/DC: For Those About To Rock*, Paul Elliott quotes Malcolm as saying: "When we first came to England in '76, the record company wanted to market us as a punk band. We told them to fuck off!… You'd get these punks having a go at us, and Bon would go: 'You shut up or I'll rip that fucking safety pin out of your fucking nose!'"

AC/DC staples like *The Jack*, *High Voltage* and the bagpipetastic *It's a Long Way to the Top (If You Wanna Rock'n'Roll)* were already in their set by the time they arrived in Bath on a break from their London Marquee residency. This short tour was promoted by music weekly *Sounds*, under the *Lock Up Your Daughters* banner. In fact, few daughters - or anyone else for that matter - turned up, as the regional shows pulled an average of around a hundred people. Three months later, AC/DC would be headlining the Colston Hall (see below). Support at the Pavilion came from the classic line-up of Motorhead, playing "maybe our fifth gig" according to guitarist 'Fast' Eddie Clarke. "Motorhead's equipment wasn't great and the gig was in a fucking tin hut, so we sounded awful," he told *Classic Rock* magazine in January 2018.

Local gig-goer Jack Gibbons was there and remembers the whole show vividly. "Attendance-wise there were at best 70 people. The PA crashed part way through Motorhead's set, leaving Phil Taylor to play a drum solo. While AC/DC were playing, there was a young lady in a schoolgirl hockey outfit and a 'Lock Up Your Daughters' headband who took great pleasure in poking Bon Scott between the legs with her hockey stick as he was having a feel while still singing. During the walkabout, some guy went up and kissed Angus's bum. Then someone else knocked a pint over on the stage, so the band didn't return." He later caught AC/DC in Yeovil and Swindon. "My mates also went to see them at Van Dykes in Plymouth, but I thought that was too far to see an unknown band we would probably forget about."

Rainbow

Hippodrome, 31 August 1976

For those who liked to rock, 1976 was the year of Ritchie Blackmore's Rainbow. This sold-out, widely bootlegged Bristol Hippodrome gig was the band's very first UK show. Having recruited former Deep Purple support act Elf to back him on the first Rainbow album, Blackmore fired everyone except singer Ronnie James Dio. He then hired Jimmy Bain (bass), Cozy Powell (drums) and Tony Carey (keyboards) for the follow-up, *Rainbow Rising* - Rainbow's masterpiece, which was released in May 1976 and became a huge influence on a generation of musicians.

Alas, the "somewhat appalling" Rainbow put veteran *Bristol Post* reviewer James Belsey in a particularly foul mood by interrupting his gentle summer slumber with the sheer horror of heavy metal. "It was the noisiest, most deafening, ear-splitting show I've seen in years and the fans were in ecstasy. I retired early on the casualty list," he grumbled. Nothing was to James's taste, not even Ronnie Dio ("shrieking, painful") or drummer Cozy Powell ("boring"). But he did rather enjoy support band Stretch. Indeed, his review was headlined 'Ritchie's Rainbow eclipsed by Stretch'.

"Rainbow playing the Hippo was very odd, as virtually all the big bands did the Colston Hall," recalls Martin Jones, who was 16 at the time. "I remember there was a very large light display of a brightly coloured rainbow above the stage. But what sticks in my mind was, after a great set, Ritchie smashing up his Strat on stage. I'd never seen an artist do that live before, and while it was exhilarating I couldn't help feel that it was wanton and unnecessary (sorry). And it couldn't have done the boards of the stage much good; in fact, every time I have been to the Hippo after that I think of it and wonder if he had to pick up the bill for repairs."

"With respect to James Belsey, Stretch were OK but nobody was really interested," adds Andy Fox. "They had a single out which I seem to remember them playing twice. But there was a real sense of occasion about Rainbow's first UK show and everybody was excited about seeing them. They had two backdrops beneath the rainbow lights, with the covers from both of the albums. But the audience were transfixed by Ritchie. He wasn't just a heavy player but also switched to classical music which he picked really gently and quietly. The way he was able to change the mood so suddenly was quite brilliant. I went to see Rainbow on every tour after that."

He also witnessed the guitar-smashing incident. "Down the front, punters descended on the remains like a pack of wild animals. I have a vivid memory of this guy standing outside the Hippodrome afterwards with his hands cut to ribbons and blood pouring down his arms. He was holding aloft the scratch plate with some of the strings still attached. He looked ecstatic, as though he'd just won the Cup Final."

Rainbow went on to sell 30 million records and headline the first Castle Donington Monsters of Rock festival. Stretch struggled on for a couple more years before splitting up. Ronnie James Dio subsequently achieved the distinction of singing on three of the greatest metal albums of all time with three different acts (*Rainbow Rising*, Black Sabbath's *Heaven and Hell* and his own band's *Holy Diver*).

The Runaways
Granary, 3 October 1976

They were only together for four years, but the Runaways undertook a European tour in 1976 that included a gig at Bristol's late, lamented home of rock. Entertainments manager Al Read recalls that the Granary was full to capacity soon after it opened that night, but disappointed punters were so eager to see Joan Jett, Cherie Currie and co that they were prepared to risk life and limb: "Whilst I was in the disco booth above the stage playing records prior to the onstage appearance of the girls, I was amazed to see several eager young men climbing in through the open windows on my level. They had climbed up the outside of the Granary to what was, in fact, the third floor."

"It was completely mad," confirms Andy Fox. "The place was full of young blokes. It was massively over capacity and people were even sitting in the venue's round windows. I couldn't see much because I was right at the back. I didn't think the Runaways were very good, though. It was all about the hype."

Thin Lizzy
Colston Hall, 22 October 1976

Before the Class As kicked in, the classic Lizzy line-up were at their absolute peak as a live band during this run of gigs, which were recorded for the *Live and Dangerous* album. Despite being heavily overdubbed, this remains one of the all-time great live albums, but wasn't released until two years later. For a brief period, venerable inkie the *NME* loved Thin Lizzy. Reporter David Housham was sent to review this Colston Hall show: "Watching two thousand Bristolians exploding in a spastic frenzy, cheering, stomping, screaming for a third encore, you have to conclude that there is no better bona fide rock band in England, maybe the world, than Thin Lizzy at the moment."

Even hard-to-please *Post* reviewer James Belsey was impressed - though obviously it was too loud. "They packed the Colston Hall, they created a near-riot, they gave a deafening show and they looked very good indeed," he wrote.

The teenage Martin Jones was there for this one. "I saw Lizzy twice, the first time being when they toured the *Fighting* album (still my favourite Lizzy album). The crowd were attentive and appreciative but there was nothing like the atmosphere they would generate in live shows in years to come. The second time I saw them was on this *Jailbreak* tour. It was a complete sell out with a loud and adoring crowd. Phil's outfit, if memory serves, was an emerald green all-in-one tight-fitting cord or suede suit. *The Boys are Back in Town* was the encore. Wow - what a way to finish."

"I actually didn't know much about Lizzy at the time," adds Andy Fox. "We had seats up on the balcony and I was hooked from the moment they started with *Jailbreak*. They had this effect where pyro went off left, right and centre and it looked as though Scott Gorham, Brian Roberston and Phil Lynott had magically appeared on stage. It's a simple trick but very effective and it completely blew me away. They played pretty much what we know now as the *Live and Dangerous* set. It still ranks as one of the top ten gigs I've ever seen."

Scorpions
Granary, 6 November 1976

Four years before they achieved global fame as perestroika-endorsing, power ballad-touting whistling Teutons, Germany's finest rock band played the Granary twice in eight months. This second show came just after the release of the *Virgin Killer* album, which boasted the dodgiest, most 'what-the-fuck-were-they-thinking?' kiddie porn sleeve design of all time (ahead of Blind Faith's eponymous album). As a pimply youth, I bought my copy in W.H. Smith; today you'd probably be arrested just for owning it. Coming a couple of years before their big commercial breakthrough with the slick, melodic heavy metal of *Lovedrive*, this would have been a rare opportunity to see them with hugely talented Hendrix acolyte Uli Jon Roth on lead guitar.

AC/DC
Colston Hall, 7 November 1976

Was Bristol ready for AC/DC on their *Dirty Deeds Done Dirt Cheap* tour? It certainly was. Were the notoriously stuffed-shirt Colston Hall bigwigs ready for the band and their fans? They most certainly were not. Graham Buck of Bristol student newspaper *Bacus* managed to blag his way backstage for this one, where he observed that "the management [were] rather perturbed to find a normally passive audience leaping out of their seats." But this was hardly surprising since "it was hard to remain aloof to a performance that was highly energetic and aggressive, with an unhealthy obsession with carnal pursuits particularly evident."

He managed to grab a word with Bon Scott, who directed some sadly unspecified "healthy Australian vernacular" at the Hall's management for cracking down on audience enthusiasm. The student reporter also ventured the suggestion that AC/DC's image was calculatedly 'not nice'. Scott retorted that this had not been planned deliberately. "It started during our earlier Australian concerts where they set up some 'interviews' in the street. Passers-by would say, 'I wouldn't let my daughter go and see that band, they're filthy' and because of our name, '… I wouldn't let my son go and see them either.'"

Interestingly this was also a rare AC/DC show at which Angus Young failed to bare his backside. Apparently, such was the Colston management's disapproval of his antics that the paranoid guitarist became convinced there were members of the Bristol Vice Squad planted in the audience ready to haul him off to the clink at the slightest flash of a pallid, scrawny Antipodean buttock.

Steve Hillage
Colston Hall, 22 November 1976

The Young Ones, series two, episode two (*Cash*): Neil the hippy is forced to join the Filth and turns into a power-crazed tyrant. Busting up a party held by his former mates, he brings his truncheon down on the record player. In a moment of awful realisation, he notices the disc he's just crushed: "Oh no… Steve Hillage!"

For years, Mr. Hillage was not happy with his brief foray into popular culture. "To be quite honest I didn't really like it," he told me back in 2009. "But I didn't mind. It wasn't a big deal to me. I just thought, 'Oh god, here they go again: Hillage the Hippy'. It just seemed to reinforce this stereotyped vision of me. People who were like Neil the hippy might have thought of me as being some kind of icon, but that's not how I saw myself. Put it that way."

Subsequently, Hillage seems to have reconciled himself to his image and embraced the joke. These days, his live shows usually open with that very clip, which is always greeted with a huge cheer of recognition.

The Hillage track played in that episode is *Electrick Gypsies*, which appeared on the Todd Rundgren-produced *L*, his second and most commercially successful solo album after leaving Gong, which hit the UK top ten back in 1976. But despite this, and the fact that Hillage had recently supported Queen in Hyde Park, the *Post's* pop correspondent James Belsey had no idea who he was until he remembered Gong: "a deliberately esoteric rock band" who had "a rude album cover that was banned" (no idea what he's going on about here, though he may be referring to *Angel's Egg*, which occasionally had a sticker placed over the small female nude).

Hillage's seven-piece band at this time included his partner Miquette Giraudy, former Jethro Tull drummer Clive Bunker and aptly named bassist Colin Bass who went on to join Camel. Belsey might have been only vaguely aware of who these people were, but to his credit he was quickly seduced by that glorious glissando guitar. "He wandered onstage wearing a woolly hat, a bear-like, shambling shabby man who immediately started playing devastating guitar music," Belsey wrote of the unassuming frontman, whom he described as "a star" who "showed the confidence and unhurried talent which has been missing for so long from up-and-coming rock players".

Hillage was a regular visitor to Bristol throughout the late seventies, no doubt thanks to the city's large hippy contingent. The teenage Aidan Naughton quickly became a convert. "I was a little too late to the party to see Gong first time around. The Pete Frame Gong Family Tree which featured in *Melody Maker* to promote *Gong Live, Etc* had me rushing to the original Virgin Records below the bus station to spend £3.99 of my pocket money that Thursday night. I listened on the store's headphones and was addicted thereafter. That led me to Hillage, National Health and Here and Now."

Aidan was back at the Colston Hall to see Hillage on the *Motivation Radio* tour in 1977 ("That was a completely different band, very much in the funk mode. There were plenty of Afghan coats on display in the audience and lots of shouts of 'Wally!'") and at the Anson Rooms in 1978 for the *Green* tour with National Health. "That was an outstanding gig and my first taste of National Health, who were my gateway drug to the Canterbury scene. My brother and I got into a bit of bother with our father as he gave up waiting outside to pick us up on what was a school night. We got home at 2am. My brother was twelve."

All that local Gong/Hillage activity seems to have attracted some unlikely fans. In 2008, the reunited Gong, with Hillage back on guitar, were invited to open Massive Attack's eclectic Meltdown Festival at the Queen Elizabeth Hall.

1977

Jimmy Carter becomes US president... *Gay News* is found guilty of blasphemous libel in a case brought by Mary Whitehouse... Forelock-tuggers rejoice during Her Maj's Silver Jubilee celebrations... *Star Wars* opens in cinemas... In Michigan, Led Zeppelin set a world record for the largest indoor attendance at a concert... Marc Bolan is killed in a car crash. Three members of Lynyrd Skynyrd die in a plane crash... The tabloids and music press are obsessed with punk, but for the record-buying public this is the year of ABBA, disco (Donna Summer, Baccara), Rod Stewart, Wings and, ahem, David Soul. *Mull of Kintyre* is the top selling single and ABBA's *Arrival* the top selling album. Another decidedly non-punky album that went on to rank among the biggest sellers of all time is also released: *Rumours* by Fleetwood Mac. The Sex Pistols are dropped by EMI, sign to A&M, are dropped by A&M and sign to Virgin, who release the only punk album to top the UK chart this year: *Never Mind the Bollocks, Here's the Sex Pistols*. It stays there for two weeks - the same length of time as *Going For the One* by Yes... Bristol's first Gay Pride event is held... Her Maj opens the Royal Portbury Dock on her Silver Jubilee tour... The hasty three-week shoot of Jack Gold's daft, pleasingly misanthropic British supernatural thriller *The Medusa Touch* includes a memorable sequence filmed in Bristol Cathedral. Richard Burton plays a telekinetic catastrophe magnet who causes the Cathedral to crumble to the ground in an entertaining shower of bouncing rubber bricks. The film is released in 1978.

Lynyrd Skynyrd
Colston Hall, 31 January 1977
Following their triumph at the 1976 Knebworth Festival, where they succeeded in completely upstaging The Rolling Stones, Skynyrd had become

one of the hottest tickets around by the time they returned to Bristol as headliners on the *Gimme Back My Bullets* tour. The Colston Hall show was a complete sell-out and student newspaper *Bacus*, which had come over all rock-friendly (albeit briefly), reported that disconsolate ticketless punters were waiting outside the venue hoping the touts would turn up.

'Artimus Pyle talks!' was the headline on Julia Griffin's report. She'd been hanging around all afternoon and grabbed a word with the recently recruited drummer, who was the first member of the band to arrive. Naturally, given Skynyrd's reputation for attracting trouble on the road, she wanted to know how many hotels they'd wrecked on the tour so far. "So far, in England, there have been 113 hotels," Pyle deadpanned. "Don't say I said that will you?"

Interestingly, he revealed that the band recorded a live album in Cardiff that had never been released, as they put out *One More From the Road* instead. Julia also reported that Bad Company drummer Simon Kirke was at the Colston for the show and said afterwards that he thoroughly enjoyed it.

At the end of the performance, *Bacus*'s heroic hackette declined protective aural intervention. "During Skynyrd's encore of *Freebird*, a kindly nurse nearby (by means of sign language) offered a pair of earplugs… The concert was loud, but it wouldn't have been the same going home without the ringing in your ears - would it?"

Martin Jones had been at Skynyrd's first Colston Hall show back in 1974, which made him a lifelong fan. This time he was determined to meet the band. He'd also worked out a cunning plan. "We were in the balcony and we knew a way to get down the back stairs and access the bands' dressing rooms. We did this from time to time and met the Groundhogs and Robin Trower that way. At the end of the show, Skynyrd went back out and did another encore, so we were waiting in a corridor for them to come off stage. Next thing, the band members, exhausted and sweaty, are filing past us. The last one was Leon Wilkeson, carrying his bass. My mate spoke to him and he stopped to talk. With that, a roadie appeared and said in a deep southern drawl: 'What the fuck are you doing? Get the fuck out of here or I'll break your legs.' Wilkeson said, 'Aw hush, they ain't doin' no harm'. He turned to us and said, 'Glad you enjoyed the show boys. Git on home now.' We left starstruck and glad that our limbs were still in one piece!"

Angie Bowie
Webbington Hotel and Country Club, 27 February-5 March 1977
All the shows in this book would have been worth attending because they were brilliant. Except this week-long residency, which was a car crash. But for that very reason, it would still have been worth the trek to Axbridge. Sadly, however, these mind-boggling performances seem to have been witnessed only by a smattering of bored pensioners with no idea who was cavorting on stage in various states of undress.

The grandly named Webbington Hotel and Country Club in Axbridge was part of a circuit of rural cabaret venues that thrived in the sixties and seventies before the advent of drink-driving laws - although special coach services were laid on from Bristol and Weston-super-Mare for the more responsible drunkard. Despite its somewhat seedy reputation, due in part to regular appearances by striptease acts and 'exotic' and/or 'continental' dancers (local historian Eugene Byrne recalls his late aunt describing it as "a den of iniquity"), the Webbington attracted all the major stars. Roy Orbison, PJ Proby, Max Wall, Gene Pitney and Slade put on shows there, as did tabloid Satanist Alex Sanders with a bevy of naked ladies. Even the Bonzo Dog Doo-Dah Band had a residency from August 11-17, 1968. Frankie Howerd liked the area so much that he bought a house locally. But the biggest coup for owner Alan Wells, a former chicken farmer from Weston-super-Mare, was bagging a brace of Hollywood sex symbols, each of whom was a little beyond the first flush of youth. Curiously, both suffered a personal tragedy shortly after playing the Webbington.

Jayne Mansfield was first to appear in April 1967, flying into Bristol Airport just two months before she was almost decapitated in a freak car accident in Louisiana. She'd recently ditched notorious promoter Don Arden (Sharon Osbourne's dad, as was noted earlier) over his demands that she wear a see-through dress for the Webbington Hotel show. So it was a rather more demurely dressed Ms. Mansfield who appeared on stage singing, telling anecdotes and playing the violin. By all accounts, she went down rather well.

Next up was Jane Russell, who was as renowned for her impressive embonpoint as she was for her performances in *The Outlaw* and *Gentlemen Prefer Blondes*. Her career was on the slide by the time she arrived in the UK on honeymoon with her second husband Roger Barrett. Quite why she took time out for a week-long cabaret residency at the Webbington from Oct 13-19, 1968, remains a mystery. Presumably she was strapped for cash. One month later, Barrett died of a heart attack.

David and Angie Bowie were still married in April 1977 (they didn't divorce for another three years). But they were living very different lives. David was looking after the couple's son Zowie (later filmmaker Duncan Jones) while recovering from cocaine psychosis and sharing a flat with Iggy Pop in Berlin. Together they recorded Pop's lauded *Lust For Life* album. Angie, meanwhile, was launching her somewhat less illustrious and exceedingly short-lived career as a cabaret artiste in Loxton, six miles outside Weston-super-Mare. The poster for this historic event announced: "Following her West End theatre success, the sensational wife of international star David Bowie brings the Soul House Company to the Webbington Country Club for their first appearance in the provinces. An appearance not to be missed!"

The six-strong company included 'musical director' Andy 'Thunderclap' Newman (of *Something in the Air* one-hit-wonder fame), singer and MC Roy Martin and Gladys Shock, former star of a Soho all-nude revue. What happened on the opening night would have been lost to history had the *Melody Maker* not sent reporter Allan Jones to cover the show. This appears to have attracted little attention locally, with just a tiny *Bristol Evening Post* ad ('All this week. Star Attraction: David Bowie's famous wife'). Jones's vivid account can be found in his splendid collection of music journalism, *Can't Stand Up For Falling Down*.

Jones arrived on the blustery Sunday night to find a "meagre audience in the hotel's cavernously draughty ballroom [stifling] yawns of gasping indifference at Webbington regulars The Colin Peters Set. After another support act: "'IT'S SHOWTIME!' Roy screeches, voice going off like a fire alarm, the very shrillness of which has some of the more enfeebled pensioners in the crowd clutching their chests, mass cardiac arrests just an interrupted heartbeat away."

Angie appears, virtually naked apart from a fur stole. Together with Gladys and another mostly unclad young woman named Charlotte, she performs *Give Your Soul to a Man*. "The noise they make sounds like it belongs in an abbatoir, a cacophony of high-pitched whinnies, whines and indiscriminate yelping," winces the reporter. After a costume change that has her trussed up in S&M gear, the star of the show gets a solo spot. "What at first sounds like a parrot being disembowelled turns out to be Angie, singing."

Later, Gladys "sheds what few clothes she's still wearing and whacks her ample tits in the face of the old feller in the front row she'd earlier terrorised with her belly dancing. He almost dies of fright."

The three female members of the troupe then perform a ditty entitled *Maybe It's Because We're Soho Hookers* set to the tune of *Maybe It's Because I'm a Londoner*. After the grand, high-kicking finale of *We'll Meet Again*, they're rewarded with some half-hearted clapping. But Angie quickly returns, determined to milk this sparse applause. "She seems to be expecting someone to rush the stage with a basket of roses," writes Jones. "Most of the audience, however, is already drifting towards the bar."

Despite this, ahem, muted response, Angie must have enjoyed herself in Axbridge, because she was back again on May 18 to judge the final of a local talent contest, alongside a bunch of nightclub owners and the headmaster of Churchill School. Alan Wells sold the hotel in the late eighties and died in 2002. The venue is still going - now rebranded the Webbington Hotel and Spa - though curiously its website makes no mention of its fascinating cabaret past.

Fleetwood Mac
Colston Hall, 11 April 1977

These days, your only opportunity to hear songs from *Rumours* at the Hall Formerly Known as Colston is when one of the many Fleetwood Mac tribute acts pitch up. The 1977 album was such an all-conquering success, which rarely drops out of the charts, that it's sobering to be reminded that *Rumours* was not an instant hit in the UK, where audiences still thought of the Mac as an old sixties blues band and seemed rather confused by the new soft rock incarnation. On release, it entered the album charts at, er, number 57 on February 26, 1977. It went on to peak at number seven the following week and had slipped to number 13 by the time of this Colston Hall show, with total sales of just 80,000. *Rumours* finally went on to top the charts in January 1978. It eventually sold more than 40 million copies, becoming one of the best selling albums of all time.

The brief five-date UK leg of the *Rumours* tour, of which this was the last show, was like a little club jaunt in between playing the enormodomes of the USA. So were the three British members of the volatile band (Mick Fleetwood, Christine McVie, John McVie) pleased to be home for their first UK tour in six years? Reader, they were not. According to original bassist Bob Brunning's book *The Fleetwood Mac Story: Rumours and Lies*, the tone was set at an opening press conference at the glamorous Holiday Inn in Birmingham, which concluded with John McVie hurling a glass of vodka and tonic in Lindsey Buckingham's face.

In her gossipy memoir *Storms: My Life with Lindsey Buckingham and Fleetwood Mac*, Buckingham's then-partner Carol Ann Harris says of that opening show, which took place on the very day that *Rumours* hit number one in the US: "Backstage in the tiny, cramped dressing rooms, each member of Fleetwood Mac was letting J.C. [tour manager John Courage, whose tasks included doling out lids of cocaine to his charges] know their displeasure in their own special way. Christine was bitching about the 'nasty' theatre; Lindsey was pissed off about the audience size; John was cold and couldn't get the radiator to work in the tuning room; and Stevie, whose wardrobe changes during the show were too numerous to count, was almost in tears over the one stingy hanging rack she had been given. Last, but not least, Mick was in a churlish mood over the lack of cocaine."

Hapless Mr. Courage apologised about the size of the venue, pointing out that it was the largest hall in Birmingham (twice the size of the Colston, so one can only imagine how foul the tempers had become by the time they reached Bristol) and that coke was hard to come by in the UK.

"Mick stared at him belligerently. 'That's crap. Totally unacceptable, I'm afraid. You know I play better with it. Don't blame me if this show sucks tonight.' As he finished he pointed his finger directly in J.C.'s face.

"'What about weed, J.C.?' Lindsey asked in a surly tone matching Mick's. 'You don't expect me to just drink my way through the show, do you? *Jesus!*'"

Still, they obviously knew the album was a winner, as the Colston Hall set was completely dominated by *Rumours*, opening with *Don't Stop* and encoring with Christine McVie's delicate *Songbird*. Just three tracks from the album were excluded (*Second Hand News*, *I Don't Want to Know* and *Oh Daddy*), though interestingly they also played *Silver Springs* - a Stevie Nicks outtake from the *Rumours* sessions that originally appeared as the

B-Side to *Go Your Own Way* and was eventually restored to the album on the occasion of its 2004 remaster. Most of the rest of the songs they played at the Colston were drawn from the band's eponymous 10th album, released in 1975, with *Oh Well* being the only survivor from the Peter Green British blues era. Despite all the ructions, the tour was judged to be a great success. When Fleetwood Mac returned to the UK three years later, they were playing arenas.

Those interested in the the great Fleetwood Mac romantic soap opera may wish to note that during this UK run of dates on the *Rumours* tour, Stevie Nicks was partnered up with Don Henley of the Eagles. By the autumn, she had fallen in bed with Mick Fleetwood.

Camel
Colston Hall, 2 October 1977

Another big night for prog in Bristol during the punk era. While Peter Gabriel was playing his first solo show in the city down the road at the Hippodrome, Colston Hall regulars Camel were back on their *Rain Dances* tour. "I remember it was a sell-out, as was the Bristol show on the subsequent *Breathless* tour," says Aidan Naughton.

Never the most flamboyant of proggers, Camel notched up a string of outstanding top 30 albums during the 1970s, winning over an audience so loyal that they can still sell out the Albert Hall today. Despite their low media profile, they also had a huge influence on the next generation of prog acts, notably Marillion. *Rain Dances* featured a guest appearance by Brian Eno on piano and Minimoog and also saw a major line-up change with Caravan co-founder Richard Sinclair replacing Doug Ferguson on fretless bass and vocals and King Crimson's Mel Collins joining the expanded band on saxophone and flute. This was also the last Camel tour to feature founding keyboard player Peter Bardens.

It was certainly a great, if somewhat short-lived, line-up, as recognised by the band themselves. The version of *Lunar Sea* on their imaginatively titled *A Live Record* was recorded at this very show, as was *Lady Fantasy* on the expanded 2002 reissue. What's more, when Camel released their massive 32 disc box set *Air Born: The MCA and Decca Years 1973-1984* in November 2023, it included several more recordings from the Colston Hall show: *First Light*, *Metrognome*, *Unevensong*, *Raindances* and *Never Let Go*.

Peter Gabriel
Hippodrome, 2 October 1977

Conventional wisdom would have it that Peter Gabriel was in a vulnerable position in 1977, emerging from the protective big tent of Genesis into the hostile world of punk as a solo artist. Indeed, across town the night before this show, Johnny Thunders and the Heartbreakers were joined on stage by an unannounced Steve Jones and Paul Cook of the Sex Pistols at Brunel Technical College for a show that ended in a riot when a bunch of Bristol City fans showed up and started smashing windows as they tried to get in. How can an aging progger compete? Gabriel's secret weapons were an outstanding debut album, a hit single acknowledged even by Nick Kent in the *NME* as a "24-carat irresistible classic" (*Solsbury Hill*) and an excellent band that included guitarist Sid McGinnis and the great Tony Levin on bass.

With only one album to draw on, Gabriel played a couple of covers (*I Heard it Through the Grapevine, All Day and All of the Night*) and unveiled a brace of songs from his upcoming second album. He also started experimenting with the audience interaction that would become a feature of later, more elaborate shows, taking advantage of the ornate Hippodrome architecture to go walkabout in the circle and stalls, occasionally popping up unexpectedly from the darkness.

"Last night, Gabriel showed how convincingly he's staking his claim in the rock hierarchy," enthused James Belsey in the *Post*, describing the show as "a lucid, eloquent and above all musical event".

Hawkwind/Bethnal
Hippodrome, 3 October 1977

The Hawkwind of 1977 was a very different beast from the space rock Hawkwind of five years earlier. During the band's Charisma Records era, which began with 1976's *Astounding Sounds, Amazing Music* album, longstanding poet-in-residence Robert Calvert was now more or less at the helm, despite his ongoing struggles with bipolar disorder. The music was more disciplined, the live production more theatrical, and Calvert's witty, literate lyrics drew on science fiction themes rather than the fantasy that informed Michael Moorcock's contributions to the previous two albums. This reached an apogee with 1977's brilliant *Quark, Strangeness and Charm* album, which some rank as the band's finest achievement. After an unlikely appearance on Marc Bolan's TV show, they hit the road for a lengthy, 20-date UK tour, followed by a jaunt through Europe. Clearly eager to spend Charisma's money, they'd splashed out on their most ambitious production: the giant, multi-coloured, pulsating Atomhenge set which stretched the width of the stage and also towered over the audience.

Alas, Calvert's mental health continued to deteriorate. Three weeks after this Hippodrome show, the whole tour was abandoned in Paris after an incident with a replica gun and/or a sword (depending on who you believe).

Martin Thomas was at the Hippodrome. "When *Silver Machine* was played at the school disco, we all jumped about a bit. But I really got into the later *Quark Strangeness and Charm* album, mostly because of the Bob Calvert lyrics and the whole 'modern' sci-fi feel. Bethnal were the support band and they dressed like they had just come off a football terrace. They played heavy/punk type music. The one track that I really liked was a cover of *Baba O'Reilly*, which hit the mark. The main thing I remember about Hawkwind is Bob Calvert. He was dressed in a Biggles-type flying outfit with pilot goggles, a long scarf around his neck and a leather flying cap. He really was an impressive performer. He seemed to be as mad as a box of frogs and I really only watched him on the stage. Most of the tracks played were from the *Quark* album and my favourite one, *Spirit of the Age*, was played towards the end of the set."

"I remember he wielded a pair of sabres during the opening song, *Hassan I Sahba*," adds Aidan Naughton. "There were also dancing robots and strobe lighting throughout the show. I haven't seen anything quite like it since. It was everything I could have hoped for and more."

1978

L ouise Brown, aka "the world's first test tube baby", is born to Bristol parents... Milton Keynes welcomes its concrete cows... In Rome, a pope succeeds another pope and promptly dies, so they have to find a third pope...The first episode of *The Hitchhiker's Guide to the Galaxy* is broadcast on Radio 4. *Dallas* debuts on the telly... If you don't like the Bee Gees or John Travolta and Olivia Newton-John, this is probably the year to emigrate as the *Saturday Night Fever* and *Grease* soundtracks completely dominate the charts. At least Kate Bush becomes the first woman to hit number one with a self-penned single (*Wuthering Heights*) and Meat Loaf's slow-burning *Bat Out of Hell* finally roars up the top 30. AC/DC release *Powerage*, which peaks at number 23 in the UK chart. Two years later, their *Back in Black* hits number one and goes on to become the second-biggest selling album of all time. The only punk/new wave acts to make any real commercial impression are Ian Dury, The Boomtown Rats, Blondie and The Stranglers... Bristol Exhibition Centre hosts the first World Wine Fair... The ornate ABC cinema in Whiteladies Road is brutally carved up into three screens... Bristol Industrial Museum is opened. In the coming years it will be amply stocked with exhibits from various factories that close down around the region. M Shed is now on the site... In a Bristol pub, plans are hatched for the city's first Balloon Fiesta, which takes place in 1979.

UFO
Colston Hall, 31 January 1978
These days, UFO generally make the news when one of them drops dead. That's hardly surprising given their reputation as the hardest-living of all UK rock bands of the 1970s and 1980s. Even Ozzy Osbourne was reportedly astonished at their sustained levels of debauchery. Naturally,

there was a price to be paid. I attended the first night of one of the band's many allegedly clean'n'sober comeback tours at the Bristol Bierkeller back in the 1990s. During the first song, Phil Mogg forgot the words and bassist Pete Way went arse-over-tit. (Things got worse before they finally got better - in 2002 guitarist Michael Schenker, sporting a black eye, was too pissed to play during a show at the Manchester Apollo and the audience booed him off.)

But there was a sweet spot when UFO were at their creative and commercial peak, before the drugging and boozing dragged them down. And this Colston Hall show in 1978 was right in the middle of it. *The Lights Out* tour boasted the same line-up and much of the same set as *Strangers in the Night*, often cited as one of the greatest live albums of all time (it came second only to Thin Lizzy's *Live and Dangerous* in a *Classic Rock* readers' poll), which was recorded that October.

Henry Cow
Arnolfini, 9 February, 1978; Bristol Cathedral, 10 February, 1978

Marxist musical experimentalists who were one of the earliest signings to Richard Branson's Virgin Records (their debut album *Legend*, or *Leg End* as it was commonly known thanks to the sock cover art, bore the catalogue number V 2005) and played alongside their chums Gong at the 1971 Glastonbury Festival, the uncompromising Henry Cow have been described as both the most progressive of all progressive rock acts and not a prog band at all. They played Bristol on several occasions during the 1970s, returning just before they split in 1978 for these dates on the grandly titled *Arts Council Contemporary Music Network Tour* (the second of which, at the Cathedral, was a free show).

Among those present was curious teenager Mike Barnes, who went on to give us the exhaustive *A New Day Yesterday: UK Progressive Rock & the 1970s*. "The latter was a completely improvised performance, with players moving around, making use of the space," he writes. "It was like nothing I'd ever witnessed before. Afterwards I recall talking slightly nervously to a genial Chris Cutler [Henry Cow drummer and percussionist] as he was packing away his kit, barefoot, wearing considerable flares...I also passed by Fred Frith sitting on the floor in one of the aisles, next to his xylophone, hunched, motionless, with his head in his hands, as if overwhelmed.

I thought it impertinent to tarry and moved along, probably thinking something along the lines of, 'Wow, *heavy!*'"

Rush
Colston Hall, 26 February 1978

It became a feature of Rush's career that the great prog-metal pioneers would fly under the mainstream media radar while achieving extraordinary levels of popularity. Towards the end of their career, they would regularly appear on those official lists of highest grossing tours alongside old warhorses like the Stones and young popsters like Taylor Swift. And each time, commentators would express astonishment at how this had been allowed to happen on their watch and then forget about it until the next time the band toured. Your only chance to catch them in Bristol was back in the late seventies.

In 1978, they were touring the *A Farewell to Kings* album. Martin Thomas was at the Colston Hall that night. "A mate had lent me a few of the Rush albums before the gig and I really liked *A Farewell to Kings*. Our seats were quite close to the right of the stage. There was a backdrop with an image of mountains and I remember that Neal Peart's drum set seemed massive. He played one of the best drum solos I have ever heard. The sound mix was good that night: Alex Lifeson's guitar was spot-on and Geddy Lee's vocals were crystal clear."

"That was first time I heard *Xanadu* live," adds Ian Gregory. "OMG (as they say these days), that track still resonates with me now, well over 40 years later. That band were on another planet. What a sound for a three-piece."

The teenage Aidan Naughton had become obsessed with Rush from the moment he heard *Bastille Day* on Alan Freeman's *Saturday Rock Show*. He'd been unable to bunk off school to get tickets for this show, so his obliging mum went down and secured front row seats for Aidan and his younger brother. They turned up early for the soundcheck and managed to secure the band's autographs. "One of the things I remember most vividly about that show is that it was one of the last I saw where real dry ice was used," he recalls. "They pumped out huge quantities."

Rush returned to the Colston on their *Hemispheres* tour the following year. By then, they were very much in the ascendant and sold out two nights. Determined to get front row seats once again, Aidan and his mates decided to camp out from Saturday night for tickets that went on sale on Monday morning. "It was pretty boring. The one thing you really don't really anticipate is the level of discomfort on your hips that comes from sleeping on the concrete floor."

The aging Bill Haley and his Comets were playing on the Saturday night, so Aidan and his chums stretched their legs by sneaking in to watch him play *Rock Around the Clock*. Later, the tedium was interrupted by the arrival of a gang of skinheads and their girlfriends after the pubs closed. "They started chucking chips at us and were saying, 'Let's kick their fucking heads in!' I was bursting for a piss at the time, but we all pretended to be asleep. Eventually, one of their girlfriends said 'Leave them alone - they're not hurting anyone' and they went off into the night. As soon as they left, I jumped up and relieved myself against the wall of the Colston..."

Spirit/The Police
Locarno, 12 March 1978

Best known for their hit *I Got a Line on You*, sixties psychedelic prog/art-rockers Spirit went through enough convoluted line-up changes to keep Pete Frame very busy indeed. By early 1978, they'd reinvented themselves as a power trio featuring founders Randy California (guitar/vocals) and his stepfather Ed Cassidy (drums) alongside bassist Larry 'Fuzzy' Knight. This rather belated first visit to Bristol came at the end of a short three-date UK tour. Also making their first appearance in Bristol were The Police, a full month before the release of their debut single, *Roxanne*. On the face of it, this was an odd double-bill. But The Police's bleached-blond, punk rock stylings concealed a shameful hippy/prog-rock past which went strangely unpublicised at the time, though their obvious musical talent did arouse suspicion among punk purists. Drummer Stewart Copeland had played with the recently split Curved Air; Sting was a member of jazz-rock fusion act Last Exit and sang on the *Nuclear Waste* single with members of Gong and Hawkwind's Nik Turner; and Andy Summers - a full decade older than his compatriots - was a veteran of the '60s psychedelic scene, had been a member of Soft Machine and performed on the orchestral *Tubular Bells*.

Groundhogs drummer Ken Pustelnik was by this time running his own Zulu PA company which did the sound for this show. "I knew all about

Spirit, but there was something odd about The Police," he recalls. "With a teacher up front, they were not quite like the other punks. The Locarno was packed. Two-thirds of the audience were there for Spirit. But there was a new crowd too, who'd obviously heard about The Police - so the word was out. The ones who were there for Spirit were all sitting cross-legged in front of the stage like it's 1969. Sting introduced himself by saying: 'Hello, we're The Police. You won't know about us. All you lot sitting down don't need to applaud us because we're kind of different to what you're used to. Just rattle your beads.' I thought that was really funny. It was slightly sarky but rather gentle, and everyone laughed."

Among the punk contingent that night was callow 19-year-old student Dave Higgitt, who went on to become editor of Bristol's legendary what's on magazine, *Venue*. "I got into that gig on a freebie, just pleased to see live music. I think I'd heard of The Police, but knew little about them. I was upstairs, where it was easier to get a drink and smoke dope. I was genuinely blown away by their set. It might be uncool to admit it now, but Sting had bucket loads of sexual charisma, and the kind of ripped physique I could only dream of (he removed his shirt at some point). A star in the making, I duly noted at the time - and I guess I was right."

Planet Gong
Corn Exchange, 28 March 1978

One of the last gigs at the Corn Exchange before it became an indoor market. Planet Gong was a punky, thrashy offshoot from the Gong mothership which fused founders Daevid Allen and Gilli Smyth with free festival stalwarts Here and Now, notably for the *Live Floating Anarchy '77* album. Alas, anyone turning up to see Daevid and Gilli at the Corn Exchange was to be disappointed, as they'd both just bailed.

"It was basically Here and Now playing the *Live Floating Anarchy* album - *Opium For the People, Floating Anarchy* and so on," recalls audience member Aidan Naughton. "It was my first and only time at the Corn Exchange and there were about 200 punks and hippies present."

In keeping with the optimistic, free festival spirit, these were 'pay what you want' gigs - as were all Here and Now shows at the time. Alas, rather a lot of people chose to pay fuck-all, which was a bit of a downer. "I saw lots of other Here and Now shows between '78 and '80, culminating in a rather ill-tempered Keith da Missile Bass remonstrating with the Trinity Hall crowd that the donations weren't enough to cover their petrol to the next gig," says Aidan. "The free festival/gig ethos was coming to an end."

Blue Öyster Cult
Colston Hall, 27 April 1978

"Flaming pyrotechnics, lasers, smoke… plus great rock'n'roll; Blue Öyster Cult is the group you always dreamt about," wrote Sandy Roberston in his *Sounds* review of this first night of BÖC's 14-date UK tour. "Even though there were sound problems and the visual effects had to be curtailed somewhat… this is one band who have no trouble living up to their semi-mythical status."

The classic line-up of the band (Buck Dharma, Eric Bloom, Allen Lanier and Albert & Joe Bouchard) were on top of their game during this tour, which came on the back of the success of the magnificent, platinum-selling *Agents of Fortune* and slightly less impressive *Spectres* albums. *(Don't Fear) the Reaper* had failed to chart in the UK when it was originally released here in 1976, but such was Cult-mania that a re-release of the uncut album version reached number 16 in May 1978.

"Sheer entertainment" was the verdict of *Post* reviewer Paul Westbrook, who revealed that BÖC had brought along £200,000 worth of lighting and effects gear for their "stunning" show. "There was the novelty for the audience of being bathed in spotlights, your knees covered with green stardust, Star Wars-style 'weapons' drilling your forehead - and a monster masked drummer whose playing was transformed into eerie writhings by those versatile laser beams. Oh yes, the music was excellent too."

Somewhat bizarrely, the support act was androgynous new wavers Japan, who'd just released their debut album, *Adolescent Sex*. Reports suggest they endured a hostile reception on much of this tour, though the *Post* review noted that in Bristol they "played competently and manfully as the expectant audience yelled for the Oysters." Japan's keyboard player Richard Barbieri went on to achieve considerable success alongside Steven Wilson in modern proggers Porcupine Tree.

This was the teenage Justin Quinnell's first gig. "The heavy metal scene in Nether Stowey had yet to gather momentum in the late seventies, so my sister came up asking if I would like to see BÖC as she had a spare ticket (before she told me 'Fiona' couldn't make it and it would be £3). I remember the support band Japan quite well as the lead singer looked a bit like a woman! Quite a shock for us 1960s folk who were weaned on the latest *Carry On* films. BÖC had lasers years before anyone else, which combined with a mirror ball looked quite good. Apart from *(Don't Fear) the Reaper*, all I remember was how nice it all looked and learning how impossible it is to 'dance' when seated. Even to this day, I wait for BÖC to be *Popmaster's* 'Three-in-ten'.

AC/DC
Colston Hall, 22 May 1978

AC/DC's Bristol date on the *Powerage* tour came just a few weeks after the recording of the great *If You Want Blood You've Got It* live album at the Glasgow Apollo. By now, there was no stopping the band's rapid ascent and the UK tour had been hastily expanded from eight shows to twenty-four.

Opening with *Riff Raff* and concluding with *Rocker*, this was a splendidly relentless assault. The tour was notable for Angus Young's deployment of one of the first radio units in place of a guitar lead, which allowed him to scurry about unimpeded. But this was only witnessed by hardcore fans. By the end of the tour, AC/DC had their first chart hit with *Rock'n'Roll Damnation*, which reached a lowly number 24. Their big commercial breakthrough with *Highway to Hell* was still a year away.

Pity the long-suffering lugholes of poor old James Belsey of the *Bristol Post*. "Anyone with a nervous disposition, heart trouble or sensitive hearing would have been advised to keep away last night," he moaned. "AC/DC are not noisy by the standards I have become accustomed to over the years. They are deafening. Their volume hits peaks I never believed the human ear could accept without permanent damage."

The band were clearly new to him. "Their gimmick is 19-year-old lead guitarist Angus Young who plays one of those rare wire-less guitars which leaves him free to roam the stage and auditorium like a radio controlled asylum escapee."

Nonetheless, he conceded that "it was fresh, had a sense of humour and had a plethora of crisp riffs to satisfy the hardest of heavy rock fans."

"It *was* loud as hell - and I've been to a lot of loud gigs," says Andy Fox in Belsey's defence. "I didn't actually enjoy it as much as I thought I would, but the sheer charisma of Bon Scott was undeniable. He actually came right past me when he was carrying Angus on his shoulders during the guitar solo walkabout."

Black Sabbath/Van Halen
Colston Hall, 26 May 1978

The tenth anniversary tour by the greatest and most influential metal band of all time should have been a victory lap. But Black Sabbath were at their lowest ebb and in the grip of their various addictions, having just released their worst album, *Never Say Die*. To make matters worse, the incredible support act kicked their collective bottom every single night for nine long months. Young and hungry upstarts Van Halen had just released their first album, which went on to become one of the most commercially successful and critically acclaimed (except by the reliably wrong *NME*, still in thrall to punk/new wave, who considered it "vaguely bearable") debuts of all time. Eddie Van Halen was already being hailed as one of rock's greatest guitar innovators, while high-kicking, motormouthed David Lee Roth was the most charismatic frontman of his generation. This was the ninth date of what must have been an especially gruelling tour for the lacklustre, drugged-out Sabs. During the following night's show at the Lewisham Odeon, over-excited Roth came out with one of his most memorable stage raps: "Lewisham! The rock'n'roll capital of the universe!"

On the first night of the tour at Sheffield City Hall ten days before the Colston Hall show, Sabbath had watched in slack-jawed silence from the side of the stage as Eddie Van Halen played his innovative solo showcase, *Eruption*.

"We sat there going 'That was incredible . . ',' Ozzy Osbourne recalled in Paul Brannigan's biography *Eruption: The Eddie Van Halen Story*. "and then it finished, and we were just too stunned to speak."

"Van Halen were incredible and Sabbath were awful," confirms Ian Gregory, who was there for this one. "What a mistake it was to take these American upstarts on tour with them. David Lee Roth's parting shot? 'Thank you Bristol - we'll see you again'. Er, no we didn't - at least not in Bristol."

Aidan Naughton offers a dissenting voice from the consensus view of Sabbath at this time. "That's a source of continued annoyance to me. I suppose older, more hardened fans might say they were not at their peak, but I thought they were fantastic. The audience reaction was ecstatic, certainly where we were standing. But we were sharing a bottle of whisky with a bunch of bikers…

"I don't think anyone really knew who Van Halen were at the time. I'd got the album on import so I knew what we were in for. I remember the Hall was empty when they came on, but after three minutes people came flooding in from the bar. David Lee Roth was chucking bottles of champagne into the audience. I believe he stopped doing that a few shows later when someone got injured…"

Johnny Cougar
Granary, 1 June 1978

These days, John Mellencamp is a justly well-regarded heartland rocker, who's been inducted into both the Rock and Roll Hall of Fame and the Songwriters Hall of Fame, was nominated for 13 Grammys (winning one) and shifted 60 million records worldwide. Back in 1978, however, he was manufactured aspiring pop star Johnny Cougar, whose previous manager Tony Defries (best known for managing and subsequently falling out with David Bowie) refused to allow him to use his real name because it was too difficult to market. They parted ways after a couple of grotty albums and Mellencamp was subsequently picked up by Rod Stewart's manager Billy Gaff. Gaff insisted that he relocate to the UK to record and tour his next album, the equally grotty *A Biography*. And that's how John Mellencamp got to play his one and only Bristol show.

"Direct from the John Miles tour - an incredible new rock star," screamed the ads. For once, the hype was true, if somewhat premature. Mellencamp's incredibleness wouldn't become apparent for another four years. His breakthrough *American Fool* album was released in 1982, topping the US Billboard chart for nine weeks.

In the meantime, this tour proved a thoroughly miserable experience for the volatile aspiring star. He was unimpressed with the punk-era fad for gobbing on performers and would frequently jump into the audience to wallop expectorating offenders.

Dire Straits

Granary, 29 June 1978

How could you lose money putting on Dire Straits? The Granary did, back in 1978 - even though the band's fee was just £125. Practically nobody turned up. A year later, they were headlining the Colston Hall on the *Communique* tour. Dire Straits went on to sell 120 million records. Eventually, Mark Knopfler disbanded the group because they were too popular.

Interestingly, this wasn't Knopfler's first appearance at the Granary. He'd played here during his brief tenure with his first band Brewers Droop, whose line-up also included future Dire Straits drummer Pick Withers. This show was likely to have taken place on 30 August 1973. The Granary's Al Read always rued the fact that no photographs were taken and he hadn't bothered to make a bootleg recording. Amusing trivia fact: before Knopfler joined, Brewers Droop played their first show at the Granary on February 1, 1971, supporting a band called Balls. These band names proved too much for the pearl-clutchers in the advertising department of the *Bristol Evening Post*. After some negotiation, they eventually agreed to print a censored version of the Granary's ad, which invited punters to come and see ***** and ******* *****.

The problem Dire Straits faced in those early days seemed to be one of promotion, as I discovered for myself at one of the very first gigs I attended. It wasn't that they weren't getting any promotion; they were just being pitched at the wrong audience. I caught them supporting the Climax Blues Band at Torquay Town Hall the previous month, on a tour that arrived at the Bristol Hippodrome two days later on May 14. They'd been billed in the music press as some kind of 'new wave' act. Consequently, my expectations couldn't have been lower. The rest of the audience had clearly formed the same impression and headed straight for the bar, which was in another part of the building. Largely because I was too young to get served, I stayed to watch them alongside around 25 other punters. I recall being astonished at how effortlessly brilliant they turned out to be. Indeed, I enjoyed myself so vigorously that Mr. Knopfler shot me a smirk as he played that solo in *Sultans of Swing*.

Girlschool

Granary, 1 July 1978

"Cheers you lot!" Someone really ought to make a film about Girlschool, because there's never been another band like them. The number of all-female heavy rock bands who don't sell themselves on sex appeal is vanishingly small. The number of all-female heavy rock bands who don't sell themselves on sex appeal and are still out there doing it in late middle age? Just one. They were often described rather dismissively as Motorhead's little sisters. But as Lemmy never tired of pointing out, the first all-female band to headline the Reading Festival could play better than most men he knew. And as former *Guardian* Music Editor Michael Hann reminds us in his excellent book *Denim and Leather: The Rise and Fall of the New Wave of British Heavy Metal*, one of their earliest champions was a certain John Peel. Those who take it upon themselves to curate rock history choose to forget that Peel's taste was much broader than the punk and weedy indie for which he's mostly celebrated. Many NWOBHM bands were featured on his show. This writer remembers hearing the likes of Def Leppard, the Tygers of Pan Tang and Dire Straits played regularly by Peel in the late seventies. It seems that these acts' independent spirit in defiance of the new orthodoxy was what appealed to the legendary DJ.

Enid, Kelly, Denise and Kim had only just formed the band and hadn't even released their debut single, *Take It All Away*, when they played their first show at the Granary, for which they were paid a princely £75. Lemmy quickly took notice and by the following year Girlschool were supporting Motorhead on the *Overkill* tour. By 1981, they had a hit album of their own, *Hit and Run*, and were headlining the Colston Hall.

Ashton Court Festival

Ashton Court, 7-8 August 1978

After the first four-day Ashton Court free festival in 1974, organiser Royce Creasey departed for pastures new and the event was pared back to a more manageable weekend affair. The festival then continued to trundle along for the next few years. Strange as it may seem from a modern perspective, music festivals were considered deeply uncool by the late seventies. The Style Fuhrers of the time dictated that these were ideologically suspect events that were the preserve of filthy hippies. But local punks could see the appeal of getting off your face and listening to live music for free in an al fresco setting. So it was no surprise that 7,000 people turned up for Ashton Court 1978.

Ken Pustelnik, who'd supplied his Zulu PA company's sound equipment for free from the festival's outset, recalls that the audience was pretty evenly divided between punks and hippies. This was reflected in the musical line-up. Steve Hillage was by far the most commercially successful musician ever to play the festival by this point, and was joined by free festival stalwarts Here and Now. The punks got The Only Ones and the Glaxo Babies. In truth, the great punk/hippy divide was largely confected by the media. Many of the musicians had much in common (Hillage was great mates with Jimmy Pursey of Sham 69) and the audiences rubbed along perfectly happily.

After that, the festival suffered some lawless years and eventually rebranded itself as the more respectable - deep breath - Bristol Community Festival at Ashton Court. For a while, it prided itself on showcasing only local acts. A few mavericks got to sneak in, such as the colourful and frequently naked Moonflowers, while Bristol's wittiest punk Bear Hackenbush had some success in terrorising the picnicking middle classes with outbursts of punk-o-metal noise on the festival's margins. But most of the bands were pale imitations of whatever was fashionable in indie music at the time, with matching haircuts and egos.

Ashton Court continued to rely on public donations and benefit shows, which meant that financial crisis was never far away. By the late nineties, the decision was made to book national headliners. This by organisers who'd prized their local purity so much that in 1986 they'd smugly rejected Hawkwind when the space warriors offered to play for free. Attendance was certainly boosted, but the tensions between free festival idealism and the necessity to provide infrastructure for a crowd that had swollen to 50,000 soon reached breaking point. Eventually, bad luck, bad weather and the logistics involved in enforcing a controversial entrance fee did for the festival, which declared bankruptcy in 2007. Still, at least we got to see a great headlining set by Robert Plant, who pulled one of the biggest crowds Ashton Court had ever seen back in 2003.

Nutz
Granary, 10 August 1978

Nutz were a fine bunch of Scouse rockers who never managed to achieve the success they deserved. Just as Nazareth had repurposed Joni Mitchell's *This Flight Tonight* as a hard rock anthem, and Judas Preist rocked up Joan Baez's *Diamonds and Rust* (her belated metal cred reportedly delighting her son), so Nutz turned Bob Dylan's *One More Cup of Coffee* into a reliable rock club dancefloor-filler. Alas, this became the band's best-known song, and not even a NHOBHM-era name change to Rage could improve their fortunes.

The Granary show is included here because of a story Al Read told in his wonderful book *The Granary Club: The Rock Years 1969-1988*. It was one of those heaving nights at the club when the audience were jumping up and down and having a fine old time. Trouble was that they caused the ramshackle speaker stack on the balcony side of the stage to lean precariously. Public-spirited punters reached over the balcony to steady it, but to no avail. The top speaker was eventually dislodged and plummeted onto a headbanger below. This unfortunate fella was now lying on the ground without moving. Al and chums feared the worst but were unable to fight their way through the packed throng and no one could hear them shouting or noticed them gesticulating. Fortunately, a couple of roadies were down below. They charged heroically through the crowd and... stepped over the recumbent, unconscious headbanger to rescue and replace the speaker. The story does have a happy ending, though. The stricken punter recovered of his own accord, got up, dusted himself down and carried on headbanging as if nothing had happened.

Motörhead
Tiffanys, 18 October 1978

After years of slog, things were finally beginning to look up for the trio once voted the Best Worst Band in the World by *NME* readers when they pitched up at Tiffany's on the Downs to play the regular Wednesday Boobs rock night. Lemmy, Eddie and Phil had been given a stingy one-single trial deal by Bronze Records and recorded a cover of *Louie Louie* with *Tear Ya Down* on the B-side. Remarkably, this reached number 68 in the singles chart. Even more remarkably, they succeeded in finagling their way on to

Top of the Pops a week after this show on their lengthy *Beyond the Threshold of Pain* tour.

Combined with a John Peel session recorded in September, this sparked a jump in the greasy rockers' cred and profile. Just one month later, they were headlining the Hammersmith Odeon in front of more than 3,000 fans.

"The main recollection I have of the Tiffany's show is the volume - bloody hell!" says Ian Gregory, who was lucky enough to be present. "They started with the track *Motorhead*, which was originally written as a Hawkwind song. They were back headlining the Colston Hall in what seemed like months after *Overkill* came out."

Motörhead never forgot their roots. At the height of their fame on April 6, 1981, they returned to Bristol to play a secret show at the Granary. This was a benefit for the local chapter of the Hells Angels, whose clubhouse in Knowle had burned down.

Whitesnake/Magnum
Colston Hall, 14 November 1978

Think of Whitesnake today and you'll likely picture a poodle-permed David Coverdale backed by hunky young American hair metal bucks while his (now late ex-) missus writhes suggestively on the bonnet of his car in soft focus. Back in the late seventies and early eighties, however, their greatest music was created by a bunch of rather more spoddy British fellas, including ace guitarists Mickey Moody and Bernie Marsden, bassist Neil Murray and Coverdale's old Deep Purple mucker Jon Lord (whose moustache alone would disqualify him from appearing in any MTV-era video).

Whitesnake by-passed Bristol on their one and only UK club tour early in 1978, so this Colston Hall show was the first of many in the city. They'd just released the breakthough *Trouble* album and *Snakebite* EP, the latter containing the slowed-down version of Bobby Bland's *Ain't No love in the Heart of the City* that was to become a singalong fan favourite. Half of the platinum-selling *Live in the Heart of the City* album, eventually released in 1980, was recorded at the Hammersmith Odeon a week after this show.

"David Coverdale was phenomenal back then," affirms Ian Gregory. "I remember *Ain't No Love In the Heart Of The City* being played quite early in the set. We also had the obligatory solos and the instrumental *Belgian Tom's Hat Trick*, which showcased the wonderfully talented line up."

Support came from Magnum on their *Kingdom of Madness* tour. Veteran Brummie contemporaries of the likes of ELO and Wizzard, to whom they donated band members, Magnum would have to slog away for a further six or seven years before finally achieving their well-deserved chart breakthrough, which saw them propelled, albeit briefly, into arenas.

Judas Priest
Hippodrome, 12 November 1978

Incredibly, back in the 1970s some people imagined that Rob Halford was straight. For this *X-Certificate* tour, the fella who sang *Hell Bent for Leather* on stage every night unveiled the iconic look pilfered from the Tom of Finland macho wing of gay culture that could only be described as "hiding in plain sight": biker's jacket, leather trousers, cap and shades. For photo shoots he posed with a bullwhip and handcuffs. In his hilarious autobiography *Confess*, Rob describes the late seventies as his "Shirley Bassey leather years" and tells a story about how a horrified Marie Osmond unsuccessfully attempted to get him banned from brandishing the bullwhip on *Top of the Pops*. Commentators who like to stereotype and pigeonhole metalheads frequently push a narrative that the Big Gay Rob's sexuality sparked a homophobic backlash. In fact, Priest's popularity was completely unaffected. We didn't care what he got up to after he peeled off those sweaty leathers. To us, he was always the Metal God. Had he denounced metal and embraced disco, however, things might have been very different.

There are those who claim, with some justification, that 1980 was heavy metal's greatest year. But the seeds of the genre's signature sound and style for the next decade were sown right here in 1978 when Judas Priest toured the breakthrough *Stained Class* album, whose opening song, *Exciter*, pointed the way to thrash metal. Aidan Naughton had won tickets for this gig on Al Read's Sunday afternoon rock show on Radio Bristol. "We were up in the balcony and that was the best show I saw by Priest," he reckons. "It wasn't a particularly theatrical presentation, but they played all my favourite songs, from *Sinner* to *Beyond the Realms of Death*, and Rob Halford's vocal range was amazing."

AFTERWORD

"Yes, but will anybody still be listening to this stuff in a hundred years' time?" That's what they used to ask. Actually, they didn't. In the early days, nobody expected pop and rock music to last very long, not even the musicians who played it. John Lennon famously remarked that he thought The Beatles were no more than a fad. He wasn't alone. In February 1967, philosopher and politician Bryan Magee wrote an article for *The Listener* in which he asked, presumably rhetorically: "Does anyone seriously believe that Beatles music will be an unthinkingly accepted part of daily life all over the world in the 2000s?"

Putting aside the question of whether longevity is a measure of quality, we now find ourselves in a position where much of this music is closer to that century milestone than it is to the year in which it was composed. Over the next decade or two, we'll also see the severing of those tethers of nostalgia as the aging rockers and their original audiences shuffle off this mortal coil. The music will then be left to stand or fall on its own merit. Will these artists go the way of the music hall stars who commanded huge audiences in their day but are now completely forgotten? Or is there something in the music itself, possibly as a consequence of the unique circumstances of its creation, that ensures its continued popularity?

We can all agree that 'classic rock' is a pretty horrible term, but if it means anything it must surely describe music that has an appeal beyond its original audience. Will anybody still be listening to Ed Sheeran, James Blunt or Amy Winehouse in 50 years' time? I'll leave that as a rhetorical question. But it is instructive to go back just a couple of decades to consider the fleeting nature of much modern musical fashion, as Andy Warhol's 'famous for 15 minutes' axiom becomes more literal than figurative with each passing year. At the turn of the millennium, when glossy music magazines sold tens of thousands of copies each month, there was an obsession with compiling lists of 'greatest albums of all time' and the like from votes cast by readers and/or journalists who ought to know better. A sensible rule might have been to exclude anything released in the preceding five years to ensure that voters have time to sober up and recognise that fad acts might not have been quite as magnificent as hype led the easily influenced to believe. But inevitably, those sixties and seventies classics were interspersed with contemporary releases. When the exercise was repeated, as it inevitably was a few years later, the only real change was that most of the new 'classics' disappeared to be replaced with whatever was fashionable that year.

I have in front of me a yellowing copy of Q magazine cover dated August 1999, which announced importantly that it contained a list of the 100 Greatest Stars of the 20th Century. Lennon and McCartney took their rightful places at the top. But as you scroll down the list, it becomes increasingly absurd. Madonna bags seventh place, ahead of Keith Richards, Bob Marley and Jimi Hendrix. Cerys Matthews is ahead of Nick Drake. Nicky Wire beats Jimmy Page. And Bez, a gentleman renowned principally for his instrument-free onstage cavorting, is considered by Q readers to be 'greater' than Igor Stravinsky, Eric Clapton, Frank Zappa and Muddy Waters. It's all a bit of fun, of course, but underlines how careful we need to be in according 'classic' status.

Not all of the artists I've covered achieved the level of success of The Beatles, the Stones, AC/DC, Pink Floyd or Fleetwood Mac. Some (Comus, Gentle Giant, Nick Drake) sold poorly but have proven to be enormously influential upon generations of musicians who followed them. In many cases, they have a higher profile today than they enjoyed in the 1960s and 1970s.

Others who were hugely popular in their day have mysteriously slipped off the radar. The clever, funny, imaginative pop-rock of Supertramp and the musical breadth and thrilling theatrics of the Sensational Alex Harvey Band seem unfairly forgotten today. But these fortunes can swiftly be reversed, allowing young listeners to discover rich back catalogues of which they were previously unaware. The success of Edgar Wright's Sparks documentary, *The Sparks Brothers*, is a case in point, as is 63-year-old Kate Bush's unexpected return to the top of the singles chart after 44 years in June 2022, when *Running Up That Hill* was featured in the popular Netflix series

Stranger Things. In the same week, her *The Whole Story* compilation re-entered the UK top 30, where it joined The Beatles' *1*, Bob Marley's *Legend*, Queen's *Platinum Collection* and *Greatest Hits*, Elton John's *Diamonds*, Fleetwood Mac's *50 Years - Don't Stop* and David Bowie's *Ziggy Stardust and the Spiders From Mars*. Alas, Ms. Bush's one and only live show in Bristol - at the Hippodrome on April 9, 1979 - falls just outside the scope of this book.

Some bands make a comfortable living from a single hit or signature song. For as long as Hollywood romcoms include the scene where a Routemaster bus drives past Buckingham Palace to the strains of *London Calling*, Mick Jones and the estate of Joe Strummer will never want for filthy lucre. Lessons about the importance of publishing, and ownership thereof, have also been learnt - albeit often belatedly. That's why Noddy Holder enjoys a comfortable retirement, with a particularly Merry Xmas each year, while Dave Hill continues to slog round the live circuit with various incarnations of Slade.

That great innovator David Bowie was first to recognise the potential to cash in on his publishing via 'asset-backed securities' with his 1997 Bowie Bonds, which offered purchasers shares in his future royalties. Today, the concept has been seized upon by giant entertainment corporations (Sony, Universal, etc) and 'investment vehicles' like the Hipgnosis Songs Fund, who've shelled out vast sums for the rights to music by the likes of Bob Dylan, Neil Diamond, Bruce Springsteen, Sting, Neil Young and members of Fleetwood Mac. These investors aren't dewy-eyed boomer nostalgics eager to dole out cash to their childhood faves, but hard-nosed businesspeople who calculate that there are rich profits to be made from the popularity of this music for decades to come. Their interest is not in one-hit wonders but artists with extensive and consistent catalogues. And that generally means those who started out in the period covered by this book. In October 2022, Genesis sold their catalogue to the Concord Music Group for more than $300m and it's been reported that Pink Floyd could be due the biggest-ever payday when a deal is reached.

At the same time, the advent of streaming was heralded by its evangelists as a utopian opportunity for emerging musicians to engage with their audiences without the interfering mediation of record companies. It hasn't worked out like that. According to BPI research, back catalogue albums accounted for 62.6% of all purchases and streams in 2019. By 2020, this figure had risen to 68.2%. (For clarity: 'back catalogue' also includes recent releases, but the point about emerging musicians still stands.)

Many of the artists included in this book have another advantage: their music and performances had no precedent in the history of popular music. The stage antics of Screamin' Jay Hawkins, The Who, The Move and Jimi Hendrix were unique. Nobody had ever heard powerchords as crushingly heavy as those conjured by Black Sabbath's Tony Iommi. And the musical and thematic ambition exhibited by the pioneering prog bands was apparently without limit. Today, no bedroom miserablist will ever go without being compared, favourably or otherwise, with Nick Drake. And anyone pursuing a career in slick, literate, sardonic rock had better prepare to be measured against Steely Dan.

Glum prognosticators see all this as heralding the Death of Rock. As I made clear in the introduction, I'm not among them. In my view, rock will persist for as long as young people pick up electric guitars and find they can produce an exceedingly pleasing loud noise. It's the changes in the way music is distributed and 'consumed' that make it more difficult - but not impossible - for them to make any lasting impact.

Although the popularity of the greats shows no sign of waning, the artists themselves are only too human. The challenge facing the industry is how to 'maximise revenue streams' by keeping their music alive on stage after they've gone. At the time of writing, much attention was focused on the 'ABBAtars' who perform ABBA's music in a specially constructed concert hall. When you drill down into it, this is little more than a projected film. It also requires the musicians to be (a) still alive and (b) prepared to undergo a gruelling production process.

Then there's the 'no original members' band. This isn't anything new. Gene Simmons, for example, used to muse that he could have several franchised versions of Kiss performing on different continents simultaneously, while he stayed home to count his money. Who knows who's really behind that make-up, anyway? To many, the distinction between this phenomenon and tribute acts is a hair-splitting one. And it clearly wouldn't work for all bands. Good luck in persuading anyone to pay to see a Rolling Stones without Mick Jagger or Keith Richards.

But the mainstream media seems not to have noticed that 'brands' are already being continued by younger musicians personally anointed by founders before they croaked, notably Tangerine Dream and Gong. This also allows new music to be composed. TD have yet to cut the apron strings completely, but have released a brace of creditable albums. More interesting are Gong. Never exactly huge stars in their day, they nonetheless retain a large and loyal audience. Before his death, founder Daevid Allen personally selected talented British Iranian musician Kavus Torabi to carry the torch. Torabi took a risk by very deliberately not attempting to emulate his predecessor or sticking to the back catalogue. Instead, he chose to retain the *spirit* of the original band, while moving it in a slightly different direction. The gambit paid off: Gong retained its old fans and is now winning over younger ones too.

It's difficult to predict where this will lead, if anywhere. But it's probably safe to suggest that, for years to come, those of all generations who love this music will continue to be intrigued by the fascinating, funny and frequently eye-opening stories of when it was performed on their doorsteps for the first time, all those years ago.

APPENDIX

MY ROCKIN' LIFE

I didn't grow up in a particularly musical family. My father could be relied upon to nod off in front of the New Year's Day broadcast of the Strauss concert from Vienna each year. My mother's idea of groovy sounds was Glenn Miller's orchestra and Josh MacRae's *Messing About on the River*, though she did have copies of the first two Beatles albums. Like parents and grandparents everywhere, she thought the Fabs were nice, clean lads with some jolly tunes. Later, she bought a copy of *Sgt. Pepper*, but I don't remember her playing it much. The only records I was given as a child were novelty songs like Ronnie Hilton's *A Windmill in Old Amsterdam* and *Don't Let the Rain Come Down*.

What my parents didn't know was that Janet the babysitter permitted my brother Carl and I to stay up late and watch whatever we wanted on the black and white telly, because she was mostly interested in talking to her boyfriend on the phone for hours on end at our dad's expense. I recall being transfixed by The Move and Arthur Brown on *Top of the Pops*. We also watched the *Happening For Lulu Show* on that legendary occasion in January 1969 when the Jimi Hendrix Experience broke off from playing *Hey Joe* to rip into a cover of *Sunshine of Your Love* in tribute to Cream, who had just split up. That was broadcast live at peak time on BBC1. It remains my top sixties telly memory, next to *Doctor Who* and the moon landings.

After that, I badgered my mum to buy me "a pop record". Any pop record would do, especially as it was bound to annoy my dad. But what she returned with was an Isley Brothers compilation on one of those cheapo Music For Pleasure-type labels. Okay, so it had *Twist and Shout* on it, but this wasn't what I craved at all. I was completely unaware of the Hendrix connection at that age. After some more nagging, she bought me another album: *David Bowie*. Now this was way too early for Ziggy Stardust. In fact it was Dame David's first solo album on Deram. This had not been a success, so I imagine mum got it cheap and was attracted by the photo of the relatively clean-cut young man on the cover. I struggled with his arch Anthony Newleyisms, but enjoyed the psychedelic nursery rhymes which, unbeknown to me at the time, were heavily influenced by Syd Barrett. (Later, I was to develop quite an obsession with Bowie, at least until *Young Americans* put me off altogether. At the age of 12, I even attempted to pass off the lyrics to *Memories of a Free Festival* as my own poetry. "I don't know who writes this David Bowie's material," remarked my crusty English teacher, having hauled me out in front of the class. "It's very good, but it's not yours!" Colour me admonished.)

Then along came the movement that was to light up my pre-pubescent life: glam rock. The cool kids all loved T. Rex, as did I from *Telegram Sam* onwards, though I found Marc Bolan's Larry the Lamb bleat a little off-putting. I also enjoyed The Sweet and Gary Glitter (hey - nobody suspected, though I do remember seeing the Bewigged Bacofoil Buffoon much later headlining a mid-eighties Bristol University freshers' ball that seems to have been written out of history). But my band was Slade. I was completely hooked from the moment I heard *Coz I Luv You* - one of the few chart-topping songs to feature a violin solo. I sneaked my little red transistor radio into junior school to listen to the lunchtime chart rundown and cheered it all the way to number one. I also formed the view that Dave Hill was the coolest man alive - a claim that doesn't really stand any historical scrutiny. To complete my glam obsession, mum ran up a pair of furry purple trousers from some old curtain material, though I don't recall having the courage to wear these outside the house.

At around the same time, I formed a short-lived 'band', of the 'miming with tennis racquets' variety, with my brother and a couple of pals. My song was always *Paper Plane* by Status Quo, possibly because I had an instinctive feel for the glory of the riff from an early age.

By the early seventies, my pocket money had funded an enviable collection of seven-inch singles at 50p a pop. But as puberty beckoned, I was also becoming aware that beyond glam there was a whole world of serious 'progressive' rock music favoured by older kids. Some of these acts had already encroached on my world when they released singles, notably Argent with *Hold Your Head Up*, Atomic Rooster with the great *Devil's Answer*, and, later, Genesis with *I Know What I Like (In Your Wardrobe)*.

There were three places where you could buy records in my grotty Devon seaside home town. The first, obviously, was Woolworths, with its limited, chart-oriented stock and know-nothing staff. The second was a hi-fi shop run by an old boy with a comb-over who considered himself to be something of an audiophile and wore an expression of permanent disapproval. He had very little stock but could order stuff in quite quickly. This was where my mother had found the Isley Brothers and Bowie records. Whenever anyone bought an album here, an elaborate ritual was performed in which the vinyl was removed from its sleeve and thoroughly inspected and cleaned before being replaced. I once watched him struggle with the fold-out gatefold sleeve of the first Wishbone Ash album while a hairy punter almost dropped his stash as he counted out his loot in crumpled old pound and ten-bob notes.

The best shop was in a room above a general electrical retailer's shop. This was run by a lovely young gay guy whom I shall call Paul, because that was indeed his name. Paul genuinely loved music as much as his customers did, which probably got him a free pass on the homophobia front, and on Saturdays the place was always full of people talking about the latest new releases. I vividly remember going in during the week when *Tubular Bells* was released to find him totally blown away by it. Paul was very tolerant of snot-nosed little kids like myself and allowed me to pay for albums in installments. The going rate for an album back then was generally £2.50. So if I paid him 50p a week the prize would be mine in five weeks. And sure enough, there it was waiting for me, all packaged up in a brown paper bag with my name on - my very first proper grown-up album bought with my own hard-earned pocket money: *Journey to the Centre of the Earth* by Rick Wakeman. I adored that record and still do today. I can also still recite huge chunks of the David Hemmings narration. Next up was Hawkwind's *Hall of the Mountain Grill*. I never looked back after that.

My collection swiftly grew and I wound up selling all the old glam rock singles to fund future album purchases - a decision that I bitterly regret today. The punk years were brilliant; not because of the music, but because fashion victims were disposing of their rock collections, which could be bought for a pittance and are now worth a fortune. By this time, I had a Saturday job at a greengrocer to finance my vinyl addiction but the nearest good second-hand record shop was two bus rides away. I soon took to haunting the place in search of treasure. One day, I walked in and my jaw dropped as I beheld the mint condition new stock in heavy-duty protective plastic sleeves on the walls. I can see it all now. Literally, because I still have all those albums: Deep Purple's *Fireball* with the lyric insert, Uriah Heep's *Salisbury* with the original gatefold sleeve, the Groundhogs' *Who Will Save the World?* with the comicbook art...

"What the *fuck!?*" I exclaimed, unable to suppress the expletive.

"Bloke came in this morning and said he had to sell his collection because he was getting married," the proprietor said. He beckoned me closer and added in a whisper, so no one else could hear: "He was *crying!*"

There and then, I resolved that I would never get married. Reader, I didn't.

Punk also paid rich dividends elsewhere. The dad of a fashion victim schoolmate was a rep for A&M. At around that time, there was a promotion by one of the crisps companies where you could get a free seven inch chart single in return for a dozen empty packets. Cunningly, I scoffed my way through a mountain of ready salted, bagged a copy of *Pretty Vacant*, and swapped it for a pile of great albums: Rick Wakeman's *No Earthly Connection*, *Even in the Quietest Moments* by Supertramp, Budgie's *Impeckable* and a white label copy of *Köhntarkösz* by Magma (imagine trying to market that). They all remain in my collection.

I still hadn't experienced any live music, but that was about to change when I turned 15. The first artist I saw play live was Donovan. This requires some clarification. Donovan supported my very favourite band at the time, Yes, when they played the Empire Pool, Wembley, on October 28 1977, on the *Going for the One* tour. He was fine but Yes were transcendent, opening with *Parallels* and climaxing with *Roundabout*. I'd travelled up from Devon on the train with a bunch of pals from school, having sent off for our £3.75 tickets weeks earlier. We had good seats towards the front and I'd never seen so many people gathered in a single place before. What's more, they were all there to see the band I loved. As Bruce Dickinson has observed, going to a big gig like that is like being at a football match where everybody supports the same team. We all enjoyed ourselves so much that we managed to miss the last train home from Paddington. I dutifully phoned my dad to break the bad news, half hoping that he'd offer to pay for a hotel room for us all to crash in. "You'll just have to wait for the first train in the morning," he harrumphed. So we spent a cold, sleepless night on Paddington Station, which turned out to be teeming with paedos who were absolutely delighted to see us. "Are you a juvenile delinquent?" one grinning pervert asked me while rubbing his crotch. "No. I'm waiting for a train," I replied firmly. Good job I wasn't wearing those sexy glam trousers.

I loathed punk for the same reason that others loved it: the bands' studied ineptitude. Having absolutely no musical ability myself, I was always in awe of those who could play really well, which is why I swiftly gravitated towards prog and metal. You often hear people saying, "Yeah, but it gave me the chance to get up and have a go." Which is fine. I've got no problem with equality of opportunity. But I had no more interest in watching the incompetent bash away than I do in seeing other people's children in a school play. Thankfully, some of the punks did eventually master their instruments and became a key force in the early days of thrash metal.

There were some exceptions. In an alternate universe, The Stranglers could easily have been hoary old proggers. Stiff Little Fingers were simply a great rock band whose Belfast origins possibly insulated them from London-based fashion. Only later did I learn that they started out as a Deep Purple tribute act. And I always enjoyed Tom Robinson, mainly because I admired his politics, which seemed a lot more palatable than the 'public schoolboy revolutionary' posturing of The Clash (who I've always particularly disliked).

Having lost my gig virginity to Yes, I was soon addicted to live music and went to my first festivals: Led Zeppelin and Genesis at Knebworth - separately, obviously. The Zeppelin event also provided me with my all-time favourite festival anecdote. This came at the tail-end of the era when you could turn up to a festival with crates of beer and not expect to have them confiscated. The empty bottles and cans would then make useful ammo for the massive fights that broke out while waiting for the headliner to appear. In front of us was a chap who could best be described as "a bit of a wanker". He was trying to impress his mates by catching the missiles that flew overhead. As the stage lights went up and Led Zep came on, he made a heroic leap to catch a flying plastic bag, which promptly exploded, covering him in fresh vomit. (I didn't get to Glastonbury until 1982, by which time festivals were considered deeply uncool. Tickets were £8, but most people snuck in for nothing.)

The Enid swiftly became my new favourite band and Steve Hillage was the loudest artist I saw at the time (though I was right down the front with my head practically inside the PA). I also became aware of a new movement through the pages of *Sounds*. Cumbersomely dubbed the New Wave of British Heavy Metal (or NWOBHM), it comprised all those bands who'd been lurking underground waiting for the punk fad to pass. Soon I was able to see bands like Iron Maiden, Saxon, the Tygers of Pan Tang, Vardis and many more, generally in tiny club venues. Finally, there was a subculture I felt a part of.

More than a year before I became a student at Bristol University, I visited the city for the first time. It was September 29, 1980. The Yes obsession had continued unabated when my mates and I learned that Rick Wakeman was to play the Colston Hall. We made our way unsteadily up the M5 in a car driven by a pal who'd just passed his test, gazing in awe at the Suspension Bridge as we came into the city. I felt even more awe on walking into the Hall, knowing that virtually all the bands I loved had played here. I can still remember where my seat was in the stalls. The first act of Rick's solo career was petering out a bit at this point, but he certainly didn't disappoint on the night, playing excerpts from all the concept albums we loved and finishing with music from the *White Rock* soundtrack.

In my first week as a student the following year, one mission took precedence over everything else - even collecting my grant cheque (remember those?). Having befriended the first rock chick I met in the student union - a lovely girl named Bridget - I dragged her down to the Granary Club to purchase a his'n'hers membership card (having persuaded her that this didn't necessarily mean we were a couple and could use it with other people). This was the first time I met legendary dishevelled club manager Les Pierce, who fumbled around in what passed for his office as he hunted for the cards, while I gushed something about how I'd always dreamed that one day I'd be able to see bands at the Granary.

It's a wonder that I ever managed to (just about) graduate, as the next three years were packed with rockin' (and other extra-curricular activities).

In truth, the Granary had passed its prime as a live music venue, but there were still plenty of great bands to see there. I particularly remember going to see Trapeze with Russell, a fellow rock obsessive and theology student. Naturally, we stood at the front admiring the band's gear long before they came on. Eventually, the bassist came out from the dressing room and said to us, "I don't know who you think I am, but I'm not him." Of course, we knew that Glenn Hughes had left many years earlier, but we said nothing.

Tuesday nights was Andy Fox's legendary rock disco up at Tiffany's. A whole gang of rockin' students would join forces and make our way up there from Clifton to bang our heads to Sabbath, Motorhead and AC/DC. The Colston Hall's autumn programmes in the early '80s were absolutely packed with metal and prog. You needed to be on the ball to secure a ticket (generally less than a fiver) by queuing at the box office, which became a regular ritual. The shows were invariably sold out and probably kept the place going, though this is rarely mentioned in its official history. Memorable gigs included Iron Maiden, Thin Lizzy, Dio, Hawkwind (multiple times), Sammy Hagar, UFO, Camel, Def Leppard, Gillan, Joan Jett and the Blackhearts, Marillion, Motorhead, Gary Moore, Ozzy Osbourne, Robert Plant, The Scorpions, Tangerine Dream and Y&T.

While still a student, I spent several enjoyable weeks helping to run one of the early Green Gatherings in Somerset, where I became the semi-official photographer. The same team ran the Green Field at Glastonbury, where I also volunteered. Two black guys from Bristol had a fruit stall at the event, but were stopped and searched by the police every time they left the site for supplies. It was collectively decided that we should stage a suitably hippyish naked protest against this blatant discrimination by the pigs. So everybody trooped up the road from the site entrance to the large police van which had been parked up for the duration. Faced with naked hippies dancing round them and chanting, the rozzers promptly fled - to huge cheers. Among our ranks was Nik Turner, formerly of Hawkwind, inevitably parping away on his saxophone. I took several snaps of him and, ahem, Little Nik. A couple of years later, after Nik temporarily rejoined Hawkwind, I got word to Dave Brock of the existence of these incriminating transparencies. He phoned me asking to borrow one in return for being put on the guest list for any show on their upcoming tour. Naturally, I was delighted to find that it had been blown up to poster size and displayed above the merch desk. Alas, I never got my pic back. TV news footage of the protest ended up in Julien Temple's 2006 *Glastonbury* documentary, presumably because of the abundance of naked hippy ladies, though mercifully I can't be seen.

[It's worth mentioning that the late Nik Turner was a genuinely lovely guy. I once told him that I'd been unable to buy two of his seventies solo albums because they'd been deleted. Two days later, a package turned up in the post. He'd copied both of them onto cassette tapes for me.]

One day, my Geography tutor, the famed explorer/mountaineer turned gentleman farmer Henry Osmaston (Google him!), cast an eye over one of my hastily cobbled together essays and remarked disdainfully: "Have you ever considered becoming a *journalist*, Askew?" This sprung to mind after I graduated with little prospect of gainful employment. So I wrote to Dave Higgitt, the Music Editor of Bristol what's on magazine *Venue*, venturing the opinion that his metal listings were terrible. He replied agreeing that this was so, primarily because he thought it was all shit. But I was welcome to write some reviews if I wanted to.

Thus began my 'illustrious' career as a hack. I wound up as the magazine's Film Editor, which afforded plenty of opportunity to interview famous directors and stars, though my first love remained music. Best of all, my newfound status allowed me to blag my way into gigs, though my unacceptable tastes kept me well away from the Rock pages for the most part, as the magazine slavishly followed whatever the *NME* deemed to be fashionable and celebrated the hordes of hopeless local bands who imitated them and/or claimed approved influences.

I managed to sneak in some interviews along the way, including Peter Gabriel, Ray Davies, Lemmy, Alice Cooper, Justin Hawkins, Ronnie James Dio, Mick Box of Uriah Heep, Roger Taylor of Queen and Vernon Reid of Living Colour, plus Bristol NWOBHM pioneers Jaguar - an acknowledged influence on Metallica - and our very own thrash titans Onslaught. I also interviewed Robert Plant on a couple of occasions. He proved to be very happy to chat and not at all intimidating, as I had feared. One of these interviews was picked up by *Classic Rock* magazine, which ran it as a cover feature. I also went to interview Bill Wyman at his King's Road office at the height of the Mandy Smith affair. Bill had just written the world's most boring autobiography. His parting words to me were that he just wanted to work on his marriage. News of the divorce came through just after my piece was published. Alas, my exhaustive 3,000 word interview with Edgar Froese of Tangerine Dream was cut to a little picture caption and then dropped altogether on press day. I still weep (and whine) about that.

There was plenty of music-related fun to be had during the *Venue* years. On one memorable occasion, the trophy wife of a local moneybags decided that she was going to be a great singer. So he hired a major Bristol venue for her debut performance and put tickets on sale. Inevitably, nobody turned up.

In a similar vein, a jolly local biker decided to organise a custom bike show with live music and secured a lovely hilltop site on the outskirts of the city. We pitched up in our shameful car during the late morning to find the sun shining on a huge stage, hundreds of bikes, loads of stalls and… no punters whatsoever. Turned out he'd neglected to tell anyone the event was happening and simply assumed they'd find out. I can still hear him repeating over and over again: "There'll be hundreds of bikes coming down that road any minute now." Eventually, Hawkwind arrived, surveyed the empty site, and, being Hawkwind, decided to play anyway, even though they had no prospect of being paid.

During this period, I also attended two of what I consider to be the best gigs I've ever seen. First was the brilliant King's X at the Bierkeller in 1991. I wasn't alone in thinking this extraordinary trio were destined to be bigger than the comparatively mediocre Nirvana, who played the same venue that year and dealt in a similar blend of Beatles-esque melody and heavy guitars. Alas, no one was going to mistake a six-and-a-half foot tall homosexual Texan African-American wearing a tunic and sporting a mohican for a Spokesman for His Generation, so whiny bitch Kurt got all the mainstream media attention. (Incidentally, I later interviewed Courtney Love when she was trying to be an actress, but was instructed not to mention her late hubby.) Then in 2000, pioneering US prog-metallers Dream Theater played the Colston Hall, supported by Porcupine Tree. Today, both acts can comfortably sell out Wembley Arena. DT's John Petrucci remains my all-time favourite guitarist.

For several years in the 1990s, *Venue* produced the official Glastonbury Festival programme. I wrote previews of the handful of rock bands who managed to get on the bill. Michael Eavis would regularly appear in the office to check the proofs. One of the perks of doing the programme was that we got into the festival for free (this was, of course, years before it sold out months in advance) and were even able to camp in the backstage area with all the stars. I was there when Oasis headlined. During the late afternoon, they were playing football with Robbie Williams backstage, watched by a crowd of fawning hacks. At one point, one of the Gallaghers lost control of the ball and it came barrelling into our tent. He came to politely ask for it back, so I retrieved it for him. But, typically for someone with no interest in musical fashion, I had absolutely no idea who any of these people were and was only informed later. "What did they say to you?" asked one of the fawners, possibly sniffing a world exclusive. "They just asked for their ball back," I replied, nonplussed.

Sadly, the proudly independent *Venue* was sold to the company behind the *Daily Mail*, which didn't do much for its credibility, and was eventually seen off by the internet. I did some work for the *Bristol Post* for a while, but it seemed to be locked into an endless cycle of 'cost-cutting' (i.e. firing journalists) as it turned into a clickbait factory like so many other regional papers, and I was soon jettisoned. Former *Venue* publisher Dougal Templeton had been plotting a return to the fray for a while, so I was very much onboard when he launched the online and print *Bristol 24/7* (www.bristol247.com) - one of those new-fangled Community Interest Companies, backed by readers and local investors. This gave me an opportunity to carry on reviewing gigs, which I continue to this day. Indeed, I'm often out rockin' two or three nights a week.

As I write this, the former Colston Hall is about to reopen in its new incarnation as the Bristol Beacon. Encouragingly, its 2024 programme looks very much the same as its 1974 programme: Jethro Tull, 10cc, Rick Wakeman, Yes, Steve Hackett…

The vinyl collection - thousands and thousands of albums - is now carefully stashed in the loft. My eldest nephew, who developed excellent musical taste even though I had no influence whatsoever on his upbringing, has announced that they are to be his inheritance.

Acknowledgements

I didn't go to any of these gigs, so I'm enormously grateful to those who've shared their memories. Naturally, any errors are my own, as are shameful or unfashionable musical opinions - except where directly attributed.

Several people deserve free backstage passes and unlimited hospitality for putting up with my repeated, often annoying demands for info and clarification. My old mate Eugene Byrne, editor of the *Bristol Times* supplement in the *Bristol Post*, could not have been more helpful in supplying context and suggesting further avenues of research. If there's anything about Bristol history that Euge doesn't know, it's not worth knowing. Tony Byers had the immense good fortune to be a Bristol University student during a key period covered by this book. Not only did he take excellent photographs of many of these shows but he's also a meticulous record keeper. If there were more old rockers like Tony, my task would have been a lot easier. Ken Pustelnik's career in music began in the late fifties and continues to this day with the current, excellent incarnation of the Groundhogs. Over the course of two long, hugely enjoyable conversations, he shared many fabulous anecdotes - some of them unprintable (but I printed a few of these anyway). As a cub reporter back in the 1980s, I often had to phone Michael Eavis to get his response to the latest accusations of hippy/traveller outrage levelled by the local press. There was never any bullshit with Michael. He'd pick up the phone at Worthy Farm and give you his unvarnished opinion on whatever you were asking about, with none of the oily PR bollocks you got elsewhere. I thank him for taking time out from posing for selfies with teenagers on the Worthy Pastures campsite ("It's the easiest job I've ever had!") to share his memories. The legendary Joe Boyd was enormously helpful with my queries about Nick Drake and Sister Rosetta Tharpe. Another old chum from the Venue days, Darryl W. Bullock has carved out a niche for himself with a series of excellent books offering an LGBT perspective on music history, which I cannot recommend highly enough. He was kind enough to let me see an advance copy of his *Pride, Pop and Politics*. Slade fan and Director of Bristol Ideas Andrew Kelly was an early champion of my project and kind enough to wade through the whole thing prior to publication. Without his assistance, you would probably not be holding this book in your hands now. Bristol music scene veteran Mike Tobin read an early draft of the manuscript and made some invaluable suggestions. The Granary crowd could not have been more helpful too, especially DJs Ed Newsom, Adrian Copley and Andy Fox. And let's not forget the contributors to the Granary Club Facebook page (https://en-gb.facebook.com/groups/92535065088/) for keeping the spirit of the old place alive.

I am hugely indebted to all at Bristol Books, especially Joe Burt and Richard Jones, for shepherding my words so skilfully into print.

The other members of my household (Sue, Bev, Trouble the cat) deserve my deepest thanks for tolerating my ongoing rock obsession.

I salute the extraordinarily helpful staff of Bristol Reference Library and Bristol University Library's Special Collections department for putting up with me during my Covid-era researches.

Also worthy of mention in dispatches for help, yarns and suggestions: Stephen E. Hunt, Charlotte Crofts, Dave Massey, Pam Beddard, Peter Insole, Colin Gunning, Aidan Naughton, Justin Quinnell, Jonathon Kardasz, Ian A. (not that one) Anderson, Tony Benjamin, Dave Higgitt, Ian Gregory, Steve Street, Martin Thomas, Mike Darby, Richard Jones, Nige Tassell, Jack Gibbons, Martin Jones, Peter Nunez, Peter Gibbs and Adrienne Webber.

Everybody needs rock buddies who are available to venture out into the night without having to seek permission to rock. Cheers to JK, Ian Simpson, Len Blackler, Callum Askew and ace photographer Mike Evans.

Although our musical tastes diverged dramatically in later years, I also need to acknowledge my brother Carl. He discovered Blue Öyster Cult before I did, for which I shall never forgive him.

In the text, I have drawn on several interviews that I did for Venue magazine and Bristol 24/7 over the years. So thanks again to Mark Kidel, Robert Plant, Ron Geesin, Mike Evans and James Warren of Stackridge and 'Rustic' Rod Goodway of Magic Muscle.

Should there be sufficient demand for a revised and updated second edition of this book, I'd be delighted to correct the errors I have inevitably made. So if you want to say "That gig didn't happen" or "That gig didn't happen as you described it" or demand "Why didn't you include this one?" you can contact me at robinaskew@hotmail.com.

BIBLIOGRAPHY

Banks, Joe. *Hawkwind: Days of the Underground* (Strange Attractor Press, 2020)

Bannister, Freddy. *There Must Be a Better Way: The Story of the Bath and Knebworth Rock Festivals 1969-1979* (Bath Books, 2003)

Barnes, Mike. *A New Day Yesterday: UK Progressive Rock & the 1970s* (Omnibus Press, 2020)

Bean, JP. *Singing from the Floor: A History of British Folk Clubs* (Faber & Faber, 2014)

Birch, Will. *Ian Dury: The Definitive Biography* (Sidgwick & Jackson, 2010)

Black, Johnny. *Eyewitness: The Who* (Carlton Books, 2001)

Blake, Mark. *Bring It On Home* (Constable, 2018)

Blake, Mark *Magnifico! The A to Z of Queen* (Nine Eight Books, 2021)

Boyd, Joe. *White Bicycles* (Serpent's Tail, 2006)

Brannigan, Paul. *Eruption: The Eddie Van Halen Story* (Faber & Faber, 2021)

Brown, Craig. *One Two Three Four: The Beatles in Time* (Fourth Estate, 2020)

Browne, David. *Fire and Rain: The Beatles, Simon & Garfunkel, James Taylor, CSNY and the Lost Story of 1970* (Da Capo, 2011)

Buckley, David. *Strange Fascination: Bowie - The Definitive Story* (Virgin Books, 1999)

Bullock, Darryl W. *Pride, Pop and Politics: Music, Theatre and LGBT Activism, 1970–2021* (Omnibus Press, 2022)

Carruthers, Bob. *The Bonzo Dog Doo-Dah Band: Jollity Farm* (Angry Penguin, 2009)

Carter, Angela. *Shaking a Leg: Collected Journalism and Writings* (Vintage Classics, 2018)

Clapton, Eric. *The Autobiography* (Century, 2007)

Creasy, Martin. *Beatlemania! The Real Story of The Beatles UK Tours 1963-1965* (Omnibus Press, 2010)

Davies, Dave. *Living on a Thin Line* (Headline, 2022)

Davis, Stephen. *Old Gods Almost Dead: The 40-Year Odyssey of the Rolling Stones* (Aurum Press, 2002)

Downing, K.K. *Heavy Duty: Days and Nights in Judas Priest* (Constable, 2018)

Doyle, Tom. *Man on the Run: Paul McCartney in the 1970s* (Polygon, 2013)

Eavis, Michael & Emily. *Glastonbury 50: The Official Story of the Glastonbury Festival* (Trapeze, 2019)

Elliott, Paul. *AC/DC: For Those About To Rock* (Palazzo, 2018)

Faithfull, Marianne. *As Years Go By* (Omnibus Press, 2013)

Farren, Mick. *Give the Anarchist a Cigarette* (Jonathan Cape, 2001)

Flur, Wolfgang. *Kraftwerk: I Was a Robot* (Sancturary, 2000)

Frampton, Peter with Alan Light. *Do You Feel Like I Do?* (Hatchette, 2020)

Green, Jonathon. *Days in the Life: Voices from the English Underground 1961-71* (William Heinemann, 1988)

Hackett, Steve. *A Genesis in My Bed* (Wymer Publishing, 2020)

Halford, Rob. *Confess* (Headline, 2020)

Hann, Michael *Denim and Leather: The Rise and Fall of the New Wave of British Heavy Metal* (Constable, 2022)

Harris, Carol Ann. *Storms: My Life with Lindsey Buckingham and Fleetwood Mac* (Aurum Press, 2007)

Hepworth, David. *1971: Never a Dull Moment* (Bantam Press, 2016)

Hepworth, David. *Uncommon People: The Rise and Fall of the Rock Stars* (Bantam Press, 2017)

Hill, Dave. *So Here It Is* (Unbound, 2017)

Hjort, Christopher. *So You Want to be a Rock'n'Roll Star: The Byrds Day-By-Day 1965-1973* (Jawbone, 2008)

Holder, Noddy. *Who's Crazee Now?* (Ebury Press, 1999)

Hoskyns, Barney. *Small Town Talk* (Faber & Faber, 2016)

Howe, Zoe. *Stevie Nicks: Visions, Dreams & Rumours* (Omnibus Press, 2015)

Hughes, Glenn (with Joel McIver). *Glenn Hughes: The Autobiography* (Foruli Codex, 2011)

Hunt, Stephen E. *Angela Carter's 'Provincial Bohemia': The Counterculture in 1960s and 1970s Bristol and Bath* (Bristol Radical History Group, 2020)

Iommi, Tony. *Iron Man* (Simon & Schuster, 2011)

Jones, Allan. *Can't Stand Up For Falling Down: Rock'n'Roll War Stories* (Bloomsbury, 2018)

Jones, Kenney. *Let the Good Times Roll* (Blink Publishing, 2018)

Jones, Richard *Court in the Act: Ashton Court Festival, Bristol, 1974-1992* (Ashton Court, 1992)

Kerr, Andrew *Intolerably Hip* (Frontier, 2011)

Keys, Bobby. *Every Night's a Saturday Night* (Counterpoint, 2012)

King, Richard. *Original Rockers*, (Faber & Faber, 2015)

Love, Mike. *Good Vibrations: My Life as a Beach Boy* (Faber & Faber, 2016)

Marsden, Bernie. *Where's My Guitar?* (Fourth Estate, 2019)

Marshall, Polly. *The God of Hellfire: The Crazy Life and Times of Arthur Brown* (SAF, 2005)

McDonough, Jimmy. *Shakey: Neil Young's Biography* (Villard Books, 2002)

Miles, Barry. *Frank Zappa* (Atlantic Books, 2004)

Moody, Mickey. *Snakes and Ladders* (Music Press Books, 2016)

Munro, John Neil. *The Sensational Alex Harvey* (Firefly, 1995)

Murray, Charles Shaar. *Crosstown Traffic: Jimi Hendrix and Post-War Pop* (Faber & Faber, 1989)

Norman, Philip. *Slowhand: The Life and Music of Eric Clapton* (Weidenfeld & Nicolson, 2018)

Norman, Philip. *Sir Elton* (Sidgwick and Jackson, 2000)

Pegg, Nicholas. *The Complete David Bowie* (Titan Books, 2001)

Read, Al. *The Granary Club: The Rock Years 1969-1988* (Broadcast Books, 2003)

Rees, Paul. *Robert Plant: A Life* (HarperCollins, 2013)

Rees, Paul. *The Ox: The Last of the Great Rock Stars* (Constable, 2020)

Rossi, Francis. *I Talk Too Much* (Constable, 2019)

Salewicz, Chris. *Jimmy Page: The Definitive Biography* (HarperCollins, 2018)

Sandford, Christopher. *Fifty Years: The Rolling Stones* (Simon & Schuster, 2012)

Savage, Jon. *1966: The Year the Decade Exploded* (Faber & Faber, 2015)

Sexton, Paul. *Charlie's Good Tonight: The Life, the Times and The Rolling Stones* (Mudlark, 2022)

Sheppard, David. *On Some Faraway Beach: The Life and Times of Brian Eno* (Orion, 2008)

Simpson, Rose. *Muse, Odalisque, Handmaiden: A Girl's life in the Incredible String Band* (Strange Attractor Press, 2020)

Thompson, Richard. *Beeswing: Fairport, Folk Rock and Finding My Voice 1967-75* (Faber & Faber, 2021)

Visconti, Tony. *Bowie, Bolan and the Brooklyn Boy* (HarperCollins, 2007)

Whittaker, Adrian (editor). *Be Glad: An Incredible String Band Compendium* (Helter Skelter, 2013)

Williamson, Nigel. *The Rough Guide to Bob Dylan* (Rough Guides, 2004)

Wright, Chris *One Way or Another: My Life in Music, Sport and Entertainment* (Omnibus Press, 2013)

Young, Rob. *Electric Eden: Unearthing Britain's Visionary Music* (Faber & Faber, 2010)

THE PAVILION - BATH

WHIT
MONDAY
3rd JUNE

SORRY
NO SESSION

FROM LIVERPOOL
THE
BEATLES
PLUS   PLUS
THE COLIN ANTHONY COMBO
and CHET AND THE TRIUMPHS

MONDAY
10th JUNE

ADM 6/-

MONDAY
17th JUNE

SHANE
FENTON
AND THE
FENTONES

BATH FESTIVAL of
BLUES & PROGRESSIVE MUSIC '70

BATH & WEST SHOWGROUND, SHEPTON MALLET
SATURDAY 27th JUNE   SUNDAY 28th JUNE   TICKETS

CANNED HEAT
JOHN MAYALL
STEPPENWOLF
PINK FLOYD
JOHNNY WINTER
IT'S A BEAUTIFUL DAY
FAIRPORT CONVENTION
COLOSSEUM
KEEF HARTLEY BAND
MAYNARD FERGUSON BIG BAND
COMPERED BY JOHN PEEL AND MIKE RAVEN

LED ZEPPELIN
JEFFERSON AIRPLANE
FRANK ZAPPA and
THE MOTHERS OF INVENTION
MOODY BLUES
BYRDS
FLOCK
SANTANA
DR JOHN THE NIGHT TRIPPER
COUNTRY JOE
HOT TUNA

WEEKEND IN ADVANCE
WEEKEND ON DAY
SUNDAY ONLY IN ADVANCE
SUNDAY ONLY ON DAY
TICKETS AND ADDITIONAL
INFORMATION AVAILABLE
BY POST FROM
BATH FESTIVAL BOX OFFICE
LINLEY HOUSE
PIERREPONT STREET
BATH (S.A.E.)

HAROLD DAVISON and TITO BURNS present

HENDRIX
Experience

The
MOVE

THE PINK FLOYD   THE NICE   THE EIRE APPARENT   THE AMEN CORNER
THE OUTER LIMITS Compere PETE DRUMMOND

POP
Folk &
BLUES

WORTHY FARM
PILTON Shepton Mallet
Somerset
starts on **Saturday,
19th. September**
and goes on over

Sheltered fields for camping!
All food at fair prices! Ox roast!
All farms milk FREE.

THE KINKS
STEAMHAMMER
DUSTER BENNETT
ALAN BOWN
WAYNE FONTANA
STACK RIDGE
AMAZING BLONDEL

IAN ANDERSON and
IAN HUNT
MARSUPILAMI
ORIGINN

with MAD MICK
and DEREK JAMES

Lightshow·Lightship
Diorama and Films,
Freaks and Funny Things

TICKETS
£1 each

THE MOST FAMOUS CLUB IN EUROPE
BRISTOL CHINESE R & B JAZZ CLUB
EVERY TUESDAY AT THE CORN EXCHANGE, CORN ST.

TUESDAY, 9th NOV.   The Raving R & B of
GRAHAM BOND ORGANISATION

TUESDAY, 16th NOV.   From London's Marquee Club
THE VAGABONDS

TUESDAY, 23rd NOV.   "You've Got to Hide Your Love Away"
THE SILKIE

TUESDAY, 30th NOV.   Girls! Girls! Girls!
THE BIRDS

TUESDAY, 7th DEC.   The Greatest Show on Earth
THE STEAM PACKET

LONG JOHN BALDRY   BRIAN AUGER TRINITY
ROD STEWART   JULIE DRISCOLL

Students admitted on Student Cards   Nurses Half-Price
Crocodile Sandwiches   Fly Lice   Chop Chop   Uncal Bonny